TIME BOMB

Philip Davies

CONTENTS

CHAPTER 1: NORTH SEA OIL RIG

Underwater…

… light rays flickering… glistening…

… shadows dancing in the water…

… seaweed waving, barnacles clinging on…

… a fish flitting past… a school… another… another…

Quiet.

Calmness underwater… light rays… flashing…

… bubbles… bubbles skipping, rising randomly to the surface; you can hear them…

… and breathing…

… controlled breathing…

… regular… regular breathing…

… bubbles…

The tranquillity was suddenly broken by a diver bursting through the surface of the water, blowing out a mouthful of water and shouting. "Jack! Jack, that's it, we're done. Get me out of here; we're going home."

Jack was looking down from the rig as Amos appeared on the surface of the water. They had just completed the final inspection of the support stanchions to Block 22/17 b.130 Montrose Alpha platform in the North Sea.

Amos swam slowly towards the rig, Jack pulling him in with a rope. On reaching the platform, he passed Jack a camera and his sample bag. "Look after those, Jack. I'm not going down there again," joked Amos.

Jack and Amos were partners (and the only staff) in an oil rig inspection company that they had set up eight years ago. They made a living checking the underwater structures to oil rigs and gas platforms. This meant that they could travel throughout the world, but most of their work was in and around the North Sea.

They had just finished the final dive of a ten-week contract. Amos was American, medium height and build, with dark hair that was slightly receding and greying on the edges. He had turned to diving as a career a couple of years after he pulled out of his engineering design course at Harvard which he said wasn't doing anything for him. He told his parents that he wanted a more "outdoor life" and went off to learn how to dive.

He began at the local swimming pool and then in downtown Houston at the Gigglin' Marlin Dive & Swim Centre on Almeda Road. *With a name like that*, thought Amos at the time, *you've got to be able to learn how to dive*. Amos was fortunate that his main diving instructor had over twenty-five years' experience of working on rigs and taught him everything he knew.

Jack, Scottish but now a converted south-west Londoner, stood at five foot ten, medium build with curly ginger hair and was heavily tanned, with tattoos along the length of his right arm. Although not tall, he had the strength of a lion, which was regularly needed when diving.

The two of them met in Aberdeen whilst celebrating a strike for one of the big oil companies in 2012. They decided, after a beer or two, to try and make some real money in partnership as they were both working for bigger organisations who would take the cream on every contract without doing much… and the level of cream was sometimes very thick.

This particular contract had involved spending eighteen days on the platform and then three days off. Normally, their three days off were spent catching up with paperwork and trying to see their families. They had been doing this for over two months now, but Amos hadn't managed to get back to see his family.

Jack hoisted Amos out of the water and onto a lower platform, just above the water's edge. Amos sat with his legs in the water, pulled off his mask and headgear. They gave each other a handshake and an embrace. Jack slapped Amos's shoulders, and they exchanged big smiles, both thankful they had finished without too many problems.

"This is what it's all about," said Amos, "finishing off a contract and heading back to see the family."

Jack acknowledged with a nod, and without saying anything, he helped Amos out of his diving suit and started packing up all the gear ready to move it away from the water's edge. He was aware that a big swell was building up and glad that Amos had got out before any bad weather hit them.

The pair of them dragged their gear up to a higher level and then clambered up the open-tread metal stairway, battling against the sea spray that was now blowing across their faces.

They reached the central control office and Amos pulled the heavy metal door open. As they entered, they could see a bearded man leaning back on his chair. He was wearing a chequered shirt and braces that stretched across his chest and protruding stomach, his fat gnarled fingers were holding a cup of coffee and there was a battered laptop open on his desk.

"That's us done," said Amos, unfastening his top. "Glad to get out when we did; it looks like there's a bit of a storm coming in."

"There's a force 4 to 5 due to blow in this evening, Amos, with a heavy 12 to 15 foot swell" said the bearded man in a broad Glaswegian accent. "You're lucky. If you hadn't finished today you probably would've had a two to three-day delay in finishing."

Both Amos and Jack signed the divers' record log, along with the time leaving the water and noted any observations.

"You know, Hamish, this is our last one," said Amos, standing up and looking down at him with his hands on the table, "and it's a good one." He chuckled to himself as he moved to shake Hamish's hand.

"When are you boys going to get me my report?" said Hamish, swinging back in his chair again and chewing his pen.

"Will be a couple of days before the samples can be with the lab, then checked and results back. We can upload photos tomorrow if that helps," replied Jack. Amos and Jack glanced across at each other.

"So yeah, maybe… what do you think, Jack? Five to seven days for our report?" suggested Amos, raising his eyebrows. Jack nodded in agreement.

"You know," said Hamish, sitting back down at his desk and no longer swinging on his chair, "that I and the company need this report urgently."

"Yeah, yeah, yeah, but we've got some holiday to take and we're going to enjoy it," said Amos, rubbing his hands together. "Yee-ha."

The key aspect of Amos and Jack's business was identifying degradation of the steelwork and protective surfacing to rig underwater structures. If this showed degrading faster than expected, repair work would need to be scheduled and undertaken, usually within six months of the date on the report, depending on the severity of the defects.

"So, what's it look like down there, Amos?" sighed Hamish apprehensively.

"Pretty good down to the thirty to thirty-five-metre depth," replied Amos. "Considering that's the side of the rig taking most of the storms and the number of barnacles clinging to the support legs."

"That's good," said Hamish more cheerfully as he laid his hand on the steel window frame next to his desk. "You feel and hear creaks and groans from the old girl from time to time and you wonder if you're gonna be in for an early bath!"

They all laughed.

"It's at night that it really gets to me," added a young lad standing by the window at the far end of the room, drying his hair with a towel. "I'm stuck in sleeping quarters where you can hardly hear anything from the rig's loudspeaker system, but you can feel the rig moving."

"You worry too much," said Jack. "These structures are really solid, built to last over forty years."

"That's provided the maintenance is done," said Hamish, throwing his pen down onto his desk and swinging back on his chair again. "And head office is bloody slow in giving me the OK to carry out maintenance and repair work at the moment. One dip in the oil price and head office is panicking and saying they can't afford to spend any money. Those 'suits' in London need to get their heads in gear." He pointed towards the mainland, spitting feathers. "No rig, no oil, no money. It's as simple as that and they've been risking it recently."

"So what about below thirty metres – why hasn't that been cleared as per our last report?" said Amos as he placed his hands on his hips and leaned in towards Hamish.

"Well," said Hamish, looking down into his folded hands, then starting to twiddle his thumbs. "We started to use the environmentally friendly stuff to clear the barnacles that you recommended in your last report, and you know what, there's two types down there now? But when head office got wind of the extra time it was taking to clean the steels, and the extra cost, they told us to stop."

Amos didn't respond to Hamish initially. This was one of the biggest issues that he had: organisations not actioning his reports recommendations – that and the weather! If he had replied straight away, he would have lost his temper and he wasn't in the mood for that. He didn't want a half hour or so discussing the whys and wherefores of oil company policy; this was not on Amos's agenda.

Amos stood up to leave and then started to pace around the room. He couldn't contain himself. "Crazy, company greed, money, money, money that's all they are after. What about the environment? And health and safety?" He gesticulated with his hands. "Right, I'm off to have a shower before I get really cross," said Amos, shaking his head in disbelief.

He pulled the door open and it blew back sharply, almost crushing his hand on the wall. "That was close," shouted Amos. "Get this door closer sorted, Hamish – put it on your list for head office."

Jack and Amos left the control room and with the wind gusting strongly, Amos had to pull the door behind him with considerable force to close it.

Outside again and facing the elements, Amos and Jack headed towards the locker rooms, passing a number of workers on the way. Two of them were sheltering from the blustery squall that had quickly developed, making it difficult to speak and hear, so there was a lot of acknowledgement from passing crew with hand signals, smiles and high fives.

Jack leant into the door to the changing room, letting Amos slip past him before the door closed with a loud slam. Suddenly, everything was quiet other than their bags and jackets being thrown to the floor.

"Phew, that was a close one; we did well to get out when we did," said Jack, making his way across the room to his locker. "Hey, Martin. How you doing?" asked Jack.

"Good, thanks," he replied, closing the door to his locker. "You guys off today? Lucky so-and-sos – have a beer for me when you hit the mainland."

"Sure will!" Jack smiled back at him.

"There's one downside at the moment," said Amos.

"What's that?" replied Jack, starting to strip down for the showers.

"When can the helicopter get here to pick us up? Damn weather up here, one minute it's calm and the next a squall develops, it's so, so changeable. Let's get ourselves sorted and up to talk to Pete in the director's office and see what's doing."

There's one crazy thing to get showered and cleaned up after a dive, thought Amos to himself. *The trouble is, you're likely to get wet again when you come out of the changing room: a continuous process of getting wet and dry and wet and dry again, and then wet and even more wet!*

Amos made his way into the showers once he had got the controls working at the temperature he wanted, which could be rather temperamental in the middle of the North Sea. There then followed a raucous sequence of karaoke songs one after the other.

Jack chuckled to himself as he listened from the adjacent shower cubicle to Amos's rendition of a few verses from "Singin' in the Rain", ending with his own words, "… I'm heading home again." There was a short pause for breath and loud humming; Jack thought to himself that Amos actually had quite a good singing voice. There was a deluge of water and splashing and then Amos was off again with his version of "The Sun Has Got His Hat On".

"Hey, Jack?" shouted Amos suddenly.

"Yeah."

"Did you manage to speak to Sally? Not long to go now, is it?"

"Still about four to five weeks to the due date so all OK at the moment, thanks."

"That's good," said Amos, "that's good." He then continued singing and dancing and slapping his feet on the shower floor.

"I know what's next on today's *X Factor* auditions," called out Jack. "Amos's version of 'Happy Feet.'" Amos continued to sing and slap his feet on the shower floor.

"Do you think Fred Astaire practised tap dancing in the showers?" shouted Amos. He then followed "Happy Feet" with "Singin' in the Rain". There was no let-up in his singing when Amos was in this mood. "Yee-ha." He probably wouldn't stop until the water to the showers ran out.

Jack just grinned, laughed to himself and continued showering. When Amos was like this, he had returned to being a ten-year-old, ready to go on holiday and just needing to put the last bit of packing together.

I just hope that the helicopter can come and take us back to the mainland, thought Jack, *there'll be all hell to break loose if it doesn't. Amos will not be a happy man with happy feet.*

After they had finished showering, the two business partners sat opposite each other as they got dressed into their casual wear.

"Hey," said Amos, "what's the problem, buddy? Why are you looking so glum? We're finished and going home."

"Nothing really," said Jack, with a shrug of his shoulders whilst doing up his laces on his boots. "It's just, well… we haven't had our last three invoices paid and we're behind on the payments for the new inspection gear."

"Hey now… don't you worry," said Amos with a smile on his face. He leant forward and began roughing the hair on Jack's head. "I'll have a word with Hamish and he can get it cleared from head office. If they want our report, they had better get up to date with paying for our services; it will sort itself out, Jack. Always does. Come on, let's go."

They both picked up their bags and wrapped their coats around themselves, hoods pulled over their heads.

"Ready to run the gauntlet?" said Amos.

They opened the locker room door and were met by a sheet of spray across their faces. They stood back for a few seconds and then decided to go for it.

The route up to the director's office wasn't the most straightforward, requiring Amos and Jack to head down towards the water and then up and around a large equipment area, but at least it gave them various places to shelter from the wind and rain on the way.

The important thing was not to slip over!

Another heavy metal door to pass through and close and they were in the director's office.

Amos and Jack pulled back their rain hoods and stamped their feet.

"Amos, Jack," called out a portly man with a strong Scottish accent. He was standing up in jeans and a chequered shirt with rolled-up sleeves, showing off a myriad of tattoos down both arms and desperately trying to hold onto a stack of papers. "How are you both doing?"

"Great, Pete, thanks," said Jack.

"Are you boys all done now?" asked Pete, shuffling his papers together on his desk.

"Yep, we're done and on our way home. Free at last, haha," replied Amos, moving a chair and sitting down opposite Pete's desk.

Pete was a middle-aged Aberdonian with a tanned and pitted face that held the scars of a severe attack of chickenpox. His greying bushy beard made up for the lack of hair on his head. It made him look a little like a walrus. Pete was probably in his mid-fifties and had been in charge of the rig for over five years now, a solid and committed guy previously in the SAS, so he was well versed in the discipline requirements which were much needed on a rig. He didn't have a big family, and although quite outwardly communicative, he kept himself to himself. The responsibilities of a wheelchair-bound daughter back home weighed heavily on his thoughts.

"Now, what I want to know…" enquired Amos.

"I know, I know, Amos. When is the chopper gonna come in and whisk you guys away," said Pete.

"Yeah, how did you know that?" said Amos with a big grin on his face.

"Well, it ain't going to be today, you know that." As he put his papers on the table and sat down, looking at the screen on his desk, he pressed a few keys and called up the latest weather forecast. "It's not looking good tomorrow either, although… there's possibly a window of opportunity in the weather between about eight and nine tomorrow morning, so we're hoping they'll be running in supplies then and they can take you both back to Aberdeen," said Pete, looking up at the two of them from his computer screen. "Amos, the timing is good for you, you know that, and it's as early as you're going to get with your no-flight time from diving, so you wouldn't be able to fly any earlier anyway," he continued.

Pete stood up and moved his arms to wave the two of them away. "Go, go, both of you go and celebrate, but not till you get back on land," said Pete. "You know the rules, no alcohol."

"Yeah, yeah, yeah, yeah, yeah," said Amos, standing up from the chair.

"We know," said Jack. "It's never a problem and it's always been a good way to save money working on the rigs – nothing to spend it on!"

"Looks like we're heading back to the dorm tonight," said Amos. "Let's hope it's the last time, Jack. What's the film tonight?"

"It's not good," said Pete, who then stood up. "*Jaws*."

"Yeah," replied Amos, and immediately started to circle Pete as a shark would do, suddenly grabbing at his arm.

"Hey, get off," said Pete. "You're the one who should be scared; you're a lucky bugger, you know that."

"I'm only messing around, and yeah, you're right, it was a close one," said Amos. Jack smiled at the two of them and shook his head from side to side.

Pete lifted an arm and motioned them both away. "See you boys later and enjoy the film. No attacking the audience now, Amos, you'll spoil it for the rest of us."

Amos turned to Pete. "You tell us as soon as you have confirmation of the chopper coming in. I've got a plane to catch out of Aberdeen tomorrow."

"No problem," said Pete, "now away with you."

Amos pulled at the door to the director's office, letting in a gust of sea spray. Jack and Amos left the office as the door slammed shut behind them.

"Here we go again," said Jack, "let's go," as another cloud of spray came off the sea. "Come on. Let's run after the next one."

They scurried along with the rain starting to turn to sleet, eventually reaching the mess with a very swift opening and closing of the door.

They threw their bags to the floor and took their jackets off and shook them before hanging them up.

"How are you doing, Amos?" came a garbled shout from across the mess room floor from a man with a mouthful of food.

Amos looked over and it was one of the riggers who he had worked with on a small job with Jack over in the Norwegian Sea about two years ago. It was a small world in the oil industry: you regularly came across people that you had met before.

"I'm good, I'm feeling real good," said Amos as he went over and shook the man's hand and stole a chip. "That's us done, just gotta get off this darn rig," said Amos.

Amos walked towards the counter serving food; Jack, who had been chatting away with a couple of other guys, followed shortly after.

Out of the corner of his eye, Amos could see through a window, a rig in the distance together with grey, grey and more grey. It was like a desert, nothing here except grey, sea squalls and rain, thought Amos.

Come on, he said to himself. *Clear up, I wanna get home and see my family.*

Whilst Amos was daydreaming, he got a jab in the ribs.

"Amos."

He turned sharply, as it hurt. "Owee."

"Amos." It was Pete. "Between nine and nine thirty tomorrow morning, all being well. The forecast is for snow and sleet showers in the morning, rather unexpected."

Amos rubbed his ribs and a big grin appeared on his face.

"Magic, real magic, thanks, Pete," said Amos. "I was just thinking of home."

"I know, Amos," said Pete. "You've had a long spell out here and we appreciate it; we've had our moments but you're welcome back anytime."

"Hey, that's real kind of you, Pete, thanks," said Amos. "Just leave my ribs out of it next time; and can you do us a favour and have a word with Hamish to get onto head office to pay our invoices?"

"OK," said Pete, turning to go.

"They're behind," said Amos, "and I presume you are going to want our report?"

"I'll see what I can do," replied Pete, "and yes, we need your report."

Jack came up to the two of them and gave Amos and Pete trays for their food. Pete motioned with his hand to say a "no thank you".

"Did you hear that, Jack?" asked Amos. "Pete wants us back."

"Nice… but not too soon, Amos. I want some time with the family, like you," said Jack.

His senses picked up sizzling bacon and he licked his lips. "I want a break from this artificial lump of iron planted in the middle of nowhere, find me a bit of sunshine," said Amos.

"OK, you guys, see you in the morning." Pete left the mess room to head back to his office.

"He's had a tough one," Amos said to Jack.

"Who?" said Jack, shuffling in the queue behind Amos.

"Pete – he's worked so hard to keep his wife and kid, you know the kid's got cerebral palsy?"

"Yeah, I knew she was disabled," replied Jack.

"And the house they've got, he's done it all himself. Lifts, bathrooms, ramps, overhead tracking gear, you name it, all by himself. Don't get me wrong, he loves them both but I'm sure he has some rest and finds a bit of quiet when he is here. Just glad my kids are in good shape; well, they were when I last saw them almost three months ago now. Three months. I'm not going to leave it that long again," said Amos.

"Amos," called out a guy sitting and eating with a few companions over to the centre of the canteen. "Get some meat down you. You Americans are fading away eating nut roast." Raucous laughter then followed from the table. "Get some proper food down yer and learn how to down a pint of 80 Shillings."

The guy was a "big" Scottish roughneck. On a couple of days off in Aberdeen last month, Amos and Jack had had an altercation with him in a bar. The guy had had too much to drink and was showing off to his mates, which ended up with Jack getting punched on his right jaw and Amos taking a heavy blow into the pit of his stomach. The brawl was broken up by a couple of very able bar men; the roughneck was not to be mixed with again. Amos looked up and smiled. He turned back again, not taking the bait.

Amos and Jack chose their food, with Amos avoiding anything with meat in it. They went and sat next to a window away from the others for some peace and quiet, tucking into their food.

Amos was almost a full-time vegetarian. It had been nearly two years now, partly because of his high cholesterol levels and partly his wife's reasons for not eating red meat and keeping off dairy products as much as she could. Better for the environment as well as ourselves, she said.

Amos had a big slice of a nut roast on his plate and the rest of his plate piled high with vegetables. They found a table away from the roughnecks.

"Hope you're going to report this back to Bernie?" teased Amos, nudging Jack with his arm.

"Sure!" said Jack between mouthfuls. "When we Skype later confirming the flight arrangements."

Bernie was Amos's wife and Jack's sister. Amos had met her

when he was working for Ranger Oil in Guildford, Surrey, UK whilst attending a health and safety conference on oil rigs and platforms. She had been one of the organisers managing the event and Amos and she just seemed to click from the first time of setting eyes on each other.

Amos thought back to the event; he remembered coming into the room late, and with all the seats at the back taken having to sit at the front. Bernadette was already on stage just about to start; she smiled at him but didn't make any comment about him being late. Amos smiled back and she tried to start but stuttered her words and with that, some of her papers fell off the lectern.

A number of the guys started laughing, at which point Amos stood up and said, "Come on, you guys, give the lady a chance." She then collected herself and introduced the event.

"Health and safety on unoccupied platforms. Are you aware that over 25 percent of platforms are unmanned, with…"

Amos came back to himself and the canteen but not for long.

At the first coffee and comfort break, she had come up to him and said, "Thank you for stepping in when I dropped my papers. I don't know what it is about men at conferences; something goes wrong and there is a tendency to take the mickey about the person up on stage!"

They finished their drinks and were heading back for the next session when Amos asked if she was doing anything later, and that was it.

Bernadette was a vivacious, fiery, ginger-haired lady and, at five foot four, she knew what she wanted and would move heaven and earth to get it – definitely the Scottish blood on her father's side of the family. She had lived and worked in Scotland all her life until she met Amos. With Jack, her brother, also being involved with the oil industry, Amos integrated into the family with ease.

Bernadette and Amos married the following year in Rosemarkie, north of Inverness overlooking the Moray Firth. After a six-week honeymoon in Scotland, visiting Bernie's relatives at Spey Bay with the amazing bottlenose dolphins chasing the salmon so close to the coastline and then on to Aviemore, Spean Bridge, Fort

William, stunning Glen Coe and timeless Loch Lomond, then finally Glasgow, they then flew to Houston, Texas where Amos had his business.

Moving to a town called Waverly in the Sam Houston National Forest, an hour's drive north out of Houston, Amos's hometown, allowed him easy access to his business contacts.

"Oi. Oi, Amos. Amos, are you OK?" called Jack, shaking his arm.

Amos came round. "Er, yeah, I must have been dreaming, I was just… Argh, never mind." He took another mouthful of food. "I'm just glad we're finished. Dreaming of home again. I'm tired and I'm gonna Skype Bernie and the kids, then head off to bed. Enjoy the film and see you in the morning, Jack."

Amos dropped his knife and fork down heavily onto his plate – he hadn't finished his meal – then stood up to leave the canteen, at which point followed further comments from the loud-mouthed roughneck. Amos viewed the comments as a joke and shook his head slowly from side to side. He smiled, put his coat on and left the canteen with his bag.

Amos got back to his room, threw his coat and bag to the floor and slumped down on his bed. He reflected on how lucky he had been meeting Bernie and then working together with Jack. He'd been in partnership now for almost eight years and it worked really well for both of them: Jack in London, close to the oil company contacts in Woking and Guildford, south west of London. And then Amos, with his links in the USA, and in particular Houston, to the work in the Gulf.

They had both worked for larger companies but felt they were just a number in their respective organisations and not appreciated as real people.

They hadn't yet managed to break into the big time of platform inspections but were building a solid reputation. They really did need to get some work in the Gulf. Their last three commissions had all been up in the North Sea, good money, but for Amos, just too far from friends and family, and he reflected on missing the children growing up.

Perhaps after Jack's baby was born they could all come over and spend some time together with his family and get their next job in the Gulf of Mexico.

Now there's a plan, he thought, rolling off the bed to sit at his desk.

Skyping from the rigs never guaranteed a connection and the link would regularly break up or cut out on the screen.

Amos called home and got through after about fifteen minutes of trying and was surprised that there was only his youngest there.

"Hi, Henry. Henry, it's Dad – how you doing?"

"Hello, Dad... I wanna see you... when you... er... coming home?"

"In the next few days, Henry; I've finished here and on my way back... Where's Mom?" said Amos.

There was a long pause.

"She's out," said Henry, "and I'm looking forward to our holiday."

Henry was eight years old and regularly insisted on the fact that he knew everything about Skyping, IT and in particular the Xbox – and often dealing with them all at the same time.

"When's she back?" said Amos.

There was another long pause. Amos knew it.

"Henry, Henry, listen to me... when is she back?"

Another pause... Henry was playing a computer game and his head was moving from side to side, looking at a screen!

"Don't know," said Henry, the line and picture crackling up.

"Tell her I'll be back on Thursday... you got that, Henry?"

"OK," said Henry with a touch of attitude in his response.

"Thursday, Henry... Henry, Thursday... you got that? ... And get me a cab, OK?" The connection crackled... and cut out.

"Come on... come on... argh, damn it," said Amos.

Amos tried to Skype again – no luck – and then a bit later, again, with still no joy. He sat back in his chair, looking out of the window towards the grey horizon.

Soon be home, soon be home, he thought to himself, *gotta make sure it's not so long next time.*

He sat up and decided to check on the weather forecast for

tomorrow. *Pete was right*, he said to himself. *Still looking good for about nine-ish in the morning...* His eyes were looking at the screen and tapping the keyboard. *Let's get those flights booked*, he said to himself.

Lying on his bed with his computer, he quickly managed to book his flights and then turned the radio on for the shipping forecast.

Amos always liked to listen to the forecast when he was out on the rigs as it gave him a feeling of assurance and an understanding of the elements when it came to going underwater.

He reflected on his dives over the last ten weeks, but in particular the last week or so. The water seemed or felt to be getting colder and somehow tasted saltier – maybe he was just getting too old for diving. *Oh heck... Jack can check the results when we come back and look up those odd-shaped barnacles. Pete has noted them as well; there seem to be more of them down on this rig than before... amazing what you can see below the water's surface... when it's clear.*

The radio crackled and spoke.

"*Viking... 5 showers north by north-west easing to 4. Fair Isle... 5 sleet north by north-west easing to 3 sleet turning to snow. Faeroes... 3 sleet north north-east. South-east Iceland...*"

With the forecast continuing in the background, Amos reflected once more on his family. He had met Bernie when he was forty-four and she had just turned thirty.

Having children later in life kept him young if sometimes not in body. He chuckled to himself.

He visualised throwing a football across the lawn to the kids in the garden at home... with the boys that was really nice. He smiled to himself. Amos lay down on the bed and was instantly asleep... Exhausted.

***

"Morning, Amos," said Jack on opening his door.

"Mmm... what do you want?" said Amos as he rolled to the other side of the bed, holding a pillow around his head and ears.

"Come on, Amos," said Jack, leaning over the bed and shaking Amos's shoulder, "it's looking good to go... hey, what's up?"

"Not the best night's sleep," said Amos. "Kept dreaming about that darn great white shark that attacked us whilst inspecting Rig 56 in the bay of Mexico... there are times when I just can't get it out of my head."

"Shit. Yeah, that was a close one – just fortunate that he didn't like meat either! Ha ha. Anyhow, I'm going down for breakfast," said Jack.

"Argh... OK, I'll see you there in ten," said Amos, moving back across the bed.

Jack closed the door.

Amos rolled himself out of bed, stood up and, standing in front of the mirror, moved his hand over the scars on his left side and shoulder. *That was a near miss,* he thought as his mind flashed back to the image of the shark in front of him swishing his tail and then turning and attacking... He shivered, changed quickly and went to the mess for breakfast.

"That was quick," said Jack.

"Yeah, there's no way I'm missing breakfast even if the flight is a bit bouncy."

The door to the mess room flew open. It was Pete, looking for Jack and Amos.

"Hey, you guys," he said with both thumbs up. "08.50 it is, and be on time." The door slammed shut.

"You know what I'm going to miss... these breakfasts," said Amos. "The beauty of it is: no cooking or washing up!"

They started what they thought would be a casual breakfast, no rush and plenty of banter with a lot of the team in the canteen.

Outside it started to sleet again.

What's new? thought Amos.

"When it's eighty-five degrees in Houston, you know what... I'm going to miss this weather," said Amos.

"No way," shouted a couple of guys sitting close to them.

Pete then came back into the canteen in a fluster. "Amos, Jack, the helicopter is coming in early – and it's going to be a quick turnaround as there's a squall picking up off the coast of Aberdeen and the pilot doesn't want to be hanging around to get caught up in it on the way back."

"Twenty minutes," said Amos. "You've got to be kidding, I've only just started breakfast."

"Take it with you!" said Pete.

After a short while he stuffed the last of his scrambled eggs on toast into his mouth and they got up from the table and dumped their trays, saying their goodbyes to colleagues in the canteen and then off to get their gear packed and ready to load up.

Amos and Jack were both quick to get to the helideck with their gear ready to load onto the helicopter; there was no way they were going to miss their flights home.

The wind was picking up again and, with it, sheets of sea spray blowing across the deck.

"If this gets any worse," said Jack, "I'll change my mind… I'm not going."

They could hear the chopper coming in, but couldn't see it until the noise became deafening.

Amos looked Jack in the eye. "I know you're not keen on choppers but I'm going. If you want to stay, stay – don't mind me – but I'm going," said Amos.

Jack wasn't the best of passengers when it came to helicopter flights. The fumes from the engine were the worst part of it, but he was as keen as Amos to get back home to see his expectant wife.

"I'm with you, Amos… just make it a larger paper bag than usual – I may need it!" shouted Jack with the helicopter and noise getting closer. He chuckled.

They had both seen some horrendous landings in the past with helicopters pushed around in the wind like autumn leaves – you wondered how on earth the pilots managed to keep control – but this pilot was well in control of the chopper and managed to land with relative ease.

"That's a pretty good landing; gives me confidence," said Amos, trying to help with Jack's concerns.

"All part of the skills of flying. And me, being a reluctant passenger having to put up with it, I suppose," replied Jack.

The high-pitched sound quietened down and the blades started to slow.

A couple of guys ran in towards the chopper with their heads and shoulders hunched and bent low to make the helicopter secure.

People then emerged carrying boxes and equipment.

"Hey," shouted someone carrying filming equipment. "Amos, Jack, what are you doing here? How you both doing? I never thought I would see you guys again after the Mexico Bay incident."

"We survived," said Amos, "and got the scars to prove it... do you wanna see them?" Amos motioned to take his jacket off.

"Good to see you, Dave." Jack vigorously shook his hand. "What brings you here?"

"Filming a health and safety video... do you guys want to be in it?"

"Yes we do, but no thanks," replied Jack.

"It's good money," said Dave.

"No thanks... we're finished here and that's enough for us... we're gonna find us some sunshine," said Amos.

"OK, you guys, take it easy and take care of yourselves now."

Jack and Amos started loading their equipment and bags up onto the helicopter. It was a twenty-seater so plenty of room for all their gear, assuming there weren't too many others on the trip to the mainland.

Pete came out onto the helipad and had a word with Jack just before they closed the helicopter doors ready for take-off.

He then stood back away from the chopper with his hands on his hips, gave a short wave and a thumbs up.

The Bristow Helicopter pilot revved up the engine, and with that, the blades then commenced their slow winding up to that head-thumping sensation.

The pilot turned around and shouted to the passengers to put their ear defenders on. He then motioned to everyone to strap themselves in with the safety belts.

Before Jack and Amos realised, they were off the deck and on their way, spray flaying in sheets off the blades then the helicopter banking up and away from the rig towards Aberdeen.

"There go a couple of good guys; you could always rely on them to deliver," Pete said out loud to himself, looking up from the deck; he gave them a wave.

Hamish walked up to him on the deck. "Let's hope their report gives us the thumbs up otherwise we're all out of a job."

CHAPTER 2: HOMEWARD BOUND

Amos nudged Jack and gave him a smile and shouted, "Only sixty minutes to go, Jack… did you know this is a Sikorsky S-92 registered with respect to a member of the royal family?"

"Oh, really?" Jack replied in a questioning and very disinterested and dismissive way. His mind and his stomach were elsewhere.

"Yup, a royal baby – George Alexander Louis Cambridge."

"That's good… I'm very… pleased for him," said Jack, turning to look out of the window and not really interested. He then widened his eyes a few times and moved his eyebrows up and down, then his hands to his stomach. He then motioned that he was going to be sick, looking for the sick bag, and then towards Amos.

"Ha… only joking, Amos. So far, no need for the bag." Jack grinned at Amos, pleased he had got one back on him.

Amos smiled and looked away, shaking his head. *Cheeky so-and-so*, thought Amos.

Behind Amos and Jack was a row of seats occupied by three very large riggers. Amos vaguely recognised them as there were so many people on the rig, they only occasionally made contact with them. He gave them a nod of acknowledgement. *Thank goodness there's only three of them*, thought Amos, *otherwise the twenty capacity, and weight, might be a problem.* Amos chuckled to himself.

There was plenty of banter between the men sitting behind Amos and Jack, mostly about how much they were going to drink when they got to the mainland.

The riggers were off to Aberdeen for a few nights on the town before returning to the platform, once they had sobered up!

"I'll bet you five pints of 80 Shillings that the rig gets shut down by the end of the month," said one of them.

Amos's ears pricked up and he was suddenly interested in the conversation.

"And if it doesn't?" was a reply from one of them.

"Then… I'll double the bet to… ten pints."

"You're on," came the reply.

The banter and shouting between them got louder and continued for most of the journey.

The constant pounding and drone of the engine and blades turning became mesmerising, together with the regular buffeting of the helicopter by the wind, although this was par for the short journey to the mainland.

They passed close to two other platforms, both gas by the look of them, thought Amos, with their flares flickering away, and then a tanker making its way back to the mainland.

They soon caught the first glimpse of land.

"That will be Peterhead," said Amos, pointing through the window.

Amos turned and saw Jack had his eyes closed and didn't stir other than a motion of his hand acknowledging that Amos had spoken. "Another twenty minutes or so, Jack, and we'll be on terra firma." Jack didn't respond.

Pete was right, reflected Amos. The turbulence and side-to-side buffeting had started to pick up as they approached the mainland.

Amos was thinking again about their report that they needed to prepare. *Got to reiterate the lack of cleaning below thirty metres… and the impact on the life of the rig of them ignoring what we had recommended; they have an obligation… yeah, that's a good word… yeah… moral obligation to use the environmentally friendly stuff… yeah, but will they do it? It's all short-term decision-making… money, money, money…*

Gotta speak with Jack on the water temperatures recorded; they did seem to be out of the expected range limits, and the salinity levels. It was not directly related to the testing and sampling, although he felt sure there was some link to the number and now different types of *Balanus crenatus,* i.e. barnacles, growing on the steels. A lot, he reflected, to sort out before he could relax on holiday… although Jack was a lot better at the paperwork than he was.

They were now only about five minutes out from the heliport at Dyce Airport. Amos looked across at Jack; he opened his eyes momentarily and moved his hand to give a thumbs up and then closed them again and turned away.

There were three helicopter operators out of the airport and the pilot checked in with the Bristow heliport control tower.

With the amount of crosswind they were experiencing, the pilot was constantly looking at the screens on the dashboard, pressing buttons and flicking switches. Amos could see instruments showing temperature, wind speed and direction, cloud cover and squalls of rain sweeping across the airport.

The information was definitely assisting the pilot with his understanding of the landing conditions. *Makes you wonder how they would get on without all this technology.*

"Control tower to Bristow Thirty-two, over."

"I'm reading you, over," responded their pilot.

The conversation woke everyone up who wasn't already awake.

"Pad Three, please, is good in about two to three minutes, just a little bit busy this morning, hence a queue, and watch out for the crosswind from the west – it's very intermittent and changeable."

"OK, over," said the pilot.

They could see a helicopter taking off from around their landing area, swirling with the wind and rain.

"OK to come in, Bristow Thirty-two… gusts of ten to fifteen, sometimes to twenty from the south-west now, over," said the control tower.

"Roger, got that over."

Looking out of the window, Amos could see a helicopter manoeuvring to land on another pad and a plane taxiing onto the runway; they soon moved into position over the pad and the pilot lowered the helicopter. It landed with a heavy jolt.

The sound of the blades slowing was a relief. So much noise travelling by helicopter, thought Amos, compared to the general quiet of the rigs, and it was even quieter working underwater.

Amos gave Jack a high five as they unclipped their safety belts and disembarked, heads bent and walking quickly over to the terminal building, trying not to get too wet. Their equipment and baggage were being offloaded by porters due to the size and weight as well as the need for transporting to their next flight out of Aberdeen.

They approached the terminal building, sliding doors opened and they entered, shaking their wet coats and stamping their feet. They walked up to the passport control zone.

"Amos, Jack, good to see you both… Where are you off to now? I thought you had taken permanent residence on the rigs, ha ha ha," said the passport control guy, who recognised them.

"We're going to find some sunshine," said Amos, handing over his passport for checking.

"Hopefully a Little Miss Sunshine for me," said Jack, taking back his passport. "Expecting a baby girl in about four weeks' time."

"Flights to Heathrow on time?" said Amos.

"Couple of minutes behind at the moment but generally all good this morning," said the passport control guy.

They looked up on the departure board. "Yes… looks like you'll be boarding around 10.15."

"Good, that gives us time to have a quick drink," said Amos. "It's my turn to feel apprehensive about travelling," he added, looking towards Jack.

It was a short drive round to the main terminal from the heliport, but they waited until they could see that all their gear had been loaded up for the transfer to their flight before walking to the courtesy car.

"Looks good, let's go," said Jack. The two of them scampered out of the terminal building, shielding themselves from the wind and rain with their coats to the Bristow courtesy car picking them up and taking them to the main terminal buildings.

"I'm really not gonna miss this weather," said Amos.

"Count yourselves lucky," said the driver. "I'm here 24/7."

"OK," said Amos, smiling. "We will be thinking of you when the sun comes out."

Amos tapped the driver on the shoulder and thanked him as they got out of the car.

Covering their heads with their coats, they headed straight for Granite City.

They reached the bar very quickly as it was now Amos's turn to feel apprehensive about flying and he needed a drink.

"A double tight-spot bourbon and a lemonade with ice and a slice, please, thank you," Amos said to the barmaid.

She opened her mouth with an astonished look on her face and put the glass she was holding down onto the counter, and then spoke in a stuttering and flustered Aberdonian accent.

"Can yur say that again? I can do yur a lemonade but… what's a 'tight-spot'?" she asked.

"Ah, ahh. OK," said Amos, with Jack looking on and smiling back at him. "Let's see if we can solve this problem; get me a small jar of blueberry jam, a sprig of mint, a lime, lemon and a knife and a can of ginger beer… I'll do the rest, OK? And then you can get me a double bourbon."

Amos and Jack sat down at a table near the bar.

"How long do you think it's going to take her, Jack?" said Amos.

"My guess is in about two minutes – she looks like a smart girl and might know what she's doing."

Shortly after they had sat down, she arrived with all the ingredients. "Within two minutes," said Amos, nodding and looking at Jack. "That's pretty good."

Amos invited the barmaid to sit with them and watch whilst he made the drink. "This way you'll know next time I pass through here, OK? What's your name?" said Amos, taking the lid off the jar and taking a spoon to the blueberry jam.

"Joanna," came the reply. She looked over her shoulder apprehensively – there was no one else at the bar.

"Come on, pay attention – they won't miss you for a few moments. Anyhow, you'll learn something. Right, let's give this a go now," said Amos.

Amos busied himself and prepared the drink with both Jack and Joanna looking on.

"Right… there you go." They were all looking at the drink on the table. "Next time I come through – under two minutes." He picked up the drink and sipped it, closing his eyes and smiling.

He put the drink back on the table.

"Mmm. Taste that, Joanna… it's so, so good," said Amos.

"I'm sorry, thank yur anyway," said Joanna. "I'd better not, I'm on duty… but I believe yur and I'll make sure it's under two minutes."

She stood up, wiped the table and cleared the remnants of the ingredients and mess Amos had created onto a tray, leaving Amos and Jack to enjoy their drinks.

She walked back to the bar.

"Oh well, I've helped someone with their job today," said Amos.

"Cheers, buddy," said Jack. Their glasses clinked together.

"Our report," said Amos. "You know we're going to need to get it out quickly. What do you think about expanding on the aspect of the conditions that we took the samples in… not just the weather and swell, etc. – you know, the salinity and water temperatures. You know my feelings that the information will be useful at some point; we just need to get a good run of statistics together."

"Sure," said Jack, "that's a good idea and we can relate that to, say, the types of barnacles on the steels."

"Hey, that's what I was thinking, particularly the different type that we spotted… you've got the pictures, Jack, haven't you… be good to find out what they are."

"Sure," replied Jack, taking a handful of peanuts from the bowl on the table.

"How long we got?" said Amos, stretching his neck as he couldn't quite see the departure screen.

"I think we should be heading through security now as the 'now boarding' sign has come up," replied Jack through a mouthful of peanuts.

They swiftly finished their drinks.

"Wow, that was a strong one," said Amos, standing up. "That was good, real good."

Amos gave a wave to the barmaid and called over to her, "I'll buy you one next time I'm over, Joanna."

She smiled back at the two of them whilst wiping clean the bar counter.

Amos put up with helicopter flights but he had a bigger fear of flying, particularly long haul, caused mainly by the claustrophobic atmosphere on board and the inability to really go for a proper walk around. At least when he was diving he was in control; flying meant he had to rely on the competence of others.

"I'm gonna need another couple of bourbons when I get on the plane," said Amos.

"It's only an hour flight to London," said Jack.

"Yeah, thanks, I know… it's the long haul to the States that I'm preparing for," said Amos.

"Hey, Amos, I've got through security without being stopped," said Jack, starting to put his wallet and phone back into his jacket pockets.

"Nice… looks like it's my turn today."

Amos realised he hadn't taken off a silver locket that hung around his neck and that he kept with him at all times. It showed a picture of Bernadette and their three children. He put the locket onto the security tray and collected it quickly as it came through.

"Can't go anywhere without this," said Amos to the airport security guard. He picked up the locket, gave it a kiss and put it back around his neck.

"Have a good flight," said the security guy.

"Jeez, thanks for reminding me," said Amos.

"Amos, that's £20 you owe me," called out Jack.

"Yeah, yeah… I know," said Amos. The two of them had a running bet around who would be stopped through security.

Amos headed straight for The Distilling House. "Ginger mule and make it quick – I've got a plane to catch," said Amos.

"Coming up, sir, coming up," said the barman.

Jack looked up at the departure board.

"Would final passengers for the 10.35 British Airways flight BA 1307 to London Heathrow please go to gate seven."

Amos beckoned the barman to hurry up and put £10 on the

bar.

The waiter brought over the cocktail. "Never mind all that," he said as the waiter was about to start shaking the drink. The barman poured the contents into a glass and gave it to Amos.

Amos immediately picked it up and downed the drink in one, putting the glass down on the table with a clunk and leaving the ice steaming in the bottom of the glass.

Amos reflected that the drink hadn't really calmed his nerves but the warmth inside made him breathe more easily.

"Right... I'm ready, let's go," he said to Jack.

They made their way to the gate, passports and tickets finally checked and then straight through to the waiting area and onto the plane.

CHAPTER 3: OILY

The flight was up and off the ground before Amos was able to think about his fear of confined spaces; he had got used to being patient, calm and collected with the diving bell and decompression procedures, but that was perhaps because he knew it was essential for his health.

Maybe, he thought to himself, *I should take some flying lessons and learn to be a pilot? That might give me a better appreciation of flying and calm me down? I'd know what's going on then.*

Looking out of the window, he thought, *Soon be home, the kids and Bernie.*

"Any food or drink?" came the voice of a stewardess from behind him.

"I'll have a lemonade and a bacon sandwich," said Jack.

"Ice with the lemonade?"

"Yes please," replied Jack.

"A toasted cheese and a double whisky would be good. Thank you," added Amos to the order.

The flight to London was quiet and pretty uneventful, as most of the passengers were workers off the rigs, tired and on their way home, ready to see their families – so there were no difficulties with elderly passengers or trying to shut out the noise of screaming children.

Amos was resting his head back and looking out of the window and reflecting on their contract and sipping his drink.

"Thanks for organising the final dives at five to six metres, Jack; it's made sure we get home quickly."

"No problem," replied Jack. "The biggest challenge of the last few days was working around the weather but we made it."

The depths of dives over the last few days meant no decompression stops.

The Divers Alert Network (DAN for short) and the Professional Association of Diving Instructors (PADI) both gave guidelines and recommendations not to fly after single or multiple dives until at least twelve to eighteen hours respectively; Jack had planned the diving schedule to make sure all the deep inspection dives were dealt with early on, leaving the shallow sampling and final inspections until the last couple of days of their contract.

"I was just thinking… and it's been nagging at me," said Amos. "You know we've been taking the additional readings for water temperature and salinity?"

"Yeah," said Jack.

"Could you run those through back to when we started taking them, around seven or so years ago, instead of just reporting on the latest levels on this contract? I don't know whether it's just me getting older or more sensitive, but this trip, I really did feel that I noticed changes… what about you, Jack, did you notice any difference?"

"No, not really during the dives… other than those different barnacle growths and the amount of seaweed on the steelwork, but I put that down to the lack of proper maintenance… although come to think of it, it did feel and was actually colder than we've had previously, very noticeable when out of the water. But you know what it's like, it varies with every contract… I think you are just getting old, Amos."

"Hey." Amos nudged Jack in the ribs. "Don't you start… I had enough of those roughnecks back there ribbing me about the colour of my hair and my diet."

"Sure, Amos, I'll run the data through over the next couple of days when I get back and overlay them and see if it shows any changes or trends."

Amos lifted his drink and tapped it against Jack's. "Been a really good contract… Thanks for looking after me."

"And you too, Amos, we're a good team," replied Jack.

"We will be shortly starting our descent into London Heathrow," came blurting out over the tannoy system. "Would all passengers please return to your seats and fasten your seatbelts."

"That was loud," said Jack.

"Nice and quick, though, just how I like it," replied Amos.

He opened the shutter to his window… grey and misty… with glimpses of buildings and roads below.

Touchdown at Heathrow was on schedule and would leave a reasonable time for transfer to Amos's flight to Houston.

The internal domestic to international flight arrangements at Heathrow usually meant a change in terminal, but Amos had managed to organise both his flights with BA to minimise the risk of missing his flight connection to Houston or losing his luggage.

Jack didn't have this transfer problem as he was going back to Guildford and being picked up at the airport by his wife, Sally.

They disembarked the plane and headed for the baggage reclaim. Amos joined Jack at the carousel where Jack was collecting his luggage and also to check, just in case any of his luggage had inadvertently ended up on the carousel instead of being transferred to his flight.

"That's the last of my bags," said Jack.

"All looking good to go then," said Amos to Jack. "Can't see any of my gear. Jack, I'll call you from Houston in the morning UK time and we can have a chat about the report… send my love to Sally and hope it all goes well for you both if I don't see you before the baby arrives."

"Thanks, Amos, will do… and you go easy on the bourbon. Give my sister and the children a big hug from me."

"Sure thing, Jack." They high fived, hugged and slapped each other on the shoulders.

Amos gave a wave to Jack as he headed off towards the "nothing to declare" zone with a trolley piled high with equipment and luggage, and then looked for directions to the departure lounge for his flight.

Amos arrived at the lounge and looked up at the board… there it was, Houston BA 0197 14.05. *That's good,* Amos said to himself. *Now let's find something to eat.*

He looked across the seating area towards the shopping and restaurant area and could see Pilot's Bar and Kitchen. *That will do, let's go and check that out.*

He sat down at a table occupied by one other person, who moved their coat and bag off the seat to allow Amos to sit down opposite him.

Amos picked up the menu and started reading it and then flipping it over, and then over again.

He couldn't decide. *What to eat, what to eat… eggs Benedict… fish, pizza, a good selection of meats, mmm, well, that's off the eats list, thanks to Bernie.*

Meat had been off the list ever since they went to a classmate of Robert's tenth birthday party barbecue… they all went down with food poisoning and then Bernie started researching everything that was put into meat to preserve it.

The inhuman way man was looking after animals, the killing of them; all this, plus the impact it had on the environment, forests cleared, our oxygen levels reduced, carbon dioxide increasing and, added to this, the cost of transportation! *What a crazy world we live in.*

It goes on and on, thought Amos.

So, they turned into 99 percent vegetarians… not overnight mind you, but over the next three to four months.

The nice thing about it was the kids had now embraced it – well, most of the time – and when they did have meat on special occasions they tried to make sure it was organic and sustainably sourced… a big step for him, but the kids, they really seem engaged with it all.

"Too much choice," said Amos, putting the menu back down. "I'll get something on the plane."

The man sitting at the table didn't say anything and just smiled back – probably because he couldn't understand what Amos was saying.

After a few seconds of looking around, he picked up the menu again. "Perhaps just a snack," he said to himself.

Amos stood up and walked over to the food counter to order.

That looks good, he thought, looking at the food on a waiter's tray. "What's that on the tray?" he said to the lady at the till.

"It's a black bean burger with roasted potatoes, a smoked paprika patty, baby gem and tomato."

"That looks good… I'll have one of those… together with a Jack Daniel's."

Amos paid the server by card. It was accepted, much to his relief.

"Your food will be with you shortly," she said.

Amos walked back to his table with his drink, neatly sidestepping the wheels of a buggy and dodging a piece of luggage rolling across in front of him.

He returned to where he'd left his things and the person who was sitting at the table had gone.

"That's good," said Amos, "plenty of room to spread out… all to myself."

Amos sat down and relaxed, took a sip of his drink and looked around the restaurant at the number of people slowly making their way around, mixed with others obviously on a last call for a flight and probably rushing off to the washroom.

Then… there… out of the corner of his eye… he looked, blinked and looked again and to his amazement…

It can't be…

Yep…

It has to be…

There's no one else like him…

Amos had now caught his eye.

"Amos," a voice bellowed from some thirty feet away across the restaurant. "Amos, what are you doing here?"

"Oily, what are you doing here?" shouted Amos.

Oily, for his size, moved surprisingly quickly towards Amos.

"Same as you, but I'm going home to see Mama," said Oily.

Amos stood up and they looked at each other with beaming faces and gave each other a hug.

"You on the 14.05, Oily?"

"Sure am," replied Oily, "and looking forward to tucking into some good old American food."

A waiter came over carrying a tray with Amos's food.

"Ticket fifty-six?" said the waiter.

"Yeah… that's me," said Amos, holding up his ticket.

"Hey, that's very kind of you, Amos, thank you for thinking of me."

Oily had already picked up the burger and took a huge mouthful.

"Argh… what's this? Where's the meat?" said Oily as he put the burger back on the plate.

"That's why I bought it," said Amos. "So that people like you don't eat my food," he said with annoyance in his voice and on his face.

"Sorry, Amos, I couldn't resist it… it looked so good."

"Yeah, and it's mine," said Amos. "You haven't changed, have you, Oily? Go and get your own."

"What's in it?"

"For your information, it's a bean burger… and it's actually good for me, you should try it."

"Actually, I have," said Oily, "and you can have it."

Amos pulled the food tray back to his side of the table and promptly started to eat it before Oily changed his mind and got his hands on it again.

"I'll get my own then." Oily went off to the food serving counter.

Oily had been in the oil industry since, well… well, probably since he was born.

Amos and he met on a rig in the Gulf of Mexico some twenty to twenty-five years ago.

Oily was a roughneck and, at eighteen stone plus, it had been an ideal job for him, whilst Amos had been a trainee rig design engineer for Exxon on a couple of months' work experience out of Harvard.

"Amos," said Oily, returning, "you haven't changed a bit… maybe a few grey hairs here and there."

"Oily, you have," said Amos rather abruptly.

"How?" said Oily.

"Well… to start with, you've put on a few pounds."

"Hey, that's not fair," said Oily.

"Well, you've just eaten half my lunch!"

"OK, so I like my food. I'll get you another veggie burger or whatever it was you were eating," said Oily. "Anyhow, you know that working on the rigs brings on a big appetite."

"What are you doing now?" said Amos.

"It's a long story… but I'm directing well operations out on a—"

"You're what?" said Amos, interrupting Oily. "Did I hear you say 'directing operations'?"

Oily nodded with a big smile on his face.

"That's amazing, that's absolutely brilliant – how did you get that job?"

"Slow but steady wins the race, that's my motto… and what my mama always says," said Oily.

Two quarter-pound burgers and chips then headed towards their table.

Oily had already taken one of the burgers off the plate before the tray had been placed on the table.

Amos sat watching Oily devouring his food. *He's going to have to be very careful with his body*, thought Amos. *He's putting himself at risk even though he burns off a lot on the rigs.*

The gate number for their flight to Houston came up on the departure board.

"Looks like we're gate forty-two," said Amos. "Come on, we had better get going. I've got some presents to buy for my kids."

"You've got kids?" said Oily.

"Yep, three lovely children," replied Amos with a big smile on his face.

They stood up from the table and Oily's hand moved across to Amos's plate and took a handful of chips that Amos had left.

"Hey, Oily… that's mine." Amos dropped his knife and fork onto the plate with a clatter and gave a look of disgust towards Oily.

"Oily, buddy," said Amos, "you've got to be careful – you can't just eat food every time you see it, it… it's not good for you in the amount you eat. You're gonna have a heart attack – have you worked out how much you're eating? Just look at yourself."

"Yeah, I know, I do try, Amos, have done for years but it's so difficult for me, Mama always gives me big portions when I get home, she says I need… 'building up'. Anyhow, where are you sat, Amos?"

Amos fumbled in his pocket and pulled out his boarding card. "Looks like… er…15B."

"Hey that's great, I'm in row twelve… we can have a proper catch-up when we get going."

Amos thought, *There goes any idea of sleep on the plane; never mind.* Oily, from what he remembered of him, was always good company and he was sure he wouldn't have changed; well, he definitely hadn't regarding food.

They headed off to the gate and Amos stopped along the way to buy some presents for his wife and children.

Give Oily his due, thought Amos to himself whilst looking ahead at him, *he walks pretty quickly.* He was ahead of Amos all the way to the gate.

Amos only caught up with Oily at the final checking of tickets.

They slowly shuffled along in the queue. "Come on, Amos, what's keeping you? You were always quicker than me. Do you remember the Rig Olympics? When you and me were in the relay team together, and the guy leading slipped over and we came in first?" said Oily.

"Yeah… and the reason he slipped over and fell?" said Amos with a quizzical look on his face.

Oily paused with his reply, his cheeks reddened and he moved his head slowly from side to side. "Well, yeah," said Oily. "I was just trying to give him a helping hand round the corner and he just… well… he just didn't make it… say, though, that was good fun."

They cleared the ticket checking and sat down in the waiting area ready to be called.

"Amos, do you remember when we had that explosion on the Galveston Platform A 244? You near as damn it saved my life."

"Hey, I only threw you a life jacket."

"Yeah, seven of them," replied Oily, "if I remember correctly." They burst into laughter together.

There was a sudden crackling of the tannoy system.

"BA flight 0195 to Houston is now ready for boarding; would those passengers in rows one to six please make their way to board the plane. Thank you."

"Here we go," said Oily. "Looks like we're going to be on time."

Amos suddenly remembered that he didn't like flying. Oily had distracted his thoughts and he had left his Jack Daniel's at the table in the restaurant... what a waste.

"Rows seven to fourteen, please."

"That's me – see you on the plane, Amos."

Oily muscled his way to the front of the queue; no one was going to get in his way, he just had such a nice way of doing it. Oily turned his head round and Amos shook his head and smiled back at Oily.

"Rows fifteen to twenty-one, please," came over the tannoy. Amos left it until rows twenty-two to thirty were called and then joined the queue to board the plane.

The usual melee of storing luggage in the overhead lockers was in front of him. He soon passed where Oily was sitting and saw that he was already busying himself with the food menu and in-flight magazines.

Amos got himself comfortable and the flight attendants went through the standard routine of safety checks, landing on water and baggage below the seat in front of you.

Oily got up from his seat and came over to Amos. "Do you follow all that stuff? If we go down, I'm sunk anyway."

"Hey, you should pay attention, Oily... it may not mean you survive but you could help someone else."

"True, very true... you're right there, Amos," said Oily.

"Could you please return to your seat, sir, thank you," said a male flight attendant.

"Owee," said Oily to Amos, "these British flight attendants do have a way with words. I'm usually told to move my big butt."

Amos laughed. Oily really hadn't changed a bit... he still retained a fun sense of humour – essential in life and particularly during those long periods when on the rigs.

Oily returned to his seat and the plane was soon off the tarmac and into the air.

After a short period of turbulence, the plane calmed down and the safety belt sign turned off.

Oily was immediately up and out of his seat to speak to Amos.

"Have you noticed, Amos, that the flight attendants are always whispering to each other? It does make me laugh. What do you think they are saying? When are the refreshments coming through?" said Oily to a stewardess.

"Very shortly, sir," she replied.

"Because this man here needs a drink" – he pointed at Amos – "as he left his in London." Oily chuckled.

"And some food, please," added Amos, "as this man ate mine in London."

How Oily is still alive after all these years, I will never know, thought Amos, *and a director of operations… wow, he has done well for himself.*

"Amos, you married?" said Oily.

"Yeah… I told you that earlier, three children."

"Oh yeah, nice, that's cool… my mama always said I should get married and have kids but I never got round to it – you know what it's like, always away from home."

"Oily, you've still got time to get married. Anyhow, how's your mother? Is she still around?"

"She sure is," said Oily very proudly, "but she's not in a good way; she's been in and out of the Kindred Hospital Spring on Hollow Tree for almost two years now… and now…" Oily paused. "And now she's put on so much weight, Amos, I'm very worried for her. My sisters don't help; she asks them to bring in extra food as the hospital portions aren't big enough."

"That's sad… I'm sorry to hear that," said Amos. "How long are you home for, Oily?"

"I've got two weeks of vacation," said Oily.

"Well… how about you take over the extra food duties and take her food that's good for her, if it helps her get better."

"Yeah, I might just do that, Amos, thank you."

"Hey... here comes the drinks trolley, Oily, you had better go and sit down."

Oily returned to his seat.

"A double bourbon and ginger ale if you've got them and a slice or two of lemon and lime, please," said Amos.

"I'll just check we have some lime, sir... er, yes we do." She prepared the drink and gave them to Amos, much to his relief.

"There you are, sir."

"Thank you; when will you be serving food as I'm seriously hungry?"

"The food should be along shortly, sir. Would you like any snacks before your meal?"

"No thanks, I'll leave it, thank you."

Amos wasted little time in making up his drink... took a slow sip and closed his eyes.

His mind drifted off again to thoughts of what each of his children had been up to and also how Bernadette's perfume business had moved on since they last spoke.

She was going to meet a company that made natural, preservative-free products to see if that would help her business, as the online side of the business had been very slow of late and she felt she needed to take a different, more environmentally friendly approach to her products and packaging. Their daughter Elizabeth strongly encouraged her in this and supported her in what she was trying to do.

I wonder how Robert and Henry are getting on with their football? Robert had a semi-final... heck... I should have asked about that... I haven't seen them play for months now... I must make sure I go to a game and Elizabeth, her dancing. I wonder if she has passed her advanced certificate yet... damn, I should have asked before rather than waiting until I get home... that will be a telling-off from Bernie.

Amos smiled to himself and remembered that Bernie always struggled with him when he got back from a long trip... and that it took a couple of days to "acclimatise" to each other again and then back into their good, happy relationship.

He knew he was very lucky to have found Bernadette and that

they were definitely made for each other.

Amos opened his eyes and picked up his glass and took another sip of his drink; he caught a glimpse of Oily looking down the corridor with the food menu in his hand, looking to see when the food trolley was going to get up to him.

He looked out of the window again and became aware that the lady sitting next to him, whom he had hardly noticed before, was making a strange clicking sound.

Amos turned away and partially closed his eyes, wishing the journey was over, but kept being drawn to listening out for the clicking sound.

He sat up abruptly, turned and was about to say something when he saw that it was an old lady and that she was knitting.

"Hello, young man, have you had a nice sleep?" she said. "I saved your drink from tipping over… you must be very tired?"

Amos was slightly taken aback and wasn't expecting the level of her conversation.

"Thank you… I was, er, miles away… in my dreams."

"I suppose you are looking forward to getting back to see your family," she said.

"Yeah, I am, been away for over two months now," replied Amos with a questioning look on his face.

"Oil?"

"Yeah."

She continued clicking. Amos took a sip of his drink.

"My late husband was in oil; he worked in the Gulf of Mexico in the seventies and eighties then a short while in Arabia and then back to build one of the first jack-up rigs when they went into deep water; that's when he had his accident. A long time ago," she sighed.

"I'm sorry to hear that," said Amos.

"He passed away shortly after the accident – a bang on the head from a steel stanchion. That wouldn't have happened today, and even if it did they have the technology in the hospitals to help. Anyhow, got to move on; this scarf is for one of my grandsons – he's just seven years old. I promised him I would get it finished for when I got back home to see him."

Eight hours of clicking... *How could she?* Amos thought to himself. *When am I going to get any sleep?*

Amos unbuckled his seatbelt, got up and went over to see Oily.

Oily was sitting in the middle of a row of three seats. Amos couldn't sit down even if he wanted to... no room!

"How did you get the spare seats either side of you?"

"Well, they're not actually spare," said Oily through a mouth of chicken tikka masala. "I get all three seats... gives me plenty of room and no complaints from anyone and on top of this I get a bonus..."

"Oh yeah, what's that?" said Amos.

"Three meals!"

Oily wiped his mouth with a serviette and pushed the empty plate away, then lifted his second plate of food onto his table.

Amos stood over Oily, chuckling, and slapped him on the shoulders then shook his head from side to side.

"I'm going for a walk... I'll leave you to it, Oily, you're obviously on a mission."

As he started walking away, he had to squeeze past a stewardess tending to the food trolley and said to her, "Just the one meal for me, please, the vegetarian terrine and a ginger beer, thank you, and oh yes... I forgot... a couple of bourbons if you can spare them, thank you... row fifteen, next to the knitting lady." Amos looked across at her and she smiled back at him.

Amos always liked to keep moving when flying; it gave him a feeling of more space. He found that when sitting he would continually move his toes and always be turning and twisting his ankles and then his legs; it drove Bernie mad at times. He wasn't sure if it was the diving or just general apprehension of flying but it seemed to get him through flights.

He strolled around the plane, chatting to a few people as he worked his way around back to his seat.

He spotted the federal agent close to the front having a nap – *Why not?* he thought. *A tough job if you're called into action* – and then came across a large group of men from Wales with their bright red tops and smiley faces. "We're going to teach the Americans how to play rugby," one of them said to Amos.

"Good luck," replied Amos.

When he got back to his seat, his food was waiting for him. He could see Oily still busy eating his meal – which one, he wasn't sure. Amos moved carefully past a passenger standing in the aisle and then sat down in his seat.

"Well, this looks good," said Amos.

"I had the same," said Knitting Lady. "Have tasted better, but it's pretty good for an airline meal… and… I had a bourbon and ginger," she said with a broad smile on her face, "and that was good too."

Amos didn't reply, and just got on with his meal, finishing off with a sip of his drink and then another as he drifted off, in and out of sleep again.

***

He was woken by the intercom. "Please return to your seats and fasten your safety belts, please, as we are expecting some turbulence."

Amos noticed that his food tray had gone.

"I saved your drink again; you almost spilt it falling asleep," said the knitting lady.

"Oh… Thank you," replied Amos, taking another sip and then trying to stop the rest of his drink from spilling with the jolting motion of the plane.

The turbulence didn't last very long and Amos decided he would see what film entertainment was available. On scrolling through he saw *Happy Feet*. He started humming the tune to himself and mimicking the penguin movements in his seat.

"I like *Happy Feet*; one of my favourite films," said Knitting Lady. "I used to take my grandchildren to see it at the cinema every time I visited them when they were younger… such a nice, happy film."

"Yeah… a lovely movie… nice music," replied Amos.

He decided not to bother with a film and drifted off to a

nodding, dozing, disturbed sleep mesmerised by the tapping of knitting needles… not the tapping of happy feet.

***

"Amos." He was nudged on the shoulder. "Amos." He opened his eyes to see Oily looking at him. "Amos, I thought you were going to come over and catch up with old times?"

"Yeah… yeah, I will," said Amos, wiping the sleep out of his eyes and stretching his arms. "Just give me a few minutes, Oily, I've been asleep."

"Sorry, Amos, you didn't look it." Oily went back to his seat.

"I've not seen him for over twenty years," said Amos to the knitting lady.

"He seems like a nice boy."

Amos got up and walked over towards Oily's row of seats.

"Got room for me, Oily?" said Amos.

"I got a couple of your favourites ready." There were two bourbons on the table at the back of one of the three seats occupied by Oily.

Amos sat down. "Cheers, Oily, that's kind of you; you remembered?" said Amos.

"How could I forget." He clinked his drink with Amos's. "Even after all these years, I still remember our first meeting when you helped me when I got into a bit of trouble down at Clear Lake Shores in the Bay Area Houston. Do you remember we were trying to negotiate a pay rise and you said like my mama says, 'Be patient, Oily,' that's what you said, 'be patient,' and you were right, and we got that pay rise and that's what I've been doing. I've been patient with people and my job, waiting for the right opportunities and now, well, I'm near enough a top dog. Pretty good, huh?"

"You've got a good memory, Oily, and I'd say you've done fantastically well for yourself," replied Amos.

"Thank you, Amos, that's really appreciated and I know you mean it. What about you, what have you been doing?"

"Well, I run a rig inspection outfit, not doing badly, but I'm getting older and not as quick in the water as I used to be, and that's probably just as well as you can't rush the inspection dives and sampling – the implications of missing something would be quite horrendous. Anyhow, I enjoy it. Jack – my partner, he's my wife's brother – and I get on very well."

"Hey, that's great, Amos. Did you ever come across Pete the big Scottish guy with a long beard?"

"Yeah," said Amos, "me and Jack have just finished working with him over on Montrose Alpha… He's doing pretty well for himself, but still has a big family commitment with his daughter."

"Yeah, I remember, she must have been two or three when I last saw Pete," said Oily, taking another sip of his drink.

The tannoy broke into action, disturbing the conversation. "Would passengers please note that we will be starting our descent into Houston in about fifteen minutes and the cabin crew will be coming through shortly to allow you to buy any final duty-free purchases. Thank you."

"That was quick… haven't even had breakfast yet?" said Amos.

"Well… as it happens," said Oily, "you missed it… you were asleep, and me and that nice lady said that you shouldn't be disturbed… so… well… there was a spare breakfast and I…"

"No, no, noooo," said Amos, "you've got to be kidding me."

Amos headed back to his seat. "Did I miss breakfast?" he said in a shocked manner.

"You did fall asleep, young man," said Knitting Lady as he squeezed back into his seat. "Look." She held up a very long scarf. "I've finished it."

"There, you see," shouted Oily, pointing across at the scarf.

"We've now started our descent into Houston," a voice bellowed over the tannoy. "We will be landing in ten minutes would passengers please return to your seats and fasten your seatbelts; the cabin crew will be coming through shortly to collect any rubbish; please put any bags into the overhead lockers or under the seat in front of you. Thank you."

The TV screens flickered and then went blank.

"Seat in the upright position, please," said a member of the cabin crew to Amos.

Amos obliged but was still very miffed about missing his breakfast.

Knitting Lady offered Amos a boiled sweet. "I always find these help my ears," she said.

"Oh… right, that's kind of you, lovely, thank you," said Amos, taking one, unwrapping it and putting the sweet into his mouth.

Amos could see land out of the corner of the window. It relaxed him straight away; he was never happy flying over water, particularly over the Gulf – strange with his job being in the water. His concern was about landing on water and sharks; the continued flashbacks of his accident stressed him out at times, even though he'd survived – one shark attack in his lifetime was enough and he didn't want any more. Maybe that's why he was happier diving in colder waters.

The plane landed with a heavy jolt and screech of tyres, taxiing off the runway towards the gate.

"You will be pleased to know," said the pilot over the tannoy, "that we have arrived on time and the temperature here in Houston is a balmy twenty-six degrees."

A huge cheer erupted from the Welsh contingent at the back of the plane.

"Hope you have enjoyed your flight with BA and we look forward to seeing you again soon; have a good onward journey."

No sooner had the plane parked at the gate than Oily was up and taking his hand luggage down from the overhead locker.

He turned and called across the aisle towards Amos, "See you in the Hubcap Grille, Amos, when you get through customs."

"Hey, sorry, Oily, I can't, I've got a cab booked and wanna get back to see my family… I'll give you a call and we can arrange to meet up." Amos then gave Oily one of his business cards.

"Sure, Amos, will do, good to see you again and you take care now," said Oily.

"You too, Oily… and make sure you organise the food for your mother," replied Amos.

Oily was gone.

CHAPTER 4: WAVERLY

The plane slowly emptied of passengers and Amos joined the queue of people jostling to get off.

He breathed in deeply and was relieved he could now start to feel fresh air blowing into the cabin. The constraints of the plane now almost over, he started to leave the stress of flying behind him.

At the bottom of the exit steps from the aircraft he said out loud, "Terra firma," closed his eyes, relaxed and smiled to himself. The walk up to and through border control was straightforward and then off to pick up his luggage. He made his way through the "nothing to declare" zone; he knew the routine well enough, he could have walked it in his sleep.

Upon entering the airport concourse there were dozens of people with cards held up with names on them, waiting and eagerly looking for friends, relatives or a business colleague… eyes looking here and there… faces lighting up… children running up to a grandfather… some people pointing and waving…

He looked at the names on the cards. *Jackson, Robins, Davies… Come on… Greenhill, Birch, Grant… Hooper… Come on, where is it?* said Amos to himself, scanning back and forth along the crowds of people. *Come on…*

Ahh… there… at last… yup… behind that group of tall guys with odd-shaped hats… There was a card held up: *AJ Rig Inspectors.*

"Perfect," Amos said out loud. He carefully bustled his way through groups of people with his overloaded trolley, very mindful it could collapse at any time.

As Amos approached, "Mr Amos?" said the casually dressed, unshaven, elderly guy holding up the card.

"Yeah, that's me."

"I'm here to take you to Waverly."

"Yeah, that's right, thank you."

The driver took some of the bags off the trolley and Amos followed a couple of paces behind, slowly pushing the trolley.

As they headed for the exit, the driver turned to Amos and said, "Good flight?"

"Not bad, could have done with a bit more quiet... but can't complain."

Amos saw Knitting Lady off to his right. She gave him a wave. Amos acknowledged and smiled back at her.

"This way, sir," said the driver, directing him over to a large yellow Ford with *Yellow Cab Houston* printed on the side.

"Just as well it's a big cab... there's a lot to load up," said Amos.

As Amos was lifting a bag into the cab, there was a loud *beep beep beeeeeep*. He turned and there was Oily driving away in a bright red Ferrari. *Lucky guy*, thought Amos to himself with a touch of envy.

The luggage filled the boot as well as the rear passenger seats and Amos had a couple of bags of presents he had bought for the family on his lap in the front seat.

"Phew... that was a close one; I didn't think we would get it all in."

"I'm used to it," said the driver. "With so many people like you flying in from the rigs there is always a lot of luggage, especially at the end of a contract. I guess you've finished now?"

"Yeah, that's me done... till the next one. Just gotta make it closer to home next time."

The advantage of Amos living in Waverly was that with George Bush Airport some twenty miles north of Houston, it was a pretty straightforward journey home. Basically, north, avoiding the traffic and general hubbub of the sprawling city of Houston. It should take just under an hour to get home to Waverly when the interstate highway 45 was clear.

Amos looked out of the cab. *Clear blue sky... when was the last time I saw that?* he thought to himself.

"When did it last rain?" said Amos to the driver.

"I don't really remember," replied the driver. "Maybe two to three months ago?"

"Hey, that was probably the last time I was home," said Amos, shaking his head. "All I've seen is rain, grey, rain, and more grey whilst I've been away."

"Where have you been?" asked the driver.

"North Sea… inspecting oil rigs," replied Amos.

"I'd try the Gulf next time," said the driver.

Amos nodded and gave a slight smile. "You've been talking to my wife," replied Amos, looking out of the cab.

Up the Hardy Toll Road through Spring, Amos caught glimpses of recognisable landmarks.

Off to his right was signposted *Old Riley Fuzzel Road Reserve*.

"I remember the last time I visited there; a great place to take the kids."

The driver didn't reply and seemed more intent on getting the driving out of the way.

Amos was looking at both sides of the road now. *Wow*, the size of Houston and outlying towns… houses, industrial parks and malls and more houses… towns expanding so fast in such a short period of time… it jolted his thoughts as to how man had just continued growing and growing out of the city centre and spread like a swarm of locusts, consuming all the land, and so quickly from nothing really notable fifty years ago.

At least where he lived with his family, he, and they, could escape from the rat race, and with them living closer to nature it provided them with a better quality of life.

So much calmer up in the forest areas than downtown, the air so noticeably cleaner; we've got to do something about this, he thought. *We're basically choking ourselves with the amount of vehicles and air pollution.*

Picking up on the A45, it was now pretty much a straight run up to Waverly… Woodforest Bank Stadium… Three Palms Action Sports Park…

"Yeah… with the boys, I must do that, but it does get a bit noisy down there," he said out loud.

Amos's phone bleeped with a message. He pulled his phone out of his pocket and saw it was Jack.

Hope your flight was on time? Started the report and checked the readings that you asked me to and you're right, Amos, both salinity and temperatures are showing changes from our previous readings, will expand in the report. Regards, Jack.

Amos looked out of the cab, reflecting on Jack's text.

Through Conroe and Panorama Village... "Where did it get that name from?" Amos said out loud, shaking his head. *There are no views. Perhaps when they named the town, then followed what I suppose we call "progress".*

"Lake Conroe Park – oh yes, last summer's birthday barbecue with Bernie and the kids; that was a good day."

Still no response from the driver. He definitely had other things on his mind.

Through the town of Ada... RV parks and trailers... Waverly Road...

"Roadworks," said Amos out loud. "Come on, I just want to get home."

"It should be only five minutes to get through this," said the driver. "It looks worse than it is. I was up here a few days ago and it will clear."

"Thanks," said Amos. *Just need to be patient*, Amos said to himself.

Amos was now looking out toward New Waverly, the 1375... the driver was right, the traffic was clearing and they were now moving at a reasonable pace... and then onto the 150. *Almost there... almost there*, he said to himself.

Forests started up on his right-hand side, then on the left, followed by the town sign.

WAVERLY.

Up to the old town... He caught a glimpse of a neighbour and gave a smile and wave – "Hey, that's Mrs Jenkins" – expecting the driver to have the same amount of enthusiasm as he... but nothing doing.

Left into Browders Loop West. "It's about a quarter of a mile up on the right," said Amos.

"Up near the big tree?" said the driver.

"Yeah, that's it… the cedar, yee-ha, made it back. How much do I owe you?"

"It's paid for, your company account," said the driver, coming to a stop.

Amos thought, *Phew, at least the bank is supporting us; we're quite a bit in the red at the moment. Jack's right… need to get those invoices paid.*

"Gee, thanks," said Amos.

The driver and Amos got out and started to unload the baggage onto the pavement outside the house.

Up at the house he could see his youngest, Henry, at the front door.

"Daddy, Daddy, Daddy," Henry called out whilst running down the drive towards him followed by a lumbering old red setter.

As he got to Amos, Henry jumped up.

Amos caught him in his arms and swung him around.

"You're home," said Henry. "Daddy's home, everyone."

"Sure am, Henry – you've grown," said Amos, giving Henry a big hug. "Where's everyone?"

He heard a car engine and turned.

"Hey, thanks, driver," he said as the cab pulled away.

Oh well… he must have another job to get to, and just left the luggage at the bottom of the drive.

"Robert's in the shed making his surfboard and Mommy's gone to pick up Elizabeth from dance class… you're growing a beard, Daddy, you're very rough." Henry rubbed both his hands on Amos's face.

Henry started to struggle in Amos's arms and wanted to be put down. Amos obliged before he got kicked somewhere that hurt.

"Dad, Daddy, I've got something to show you, come on." Henry grabbed Amos's hand and pulled him up the driveway into the garage.

"Look, the bright red one," said Henry, pointing to the clothes rack hanging from the wall of the garage.

"Wow, when did you get that?"

"For my birthday, silly, you bought it for me," said Henry.

Drat, thought Amos, *I forgot it was from me and Bernie.*

"It's really good for when we go snorkelling," said Henry.

Henry pulled the wetsuit off the hanger and started to put it on when the noise of a car turned Amos's attention away from Henry. Up the drive came Bernie in the family car, narrowly missing Amos's luggage.

She parked up and jumped out of the car, leaving the door open, and ran straight over to Amos. They gave each other a big hug and kiss.

"I've missed you, Amos… don't go away for so long next time," said Bernie with tears in her eyes.

"I've missed you too, honey."

Their daughter Elizabeth then came running over. "Daddy, Daddy." She ran and jumped into Amos's arms… just after he had managed to let go of Bernie.

"Look, look, I've got a certificate," she said, waving it in her hand. "Silver grade star."

"Hey, that's wonderful news, Elizabeth, well done," said Amos.

"I'm going to put it up in my bedroom today so everyone can see it," she said very proudly.

They slowly meandered up to the house followed by Lucy, the dog.

Once inside the front door, he gently put Elizabeth down and she ran upstairs holding her certificate… with Lucy following behind.

They could hear noises of drilling and sanding coming from the workshop at the back of the garage.

"I must go and say hi to Robert," said Amos, one arm around Bernie and Henry still holding onto his hand.

"OK, tea will be about twenty minutes," said Bernie, giving Amos another kiss and making her way across the hall to the kitchen.

Amos and Henry headed towards the back of the garage and through the door into the workshop, the noise getting louder and louder as they got closer.

Robert saw his dad and Henry come into the workshop and he turned the sander off.

There was dust everywhere but at least Robert had the sense to be wearing goggles and a mask, windows open and the extractor fan was on.

He lifted up his goggles and pulled down his mask, revealing eyes, nose and mouth all clear of dust but the rest of his face and clothes had a slight coating of white dust.

"Hey, Dad, good you're back."

"Hi, Robert, great to see you… you've been busy."

Amos went over to him. They looked at each other and he gave his son a big hug despite the dust all over his clothes.

"Robert has been doing this for ages," said Henry.

"I've almost finished, Dad," said Robert.

"Yeah, I can see that, it looks very good." Amos ran his hand along the board.

"I was hoping to finish it before you got back and give the workshop a tidy-up but I put a bit too much filler on the board and it's taken a lot longer to sand it down."

"Hey, no problem." Amos put his hand around his son's shoulders. "It really does look professional, the board is so smooth," he said as he ran his hands over the board again in admiration.

"I just need to finish off this last bit of sanding and then onto the fins. I've used some of the wood from the tree that fell down last year," replied Robert.

"What colour are you going to finish the board?"

"Blue on the backboard and then put some gecko logos on the top."

"Look at all these geckos," said Henry, holding up a series of different-sized geckos on laminate paper.

"Then once they're on, seal it and let it dry; won't be ready for holiday, though." Robert showed Amos how he was going to do it.

"That's a shame. Hey, we've got tea shortly so you had better take a shower and get a change of clothes with all that dust."

"Sure," said Robert, "just got this final section to finish off, will only take a minute or two."

"Daddy, let me show you what Lucy's been doing in the garden." Henry grabbed Amos by the hand and led him out of the workshop and into the garden whilst Robert finished off sanding.

They walked towards the garden shed which was located behind the kidney-shaped swimming pool.

As they got to the shed, "Look, Dad," Henry shouted out and pointed at a huge hole in the ground.

"Are you sure Lucy did this, Henry?" said Amos.

"Who else... not me, and it smells so poohy," said Henry.

Amos knelt down and looked at the scraping on the ground and thought for a moment. *I wonder if there might be a break in the fence... could be hogs have got in.*

He stood up. "Henry, let's have a look around the fence and see if it's all still up because that smell might be a wild animal's got in."

"Wow, can we keep it if we find it?" said Henry.

"I don't think so," said Amos. Henry was disappointed. "If it's hogs then they can be dangerous, so it's probably not a good idea, Henry."

They followed a worn path and Amos pointed out hoofprints in the soil to Henry. The path led them to where there was a hole in the fence.

"There you are... it is hogs and they've been coming in here."

"Wow, I'm gonna tell Robert. Could we catch one, Dad?"

There was suddenly a big splash behind them: Robert had decided the simplest way to get clean was to have a swim in the pool. Lucy was parading around the edge of the pool, wagging her tail as Robert swam.

"Come on, you guys, tea's ready in a couple of minutes," came Bernie's call from the house. Henry ran back towards the house.

Amos turned and saw his wife, the sun on her face; she was wiping her hands on a tea towel and they smiled at each other. *That's such a lovely sound and sight to be home, and good timing,* thought Amos. He was also very hungry.

Robert got out of the pool and dried himself whilst making his way into the house to change with Henry by his side describing how they were going to catch a hog.

Amos opened the shed door and picked up a hammer and a bag of nails and went back to the hole in the fence and nailed some wooden boarding criss-crossing over the opening. "That should do it for the time being," he said.

"Come on, you guys, it's on the table," came Bernie's call from the house.

"OK, honey, coming now."

Amos walked back to the house, pausing to take a look around the garden, taking a deep breath, satisfied that they had bought a place in the country to live and bring up their children rather than in the city.

Henry was already sitting at the table when Amos came in.

"Dad."

"Yes, Henry."

"Who cooked your meals whilst you were away?"

"Gee… I don't really know, there were probably two, maybe three chefs, but it was pretty good food. I hope Jack has kept you posted that I've been sticking to a vegetarian diet?" he said to Bernie.

"Yeah, he said something a couple of weeks ago… that you had told him to mention it to me." They smiled at each other.

"Did you have to clear the table and wash up at meal time?" said Henry with an impish grin, knowing that was what he had to do at home with the others after a meal.

Amos washed his hands at the kitchen sink, trying to keep out of the way of Bernie, dried them and sat down at the table.

"Well, Henry, we would have to clear our trays away after every meal in the usual way."

"That's not very much," replied Henry. Elizabeth and Robert arrived at the table.

Bernie opened the oven and brought over two trays of food.

"My favourite," called out a satisfied Elizabeth as she sat down.

"Mine too," said Amos.

"Nut roast," said Robert. "Argh… Mom, can I have a burger?"

"Just sit down and eat this first and if you're still hungry I'll make you something else," said Bernie with an annoyed look on her face. "I've just spent a lot of time making this meal and you haven't even tried it yet."

"OK, Mom, sorry," said Robert reluctantly, sitting down like a sack of potatoes on his chair. Bernie was standing up with a bowl serving vegetables.

"Why has Elizabeth got more nut roast than me?" said Amos, with a slightly taken aback expression on his face and leaning back in his chair.

"It's my favourite, Dad, nothing left on my plate when I finish my meal… and… no dead animals either." She stared across to Robert.

"I haven't said I don't like it," said Robert. "Just because your teacher at school's a veggie doesn't mean the whole world has to be veggies."

"She's not a veggie," replied Elizabeth, folding her arms in a huff.

"What's a veggie?" said Henry.

"It's someone who likes food with no meat in it," said Bernie.

"I like being a veggie," said Henry.

"Now, you two help yourselves to vegetables," said Bernie, looking at Robert and Amos.

Elizabeth poked her tongue out at Robert.

"Hey, hey," said Amos, "come on, you two, Mom said she would make you something else if you didn't like it. Now tell me what you've been doing at school, Elizabeth."

Amos hoped the change of subject would calm them down so they could all enjoy their meal together. Amos and Bernie smiled at each other from across the table, glad that they were all together again safe and sound.

"I've started learning French this term, Dad, and doing quite well… can we go to France? I want to practise," said Elizabeth.

"You don't have to go to France to practise speaking French," said Robert. "Parts of Canada only speak French around Ottawa."

"I also came second in a cooking competition at school," said Elizabeth.

"Well done," replied Amos through a mouthful of food. "What

did you cook?"

"Bread and butter pudding; we've got some left unless the boys have eaten it all?" said Elizabeth with a glare across the table at both of her brothers.

The boys looked at each other and both smiled, with Henry looking down at his food.

"We did leave you some, Dad," said Robert, pleasantly surprised with the taste of the nut roast.

"I'm looking forward to it," he said with a smile and a chuckle. "Thanks for organising the cab today," he added.

"Henry told me you had called and we tracked the connections… perfect timing," said Bernie.

"How's everyone been?" said Amos, looking around the table.

"Chaos," said Bernie, "from the moment you left, to the moment you got back."

"So, normal then," said Amos, putting a forkful of food into his mouth with a smile on his face.

Bernie gave him a stare across the table.

"Dad?" said Elizabeth.

"Mmm," replied Amos, looking away from Bernie and continuing to chew his food.

"Did you know that just using concrete in buildings produces 10 percent of the world's carbon emissions and greenhouse gases."

"Gee, that's a lot of pollution. So no more buildings then? What did your teacher say to that?"

"Do we have to?" said Robert with a bored tone of voice.

"Robert, enough of that. Let's listen to what Elizabeth has to say," replied Bernie. "You might learn something."

Elizabeth continued. "She said that it's not just carbon dioxide, but methane, and that a single cow produces over a hundred kilograms of methane every year just so Robert can have a burger, and there's almost one cow for every seven people on our planet." She poked her tongue out at Robert.

"That's a lot of poohy smell," said Henry. They all laughed and joked about cow smells.

"Let me finish," said Elizabeth crossly and then paused to

compose herself. Bernie held her hand up to try to keep everyone quiet. "And the problem is that methane produces over twenty-five times more pollution-trapping heat than carbon dioxide, but it does only take about ten years to clear in the atmosphere compared to carbon dioxide, which is a lot longer, about—"

"Ha ha, so I can have my burger then," laughed Robert.

Elizabeth started to argue with Robert.

"Hey, you two calm down now."

"Daddy," said Henry, "when we go on holiday will you take me to see a moray eel?"

"Me too," said Elizabeth.

"Well, I'm sure we can sort something out but that's not for a while yet anyway," said Amos.

Bernie looked at Amos from across the table, aghast, putting her knife and fork down loudly on her plate, eyebrows raised and mouth open.

Standing up from the table, she said, "It's tomorrow, Amos, tomorrow; you've forgotten, haven't you? We've planned this vacation for ages and we leave here tomorrow at 6.30 sharp for the 11.50 flight out of Houston." Bernie's voice reverted to a sharp Scottish accent when she got cross.

"Hey, hey there, I hadn't," said Amos. "It's just that with my work getting extended… I hadn't quite realised it was so soon." Amos sat back in his chair and his shoulders slumped.

Bernie gave Amos a glare, which Amos knew was challenging his answer.

"Well," said Bernie, "you had better get packing, otherwise you're going to be last as usual."

"But honey, I've only just got back, and we're still eating."

"I'll help you, Daddy," said Henry.

"Me too," said Elizabeth with a big smile, taking away Amos's clean plate.

Bernie walked away from the table, taking plates and cutlery and putting them into the dishwasher.

"Come on, you guys, early night tonight so let's get going." Bernie looked out of the kitchen window. "Look! Your luggage is still out there on the driveway." She pointed out of the kitchen window. "How are we going to get away tomorrow?"

Robert got up from the table and put his plate into the sink.

"Dishwasher," said Bernie sharply.

Robert took his plate out of the sink and put it into the dishwasher.

"I'll get your bags, Dad," said Robert, looking down the drive from the kitchen window.

The family spent the rest of the evening unpacking and then washing and sorting out Amos's clothes for the holiday.

It was almost midnight by the time Bernie had taken the last of his clothes out of the dryer.

"So much for an early night," she said, walking out of the utility area and into the lounge and there… Amos was asleep on the sofa with his head back and mouth open, Lucy curled up to one side and Elizabeth the other.

Bernie gently lifted Amos's hand from around Elizabeth and led her up to bed.

CHAPTER 5: THE CAYMANS

The front door bell rang.

There was no movement downstairs.

But doors were opening and slamming above, voices calling out to each other and the family rushing about.

No one had heard the bell, except for Lucy the dog, who gave a loud bark, but this was lost by the family as they were all busy trying to get dressed and complete their packing.

Amos was stirring beneath a blanket on the couch in the lounge.

Another ring of the doorbell and a loud *rat-a-tat-tat.*

"Cab for Houston," bellowed a voice from outside.

"Amos… Amos," screamed Bernie from upstairs. "Are you up yet? Can you open the door? It'll be the cab for the airport. I told you last night that we have to leave by 6.30."

Amos woke with the noise, yawning and calling back, "Yeah, yeah OK, honey… I'm up… I'm up… I'll get it."

Amos rolled from his sleeping position and sat on the edge of the couch, rubbing his head and the sleep from his eyes and looking at the clock on the wall; it read 6.16.

Slowly getting up and slightly unsure on his feet, he walked towards the front door. He unbolted and opened it.

"Cab for Houston, sir?" came a wonderfully cheerful voice from a man with a big smile on his face.

"Yeah, sure, that's right… hold on a minute, we'll be right with you," replied Amos, turning back into the house.

"You look like you had a late night on the town?" said the driver.

"No, just asleep on the couch."

"Ahh, an argument with your other half. I know I sometimes—"

"No, nothing like that," responded Amos sharply, a questioning look on his face. "Hold on a minute, you're just guessing... I had a long day flying in from the UK."

The driver smiled at Amos and nodded quietly to himself. He thought he knew otherwise.

"The lady who booked the cab said I had to be here early so you could leave on time. Otherwise..."

"Yeah, yeah... I know... that's fine... just give us a few minutes."

Amos turned back into the house to get showered and dressed. Scratching his shoulder, he headed towards the stairs. As he did so there was a loud thumping sound. A suitcase appeared bouncing down the treads of the stairs and hitting the hall floor.

Elizabeth followed the bag at a gentle, sedate pace; she was the first to be ready, although her bag reached the hall before she did.

"Taxi to Houston airport?" called out the cab driver, seeing the piece of luggage, and sounding rather desperate now, hoping someone would react sensibly this time.

"Yup, that's us," replied Elizabeth, grabbing the handle of her suitcase and wheeling it across the hall to the front door. "Well, I'm ready and going if no one else is," she said smugly to the cab driver. The driver took the suitcase from Elizabeth with a relieved look on his face.

A few paces behind Elizabeth was Robert. He was dragging his luggage across the hall, with one of the suitcase wheels caught in a rug. Slung over his head and one of his shoulders was a pair of goggles and various snorkelling gear.

"I'll take this one," said Robert as he manoeuvred himself through the front door, treading on the rug and pulling the suitcase up to release the wheel. He followed the driver down to the cab.

"Can someone help me?" came a desperate shout from upstairs. The call was from Henry's bedroom.

"Can you go and see to Henry, please, Elizabeth?" bellowed Bernie's voice.

"I'll do it," said Amos.

"No you won't, Amos... you need to get ready. Just look at you!"

"Just coming, Henry," called Elizabeth. "Dad, you're not even dressed yet."

Elizabeth ran across the hall and up the stairs into Henry's bedroom, passing her mother, who appeared out of the kitchen with a pile of Amos's cleaned clothes.

"I can't get Shadow into my bag." Henry was sitting on his bed trying to force his big black teddy that he had won at the end of term raffle into his suitcase. He was a BIG teddy.

"Henry, you can't take Shadow, he's too big. Why don't you take RuRu instead?" said Elizabeth.

"I want to take Shadow." Henry folded his arms and started to sulk.

Amos walked into the bedroom with a towel around his waist and remnants of shaving foam around his ears and neck.

"Henry, Shadow's too big, buddy."

"I wanna take Shadow." Henry started to cry.

Amos looked across at Elizabeth and then sat down next to Henry and comforted him.

"Maybe next time… when you've got a bigger bag… and I'm sure he doesn't want to get squashed and crushed up. Anyhow, he doesn't have a passport."

Henry sat up and wiped the tears from his face.

"Come on, let's go," said Amos, giving Henry a cuddle and getting up from the bed. "We can see if there are any cuddlies on holiday."

Elizabeth gave RuRu, a small white rabbit, to Henry, and he held it to his face. Amos zipped up the bag.

"Hurry up, everyone," shouted Bernie from the bottom of the stairs. "The driver's waiting." She dropped the pile of Amos's washing at the bottom of the stairs.

"Just finishing up, honey. I've only just got up; if I had woken earlier…" Amos replied. In fact he still had to finish shaving and dry his hair; he had a lot to do, like get dressed and pack his clothes, for instance!

"We let you sleep in, Amos, as you needed to rest," called Bernie.

Robert took Bernie's bags to the cab. He was followed by Elizabeth and Henry together with their hand luggage, Henry with his rabbit held to the side of his face.

Henry and Elizabeth got themselves into the cab whilst the driver was loading the luggage into the back of the SUV.

"Anything else, Mom?" called out Robert, walking back up the drive and through the front door.

"Yeah, could you take Lucy round to Mrs Courtney and then see to Dad, he's the one that needs help… he's last as usual."

"Where's my shorts and tee shirts?" came a flustered shout from upstairs.

"At the bottom of the stairs… and hurry up, Amos, you're always late," Bernie shouted back.

"OK, Mom," replied Robert as Lucy came meandering up to him.

"Come on, Lucy, old girl… you're going on holiday as well." He stroked and patted her soft silky head. Lucy followed him out of the house and up the road to the neighbour.

Robert reached the neighbour's front door and pressed the doorbell.

"You'll have fun playing with Mrs Courtney's dogs." The door to the house opened and an elderly, grey-haired, slight lady stood at the doorway with hands on her hips and one of her spaniels by her side, wagging its tail.

"Hi, Robert, I can see you're all ready to go, then." She looked down the road to the cab being loaded up.

"Well, almost," replied Robert, "just waiting for Dad but he only got back yesterday afternoon."

"Well, you all have a good time now, and I'll see you all when you get back."

Lucy walked casually into the house. She had been there before.

"Thank you, Mrs Courtney, here's Lucy's food and blankets. Thanks for looking after her." Robert handed Mrs Courtney the bag, turned and ran back to the house.

"Nice children," said Mrs Courtney out loud to herself, watching Robert return to the house and looking at the chaos of luggage being taken down the drive to the cab.

Elizabeth was already sitting in the cab and gave Mrs Courtney a wave. She waved back, reflecting briefly on her own family holidays and then turning back into the house and closing the front door.

"Amos, it's not just the money wasted with the meter ticking on the cab… I'm worried about us missing the flight. Now come on, hurry up, it's gone 6.30," came Bernie's loud voice from downstairs.

Amos was almost ready and grabbed a mouthful of coffee from the mug on the window sill. He got a shock when he found it was cold and spat it out into the wash basin.

"Ah, yuck." He wiped his mouth. "Just a couple more minutes… almost there," came the muffled reply from upstairs, Amos now cleaning his teeth.

"Dad, shall I take this down?"

Robert had Amos's bag at the top of the landing.

Amos appeared around the bathroom door and gave a thumbs up and finished off in the bathroom.

Robert took the bag down the stairs and passed it to the cab driver, who then stood scratching his head by the car, bemused by how he was going to fit the last bag into the cab.

After a short period of contemplation, he then proceeded to empty the boot of all the luggage and reload. The final bag was heaved in with considerable force.

"There, I knew it would all fit in," he said out loud, pleased with himself and wiping his brow before forcing the tailgate shut.

A thumping of feet in the house preceded Amos appearing at the front door.

"Honey, have we got everything? Er, tickets, money, er…"

"Yes, come on, we're ready to go," replied Bernie from the cab.

Elizabeth joined in. "Dad, come on hurry up."

Amos closed the front door and turned the key to double lock and set the alarm.

That should do it, he said to himself, taking a final look at the windows at the front to see that they were all closed.

"Come on, Dad," shouted Elizabeth out of the window of the cab.

He turned from the house and ran down to the cab, got in and slammed the door shut behind him.

"You're always the last one, Dad, why'd you take so long?" said Elizabeth as the driver turned the car around.

"Just had to check the house one more time…"

"I'd already done that," said Bernie with an exhausted tone in her voice.

The cab moved off.

"Yeah… well," replied Amos, still unsure that he had everything.

"Passports," he called out, "have we got the—"

The cab screeched to a halt.

"I've got them," replied Bernie in a very annoyed voice. "It's all sorted. If you'd got back earlier you could have done it all, Amos, then we wouldn't have this last-minute rush and panic… we're supposed to be relaxing."

"OK, OK, I'll not ask any more questions."

The cab driver accelerated away from the house for the second time. After a short while they reached smoother roads and then the freeway.

Amos was still very tired and despite the children all being very excited and constantly talking to each other, he dozed off, drifting in and out of sleep.

Bernie motioned to the children not to disturb him and to let him sleep.

Eyes closed but listening intermittently into their conversations, Amos suddenly realised that he felt very isolated. He hadn't seen his family for such a long period of time that it felt like he didn't know them. He knew he would have to spend some quality time catching up with each of them again.

The nattering and chatting between the family continued unabated for the whole journey.

A jolt from a speed bump in the road woke Amos.

Opening his eyelids and seeing cars passing the cab leading up to the departure terminal drop-off, he immediately knew where he was.

He turned his head slowly, finding he had a stiff neck from having dozed off in an awkward position.

"Wake up, Dad, we're almost there," said an excited Elizabeth.

The cab slowed up, hitting a few more speed bumps and then parked up at the departures drop-off zone. By now Amos was fully awake.

The airport was busy, always was, particularly this time of the morning.

The children and Bernie got out and the driver started to unload their luggage onto the pavement.

"How much do we owe you?" said Amos to the driver.

"That'll be $72, but I can put it onto an account if you want?"

"No, no… that's fine, we'll get it out of the way now." Amos was mindful that his business account was in the red at the moment and that this wasn't strictly business. He handed over two $50 bills.

"Take $80."

"Thank you, sir," said the driver.

"We'll get going, Amos," said Bernie, "as we are running late and the kids will want some breakfast; see you inside at the check-in desk." Bernie pushed one of the trolleys whilst the children charged ahead of her.

Amos put the $20 back into his wallet and followed behind them, eager to catch up.

"Hey, wait for me."

Bernie turned around and smiled at Amos, who was trying to catch up; she had been waiting so long for Amos's return from Scotland and was very thankful that they were now all together again and he was back safely.

They dropped off their hold luggage and immediately headed for security and border control.

Bernie looked up to check the departure board. There it was: 11.45 United Airlines flight to Grand Cayman.

"Great, we've got enough time for some breakfast. Let's go and get a burger from over there," said Robert, pointing towards a fast-food area.

"Yuck, if that's where we are going for breakfast, I'm not having any," replied Elizabeth. "I want to sit down with a knife and fork and a plate, not plastic cups and fatty burgers; you know they should stop selling beef burgers and use recyclable materials for the cups and plates."

"Hey, you two, cut it out," intervened Amos as the two of them were getting very heated.

Bernie stepped in quickly. "Hey, that looks like a nice place over there; let's go over and have a look at the menu."

The family manoeuvred their way over to the menu stand at the restaurant and after a five-second reading of the menu by Elizabeth, she announced, "This will do," and led the family to an empty table.

"I want a burger like Robert," said Henry before he had even sat down.

"That's fine, Henry," replied Amos. Bernie looked up and glared at Amos. Amos gave a sort of acknowledging nod of the head and shoulders.

"He can have a halloumi burger; that's what I'm having," chirped Elizabeth and put her menu back down on the table.

Robert and Amos chatted briefly to each other at the table whilst Bernie helped Henry with the choices on the menu. To keep the peace Robert chose a halloumi burger as well, which meant Henry followed suit... as did Amos. Bernie went for a beetroot "power" salad, which she felt she definitely needed after the stress of getting everyone to the airport on time.

Drinks (water) arrived in a jug together with five glasses, much to Elizabeth's satisfaction as it complied with her values on sustainability and the environment.

"I want a fizzy drink," said Henry.

"We'll get you something on the plane, Henry, you know this is better for you when you're eating," replied Bernie.

"Er... four halloumi burgers and the power salad, please," said Amos, pointing at the menu and looking up at the waitress. She had already registered the table and tapped in the food order with the electronic device hanging around her waist.

"That'll be about ten to fifteen minutes, sir, I hope that works with your flight time... where are you guys heading?"

"We've got three weeks in Grand Cayman," said Bernie, "and boy do I need it."

"And I'm going snorkelling," said Elizabeth.

"Me too and I'm going to see sharks and stingrays," added Henry, moving his hands through the air, imitating sharks. It made Amos give a slight shiver.

"Hey, I've never been, but I'm told it's a stunning island to visit and lots of things to do," replied the waitress.

"It's our first visit, so it should be interesting. Kids, now stop messing with the salt and pepper – it's for your food, not the floor." Bernie took the salt and pepper pots and placed them on her side of the table. "Now behave yourselves."

"The food will be here shortly." At which point the waitress swivelled on one of her heels and walked away.

"How did she do that?" said Henry. "She just turned around without moving her legs."

"You'll have to ask her when she brings the food," said Robert.

Elizabeth got out some cards and started dealing them out to Henry and herself. "Does anyone else want to play?"

With all the interaction and conversation with the family, Amos had forgotten about his fear of flying.

"Go on then, deal me in." Amos stretched across the table.

"Hey, you're not supposed to see my cards," said an annoyed Henry, now holding them close to his chest.

"How long's the flight?" Robert asked his mother, whilst looking across the table at the card game the others were playing.

"Just over three hours, depending on the weather, but a tropical storm or two could add to that and you could end up landing on another island if it's really bad. That's what happened to Jose when she was visiting Jamaica a few years ago... it was that bad that the plane turned back and she ended up in Cuba for two days in the airport lounge... not a great start to their wedding anniversary celebrations."

"That would be cool – so I should get enough time to watch at least one film?" replied Robert.

"Yes... oh... there, looks like that could be our food," said Bernie.

The waitress held the plates up over the table and served Henry and Elizabeth first. They tucked in straight away; she disappeared and then returned with the rest of the meals.

"You've got a couple of hungry children," said the waitress.

"Yeah," replied Amos, "not much breakfast this morning; we had to leave home in a bit of a hurry, and—"

"Only because you were late, Dad," interrupted Elizabeth.

"And he hadn't packed his bag," said Henry with his mouth full of food and starting to giggle.

"Henry, mind your manners, now, don't speak with your mouth full." Bernie was a stickler for good manners, particularly at the table.

"Enjoy," said the waitress and she turned like she did last time and walked away.

"Argh, drat," said Henry, "I meant to ask her how she did that."

"Don't worry, Henry, she'll be back."

Their timing for food and the flight was perfect: no sooner had the last mouthful been devoured than the call came up for them to proceed to gate thirty-seven, as the plane was ready for boarding.

They finished up and made ready to go to the gate and the waitress appeared with the bill. Amos duly sorted it out and Henry remembered, following a nudge from Elizabeth.

"Excuse me, excuse me, miss… can you show me how you turn from the table, please."

The waitress turned around and looked down towards Henry and placed her tray on the table.

"Right, now watch carefully."

She turned.

"You got that?"

"Well, I think it was… you didn't move your leg but twisted," said Henry.

"That's right. You've got a smart one there, madam," she said, looking at Bernie.

She picked up her tray and turned to go.

Henry watched her again.

"Got it!" shouted Henry. He pushed his chair back, making a horrible high-pitched screeching sound, and stood up and mimicked the waitress. The family looked on and laughed.

Robert announced, "I'm going to buy some snacks for the flight." He stood up and headed towards the shopping area.

"You've only got a few minutes, honey," said Bernie. "Be quick now, remember it's 11.45, gate thirty-seven, so we will have to be boarding around 11.15 – and get something for Henry and Elizabeth, please."

"Yeah, sure, Mom," replied Robert.

"I bet he's going to buy another burger," said Elizabeth. "He finished that one so quickly. Probably one with beef in it – I'm going to quiz him when he comes back."

"Remember, honey, that we hardly had any breakfast and we may have to wait a while on the plane."

Robert did return quickly with a bag full of goodies, with no sign of him having visited a fast-food chain.

"Come on, let's get going now," said Bernie.

They made their way through crowds of people and towards their gate, joining the queue for checking in at the waiting area and eventually the call came for them to board the aircraft.

"I'm so excited," said Elizabeth as they shuffled towards the entrance to the plane. "I can't wait to get onto the beach and see some turtles."

"I wanna sit by the window and pretend I'm a pilot," said Henry.

"OK, kids," said Amos, showing the tickets to the air stewardess. "You three are together in row seventeen and the two of us behind you in nineteen, so no misbehaving."

The children raced ahead as best they could up the central aisle and found their seats; they were soon all settled with the rest of the passengers.

In fact, there was plenty of room on the flight; it wasn't full, but the children were happy to stick together rather than move into spare seats closer to their parents.

Amos suddenly remembered that at this time of year there were more tropical storms and that because of this, less people travelled. "I need a drink." His fear of flying suddenly clicked in.

"Amos, it's only a short flight," said Bernie, patting him gently on his arm and leaning across to kiss him on the cheek.

"Yeah, yeah, I know, Bernie, but I need a drink." His brow was starting to produce sweat beads and his hands were beginning to get clammy.

"Calm down, honey, it's gonna be fine. Anyhow, they'll be serving drinks shortly," said Bernie.

It wasn't long before the plane was taxiing onto the runway and up into the air.

Once the plane had levelled off, the drinks trolley started meandering its way towards them, much to Amos's relief.

"Kids, what would you like?" said Amos as the stewardess reached the children.

"And be sensible, we'll be getting some food a little later," added Bernie.

Amos and Bernie smiled at each other. "We've all been so looking forward to this, Amos," she said.

"Me too; I promise I won't leave it for such a long time next contract. Gotta try to get work in the Gulf if we can. Once Jack and Sally have had their baby, they can come over and stay with us; that would be good." He gave Bernie a kiss.

They were interrupted by the stewardess. "Anything to drink, sir? Madam?"

"Yes, please," replied Bernie. "Just an orange juice for me."

"And a bourbon, thank you – could you make that a double, please? Thank you," said Amos.

"Sure." The stewardess smiled with her reply.

"Dad." Henry appeared on the empty seat in front of them.

"Hey, you made me jump, how did you get there?"

"Dad, can I go snorkelling and diving with you when we get to the beach?"

"Yeah, we sure can, we'll have plenty of time for that," replied Amos.

"Yippee, yippee, yeah!" And Henry disappeared to sit back with the others.

Amos took a sip of his drink.

"He's so pleased you're back, Amos. Robert's been really good with him whilst you've been away – they've been doing a lot together, mainly swimming and football in the yard, plus going for walks and building a camp up in the forest."

The flight path was over the Gulf of Mexico, towards Cuba, skirting around the mainland through the Yucatan Channel before heading towards Grand Cayman. Plenty of open sea.

With the flight only partly full, the food trolley quickly followed after the drinks.

Elizabeth joined her parents. "The boys aren't talking to me – they keep changing their minds about what they want to eat and then said they are going to have burgers again and don't want to play cards with me."

"Don't worry, darling, they'll settle down once they've had something to eat. Have you decided on anything?" said Bernie as Elizabeth sat in the spare seat next to them.

She pointed at a toasted cheese sandwich.

"That would be nice," said Amos. "I think I'll have one of those as well."

"Dad?" said Elizabeth. "Do you have to travel so much? We never see you and all that flying isn't good for you or the planet."

"Well, honey, if I could get to where I work any other way, I would, and will have to see if I can work nearer home." Amos glanced across at Bernie.

That seemed to calm Elizabeth down and she settled next to her parents.

The trolley duly arrived and the boys ordered their lunch and were tucking in before the trolley had got to row nineteen.

"You've got two fine boys," said the stewardess, and then added, "and a girl; what a lovely family," when she realised that Elizabeth was sitting with Amos and Bernie.

"We'll keep it simple, as we're hungry… three toasted cheese sandwiches and some salad if you can spare some."

"Sure, we have a little more food than usual available as there aren't many passengers on today's flight."

There were a couple of jolts to the plane and the stewardess smiled at them. "The usual for this flight and time of year," she said and moved to serve the next row of passengers.

"Would passengers please return to their seats," came a steward's voice over the tannoy.

Moments later, the captain spoke over the tannoy.

"Good afternoon, everyone, this is your captain speaking and I hope you are enjoying the flight; we're going to be expecting a little turbulence shortly as there's a few tropical storms building up on our way over to Grand Cayman. We'll do our best to minimise this by flying around the storms but this may add some time to our flight. I'll keep you informed during the flight."

Amos looked out of the window and up towards the front of the plane as best he could; yup, he could see the whole sky up ahead with dark clouds, and then a flash of lightning in the distance.

He turned his head back into the cabin, looking for a stewardess.

"Excuse me, excuse me… another bourbon, please," he said as he gained the attention of the stewardess. She acknowledged with a nod whilst attending another passenger.

"Gonna get a bit bumpy, Bernie, by the look of things. Boys," Amos called out, "you got your belts on?" The plane suddenly lost height and dropped and then wobbled heavily from side to side. Elizabeth was still sitting next to Bernie.

"Robert, can you make sure Henry's belt is on and put a cap on your drinks in case it gets any worse."

A stewardess was swiftly making her way up the aisle, checking that belts were fastened and supporting herself as she went with her hands on the top of seats.

There was a sudden gasp from a number of passengers as the plane lost altitude for a few seconds. Then laughter as it gained it again. The pilot started to bank steeply to the right; he was definitely steering to miss the worst of the storm, concluded Amos. The pilot then levelled off and there then followed a period of intense buffeting.

"Are we going to be alright, Daddy?" said Elizabeth.

"Yeah, we'll be good shortly." He held onto his drink to prevent it spilling. "Just a storm or two up ahead that the pilot's flying around." Amos tried to sip his drink but it spilled down his chin and shirt, although he did manage to get a taster of his bourbon.

Bernie held on to Elizabeth's hand one side of her and Amos's the other.

"It's looking clearer up ahead; I can see blue sky," said Amos, just as the plane took another buffeting and loss of altitude.

"Are you boys OK?" said Bernie.

They both turned around in their seats and looked back at Bernie. Robert gave a thumbs up and Henry, with a big grin on his face, said, "This is really good, Mom – I wanna be a pilot."

The plane started to straighten and the buffeting slowed to nothing; a sense of calm returned to the passengers.

"Well, I'm glad that's over," said Amos, finishing off what was left of his drink that wasn't soaking into his shirt.

"That's one way to stop you having a drink, Amos." Bernie dabbed a serviette over the damp patches.

The tannoy broke the quiet.

"Good afternoon, this is your captain speaking, apologies for the bumpiness of the last few minutes, but we've had to fly around two storms that were converging on our flight path. We now have a clear run to Grand Cayman and should be arriving at 15.45, that's about ten minutes after our scheduled landing time; enjoy the rest of the flight."

The last three quarters of an hour of the flight were uneventful. Amos took a walk around the plane and then joined the boys at their seats and had a game of Harry Potter Top Trumps. Elizabeth and Bernie sat chatting together whilst flicking through the in-flight magazines.

"We will be shortly commencing our descent into Grand Cayman; would you please return to your seats for landing and fasten your seatbelts, fold your table up and stow away any luggage in the overhead locker. Thank you."

The passengers settled themselves down.

"Look… look down there." Robert leaned past Henry to look out of the window.

"Wow, so blue."

"The contrast of blues and turquoise and then the greenery

and beaches is stunning," said Bernie, leaning over Amos. "Do all Caribbean islands look as nice as this?"

"Sure looks good," replied Amos.

"Let me see, let me see," said Elizabeth as she forced herself past Bernie, not wanting to miss anything.

The pilot banked the plane and they could see pleasure boats, mangrove swamps on the edge of the island and stunning views of hotels and villas with palm trees encroaching the edge of the sea.

As the plane approached the landing strip, it got closer and closer to the water.

"Heh, there's no land," said Robert.

"I can swim," said Henry.

"It's not a problem, Henry," answered Robert.

"It's not a problem… the runway is right on the edge of the sea. Look now and you can see it," said Amos, pointing.

As soon as they caught a glimpse of the runway from the plane, they landed with a slight bounce, the plane braking quickly.

"Wowee, that was good – better than my Xbox game. I am really gonna be a pilot when I grow up," said Henry.

The plane taxied up close to the triangular-shaped timber terminal building: Owen Roberts International Airport. Puddles on the tarmac were already evaporating, the remnants of a recent tropical storm.

"Welcome to Grand Cayman, I hope you enjoy your stay and look forward to seeing you again soon." The plane's engines started to die down.

A blast of hot, humid air filled the aircraft shortly after the doors were opened.

"That feels good – definitely shorts and tee shirts this afternoon," said Amos, smiling at Bernie.

"Made it at last," said Bernie. "It's taken almost two years to get you on holiday, Amos."

"Yippee, we're here!" shouted Elizabeth, gently muscling past a number of passengers in front of her to catch up with the boys, who were already making their way down the steps off the plane.

Bernie and Amos followed. Once through customs they were

immediately confronted by a very smartly dressed, tall, dark-haired lady with a silky complexion.

"Hello, welcome, you must be Mr and Mrs Amos and family? My name is Daphne from the hotel."

Henry had a chuckle and put his hand to his mouth to try to stop laughing.

"Yeah, hi, I'm Amos and this is Bernie, my wife, Robert, Elizabeth… and Henry." Amos rubbed Henry's hair.

"Oh, I'm so sorry, I thought you had Amos as your second name – that's what I have here."

"Don't mention it, it's fine," replied Amos.

"Are you from the Grand Marriott Beach Hotel?" Bernie questioned.

"Yes, I am – I hope you have had a good flight? And if you would like to follow me, I'll take you to your courtesy coach."

The porter who was standing with Daphne, helped push the trolley with their luggage out of the terminal building to the coach.

He was way ahead of them and loading up their luggage before they had even got to the sixteen or so seated coach.

The porter scratched the back of his head, it wasn't going to be an easy job fitting them all in, as there were already other passengers seated on the coach and their luggage loaded in the boot.

The children got on first and squeezed their way past a number of people to the back; Amos and Bernie followed, with Amos having to sit with a large holdall on his lap next to the driver.

"OK. Everybody, is that everything and everyone and are we ready to go?" said the driver in a jovial voice, shoving the last bag into the boot and forcing the door shut. "Let's get going then."

There was no sign of Daphne. "Is Daphne supposed to be with us?" Amos asked.

"No, she's gone ahead, no need to worry – you'll see her soon when we get there. It's only a few minutes' drive up to Seven Mile at the most," replied the driver.

"Hey, Dad, have you seen?" came a call from the back. "They drive on the left," said Robert. "That's real funny."

The driver looked in his mirror and his eyes smiled back at

Robert as well as keeping an eye on the road.

"This must be your first time to Grand Cayman; a bit of history for you, young man. Did you know that there were once pirates living here?"

Henry's eyes lit up.

"And we were once part of the United Kingdom of Great Britain, and are still a British Overseas Territory and dependency, and in the United Kingdom… yes, man, they drive on the left, just like us over here."

The driver was carefully making his way out of the airport and onto the local roads.

"We have our own government in George Town, that's our capital, and this is the biggest island. The other two are called Cayman Brac and Little Cayman. Any questions you may have I'll be happy to answer them for you."

"He knows a lot," said an impressed Henry to Robert.

"How many people are on the island?" asked Henry.

"Sorry, I couldn't hear the question."

Robert nudged Henry. "How many people are there on the island?" repeated Henry in a louder voice.

"Well, that's a good question, young man at the back. There are over sixty-five thousand people on the islands; most live in George Town, and you know why I don't know the exact figure?"

Henry shook his head.

"Because people visit us for holidays and cruise ships carrying thousands of people arrive every day and the population goes up and down, up and down. Last year we had almost two million people visit the islands on cruise ships – that's about six thousand people every day. Does anyone know the highest point on Grand Cayman? … Well, it's sixty feet above sea level and you know, some of the cruise ships are taller than that. OK, we are nearing our destination – I said it would only be a short drive."

The coach turned off the road into the hotel grounds and headed towards a canopy-shaded area in front of the hotel entrance.

They spilled out of the courtesy coach onto the open-air hotel foyer, followed by their luggage. Daphne was there waiting for them and started to walk towards the coach.

"Woo, look at that," said Amos. Bernie gave Amos an odd look. "Fountains, waterfalls, hey, and there… look, a green parrot."

Pools of crystal-clear water reflected the sunlight and there… the view of the beach through the palm trees swaying gently in the breeze.

The children ran off past reception towards the swimming pools.

"Well, well, well, the Grand Marriott Hotel Seven Mile Beach. Wow, I never thought we would ever visit here," Amos said to Bernie whilst walking towards the reception, carrying his luggage.

"Leave that, Mr Amos, we'll take that for you," said Daphne.

"Honey, how am I paying for all of this?" He looked at Bernie.

"Well, you're not really… it's on me, Amos."

He raised his eyebrows. "How did you… I thought the business was struggling and…?"

"Well… I suppose perhaps it's not really me, but Grandma and Grandpa," added Bernie with a smile, looking at Amos.

"This way, Mr Amos," said Daphne.

Henry came running back towards them. "Dad, Dad, look at this." Henry grabbed Amos by the arm and pulled him towards a TV screen showing diving, and multi-coloured fish swimming around coral. "Is that what we're going to be doing, Dad?"

"Yes, something like that," replied Amos.

"Yes, yippee." Henry ran off back to the others, who were standing in the shade by the pool looking at two green parrots.

"This will definitely not be a busman's holiday; I'm gonna enjoy every moment, whether diving, snorkelling or just relaxing on the beach. Thank you, Grandma and Grandpa – how did they know things were a bit tight?" Amos replied to Bernie.

"They're not? Are they?" replied Bernie rather sharply.

"No, no… things are fine, we've just a few invoices waiting to be paid… Jack's looking after it."

"Well, that's good. Anyhow, the holiday is a present as Grandad reached his seventy-fifth birthday… he's done the same for Jack, but they won't be taking their holiday until after the baby is born."

"Mr and Mrs Amos, can you please register at the reception desk and we can then show you to your rooms. Anything you need, I am here every day – ask at the reception and just call me; that's what I am here for." Daphne then handed over the key cards for the two rooms and asked the porter to lead them to their rooms.

The children saw that their parents were being led up to their rooms and came running back from the pool area.

They took the lift to the first floor and were led to two rooms next to each other.

The porter opened the doors to the rooms and left the luggage. Amos gave him a tip.

The children charged into their room. "A/C at last," said Amos as the door closed.

Bernie walked up to the curtains and drew them apart.

"Look at that, Amos."

Amos lifted a bag onto the bed and then walked over to Bernie, who was standing on the balcony. What a view: swimming pools, gardens, palm trees swaying in the breeze and, through the trees, waves lapping up onto the beach.

The air carried the sweet smell of coconut. The scent of the Caribbean, with distant music from the poolside.

Amos walked up behind Bernie and gave her a hug whilst looking out from the balcony. "This is wonderful; what a great location, and the view is stunning."

Their few moments of quiet didn't last long; the children, already changed and very excited and ready for a swim, charged into their bedroom.

"Mom, Dad," they shouted, the two youngest jumping on the bed, Robert following into the room shortly after.

Bernie and Amos turned from the balcony, each of them catching a child jumping from the bed into their arms.

"Let's go down to the pool and swim?" said the two youngest in unison, both very excited.

"OK, you guys, let's see what the pool is like," replied Amos.

"Yeah, yeah."

"Let me down," said Henry. The two of them both squealed and struggled, wanting to be put down onto the floor.

Elizabeth and Henry ran to the lift, Robert following closely behind.

"See you all down by the pool," said Bernie in a bit of a fluster. "It's been a long day, Amos, I need to sit down." She grabbed her beach bag and made sure she had the suntan lotion, hat, sunglasses, book and water for the kids.

"OK, honey, let's catch up with the children and settle down somewhere and get a drink. I'm not going for a swim now," replied Amos.

The outdoor leisure area was extensive, with three pools, a slide and a hot tub surrounded by sunbathers and palm trees, a few people having a quiet swim in between sunbathing. That soon changed when the children jumped into the pool.

The three of them were all very good swimmers, particularly Henry for his age; as he was always trying to catch up with the others, he had built up both good swimming strength and stamina.

Bernie and Amos joined them by the pool and settled down with some loungers which they pulled into the shade. A smartly dressed black waiter immediately came up to them and asked if they would like any drinks.

"Definitely," replied Amos. "A Corona for me and…"

"Make that two, please. Kids, what would you like to drink?"

There was no response – they were too busy playing in the water.

"Children, what would you like to drink?" called Bernie again.

They eventually responded. "Cola, please," replied Robert.

"Me too," said Elizabeth.

"Henry, Henry?"

He didn't reply; he was focused on trying to throw a ball towards Robert.

"Make that three colas, please," said Bernie, thankful that she could now relax.

"Your room card, please, sir."

"Ah… ah, ah, I don't have it," said Amos. "I'd better go and get it."

"Don't worry, sir, your room number will do and you can sign the slip."

"Er..." Amos couldn't remember.

"214 and 216," chirped Bernie. "Amos, you really are terrible at remembering numbers, aren't you?"

"Thank you, ma'am." And the waiter returned to the bar, stopping to pick up empty plates and glasses on the way and other orders.

"So nice to see them all playing so well together," observed Amos.

"Yeah, Robert and Elizabeth have their moments as you know, mostly about food at the dinner table, but Henry seems to bind them nicely together. You know, Amos, Elizabeth's very bright and gonna make a difference when she gets older. You'll not be able to win many arguments with her, particularly when it comes to the environment. She's very knowledgeable for her age and at times almost obsessed with looking after the planet and trying not to waste anything."

"That's great to hear, honey, and sorry I've been away for so long. I'll try not to let it happen again... I miss you and the kids so much."

"Well, get some work nearer home, Amos. The Gulf is right next door to us," Bernie said with a stern tone in her voice, the frown on her forehead giving an argumentative look in her eyes for just a moment, then looking away from Amos and out to the glistening sea.

After a while, the waiter returned, placing the drinks on the table. Amos signed the chit.

"Thank you."

"Anything else I can get you, sir?"

"No thanks, that's fine, thank you."

"Children... Robert... your drinks are here," called out Bernie.

"OK, Mom," replied Robert, "be with you in a minute." They were playing keep me up with the ball. "Twelve, thirteen, fourteen, argh... so close to our record," said Robert.

"That's your fault, Robert, for hitting a tricky one to Henry," said Elizabeth.

They got out of the pool by the steps and ran over to where Amos and Bernie were sitting.

"Which one's mine?" said Henry with water still dripping from his body.

"They're all the same," replied Bernie, moving the drinks away from the edge of the table.

"Hey, Henry, not so quickly," said Bernie. Too late.

"Ooh, that was nice, let's go play some more."

No sooner had he placed the cup on the table than Henry was off, back into the water.

"He should have been a fish, that one," said Amos, chuckling to himself. "Cheers, Bernie." Their glasses clinked together.

They lay back down onto their loungers, not quite sleeping but soaking up the atmosphere and listening to the children playing in the background.

The ball suddenly bounced close to Amos and sprayed him with water and made him lift his head off the lounger.

"Hey."

"Sorry, Daddy," said Elizabeth. "It bounced off the edge of the pool and then hit my hand."

"That's OK, I needed to cool down anyhow."

"Looks like you should have come down with your swimming costume after all," said Bernie with a smile on her face.

"There'll be plenty of time for that," replied Amos, lying back down on the lounger. They rested for a few minutes until Amos interrupted the silence. "Bernie…"

"Mmm," came a muffled reply.

"I'm going to take a walk down to the sea before the sun sets, as it goes down quickly near the equator – do you wanna come along?"

"Yeah, sure, just give me a few more moments."

They got up and motioned to the children that they were going for a walk down to the sea. The children were content playing in the pool.

Amos and Bernie walked the short distance to the beach,

holding hands as their bare feet kicked up the sand.

From under the shade of a group of palm trees, they looked out to sea at the stunning colours of the sky with the sun rapidly setting.

"Three weeks of this," said Bernie to Amos.

They kissed and then hugged with the sun disappearing below the horizon. Not a cloud in the sky.

CHAPTER 6: SEVEN MILE BEACH

The following morning, Amos and Bernie were woken by the door to their bedroom slowly creaking open, voices whispering and then an excitable Henry and Elizabeth running into their room and jumping onto the bed.

"Hey, you guys, come on," said Amos, "we've not woken up yet."

Elizabeth cuddled up to Amos. "Oowee, Dad, you're nice and warm."

"Some consolation for being woken up so early," said Amos, rubbing sleep from his eyes.

Henry hugged Bernie on the other side of the bed.

"Mom, your bed is so big and warm," said Henry. "I've got Elizabeth in mine and she takes the covers when she's cold."

Robert followed Henry and Elizabeth into the bedroom and sat on the end of the bed.

"Sorry, Mom, Dad – I told both of them that you'd still be asleep," apologised Robert.

"Thanks, it's not a problem," said Bernie contentedly.

Amos gave Bernie a questioning look. "Really?"

"Can we go down to the beach today, Dad?" said Henry, looking up from the bed covers.

"Why, sure you can," replied Amos, a little more enthusiastically and with a smile on his face. "Every day if you want."

Henry cuddled up to his mom again.

"Hey, you guys are already dressed."

"Yup," replied Henry.

"We're ready for breakfast, Daddy, and if you don't get up soon you're going to miss it," said Elizabeth, sitting up and rubbing her tummy.

Amos looked across to his bedside table: 09.33.

"Breakfast is until ten, Dad," said Robert, standing up from the bed and ready to go down; he was hungry.

"Woo, OK, right, well, er… why don't you guys go down and get us all a table and Mom and I will follow you down in a few minutes."

"OK, Dad," said Henry, rolling off the bed in a hurry to get down to breakfast, calling out, "Come on, let's go," as he ran out of the bedroom.

"Keep an eye on those two, please, Robert if you could – we'll follow you down shortly," said Amos.

"OK, Dad."

"They'll be fine, Amos, don't fuss." Bernie nudged Amos in the stomach.

Elizabeth gave Amos a big kiss. "See you in a minute, Dad, and don't be late otherwise there won't be any food for you… 'cause we will have eaten it all! He he…" She got out from under the covers and chased after Henry.

Amos chuckled. "OK, honey, I won't." He moved across the bed towards Bernie.

"I'm happy here," murmured Bernie through the covers and snuggled up to a pillow, "and keep your hands off… they're cold… and no funny business now otherwise we'll miss breakfast." She laughed as Amos tickled her and gave her a cuddle.

Their bedroom door slowly shut with the door closer.

As soon as it closed, Amos was up and out of bed, stretching his arms up to the ceiling and wiggling his fingers and clapping his hands.

"Right, let's go and grab breakfast before I change my mind," he said, giving Bernie a kiss on the forehead.

He quickly removed his pyjamas, leaving them on the floor, and ran into the bathroom to shower. He glanced at a vertical mirror and briefly saw the huge scar that ran down his left side and shuddered, as a shark flashback stunned him. Bernie followed into the shower once Amos had finished and they were soon ready to join the children downstairs for breakfast.

Amos and Bernie exited the lift and could see the breakfast area set up under an array of straw parasols close to the pool area with other guests finishing their breakfasts. The sun glinting through palm trees and light Caribbean music playing in the background.

"Morning, Mr Amos and Mrs Amos, and how are we this morning?" said a waiter with a wide smile on his face and definitely happy in his job.

"Er... Yeah... er... Hi. Good morning," he replied, turning his head and raising his eyebrows towards Bernie.

"Morning," Bernie replied to the greeting.

"They already know who we are, Bernie?" said Amos.

"That's their job, Amos," she replied rather curtly and carried on walking.

Bernie was never that bright and breezy in the morning until she had showered and taken a sip of her first cup of coffee, so conversation was still rather snappy.

"Ahh, there are the kids... Just over there." Amos waved as they walked towards them.

"Morning," said an elderly couple in unison.

"Morning," replied Bernie as she recognised them both from the plane.

"How do you know them?" said Amos to Bernie.

"You were asleep on the plane, Amos." She turned her head towards him in a questioning manner and then away from him, shaking it.

The children had found a table with some shade close to the buffet area, which looked very inviting. The sun was already building up to the heat of the day, but it was very calming and relaxing with the gentle breeze of the Caribbean.

Elizabeth called out, "Dad, Dad, over here." Amos didn't hear as he was distracted, soaking up the atmosphere.

"Ok, honey," replied Bernie.

Amos and Bernie made their way to the table, after visiting the coffee machine, and sat down at the circular table the children had chosen: perfect for conversation.

"What have you got there, Henry?" said Bernie, looking at his breakfast.

"It's like a pancake, Mom, as Grandma makes, you know," he said, taking another forkful.

"And he's poured loads of maple syrup on it," added Elizabeth.

"That's just how I like it," said Amos, taking a sip of his coffee and winking at Bernie.

"But he has had some fruit, Mom, so don't worry," said Elizabeth as Henry was munching away at the second of the three pancakes on his plate.

"That looks good," said Amos, looking at both Robert and Elizabeth's breakfast bowls.

"It's a chocolate cereal, Dad, like we have at home... my favourite," replied Elizabeth. Robert had chosen eggs, bacon and tomatoes.

"I think I'm gonna go for some of what Henry's got." Amos got up from the table and headed towards the self-service breakfast area. Bernie followed, holding Amos's hand.

"We really must do this more often, Amos, it's so nice here and all of us together."

Amos smiled but didn't reply; he was thinking of breakfast, looking at the approaching display: *pineapple, mango, papaya, peaches... coconut juice, and look at those muffins... so much choice and the colours*, and then thinking of Henry's pancakes.

"Look... blueberries, raspberries and those green kiwi fruit... how do they get it all here?" Amos said out loud. "Must have cost a fortune as most of the island is jungle from my recollection."

"Sir, it comes in on ships a couple of times a week depending on the weather and the season and with the number of tourists visiting we have to import a lot of our food," said a voice from behind them. They both turned round; it was one of the members of staff.

"Morning, Mr Amos and Mrs Amos. I hope you both slept well, and everything is to your satisfaction?" He was one of the well-dressed guys who had been on reception when they arrived. Amos reminded himself of his name by a glance at his name tag.

"Thank you."

"Yeah, thank you, Dudley, that's kind of you to ask," said Amos.

"It's really lovely here… it feels like paradise and the food selection looks wonderful too," added Bernie, who was open-eyed and pointing at some star-shaped fruit.

"That's actually star fruit or carambola… It tastes a little like papaya and orange. The more yellow the skin the sweeter the fruit. You can eat the skins but me, I prefer to just eat the inside," said Dudley. "One of my favourites when I get time to have some breakfast." He chuckled.

"OK, lovely, thank you, Dudley," said Bernie. "I'll take just one to start with and see how I get on – I don't want to waste any."

"That's fine, Mrs Amos, whatever you want to do. And if you need anything just ask. Now have a nice breakfast." Dudley casually walked away from them towards another group of guests.

"Dad, try some of that orangey-coloured fruit, it's really nice," shouted Elizabeth.

"Yeah, OK… I think I know the one you mean, it's called papaya."

Having chosen their breakfast with a sample of the vast array of food, they returned to their table and were met by Henry and Robert coming in the opposite direction, returning for seconds (or was it thirds?)

"Hey, you two, make sure you only take what you are gonna eat, you got that? Otherwise it's wasteful; you can always have some more or even something different tomorrow." Bernie was aware that the boys really did like their pancakes.

"OK, Mom," said Henry in a rather flippant reply, being more intent on piling his plate with some more pancakes.

"And make sure you put some fruit on your plate, Henry. Try some of the papaya fruit – Robert will show you which one it is – you will like that," said Bernie, turning back towards Amos.

"I have, Mom and it's OK, I've got some fruit this time."

Bernie and Amos left the boys to help themselves, hoping that they would be able to eat everything they took from the buffet, and returned to their table.

"Dad?"

"Yeah," he said, taking a bite of his maple-syrup-coated pancake topped with blueberries. "Yum."

"Can we go to the beach this morning and swim in the sea?" said Elizabeth with a beaming smile. "It's so lovely here."

"Yeah, sure, once we've had our breakfast and your food has gone down," replied Amos as he sat down at the table after getting another cup of coffee.

"What's that you've got, Mom?" Elizabeth pointed towards Bernie's plate.

"Star fruit; do you wanna try a bit? It's very sweet – you'll like it." She had a piece of the fruit on the end of her fork and offered it to Elizabeth.

Elizabeth did like it and promptly got up from the table and went to get some for herself.

The boys returned with more pancakes.

"Boys, I'm gonna remind you now – are you going to be able to eat all that? You know I don't like anything thrown away."

"I can eat all of this," said Henry with another forkful of pancake about to enter his mouth. "I've got some fruit, Mom… look."

Bernie laughed. "Well, all I can see is pancakes, Henry. Robert, you'll have to help Henry out – I can't see him eating all that."

"They're mine, Mom," said Henry, becoming protective of the food on his plate.

"OK, OK," replied Bernie, now looking across to Amos, who himself was tucking into a pancake, and pointing out with his knife the fruit he had on his plate.

Breakfast continued with the children nattering to themselves about the activities available at the hotel and what they were going to do down on the beach.

"Dad?" asked Henry.

"Yeah."

"Me and Robert saw this hotel video this morning showing some divers and the colours of the fish were fantastic. It looks really cool – are we gonna go, as I would really like to, please, Dad?"

Robert's fork stretched across to Henry's plate, without complaint from Henry, and took the remains of his final pancake.

Henry had now completed his mission and was noticeably full to the brim.

"Yeah, I'm sure we can fit a bit of that in. Anyhow, we've got plenty of time, Henry," replied Amos, now sitting back from the breakfast table, holding his stomach with one hand and his mug of coffee in his other. "Hey, Bernie, this coffee is real good, ten times better than the stuff we get on the rig."

"Dad," said Elizabeth, "why do you have to work so far away? We never see you any more."

Bernie raised her eyes from her food and lifted her eyebrows with a smile on her face, tilting her head slightly towards Amos, interested to hear his reply.

"And you never see my football games," said Henry.

"Yeah, kids, you're both right. I'm gonna speak with Jack when we get back from vacation and see if we can get work in the Gulf – it'll be better and it's much closer to home."

Bernie's eyebrows lifted again; and shook her head, she had heard it all before from Amos.

"It's difficult sometimes, as you know, as I have to go where the work is…"

"But you could just get work closer to home," said Bernie, her voice raised. "You said it yourself."

Amos moved his head from side to side and paused before he replied.

"OK, you guys, point taken, and thank you. Let's finish off what's on your plates and let's get down to the beach."

"Yeah," said the children in unison.

The children charged off back to their room to get changed for swimming and to get their towels and snorkelling gear for the beach.

"They do love you being back, Amos. I know I've said this before but we do miss you so much." She put her hand onto Amos's. "And you can see already from Henry and Elizabeth that they want you to be around, and Robert, he…"

"It's been bugging me as well, but the money's not so good here in the Gulf, though, honey, you know that, and we've needed it."

"I've reached a point now, Amos, that I really don't care any more," said Bernie. "You've got over the worst of the outstanding bills on the business, haven't you?"

Amos didn't reply.

"I just want you around before the children are grown up and gone before you've even got to know them."

Amos acknowledged and held on to Bernie's hand. They left the table and returned to their room.

No sooner had they got to the door of their room, the children appeared from theirs and went charging down to the beach.

"Robert, keep an eye on those two, please; we will join you on the beach shortly."

"OK, Dad." As he ran off to catch up with the other two with a beach towel over his shoulder, a football in his hand and mask on his forehead, the others had already disappeared down the stairs.

It was only a short walk away from the pool area to a stone-flagged footpath gently meandering and then disappearing with the sand under their feet that led to the beach, where Amos and Bernie met up with the children.

"Let's find a bit of shade. It feels like it's going to be hot," said Bernie.

They pulled a number of loungers and side tables together into the shade of a group of palm trees leaning over the narrow stretch of beach and settled down. The boys were throwing a football to one another and Elizabeth was picking up seashells and coral by the water's edge, dipping her toes into the water and intermittently running back to her parents to show them what she had found.

Bernie settled down on one of the loungers, kicking off her sandals and wearing her wide-brimmed pink floppy sunhat and sunglasses, still in a tee shirt and shorts and with a handful of magazines and a book on the side table but deciding to rest from breakfast. Amos settled down on his sun lounger, once he had managed to fight his way to resolving the mechanism for keeping the back up at a relaxing angle. Tranquillity on the beach... at least for a while, Amos knowing better not to speak for a bit, letting Bernie relax.

The peace on the beach, though, was soon disrupted, but not by the children.

"Good morning, sir, good morning, madam, and how are you all today? May I get you some drinks?"

Amos opened his eyes and looked across at Bernie; they were both thinking, *When do we get a bit of peace?*

"Why, yes, of course, thank you," replied Amos with reluctance and an edge of sarcasm. They could have pretended they were asleep.

"Boys… Elizabeth," Amos called out, "what do you wanna drink?"

Elizabeth came running back to her parents.

"Could I have something cold and with fruit in it, please?" she said to the waiter.

"Why, yes, young lady… well, we've got quite a bit of choice: we've got fresh mango, pineapple, peach—"

"Mango, please," interrupted Elizabeth and ran off down to the edge of the sea.

"Make that two," came a muffled voice from Bernie.

"Three, please, waiter, thank you," said Amos.

"All with ice?"

"Definitely," said Bernie.

"Boys, what do you wanna drink?"

"Cola, please, Dad."

"Me too," said Henry.

"Three mangos and two colas, please. Thank you."

"And no straws," Elizabeth called out. "I think they are such a waste."

"OK, little lady, no straws – be with you shortly, sir, madam."

"Thank you," replied Amos.

"Anyhow," added Elizabeth. "They should be made of recycled paper, not plastic."

The waiter turned and walked back to the pool bar, clearing away empty plates and glasses onto his tray.

Bernie and Amos lay back down on their loungers, the boys went back to throwing the football to each other and Elizabeth to walking along the shoreline, continuing to collect shells and coral.

"Hey, Bernie, do you wanna walk along the beach for a while?" said Amos suddenly; he was getting itchy feet just lying down.

After a brief pause she opened her eyes. "Yeah, why not, I need a bit of exercise. That breakfast was very filling – usually happens on the first day away… eyes bigger than my stomach."

She lifted her head up and moved her book onto the table and they both wandered down towards Elizabeth. On seeing her parents walking towards her, she came running up to them.

"Look, look, Dad, Mom… look what I've found, isn't it beautiful?"

It was a lovely piece of coral and she gave it to her parents to look at.

"Do you see those red dots in it?" she said, pointing to the area on the coral.

"It's lovely," said Bernie, turning it in her hands and admiring it, then giving it to Amos.

Amos became interested and pointed at the coral. "Nature's treasure," he said. "Those small red areas are probably red coral; might be quite rare. I've not seen that before."

"Ooh, good, I will show the boys," she said, taking the coral back from Amos.

"Drinks, sir," came a call from the waiter.

Amos turned back towards the waiter and acknowledged with a wave of his hand. The boys heard the waiter's voice and ran up to the table to have their drinks. They arrived as the waiter placed them onto the table.

Amos and Bernie looked back to the view along the beach, and continued strolling hand in hand, the waves caressing the sand and washing over their feet.

"This is so peaceful," said Bernie.

"Yeah, good choice coming here, Bernie, and a really big thank you to your parents. They really have been a great help to us; it's just what we needed. We must get them to come over again, maybe at the same time as Jack and Sally do after the baby is born."

"Dad!" Elizabeth came running up to them.

"What have you got this time?" Amos said rather impatiently, Bernie giving him a shake of her hand to remind him that she wanted to be with him. Amos acknowledged.

"When can we go diving? I wanna see a moray eel, remember, you promised?"

"Yeah… we'll have a look at what they've got from the hotel and sort something out, honey, when we get back."

"You promise now, Dad."

"Yeah, yeah, I promise."

"Thank you, Daddy." She jumped up and gave her father a hug and then ran off in front of them, stopping to pick up a piece of driftwood.

"Shall we head back now, honey, as I'm desperate for a drink before they get warmed up by the sun – it's pretty hot out here," said Amos.

They returned to their loungers and Amos was right: the ice in their drinks had almost disappeared. They too were thirsty.

Amos raised his arm to attract a waiter's attention, who duly came over.

"Three more mangos, please… and, boys, would you like another drink?"

"Yes please, cola," came a very quick reply from both of them. They were still happy throwing the ball to each other. "Funny how this keeps the boys content," said Amos. "And two colas, please, thank you, waiter."

"Dad, catch!"

The ball whistled across the beach towards Amos, narrowly missing Elizabeth and, luckily, he caught it just before it hit the drinks table.

"Hey, you guys, be careful now."

Henry started laughing.

"Sorry, Dad," replied Robert.

Henry then came running over to his parents.

"Dad?" asked Henry.

"Yeah."

"Elizabeth said we are going diving, when are we gonna go?"

"Er, yeah… we will need to organise that but you know the game we play before you can go…"

"Yeah, yeah, yeah," shouted Henry and Elizabeth together out loud. "We know." And they both came rushing up to Amos.

"Robert, Robert, come on," called out Elizabeth. He made his way over enthusiastically. "We need your questions, Robert."

"Do you remember, Robert, the difficult ones?" said Elizabeth excitedly.

Bernie sat down on the sun lounger with a broad smile on her face as she knew this would be fun and always enjoyed seeing the children interacting with Amos when he gave them a challenge. He just had such a nice way about life in general that he got on with most people with ease. She looked across at them chattering away and reflected on what a great catch Amos had been.

"We're ready for you, Dad," said Elizabeth very excitedly. "We've got some interesting questions for you which you know you're not supposed to get right."

"He's not going to get that one," said Henry, pointing at the sheet of paper Robert was holding.

"Shh, we have to be quiet, Henry," replied Elizabeth with a finger over her lips.

The children huddled together, discussing what was written on various pieces of paper they had taken out of their rucksacks. They had already prepared themselves. This was a game that Amos played with the children before they could go diving. It involved a series of questions from the children and if Amos got any of them wrong, then the children could go diving.

"You know the rules now, kids – seven questions," said Amos.

"We've got eight this time, Dad," interjected Henry with a big grin on his face; his hand then came up to his mouth to try to stop sniggering.

"Eight? How come?" replied Amos.

"That's because—" said Elizabeth, who was interrupted mid-sentence.

"You know too much, Dad, and we wanna go diving," said Henry.

"So, Dad, are you listening? What we've got are two questions each and then a final two tricky questions; we'll decide who's going to ask them later."

"OK, I suppose I had better lie down for this." Amos duly took his drink and relaxed on the lounger.

"Yippee. Have you got question eight, Elizabeth? You know, the one that you and Robert found – Dad's definitely not going to get that one," whispered Henry to Elizabeth and Robert. The children were really looking forward to this, Elizabeth and Henry getting very excited. Yes, there was a bit of teasing from Amos, but he knew when not to.

"OK, Dad, here we go," said Elizabeth. "Question one… Go on, Henry, go on."

"What's the biggest oil field in the world?"

"Ah, that's I think quite a straightforward one for me to start with, thank you, Henry… er… mmm… that's the one I think in Saudi Arabia… the Ghawar Field…" replied Amos.

"Drat," said Henry, lifting his hands to his head.

"It's OK, Henry, don't worry, we've got lots of other questions. Question two." This time it was from Robert. "What was the name of the person or company that designed the first oil rig in the Gulf of Mexico?"

"Woo, that's an interesting one… so early in the game as well… er… well… there were rigs being built at the back end of the 1890s, but in the Gulf itself… mmm… and in open waters… I'd say it was probably after the war, the Second World War, 1949-ish… so… mmm… that would be John T. Hayward… and he worked for a company called Barnsdall Refining… that's my guess or answer."

Elizabeth and Henry looked across at Robert.

"Yup, Dad, you're right… well done, I thought I would catch you out on that one," said Robert.

Question three, this time from Elizabeth. "What's the name of the most environmentally friendly oil company?"

"Well, that varies from time to time," replied Amos, putting his hand to his face and rubbing the stubble on his chin.

"Yes," said Elizabeth,"whenever there's an oil spill, the company that's caused it goes bottom of the list, right?"

"There are some big companies out there… and they would find it easier to implement environmental protection requirements. Well, the last time I looked it was probably… mmm, Shell? BP? … No, maybe not… I don't think so, although they're pretty good now… mmm… Exxon… mmm… Possibly Sunoco… I think I will go with Exxon."

"Dad, you're not supposed to get that one either," said Elizabeth.

"Right," said Henry, "I've got my second question… how many gallons are in a barrel of oil?"

"Henry, now that is another tricky question. I vaguely remember learning about all that sort of stuff at school but that was a long, long time ago."

"He he he," said Henry, holding the answer on a piece of paper and looking towards his sister.

Bernie looked across at Amos, suggesting with her eyes that he should get this one wrong.

"I think it's around forty or so… But which number… This is very difficult, you know, Henry… I think it might be… maybe forty-two or forty-three, maybe more… but… I will have to guess at forty-two."

"Ahh… no, Dad, you're not supposed to guess right." Henry scrunched up the piece of paper and threw it onto the sand, then folded his arms together and dropped his head into his arms and sulked. Bernie's eyes across from the other lounger to Amos said it all.

Question five from Robert: "What is the longest underwater pipeline from land to rig?"

"Could you say that one again, please, Robert."

"What's the longest underwater pipeline from land to rig or platform?"

"Phew… another hard question." Amos sipped his drink. "Well, in the Gulf… no, it's too short a distance… mmm… Saudi is mostly on land… So it's got to be up in the North Sea somewhere… Norway to the UK, maybe… Argh, yes, it's coming to me… it's called the… it's on the tip of my tongue… Langeled, yeah, Langeled."

"Dad's right," said Robert. Bernie looked across at Amos again with a question of urgency in her eyes. *Come on, Amos, get one wrong.*

"Right, my turn," said Elizabeth rather crossly. "Which oil company caused the oil disaster off the coast of Alaska?"

Amos replied straight away, "That was I think the Valdez in 1989, Prince William Sound and—"

"You know you're right, Dad," interrupted Elizabeth. "And did you know how much damage it caused? Tens of thousands of birds died and sea otters and other animals and you might not think that's a lot but years later fish stocks like herring and salmon have gone down and been found to have defects, and we're eating the fish!"

Elizabeth turned to the others and they huddled together to discuss which would be their final two questions to put to their annoying father.

Whilst the children were busy discussing, Bernie looked across to Amos and gave a stern stare. "Amos, you might have been the rig quiz champion but come on... you're not on the rig now... It's the children, our children, and we're on holiday."

"But honey, I can't not get a question right if I know the answer – if I know it, I'm gonna say it."

"Question seven," said Elizabeth. "What goal did Brazil recently set to help stop climate change?"

"Argh, a sports question. I thought the quiz was about stuff I knew about." The children giggled together, thinking he was on the wrong track.

"What goal?" Amos repeated the question to himself and scratched his head. "Well, I don't think it would be scoring goals in soccer although they are good at that... mmm... I think it's to do with trees and the number of trees in the rainforest that they would cut down."

"Argh, Dad. You're right again," said Henry. "Dad, come on, you're too clever for us and I wanna go diving," said a disgruntled Henry. "And Dad. Did you know that they didn't even get anywhere near the target – they ended up cutting down almost twice as many trees, almost four thousand square miles."

"That's a lot of firewood, and what are they going to use it for?" replied Amos.

"Cattle farming so that Robert can have his beef burger," replied Elizabeth crossly. The children huddled together again to agree on the final question.

"Right, we're ready for you now," said Elizabeth. "We've got our final question eight for you, Dad, and you had better get it wrong…" She nudged Henry to ask the question, knowing that he was so keen to catch his dad out.

"How much… How much does burning oil pollute the air?"

"What do you mean, Henry?"

"Carbon dioxide emissions, Dad," said Elizabeth rather sternly now; she was definitely erring on her mother's side of the family, thought Amos, with the directness of her speech and Bernie's sharpness of tongue. Amos paused with his answer. Bernie was right: she definitely had a passion for looking after the environment.

"Wow… Henry, I think you might have got me with this one… carbon dioxide emissions from oil… mmm… You know what… I could have a guess." Bernie gave him another stern look. Amos saw the look in her eyes and waited a while before answering. "But I don't think I know the answer to this… But let me think…" The children were now getting very excited. "Nope, I don't know, I really don't."

"Yeah!" Henry and Robert jumped up with joy. Bernie's face was a picture of relief that she could now relax.

"Well, Dad, you should know," said Elizabeth. "It's what you are doing with your work all day long, every day… It's poisoning the air… all the time. When oil burns, it produces carbon dioxide and methane and gases that cause cancer. You should know, Dad, as you're working close to the fumes and the burning oil and gas all day on the rigs. My teacher says that the deep water horizon disaster in the Gulf of Mexico caused minute particles of the oil spill over the sea to evaporate off the surface of the sea and into the air and we are breathing it in. And it can influence climate change."

"Hold on there, where did you get that information from?"

"My teacher, Dad, I said earlier."

"Yeah, she's the veggie, Dad," said Robert.

"She's not a veggie," replied Elizabeth, very annoyed.

"Hey, hey, come on, you two, now stop that," said Bernie. "Amos, could you go and organise the diving now, please, and Robert and Elizabeth, behave yourselves."

"We're going diving, we're going diving," said Henry in a singsong voice.

Amos looked across at Bernie as the boys headed off to the hotel's reception desk; he then whispered to her out of earshot from the children, "You know I knew that one… and I didn't want the children to miss out."

"I'm not so sure you did, Amos," replied Bernie with a look of uncertainty and a slight shake of her head. "You said to me earlier that you would give a right answer if you knew it. Anyhow, you'll know the answer next time the question comes up."

Elizabeth came running over to Amos. "Dad, Dad, come on, let's go and catch up with the boys," she said, grabbing at his hand.

"Bernie, do you wanna come with us?"

"Come on, Mom," said Elizabeth.

"No thanks, honey, I'm fine here at the moment – I just wanna have a bit of time to myself for a while." She sat down on the sun lounger, lay back and opened up her book.

Amos kissed her on the forehead and followed the children up to the hotel reception. *We should have come here years ago*, Bernie said to herself.

The boys were already sitting down and looking at the dive brochures and the options available to them. Amos and Elizabeth caught up with them.

"OK, kids, the first thing we'll organise is a PADI resort course just to get us going. Robert, you'll need to do it again as a refresher and then we'll see what else we can do after."

"Yeah, we're going diving," cried out Henry.

"Shh, Henry, not quite yet, Henry, and not so loud, Dad's gotta book it up yet," said Elizabeth.

Amos got a surprise from behind him whilst he was queuing at reception. "Good morning, Mr Amos, how can I help you?" It was Daphne, who had seen the children sitting and watching the diving video on the TV screen and collecting up various brochures.

"Hey, thank you, how you doing? That's very timely, Daphne, thank you... er... we were wondering if you run PADI resort diving courses here at the hotel?"

"Ooh yes, yes we do, Mr Amos... you can go to the dive centre right next door to us and ask for James, he'll sort you out, and would this be for all of you?"

"Well, probably just the four of us – me and the children. Bernie, she's not so keen on diving as she has problems with her ears."

"OK... let me see now, I can check the reservations and see... mmm..." She sat down behind the reception desk and called up information on the computer screen. "How's your stay been so far, Mr Amos?"

"Very, very nice, thank you and the breakfast, wow, what a selection, for me it was eating like a king."

"Thank you, yes... It looks like... Yes... there are places, yes, there are six places available tomorrow morning at eleven... so yes, the four of you are available to go and if Mrs Amos changes her mind just let me know. Would you like me to book it up now for you?"

"Yes please, and thank you, do you need any money from me?"

"No, that's fine, Mr Amos, we will book it to your room." *Ouch,* thought Amos, *there's gonna be a big bill at the end of the holiday.*

"You'll need to be meeting by the pool at 10.30 and the instruction lasts about an hour to an hour and a half, maybe two hours, depending on how many others are joining the course, but at the moment it's just you guys."

"And what about the afternoon shallow dive?"

"That's meeting in reception here... Let me see now... two o'clock, and you'll be back at around 4.30, is that OK?"

"Yeah."

"But that does depend on how you all get on in the morning... Henry here looks as if he might be a bit too small, but we'll let the instructor decide what's best."

"Daphne, that's perfect, thank you, thank you very much. Which direction is the dive centre? As we may go and have a look before tomorrow morning."

"Through the doors over there," she said, pointing in the direction of the spa area, "and then to your right – it's signposted."

"Great, thank you," answered Amos with relief. *At least I've got something right.* He walked back to where the children were seated, the boys watching the diving video and Elizabeth sitting on a comfy sofa looking at the brochures.

Elizabeth looked up. "Dad, have you booked it up?"

"Yeah, all sorted, honey."

"Thank you, Daddy." Giving him a big hug.

"You've got your training in the morning and I'll join you for that, and if you pass then we can all go on a real dive in the afternoon."

"Henry, Robert, Dad's booked it for tomorrow."

Henry jumped up and brought over a brochure he had picked up from the table.

"Dad, look at this." It showed a number of divers underwater and surrounded by fish with coral in the background and a number of small sharks. Amos shuddered.

"Yes, Henry, all sorted – we'll be diving tomorrow."

"Let's go tell Mom. Maybe she'll want to come," said Henry.

Elizabeth and Henry ran back to their mother on the beach.

"Thank you, Daphne, much appreciated," said Amos.

"My pleasure, Mr Amos, and remember if you need anything just ask and I'll try to sort it out for you. James the dive instructor is a nice young man so the children will enjoy learning with him."

"By the way, what time does lunch start and where do we go for it?" asked Amos.

"From twelve, Mr Amos, and you can sit under the shade outside if you want; you don't have to be inside. You seem to like your food?"

"Yeah. Thank you. I was just thinking of the children."

"Have a nice afternoon."

"You too," he replied.

Amos turned away from the reception with a spring in his step. Robert was waiting for him. They decided to see if they could find where the dive centre shop was.

They soon found it. With a sign on the door.

"Closed, back soon."

"That's a nuisance," said Robert. "It would have been nice to have a look around."

"Just gotta get used to it. It's the Caribbean, Robert, there is no time or real timetable for anything – things just happen when they happen. It's just part of the lifestyle. OK, we may as well head back to the others." They walked through reception and past the pool area.

"Kinda cool really."

"Yeah, especially if you're at school," replied Amos with a chuckle. "Not so good if you've got business to attend to. I remember a few years ago having a four-day workshop and meetings over in Nassau, Bahamas, and I would turn up at the allotted time, 9.30 start, and we wouldn't get going until maybe ten. Come 10.30, there's a coffee and comfort break for ten to fifteen minutes and before you know it, everyone's talking about lunch and where to go for it… it taught me another lesson in how to be patient. We did manage to get the work done… eventually. But don't get me wrong, they are really lovely people to work with, and I'd be happy to work in the Caribbean most of the time."

Amos and Robert arrived back on the beach, the children nowhere to be seen.

"All sorted, I hear, Amos." Bernie sat up from the lounger.

"Yeah, tomorrow morning at 10.30 by the pool and then a shallow dive in the afternoon; are you sure you don't want to join us?"

Bernie shook her head and pointed towards the waves. "Look, Henry and Elizabeth are already practising."

Amos looked down to the sea and they had their snorkels and masks on.

"Henry, hold on a second," Amos called out and then ran down to the water's edge. "Let me check your mask."

"It's fine, Dad, Mom's done it – she always checks it," said Robert.

"I've been practising in the pool at home with them both and with Robert, so don't worry yourself – they know what they are doing," replied Bernie.

Robert joined them with his mask and snorkel. "I check it as well, you know, Dad." He ran past and dived into the sea.

Amos walked down to the seashore and called Henry in. Having done a check for his own peace of mind, Amos let Henry go back to join the other two in the water and then walked back to the loungers and lay down.

"Looks like Robert has been doing a good job on the snorkelling gear," Amos said to Bernie.

"They've been practising almost every day after school for the last month Amos; Robert's been teaching Henry the underwater hand signals as well, and Elizabeth swims like a dolphin – you'll get a nice surprise when you have your lesson tomorrow in the pool."

"That's really good, I was worried that Henry might struggle but looking from here he is doing pretty well. I meant to ask earlier – what's that you're reading?"

Bernie lifted the book and showed the cover to Amos. "*Ethical Business and How to Apply it in Practice.*"

"Woo, that's a bit heavy reading for a holiday isn't it?"

"It's been difficult finding time at home to do anything, with me sorting out the three of them all the time but, well, as you know, I said I wanted to try and get a better direction on my business."

"Yeah, I meant to ask, how's it going?"

"Well, we're just about ticking over at the moment, but it just feels like it needs some type of boost or added value to the products and this book winked at me. I picked it up from Johnstones bookshop downtown – you know, the one with the weird-looking sales staff with orange name tags that make you feel you're on another planet. There's an interesting point they raise here about using plastic containers and wrapping which I think I will move away from or perhaps get the customers to return the packaging for reuse and they get a discount on their next order. Yeah, that sounds good.

Did you know that it's your industry, Amos, that's creating all this plastic? 80 percent of it ends up in landfill or thrown into the sea so that the fish eat it and then guess what? We eat it by eating the fish that have eaten the plastic."

Amos decided to avoid the impact his industry had on producing plastic and tried to respond positively.

"Rather you than me, honey. I just hope that this doesn't turn into a busman's holiday."

Bernie responded sharply. "Oh come on, Amos, you can talk… this is about doing things with the children, and for you and me to enjoy as well as them!"

"Yeah, yeah, you're right, honey… that was probably not the right choice of words. Anyhow, I've been looking forward to it for a long time now."

Amos laid his head back on the lounger… he soon fell asleep.

***

"Dad… Dad… wake up, Dad, look what Robert's found," said an excited Elizabeth.

Amos could hear noises… and was nudged on the arm by Bernie.

Amos sat up and leant up on his elbows. In front of his face was a huge shell.

"Well I'll be… That's huge!" replied Amos. "That's quite beautiful… did you have to dive out far for that?"

"No, I was probably only up to my waist in the water and almost as soon as I went under I could see the shell."

"Children, you've had over an hour in the water – now it's time you came in, got dried and we can go and have some lunch."

"Yeah," said Henry, taking the last slurp from his drink. "I'm hungry."

The family made their way back up to the hotel and the buffet area. They must have been one of the last up for lunch, as they were starting to clear the tables.

"You'll have to be quick," said one of the waiters, smiling.

Having had a big late breakfast, a light buffet lunch was all they really needed.

***

Returning to the beach, the family were relaxed, talking, throwing the football, looking at the different corals they had found on the beach and the children out snorkelling with Amos once their food had gone down.

Amos waved back towards Bernie on the beach, who was content reading quietly and reflecting on them all being together and enjoying themselves.

Amos kept a close eye on Henry whilst in the water. He couldn't help but notice how proficient they had all become at swimming; it was very reassuring. Henry then dived down under the water and came back up and whilst treading water showed Amos what he had found.

"Hey, Dad, look what I found... a piece of coral."

Amos swam over to Henry and took a look. "Your mom would like that, you know; you could make a necklace for her."

"Henry, let Dad take it," said Elizabeth. Henry handed it over and then dived under again to see what else he could find.

Bernie then walked up to the water's edge and called out, "Come on, you guys, you'll be turning into fish if you stay in any longer... I've ordered some more drinks, so you had better come out and get dry before they get warm again." She walked slowly along the beach and back to their base.

A few minutes longer in the water and Amos and the children all returned to the loungers. Henry was shivering and soon warmed up after Bernie put a towel around him, then ran off to play football again with Robert.

"Hey, you two, come and have your drink – you know you need to get fluids down you when it's hot," called Bernie.

The boys ran back. Henry drank his drink a little slower this time, but only because Bernie was supervising. He then lay down on the sun lounger next to Bernie with a towel around him and over his head. Elizabeth soon joined him and they were messing around under the towels. Bernie moved onto another lounger and continued to read.

"Robert and I are going over to see if the dive shop is open yet," said Amos.

"OK."

As the two of them walked back up to the hotel, Amos said to Robert, "You've done well remembering all those signals, and teaching Henry; was that from when we went to Florida two years ago?"

"Yeah, although I did do a bit of reading about it again once we knew we were coming here."

They got to the dive shop.

"Closed – gone diving – open at ten in the morning – James."

"Argh no, not again," said Robert.

"Well at least we have a name and let's hope it is open in the morning, otherwise we won't be having the diving lesson."

"He's probably got a routine in the day with lessons in the pool in the morning and then out diving in the afternoon."

"Yeah, I'm sure you're right, Robert."

"Come on, let's get back to the others."

As they made their way back they could see that the sun was already starting to set.

Henry and Elizabeth were building a castle out of the coral and shells they had found on the beach. The big shell that Robert had found was placed neatly on the top.

"Look at what we've built, Dad – a fairy castle out of coral," said Elizabeth.

"Gee, that must have taken you guys some time to build and collect all those shells and coral."

"And we've built a tunnel right underneath it… See," said Henry. Amos bent down and looked through the arch of the castle. At the end of the tunnel was Henry's face looking at him.

"Wow, that must have been difficult to build. You did well there, Henry," he said, ruffling Henry's hair.

"And me, Dad," said Elizabeth. "I helped with the pieces of coral and the shells around the outside – see those pink ones there. The special one I found earlier with the red coral dots in it, I'm going to keep and take home with me. Dad, did you know that the coral is being killed by climate change?"

"How do you mean, honey?"

"Well, the sea absorbs carbon dioxide and the problem is it also becomes more acidic, resulting in sea food and plants dying; it's happening so fast they don't have time to adapt. Are you listening, Dad, as you don't seem to be?"

"Yeah, honey, I'm sure you're right."

Elizabeth continued playing with the shells and coral.

Amos leant over Bernie on the lounger. "Bernie, what do you say to an evening out at a place called Rackam's restaurant? I overheard a conversation at the reception earlier and they said that they went there with their kids and had a great time."

"I'm easy, Amos, but the Veranda restaurant at the hotel last night was so nice and it's all paid for as part of our holiday," replied Bernie.

"Yeah… You're right… just a thought. We can always come back here to the Veranda and get something to eat if it's no good; I just thought it would be nice to try out different parts of the island."

Thinking about it, Bernie replied, "How far is it anyhow?"

"Apparently it's a couple of minutes in the cab down to the edge of town."

"Yeah, OK, if you feel it's worth a try… let's give it a go."

"OK, I'll book us a table. You never know with these popular places – they can get full pretty quickly and then we will be disappointed."

Amos stood up and made his way to reception. The receptionist, who he hadn't seen before, rang the restaurant and booked a table for him.

"That's a popular restaurant, Mr Amos, you did the right thing booking. Your children will love it. I've been a few years ago for a family celebration – I think it was my husband's birthday – bit expensive but a good choice for a special occasion and the food is good."

"Thank you," said Amos. "A good recommendation."

Amos returned to the beach and announced the arrangements for their evening meal. They were very excited. When the children knew they were going out for a meal it never took them long to get ready.

With the sun now almost setting, the taxi arrived at reception to take them to the restaurant for 6.15.

The children were dressed and already in the cab with the doors open waiting for Amos and Bernie. The lift pinged and out emerged Amos and Bernie onto the hotel foyer.

"Come on, Mom, Dad, been waiting for ages," called out Elizabeth.

Amos and Bernie made their way over to the cab.

"You look a million dollars, honey," Amos said to Bernie.

"You scrub up reasonably well yourself," she replied.

"Good evening, sir and madam. Rackam's, I believe?"

"Thank you, yeah, that's right." Amos got into the front seat and Bernie joined the children in the back of the cab.

"What's it like there?" asked Amos.

"Oh man, I believe it's very good still. I went there some years ago to celebrate my wedding anniversary. Definitely try the mahi mahi if it's on the menu – it's so fresh, and the curried cheesy fries are really special, make sure you try some." The cab driver pulled away from the hotel.

"Yeah, we'll do that, thank you," replied Amos. "Sounds like we've made a good choice."

"How long are you staying on the island, sir?"

"We've got three lovely weeks of relaxing," said Bernie.

"Well, you'll have plenty of time, then, to visit places like the Turtle Farm and Stingray City."

"Yeah, we've seen that on one of the leaflets at the hotel," said Henry. "Do you get to touch the stingrays?"

"Young man, Stingray City is one of my favourites – I take my granddaughters there when they come over. If you do go, try Marvin's boat trips – he's my cousin, but he's also very good, and mention me. OK, you happy people, here we are: Rackam's."

"That was quick, thank you."

"I said it was close and I'm sure you will enjoy yourselves; it's very popular with families, especially in the evenings when they feed the tarpons. You should be able to see them – they feed them every evening about 7.30."

"What are tarpons?" said Elizabeth.

"They are big fish... Make sure you don't fall in now. Enjoy."

"How much do we owe you?" asked Amos.

"It's taken care of at the hotel, sir."

"OK, thank you." Amos leant through the window over to the driver and gave him a tip anyway.

"Thank you, sir, have a nice evening."

They were met at the entrance to the restaurant by a very welcoming lady dressed in a light green top and white shorts and with a smooth brown complexion to die for, thought Bernie.

"How are you all doing today?"

"We're good, thanks," replied Amos.

"You have a reservation?"

"Yeah, we're five and the hotel rang up..."

"Ah yes, here you are... follow me, please." She grabbed a handful of menus.

They were taken to a table overlooking the sea.

"Wow, what a view," said Robert. "And if you look down there – look at those big fish; there's so many of them."

"They must be the tarpons," said Elizabeth, leaning over the barrier from the verandah.

"Yes, you're right there, young lady," said the waitress. "Is this your first time to Rackam's?" she said as she was handing out the menus.

"We're going diving tomorrow," said Henry.

"Hey, you're lucky, that's one thing I would like to do. I've been snorkelling over at Stingray City – that's one thing you've got to try if you haven't done that yet, and there are some places where you can stand up and look at them and even touch them if you are brave enough."

"I'm gonna touch one," said Henry.

"Yeah, we're first time here in Grand Cayman, actually, and we thought we would give Rackam's a try," replied Amos, pulling out his chair and seating himself down at the table.

"Well, I'm sure you will enjoy your meal here," she said, handing out the menus to each of them in turn. "The special on this evening is mahi mahi."

"Well, that's me sorted." Amos put his menu back onto the table.

"What's mahi mahi, Dad?" asked Elizabeth.

"It's a fish, honey," replied Bernie, "and very tasty when it's cooked well."

"Would you like to order any drinks?"

"Cola, please," said Robert.

"Me too," said Henry.

"Henry, try something different – you've had that all day."

"Robert's having cola, Mom."

"OK… well… alright then. We'll have some water as well, please, bottled still water, thank you."

"What's the beer like here?" asked Amos.

"Well, we've got quite a number of local brews on island: the Cayman Island Brewery and 1981 Brewery Co. If you like a lager, maybe try a White Tip?"

"Sounds interesting… I'll try one of those, please."

"Make that two, thank you," said Bernie. "Elizabeth?"

"I'm just going to have water, please."

"That's great," said the waitress. "I'll be back shortly with your drinks and to take your food order."

"That was a nice and easy choice," said Amos. "I was hoping that they were gonna have the mahi mahi."

"I think I'll have that as well," said Bernie, closing her menu and putting it down on the table. "Children… Boys… have you decided yet?"

"I'm going to have the foot-long hot dog with jalapeño relish and some of those cheesy chips, please."

"Me too," said Henry. Amos laughed.

"You're not going to have one of those, Henry, it'll be too big for you and you won't be able to eat it," said Bernie.

"Don't worry, Mom, I'll eat whatever Henry doesn't eat," said Robert, rubbing his hands together.

"I'm going to have a Greek salad as I know it's good for me," said Elizabeth.

"Cola, cola, water and two beers." The waitress placed the drinks on the table. "Are you guys all ready to order now?"

"Thank you. Yes, I think we are," said Amos.

"Any starters or do you just want to go straight into mains?"

"Just mains, please."

"OK, what can I get you?"

"Greek salad, please," said Elizabeth.

"The foot-long hot dog with cheesy fries."

"Me too," said Henry, "same as Robert, please."

"And could you make that one without the jalapeños, thank you, and two mahi mahi," said Bernie. "Thank you."

"Could I have mine with curry cheesy fries, please," said Amos. "In both?"

"How hot is the curry sauce?" asked Bernie.

"It's quite mild but we can spice them up for you if you want?"

"No, no, that's fine, I'll have it as it comes, as long as it's mild."

"Yeah, sure," said the waitress.

"I'll have mine spiced up, please," said Amos.

"OK, you guys, if that's all, give us about fifteen minutes and your food should be with you. Enjoy the view and the fish – they should be making their way in soon."

"We've already seen some of them in the sea from the balcony," said Henry.

She was right, it was a stunning time of day to be sitting down for a meal. The sun, a bright red ball just touching the horizon, surrounded by orange and pink rays shooting across the sky and bouncing off the few wispy clouds; there was a gentle splashing of the waves and the blues and turquoise colours of the sea were slowly turning darker. A slight warming breeze in the air blew in from the sea and the lighting in the restaurant was slowly replacing the natural light.

"Amos, whoever you overheard at the reception was right – this really is quite a wonderful place."

"Look, Mom… look down there, Henry." Elizabeth was pointing down at the water.

They stood up from their seats, and all looked over the railings to see the huge fish swimming gracefully towards them, a light underneath the wooden boarding of the restaurant attracting them in.

Someone on a table further along from them was feeding them and they started to jump out of the water to catch the food.

"If we come here again I'm going to bring my fishing rod," said Henry.

"OK, you guys, let's sit down now – here comes the waitress with our meals," said Bernie. The children reluctantly turned away from the sea and returned to the table.

"Those fish are amazing, Mom."

"And so big."

"Is there anything else I can get you?"

"No, I think that's fine, thank you."

"Enjoy."

"Yeah, I'm sure we will," replied Amos.

The waitress was right, they did enjoy it.

As much as Henry wanted to finish his hot dog and cheesy chips, Robert ended up helping him out. Elizabeth and Henry left the table to get another look at the tarpons. Robert joined them after finishing off the last of the chips. Amos and Bernie had ordered a second beer each and were content just sitting there at the table and enjoying the ambience and the hubbub of a busy restaurant with Caribbean music playing in the background and the children enjoying themselves.

"This beer is surprisingly nice, Bernie; I wouldn't mind taking a few of these back with us or getting the recipe." They lifted up their glasses together.

"Cheers."

"That's weeks away, Amos. Stop thinking about home – enjoy the now whilst we're here; you know it won't quite be the same when we get back, anyhow."

"Yeah, you're right, Bernie." He took another mouthful of beer, which was aptly named White Tip, with a shark on the label.

"You know what, Bernie? I'm really looking forward to taking the kids diving tomorrow. Are you sure you don't wanna come with us?"

"No thank you, I'm fine on land, Amos… I'll let you get wet. I might come with you on the boat but I'm not going in."

"Did you all enjoy your meals? Looks like you did," said the waitress, looking down at the empty plates.

"Yes, they were great."

"Would you like any dessert?"

"Well, I did catch my eye on some rum cake as we came through earlier."

"Yeah, sure, it's made locally on the island; it's a speciality here."

"Well, if we have… say… what do you think, Bernie… three portions? Then the kids can taste a bit as well. Hey, well, make that four portions of the Tortuga rum cake, please," said Amos, "otherwise I won't get any."

"Be right back." The waitress cleared the table of their main course.

"Mom, Dad," called out Elizabeth from the railings on the verandah, "come and have a look at this one."

Amos got up and went over to where the children were looking down. The first thing he saw was the mouth of a fish opening towards the food. Amos shuddered as it gave him another spine-chilling reminder and flashback of the shark in the Gulf.

"It's real big, Dad," added Henry, pointing and looking down at the fish flopping and flapping around on the surface for the food.

"Amos? Amos, are you OK?"

Bernie got up from the table and called the children back; they were reluctant to stop looking at the fish.

"Amos?"

"Yeah, sorry… I, er, if, er… got a sharp reminder just looking down at the fish with its mouth wide open, you know, when I was in the Gulf." His hand was rubbing the side of his chest and then he turned away from the balcony to return to the others.

The waitress was wending her way past the other tables, carrying the desserts, and she placed them on the table.

"There you are, hope you all enjoy – it tastes really nice."

"Where's my pirate cake?" said Henry.

"Well, I thought we could share as we've had a big meal and we've got a spare plate."

Amos looked at Bernie, then back at Henry, and then moved his rum cake over to Henry. Henry lifted his spoon and tucked in; he was now happy. Bernie then moved her plate over to Amos. "It's OK, honey, we can share," said Bernie.

No sooner had they settled down to eat than the waitress returned and placed a fifth rum cake on the table. "It's on the house – enjoy!"

The evening had gone very quickly.

The waitress walked past their table to check on them. "I see you liked the Tortuga rum cake as well as the main course?"

"Yeah, thank you and thanks for the extra one. Could I have the bill, please, and are you able to organise a cab for us back to the Marriott?"

"Yeah, sure."

"Thank you."

Amos settled up and left a generous tip, which Bernie thought was a bit much, and then cajoled the children away from looking over the balcony rail down at the fish.

"Come on, kids, let's go, the cab's gonna be waiting and you've got a busy day tomorrow."

"Yeah, diving, come on, Henry," said Elizabeth.

The waitress returned to give Amos his receipt and with it had wrapped up a piece of Tortuga cake for Amos.

"Hey, that's really nice of you, thank you."

The cab journey back was uneventful except for the children's various descriptions of fish that they had seen earlier in the day and expectations for tomorrow.

Arriving back at the hotel, Amos paid the cab driver. They walked past the fountains and waterfalls of reception and foyer area, up in the lift and to their rooms.

"Night, Mom, Dad…"

"Night, kids, see you in the morning," said Amos.

"I'll be with you in a few minutes to tuck you up," said Bernie.

***

The following morning, Amos and Bernie were awoken again by the creaky noise of their bedroom door followed by the children running in and jumping on the bed.

It was much earlier than yesterday as Amos opened one eye and glanced at the clock by the side of the bed: 08.42. "Oh well, we should be thankful that it wasn't earlier," said Amos to Bernie.

Amos managed a "Morning, kids."

"Morning, Dad, morning, Daddy," the children responded very excitedly. Bernie did not stir; although awake, she was happy still tucked up in bed.

Amos sat up, and looked down towards the end of the bed at the children – they were all fully dressed and ready with their bags for their diving lesson in the pool.

They then piled onto Amos's side of the bed until there was no room for Amos and he fell out of bed and onto the floor.

"OK, you guys, I've got the message now. Tomorrow, no jumping on the bed – let me and Mom have a lie-in for a bit."

"OK, Dad," replied Elizabeth.

"We're going to head down and have breakfast so we'll see you downstairs, OK?" said Robert, realising that they weren't wanted.

"Yeah, that's fine by me."

"You do realise, Dad, that it's almost nine o'clock and we're ready for breakfast and then our lesson so you had better hurry up, Dad, as I don't want to miss it."

"You've organised the diving, Amos, so you had better get yourself sorted out." Bernie motioned towards Amos and then stretched her arms in bed.

"Crikey, is it that late already? Right, I'm gonna shower and I'll join you in a minute – see you down there."

"I'll follow you down shortly," came the subdued voice of Bernie, still happily resting, "and don't eat too much as you're swimming later this morning."

"OK, Mom, we know," came a combined response from the children as they raced out of their parents' bedroom.

Amos appeared out of the shower very quickly, dried and changed and headed down to join the children.

"See you shortly, honey," he said as he touched her on the cheek and kissed her on the forehead.

"Mmm, I'll be down soon." Bernie was trying to make sure she made the most of being able to sleep in… and not having to make breakfast.

The boys were already tucking into pancakes when Amos joined them. He poured himself a coffee then visited the breakfast buffet. Elizabeth was there with star fruit and yogurt in her bowl. Amos was content with a coffee to start with, as the extra piece of rum cake he'd eaten last night must have been two or three portions in one and was still feeling the effects of it on his stomach.

"Boys, remember what your mother said about eating; you know it's not good to dive on a full stomach."

"We're not gonna have any more after this one, Robert already said."

"OK, that's good, Henry – I don't want any of you sinking to the bottom."

Bernie joined them at breakfast as they were finishing.

"Mom, are you gonna come and watch us?"

"Yes, Henry, I'll be there watching you; it's only just around the corner in the other pool so let me have some coffee and something to eat and I'll come round and join you."

"Are you sure you don't want to join us diving?"

"No, honestly, Amos, I'm sure and will be happy just watching you all enjoying yourselves."

"OK, honey, we'll see you shortly."

Robert led the way around to the dive shop, which as you would expect was actually open. Elizabeth and Henry were already in and looking around the shop, picking up goggles and holding up various items of diving gear and swimming wear.

"Morning, guys, you must be the Amos family?" came a male voice from behind a hanger of waving wetsuits.

"Yes, we've booked a resort lesson this morning and then a shallow dive this afternoon, all being well with the dive this morning in the pool," replied Amos, looking around for a face to put to the voice.

"Sure, that's right – it's the four of you, isn't it?" A head appeared from behind a wetsuit.

"Yeah," replied Amos, now walking further into the shop. "Nice to meet you. I'm Amos and this is my eldest son, Robert, and somewhere over there in the shop are my other children, Elizabeth and Henry."

"Good to meet you guys; you've chosen a great day to start diving. I'm James and I'll be your instructor all day. Do you mind starting to fill in the forms on the desk here, thanks, and then we can get going. You'll be pleased to know that it's just the four of you this morning in the pool so we should be able to get through the morning session quite quickly depending on how you all get on. Henry, isn't it?"

"Yeah."

"Have you been diving before?"

"No, but I've done a lot of snorkelling and I can hold my breath underwater and do all the signals and I can swim two hundred metres," replied a confident Henry.

"Well, that's a good start. I'll test you on that later, Henry. What about you, Elizabeth?"

"I've had a try at diving about a year ago and I do a lot of swimming at school, and snorkelling at home with Henry and Robert."

"That's two out of two so far, and looks like we've got a school of fish today – that makes me a happy instructor. Robert, I'd guess you've probably been a few times, am I right?"

"Yeah, but I'll need to have a refresh as I've not been diving since last summer with Dad."

"And Amos, I'd say you've probably—"

"He does it for his job," interrupted Elizabeth nonchalantly.

"Yeah, he swims with sharks," Henry proudly added.

"Well, not quite," added a slightly embarrassed Amos.

"Cool, so your dad must be good – looks like we're in for a good session today then and you guys can teach me a thing or two," said James whilst trying to put a wetsuit back on the rack and the hanger missing the rail, now a bit apprehensive that he had a well-experienced diver in his class.

"I've got my card with me, so yeah, I get by," said Amos.

"Dad got bitten by a big shark," said Henry, moving his hands wider and wider.

"Thank you, Henry. Where are you from, James?"

"Australia, Gold Coast, just south of Brisbane – do you know it?"

"Sorry, no, I've not been there but understand it's a lovely country. How long have you been diving?"

"This is my seventh year; I quit uni after the first term and decided I wanted an outdoor lifestyle so I became a diving instructor and here I am. This is my second year over here in Grand Cayman. I tend to have about six months away from home and then back home for the rest of the year to see friends and family."

"Nice work if you can get it," said Amos. "You are doing better than me at the moment!"

"Dad, you could try doing something like that," chirped up Elizabeth, putting on a pair of snazzy sunglasses. "What do you think of these, Dad?"

"I think we should show those to your mom first, honey; maybe she would like a pair as well, but be careful with them now." Elizabeth put them back on the rack with Amos looking on.

"It's OK, nothing to worry about," said James. "They're pretty strong glasses."

"You don't know my kids," said Amos with concern in his voice; he had also seen the price tag – $85.

"Right, let me just check those forms are filled in correctly and we can get going."

"Dad," said Robert, "once we've had this lesson and dive this afternoon, are we going to be able to take any more dives?"

"Yeah, I'm sure we will and am looking forward to it… as often as we want to."

Looks like it's gonna be a busman's holiday, Amos thought to himself, but inside was very satisfied and content.

"Good. Right, let me just check… papers are all done. Are you ready to go?" said James to Elizabeth and Henry.

"Yes, please," they replied in unison.

"So we've got the resort lesson and then out where this afternoon? So that I can get my bearings," asked Amos.

"That'll depend on the weather, Amos, but probably over to Turtle Reef. It's one of my favourite shore dives – good for beginners; it's just north of Seven Mile Beach and close by to the turtle breeding centre, and it's an easy ladder entry, relatively shallow area and protected from the current. Good for first-timers."

That's a good reply, thought Amos to himself, *and the right one. Perhaps Bernie will want to come up with us this afternoon and she can go to the turtle farm.*

"That sounds ideal, James – do you want any help with the diving gear?"

"No, it's fine, thanks, it's all laid out by the pool."

James flipped the sign over on the door as they exited the dive centre shop and locked the door. *Back at lunch time… Whenever that might be*, thought Amos. *They do have a very relaxed approach to time… I should take note.*

"If you guys wanna follow me down to the pool and we'll get going." James led the way with Elizabeth and Henry in close pursuit.

"Yippee." Elizabeth and Henry were chatting away whilst following James.

"Dad," asked Robert, "will there be any chance of you and I doing some deeper dives, as I was reading up on dive sites back home and there's quite a few shipwrecks around the island and that might be interesting."

"Yeah, sure, we'll have a chat with James and see what he can organise for us; let's see how we get on and get today's dives done first."

"That'll be great, Dad, thanks. I'm happy to pay for the extra dives as…"

"Hey, Robert, don't be silly… that's nice of you to offer, though, but it'll be fine. With Grandma and Grandpa having helped pay for the holiday, we've got a little bit more to enjoy ourselves." Amos put his arm around Robert's shoulder.

They reached the pool area and James directed them to each of their piles of equipment.

"Now then, Henry, this here is your diving gear… it's like your lungs underwater so you've got to look after them properly, you got that?"

"Woo, it's soooo heavy, I can only just lift it off the ground… and… I can't… Dad, I can't," said Henry with great effort and straining to lift it onto his shoulder.

"Just wait, Henry, now careful with that, let me help you." Amos lifted the tank onto Henry's back, complete with the buoyancy compensator, and then tightened up the straps to suit Henry. Whilst he was doing this, Amos carried out an MOT on all the gear, checking the regulators, the air pressure, the volume in the tanks as well as the gauges. *All looks pretty good*, he thought.

"How's it all looking?" said James whilst fitting Elizabeth's tank and noticing that Amos was checking Henry's diving gear.

"Er, yeah, it's actually all looking pretty good; this is mainly new gear by the look of things?"

"Yeah, we replaced most of it in the early part of this year as a site-wide overhaul."

"You OK, Robert?"

"Yeah, fine thanks, Dad, a bit tight around my left shoulder but I've loosened the strap a bit so it should be OK now."

"Are you diving as well, Amos, as the gear is all laid out for you?"

"Yeah, James, thanks, I think I will as you've got it out ready for me. It'll be good to see how the kids get on underwater."

Amos was ready in the blink of an eye.

"Right," said James, "you all know how to clean your goggles?"

Henry had already started and spat into them and gave them a clean before putting them on. "I like this bit," he said. "Mom never tells me off for spitting in my goggles."

"Now test your mouth regulator and try breathing as if you are underwater. That's good. How's that for everyone – Henry, Elizabeth?"

There were a number of muffled responses and Henry gave the diver's OK signal.

"Very good, Henry," said James. "OK now, let's take the regulators out of your mouths and learn a few signals."

"I know lots," said Henry.

"OK," said James, "let's see how good you are. Henry, you tell us what these underwater signals are for. Like this…"

"That's the sign for OK."

"Right. And this?"

"That's for not OK."

"Or, I've got a problem," added Elizabeth, "and then you point to what the problem is."

"Very good, you've taught them well," said James, looking at Amos.

"And this one is…" James had both hands over his head.

"Er… Oh no… I've forgotten… don't tell me, wait… don't tell me…"

Amos put his hand up to stop Elizabeth saying as she was about to answer and he knew that Henry desperately wanted to get the answer right.

"It's… OK, I know this one… there's a problem on the surface of the water."

"Well done, Henry," said Amos. "Now let's see if Elizabeth can get a couple. What's thumbs up mean?" said James.

"It's for up," came with a beaming smile from Elizabeth.

"Or end of the dive," added Robert.

"And thumbs down?"

"That's for going down," said Henry.

"Or dive or descend," added James. "Henry, you know you're pretty good – where did you learn all of that from?"

"My brother."

"You can have my job, Robert, when you get a bit older... OK, let's do some more as I can see Elizabeth here wants to. Elizabeth, what's this one?"

"Slow down," she replied.

"And this one?"

"Stop." She motioned with the palm of her hand up vertically.

"Yes, that's all correct – or you can use a fist for stop," said James. "Two fingers pointing at my eyes is for..."

"Look," jumped in Henry. "That's an easy one."

Amos folded his arms and smiled and chuckled to himself at his children whilst the question-and-answer session went on.

"And this, shaped like a hand shake is..."

"Going in this direction."

"Come here?"

"That's easy," said Elizabeth, "it's... like this." Elizabeth motioned with her hands.

"That's right. Level off your hand waving horizontally in front of you... good. OK, we had better do some trickier ones just to see how much you know... I think we might run out of signals. Two fingers parallel with both hands says...?"

"Don't know that," said Henry.

"Nor me," said Elizabeth.

"Stay together."

"Yup, or buddy up – well done, Robert. Hey, you guys are having me on, aren't you? You already know about this stuff."

"Robert's been teaching us," replied Elizabeth.

"Well, he's done you guys a good job. We've probably done all the ones that we are going to use today, but let's see what else you know – perhaps, Robert, you can take us through some more."

"Sure. Well, a horizontal hand and three fingers underneath means...? We wait for three minutes at this level, but it also might be to check everyone's OK or maybe a safety stop. This one is a decompression stop... A fist held up with my thumb and little finger poking out."

"That's a funny one," said Henry.

"Yeah, but a very important one otherwise you might end up in hospital," added Amos.

"A fist to the chest means…?" Robert waited and then said, "You're on reserve air in the tank."

"Yes, and that's another important one to remember," said James, "or you might be low on air. Robert, thank you. How about this one?" James held his hand across his neck.

"You're dead," said Henry.

"Well, you might soon be," replied James. "It means you are out of air."

"I know another one," said Henry as he wrapped both his arms around himself. "That means I'm cold."

"And here's a final one for you." James put out his fist with just his second finger bent so it looked like a question mark "

"That looks like a… question mark."

"Yes, you're right, Elizabeth, well done – question. Some of the signals are very simple, aren't they. Did you know," said James, "that you can also write underwater? But we won't be needing that today. Now then, let's have a refresh and quickly run through these. Henry, what's this… this… this… and finally this… good, all correct – give me five. Elizabeth, this… this… and this… yup, ten out of ten. And Robert, this… correct, one hundred per cent… well done all of you. Wow, you guys are now ready to get into the water."

"Why didn't you ask my dad any?" asked Henry.

"Well, there's a simple answer to that," said James, smiling across at Amos. "He showed me his diver's card and that tells me he knows all this and more, probably a lot more than I can teach you. Right, now let's get those masks and regulators on. Henry, show me what you do when you're in the water to control going up or down in the water. Hey that's good, and you, Elizabeth… and finally Robert… OK, let's slowly get into the water."

"You're looking good, Henry," said Amos, now with his diving gear on and joining them in the water.

With the four of them settled in the water, James gave them a hand signal to go down. They stayed at the bottom of the pool for a few minutes and then James gave the signal to go back up.

When they all got to the surface, James took his regulator out and said, "Henry, for a first dive that was ten out of ten... Give me another high five. OK, this time I want you to go down and swim to the far end and then back again and up – are you all OK with that? Any problems anyone has before we get going again...? No... OK, let's do it. Masks on, regulators in."

Amos kept a close eye on his two youngest, in particular Henry. After about ten minutes they were back again.

"OK, you guys, it looks like you're teaching me how to do my job! Let's do that again, down at the deep end, and try to practise some of your underwater signals."

A further twenty minutes in the pool swimming and diving to the bottom and up again and they were back where they started. They all floated to the surface and James said that they had all passed and were ready for the afternoon session.

They got out slowly and removed their gear and placed it next to the pool.

"Do you need any help with the equipment?" asked Amos.

"No, it's fine, thanks, don't worry – you guys go and enjoy yourselves. I'll sort this out and see you in reception at, say, 1.45, as we've made good time this morning. Your children are amazing – they've picked it up so well."

"Thank you, see you later, James."

The children were already wending their way back to the beach to find their mother. Amos followed proudly. Henry leading the way.

"Mom, Mom, I went down to the bottom and then up again in the deep end... It's so easy, you could do it if you want?" said an excited Henry, running up to Bernie. "And we remembered all the signals Robert taught us that you have to use underwater and we're going in the sea to do it properly this afternoon."

"Really, Henry, that's very good and you've probably got Robert to thank for that and all those lessons he gave you in the pool."

"Hi, Bernie," said Amos, "we all got through... Even me! Well, I'm starving; are we up for getting an early lunch from the buffet, as we're meeting James the instructor at 1.45 and then heading up the top end of Seven Mile Beach."

"You can come as well, Mom, and watch us if you want," said Elizabeth. "James said it's quite close to the turtle farm, you know, the one in the brochure that we showed you, so if you get bored you can always go up there – it's next door to the diving."

"I'll think about it."

"I'm hungry," said Robert.

"Remember, you guys, not too much as you've got your dive this afternoon; save your main food for this evening when we're all finished. Oh yes, and before I forget – the waiter, you know, the really nice one…"

"Er, Dudley?"

"Yes, him; he had a message for you. Oh look, here he comes now – he looks out of breath."

"Mr Amos, Mr Amos, I'm so glad I found you – you have an urgent message from a Mr Jack."

"Amos, you had better take it… It could be a problem with Sally," said a concerned Bernie.

"OK, thank you, Dudley. Why don't you all go and get some food and I'll join you when I've spoken to Uncle Jack."

Amos followed Dudley back to reception.

"Here's the number, Mr Amos, and the phone you can use – it's on the end of the desk."

"Thank you."

Amos rang the number on the piece of paper. *Brr… Brr… Brr…* still no answer. *Brr… Brr…* He was about to hang up when the phone was picked up.

"Amos, Amos, is that you?"

"Jack?"

"Yeah."

"What do you want? I'm on holiday, you know the rules: no calls on holiday unless it's life or death. How's Sally?" he said sharply.

"She's fine."

"How are your parents?"

"They're fine as well."

"How's the report?"

"That's good and I'm almost finished."

"That's it, then, nice to speak to you, Jack." And Amos put the phone down before Jack could respond.

Amos said to Dudley and the receptionist, "No calls, right – I want some peace and quiet on holiday, OK."

Amos headed towards the dining area and could hear a phone going back at the reception.

"How are Jack and Sally?" asked Bernie.

"Both fine – can't quite work out why he called… Your mom and dad are fine as well."

"Dad, look, they've got some curried cheesy chips again and a deep-fried onion like the one we saw last night; I'm gonna try some of that," said Robert.

"Go easy on the food, children, you heard what your mother said earlier, otherwise James might not allow you to dive." Amos was thinking of a good reason to try to make sure that they didn't overeat.

With the threat of not being allowed to dive, the children ate a light lunch. It's never good to dive on a full stomach; it's not safe and can lead to not very nice consequences if you've eaten too much.

They finished lunch and as they headed back to the beach, Amos was being beckoned over by a waiter. Amos waved him away; he was having none of it.

The waiter then came to speak to Amos on the beach.

"Mr Amos."

"Yes, I said no calls, thank you. Children, what would you like to drink before we head off to reception?"

"The usual, please, waiter. Thank you," said Bernie. "Maybe it's urgent?" now looking at Amos.

"Urgent what?" replied Amos. "Jack's call? It's not; I spoke to him. Jack knows the rules about holidays we've had for years now and he just wants to go through his report as we're adding stuff we haven't put in before… anyhow, it's not life or death so whatever it is, it can wait."

Amos found it difficult to settle down on the lounger; it was nagging him as to why Jack should be so insistent.

"Dad, when we dive, can you be close to me, please? You know, it's just that it's going to be so different down there and you can't move quickly if anything scary happens," said Elizabeth.

"Yeah, sure, honey. We'll all be very close to each other when we're diving, and James will be there as well – he's a good instructor, and Robert, they've all dived before. You'll be fine once you get going."

"Good, it's just I don't want to be scared if a big fish comes up to me."

"Hey, Henry, you OK about diving?"

"Yeah, I wanna see a big fish."

Amos and Bernie looked at each other.

"You'll be fine, both of you. You know the diving signs and how to use the breathing apparatus and you can swim like fish… you just need to be aware of what's happening around you all the time and enjoy what you are seeing."

"Thanks, Dad, that's reassuring," replied Elizabeth. "Dad, I was thinking of taking the underwater camera; what do you think?"

"On the first dive I suggest you might just like to have it there and if you feel comfortable then yeah, why not take some pictures. It's just that I don't know what this particular dive is like… it might just be to get you used to using the gear in the sea first, see how it goes."

"OK, I think I'll take it along anyway. Then if I take some pictures we can show Mom."

"That's nice, I'd like that," she replied with a nice feeling of being appreciated.

"Have you decided whether to come with us, Mom?" asked Elizabeth.

"Yeah, I'll come over with you, and as you said, if I get bored I'll go and have a look at the local turtles next door."

"Ooh, good," replied Elizabeth, giving her mom a big hug. She was excited but also apprehensive about diving in the sea.

"Have you all got your water bottles and towels with you?" said Bernie.

The waiter arrived with a tray of drinks, carefully placing them on the table and removing empty glasses. He then gave Amos a note on a piece of paper and walked sheepishly away. Amos just stuffed it into his pocket without looking at it, annoyed as it was interfering with his holiday.

"What was that, honey?" asked Bernie.

"It was just the receipt from the waiter."

"Dad, which one's mine?" asked Henry.

"You and Robert have both got the same."

"I now know why the turtle is the picture that is shown on so many things – it's because of the turtle farm. I saw turtle soup on the menu last night and I don't think I want to try it," said Elizabeth.

"If it's sustainable then why not?" said Robert. Amos and Bernie looked at each other with a look of understanding and appreciation on their faces of what Robert had said.

"It's an animal and I don't want to be eating animals," replied Elizabeth, stressing the "I".

"Come on, you two, finish your drinks – we need to be getting up to reception."

"Yippee, it's time to go," said Henry.

Henry gulped his drink down, grabbed his rucksack and led the way up to reception.

"Don't get on the bus, Henry," Bernie called after him." Elizabeth, Robert, can you catch up with him, please?"

"Sure, Mom." Robert picked up his towel and chased after Henry.

"Have you got everything, Bernie – suntan lotion, hat, towel?" Amos said as they set off quickly to catch up with the children.

"Yes, that should do it. Oh, my book – I mustn't forget that." She quickly ran back to the beach to get her book and caught up with them all at the reception.

James was joined by a local guy called Steve, who was very casually dressed and was probably in his mid twenties. He didn't say a great deal but they found out later from James that Steve was a very competent diver but had recently lost his mother due to a drug overdose, and that James was trying to help him out.

The journey from the hotel took them running parallel with the coastline of Seven Mile Beach with its spectacular hotels dotted along the coast and smaller condominiums. They were surrounded by clear blue skies all the way and glimpses of the sea from the coach leading down to the beach.

"James, how long did you say you'd been working here?" asked Amos.

"This is my second season, if you call it a season."

"Ah yes, you mentioned that earlier."

"You can dive all year round here and the weather is pretty much the same, except around the August-September times when it gets a bit stormy and you get a few hurricanes around."

"Wow, hurricanes," said Henry. "I wouldn't like to be here with one of those happening; that must be very scary."

"It's actually generally OK here," replied James. "The islands are well protected by natural reefs, which take the power out of the sea. Storm surges are probably the biggest problem but the islanders are used to the weather; that's why when you look around some parts of the island, the houses have a garage and storage on the ground floor and then steps up to the living areas above. That's just in case the sea floods in, which it does very occasionally on some parts of the island. OK, here we are."

James parked up close to the area where there were a set of steps and a ladder leading down to the sea.

"Amos and Robert, if you could help me and Steve offload the diving gear that would be appreciated."

"Yeah, sure," they both replied.

"James, where's the turtle farm from here if I decide to go and visit it?" asked Bernie.

"If you follow that path" – James pointed past a group of boulders – "then walk for about a hundred metres, you'll then hit the road and you will see the signpost for the turtle farm. It's on the left."

"Pretty close then, thanks," replied Bernie.

"It'll be about a ten, maybe fifteen-minute walk… but it's pretty hot at the moment so you might just wanna stay in the shade.

Look, there's some seating over there under those palms; see how you feel."

Bernie put her rucksack and towel on the bench in the shade and then came back to the others, who were now prepared and ready for their first dive in open water.

"I'm so excited, Mom," said Henry.

"Me too," said Elizabeth.

"OK now," said James. "You guys know the routine. Can I suggest, Robert, you go first, followed by your dad then Elizabeth and Henry, and I'll follow you in at the back. Steve here will stay out of the water." Steve lifted a hand in acknowledgement. "If you've got any problems he'll come and help you; you remember the signals and how to increase and decrease the pressure in your vest?"

Henry showed him, then Elizabeth and Robert.

"Now remember when you are in the water to look out for each other – you all got that?"

They nodded back at James and were all soon clambering down the ladder and into the water. Bernie took photographs of them in their diving gear and as they were getting into the water. Looking down from the top of the ladder, she couldn't really tell who was who in the water. But after a short while she could make out Amos and Henry together, which reassured her, and then spotted James close to Elizabeth. That just left Robert, who must have dived down as he was nowhere to be seen. A few minutes later she was reassured as a fifth person could be seen in the water. They were rising to the surface and speaking and then disappearing underwater again.

Bernie decided she would wait for them to return rather than go to the turtle farm. They could all do that together another day, so she went and sat on the bench to read her book, leaving Steve to keep an attentive eye on the diving area. James had put a red marker flag down in the water so that there was a reference point for everyone.

After twenty minutes, Amos and Henry climbed up out of the water and took their gear off.

Henry saw his mother sitting in the shade and came running

over to her. "Mom, Mom, you'll never guess what! I saw a huge round fish and hundreds of small black and white fish – I hope Robert's taken some pictures. One of the fish I saw was so big… and orange-coloured with black stripes on its fins; we went down near the bottom and came up again. There were so many fish in the water. Robert, he can show them to you as well."

"How was Henry, Amos?" said Bernie, trying to avoid being splashed on by Henry.

"Well… for a first dive, very good. James has picked a very safe spot here, ideal for beginners."

"Can we go back, Dad?"

"You enjoyed that, didn't you, Henry? I thought so… let's just wait a while until the others come out and then we can go back in together. Mom's got you a drink so have some of that and rest for a while."

"This other fish I saw, Mom, it came right up to me, I could almost touch it and then I got close to some coral – it was so cool and colourful. You should try it, Mom."

They saw Elizabeth appearing at the top of the ladder, helped by Steve to remove her tank. She then pulled her mask off and shouted out, "Did you see that big fat fish, Henry?"

"Ah, you mean a puffer fish? You gotta be careful with them – spiky, very spiky, you mustn't touch them," said Steve.

Elizabeth ran over to the bench where the others were sitting. "Dad, thank you for letting us go diving. It was really good. Wait till I tell Madeline back at school – she won't believe all the fish we've seen."

"I wanna go back in, Dad," said Henry, "and I wanna see the puffer fish that Elizabeth saw, as I didn't see one."

"I saw hundreds of small zebra-type fish and an orange-coloured fish, there were so many… and… and we saw some dead coral, it was so sad. It's just… it's just nothing… no colour, and then you can see where the live coral is and the fish busy feeding and brushing themselves against the greenery, but the dead stuff…"

"Yeah that's happening in a lot of places around the world at the moment. Where James lives in Australia, the Great Barrier Reef is really suffering; they have lost over 90 per cent of the coral in some places," replied Amos. Amos and Henry got themselves ready to dive again. Elizabeth decided she had seen enough and stayed with her mother.

"We'll be about fifteen to twenty minutes at the most, Bernie, that's all we've got left in the tanks, and there's a bit of a breeze picking up," said Amos.

Bernie helped Elizabeth to dry and change and they sat together with Bernie listening to Elizabeth telling her more about what she'd seen. "Does it make you want to come with us, Mom?"

"Well, not really; I'm happy swimming in the pool at home, but I don't know, I've never been very keen on the sea. It's too rough and unpredictable for me."

With the wind picking up and then the waves, Amos kept the second dive with Henry short and they returned to the shore with Robert and James, who followed them in with the marker flag.

"I hope you guys enjoyed that; you're all very good, you know."

"It was brilliant, thank you," said Elizabeth.

"And I went out twice and saw a puffer fish with Dad," added a happy Henry.

"Did you manage to take any pictures, Robert?" said Elizabeth.

"Yeah, loads, it's very easy to use. I'll show you all the pictures later when we are dry and we can enjoy them together."

"I'm cold and am really hungry now, Dad," said Henry.

"I'm not surprised with all that swimming and chasing the fish," said Amos. "Here's your top, now; put that on and that will help warm you up. We will get something to eat when we get back to the hotel." Bernie pulled the T-shirt over his head.

Whilst the family were catching up with each other, James and Steve loaded up the diving gear. The return journey to the hotel went in a flash with the constant nattering and conversation with the children as to what they had seen.

The minibus arrived back at the hotel and they piled out, tired from their adventure.

"Thank you, James," said Amos, shaking James's hand. "Much appreciated; you're a good instructor and that was a good spot for beginners. I'm sure we'll be doing it again over the coming weeks."

"That's a pleasure, Amos, see you all soon. You've got my number so you can just give me a call on my cell phone."

"Sure." Amos waved him off as he drove away.

"We're heading back to the room now, Amos, to shower and change – you know it's almost five, and dinner on the verandah starts at six."

"That's just as well, as we've got three hungry children and a hungry dad."

The family made their way back to their rooms. On the way past the reception desk, Dudley was waving frantically at Amos with a piece of paper in his hand.

"You go on, Bernie," said Amos. "I'll see what Dudley wants this time and see you back in the room."

Amos strolled over to the desk.

"Mr Amos, Mr Amos."

"Hello, Dudley, and what can I do for you?"

"Yes, Mr Amos, it's another message and from Mr Jack again; he says it's very important."

Amos took the envelope from Dudley and read the note inside. *We've won the Rosebank contract. Call me – Jack*, was all it said.

"Yeeha." his fist punching the air and then dancing a little jig.

"Are you alright, Mr Amos?" said Dudley with a very concerned look on his face.

"Yeah, yeah, absolutely fine. Can I use your phone, please?"

"You know – over there, please."

"Thank you."

He dialled. *Brr… Brr…* No answer… *Brr… Brr.* Jack picked up.

"Jack, hi, it's me – that's amazing news. No wonder you wanted to call. I'm sorry I didn't respond better when you called earlier. That's brilliant, absolutely brilliant," Amos said, beaming all over his face, and a number of staff around him wondering what the conversation was all about.

"Amos, yes, it's fantastic news but there's only one problem…"

Amos listened to Jack and then put the phone down. His excitement had disappeared.

Dudley enquired of Amos, as he was staring out towards the sea, "Everything alright, sir? Sir?"

Amos didn't reply immediately.

"Er, yeah, thank you." And he walked away from the reception and sat on an easy chair in the foyer.

"Oh hellfire, what's Bernie gonna say? I can't... I... oh shit... This isn't supposed to happen." His fist hit the arm of the chair with a heavy thump.

"Would you like a drink, sir?"

"No, I'm fine, thank you."

The waiter walked away.

"In fact, yes I would," called out Amos. "A double bourbon, please... Thank you.

"What if I... no... maybe Jack could... that can't happen, that's not what they want... oh shit, why me... why now... why couldn't it wait? I've gotta tell her... and the kids... but when? Before dinner? After dinner? There ain't gonna be a good time... oh why oh why oh why now..." He breathed deeply again and sighed.

The waiter returned with his drink.

"Who'd go on holiday and run a business... It's just not possible. Why can't I have a break?"

The waiter shrugged his shoulders and walked away. Amos stood up and downed his drink in one. He wasn't sure which direction to walk. He eventually decided to return to the room.

Bernie was in the shower and she called out, "Everything alright with Jack? I assume it was him again."

"Yeah, yeah, all good."

The door to their bedroom opened.

"Dad, I know the restaurant here is nice but can we go to the restaurant we went to last night again? It was really good..."

"Yeah, I'm sure we can, but this evening we're gonna go to the Veranda restaurant." Bernie emerged from the bathroom wrapped in towels and rubbing her hair. She gave Amos an inquisitive look as Amos did not look himself.

"Come on, honey, your turn for the shower otherwise we'll miss our table slot."

"Dad said we could go to that restaurant again that we went to last night?"

"Yes, but not tonight, honey, as your dad said. Just give us a few minutes to get dressed and we'll come and get you on the way down."

"The boys are just watching TV… and they won't let me watch what I wanna watch," said Elizabeth.

"OK, well, why don't you just watch what you want in here whilst we get ourselves dressed."

Bernie walked round to the children's bedroom and the boys were staring at the TV.

"Have either of you boys showered yet? Well, hurry up both of you as we've got the table booked for six. Come on, hurry up, otherwise we'll miss our slot and we won't be getting any food." That got the two boys rushing for the shower.

Bernie returned to the bedroom and Amos had been quick and already emerged from the bathroom and was starting to get dressed.

"Something's up at work, isn't it?" Bernie could tell when Amos had something on his mind; he had a habit of regularly looking into space in a very contemplative fashion.

"Yeah, yeah… it's work… I'll tell you about it later, honey."

∗∗∗

All washed, dried and dressed, they were ready for dinner. Walking down towards the restaurant, Bernie asked Amos again.

"Well, are you gonna tell me or do I have to tickle it out of you?" said Bernie, smiling and tickling his stomach.

"Well, it's really good news. We've won a big, big contract – you know, the one I told you about. It's the biggest we've ever done."

"This way, sir, madam," said the waiter.

"That's wonderful, I'm so pleased for you and Jack." And she gave Amos a hug before they sat down at the table.

The children were already sitting down at the table. "I think I'm going to have… mmm…" said Elizabeth.

"Good evening. I'm your waitress this evening and my name's Kate. Here are the rest of your menus. Would you like to order drinks?"

"A double bourbon, please," said Amos without hesitation.

"Amos, really?" Bernie looked up from her menu towards Amos. "Two colas, a mango juice, please, and I'll have a Bacardi and Coke. Thank you," said Bernie.

"Coming right up, and I'll be back to take your food orders."

The children were busy looking at their menus.

"Look," said Henry, pointing at the menu. "Turtle soup. That's funny – I've never seen that."

"I'm gonna have a tuna steak," said Robert.

"Amos, tell me." Bernie had her serious voice on now and he knew the conversation was going to be a tricky ride.

"Well, we won it… the big tender we put in… and it's really good money… It's $350 and—"

"$350 what?" enquired Bernie.

"Thousand. $350,000 each, and more work to follow. But there's a problem: it's in the North Sea again."

"Well, that's OK. For that money, it's worth doing… Isn't it?"

"Yes, but… I have… well, I've…"

"Yes, Amos?"

"I've gotta go tomorrow to sign the contracts."

The drinks arrived and were put on the table by the waitress.

"You what. What do you mean, tomorrow? Can't it wait? We've been waiting months to see you, Amos, months." Bernie's voice became louder and drifted into her Scottish accent as she got cross. "Months, Amos, and now you… you… this can't be happening." She got up, threw her serviette onto the table and stormed out of the restaurant.

"Dad, what is it?" asked Robert.

"Why's Mom cross?" said Henry.

"Well, it's good but bad news. You know that contract, that big one – well, we won it but I have to go and sign the contracts and set it all up. It will take seven to ten days or so and I have to go tomorrow."

"Wow, no wonder Mom's upset," said Elizabeth.

"Yeah. You guys order your food; I'm gonna see to Mom and come back. Could you order me some mahi mahi again, thanks, and probably something salad and fish for Mom. Thanks, Robert. I'll be back shortly, hopefully with Mom."

Amos headed back to the room. Bernie wasn't there. He then went down to reception and asked if they had seen her and the receptionist pointed towards someone sitting near the pool.

"Thank you," replied Amos and walked over to her.

"Bernie, I'm so..."

"Amos, I've just about had enough. I love you but I can't keep going like this. This is supposed to be a family break, just all of us together, no interruptions, no problems, just... just... Oh, I give up." And she stood up and walked away to the other side of the pool.

Amos followed, at a safe distance.

"And what am I supposed to do now... hey? The children wanna go diving – who's gonna be taking them? It's certainly not me, Amos. This is your problem – you sort it out." She stormed off again back towards the reception area. Amos looked on and then out to sea.

Then he looked over towards the restaurant. He could see Bernie had returned to the children and had sat down and they were ordering their dinner. Henry and Elizabeth were deep in the menu still deciding what to order when the waitress returned to the table for their orders.

"God, I hope this blows over," said Amos out loud to himself, looking up to the night sky.

Amos then walked back to the dinner table.

"Dad," Robert said, "you've gotta go to work."

"That's not fair – we've only been diving once and I wanna find some treasure," said Henry.

"Yes – why, Dad?" said Elizabeth. "You've said you're going to have three weeks with us." Bernie, with a slight smirk on her face, folded her arms and looked across the table at Amos with a look of *You sort the children out, Amos, it's not my problem.*

145

Amos explained the situation. The children listened reluctantly. Bernie, now with a very stern look on her face, fidgeted from time to time and decided to just listen to Amos or she might say something she would later regret.

The waitress arrived with their food.

"We could go to the turtle farm and Stingray City. Mom, you could snorkel if you want to and we could take a boat trip to one of the other islands or go fishing..." Robert was flicking through the island tourist brochure.

"We'll have ten days whilst Dad is away so we should make the most of it and then we can go diving again when he gets back," said Elizabeth, very logically.

"I can't wait that long," said Henry in a grumpy voice.

Amos was listening intently to the children's conversation. They seemed to have worked it out better than he had. He thought that hopefully that would ease Bernie's pain and annoyance with him.

Both Amos and Bernie were subdued over dinner. The children sensed it, particularly Robert, who maintained a lively conversation all evening, which helped everyone somehow enjoy the evening as best they could.

Back in the room, Amos sat at his laptop and booked his flight. Bernie said nothing.

The children came into their bedroom to say good night.

"Do you have to go, Dad?" asked Henry.

"Unfortunately, yes... as I said earlier, Henry, they want to see me in person before they sign up."

"Can we go to the airport with you, Dad?"

"Yeah, sure you can. Night night, you guys, see you tomorrow." Their bedroom door closed. "It'll be the Cayman Airways 07.45 to Miami, and then I will pick up the connection to London."

"I don't care, Amos; you just get on and do what you want." She slammed the bathroom door.

Amos packed a suitcase and got ready for bed. Bernie emerged from the bathroom and went straight to her side of the bed with no response to Amos apologising and saying good night.

CHAPTER 7: ROSEBANK... "THE BIG ONE"

Amos walked across the tarmac and climbed the steps up into the aircraft. He stood at the top and looked back towards the terminal building. He could see his children waving and his wife lifting Henry up so that he could see. He waved back with a tear in his eye. *I hope I've done the right thing,* he said to himself. *What happens if we don't sign? What a mess. Think positive now; I'll be back in ten days,* he thought to himself, *hopefully sooner.*

"Excuse me, sir, do you mind letting on the last of the passengers as we need to prepare for take-off. Thank you."

"Oh, I'm sorry." Amos looked over towards his family, a final wave, and then entered the plane.

"Good morning, sir."

"Hi. Yeah. Good morning to you too."

"Would you mind getting seated as quickly as possible, please, sir, thank you."

Amos looked at his ticket: row eight, seat A. In fact, it didn't really matter where he sat as there were plenty of spare seats. It reminded him of Oily and his three seats. He sat down and moved across to the window seat and looked out. He could see his family; they were still there and started to wave again when they saw him. He waved back and vowed not to leave his family like this ever again.

Even though it was only a one-and-a-half-hour hop to Miami, he found it difficult to stay calm, his mind racing about numerous things. The flight. His family, and what Bernie was thinking of him... they had hardly spoken since the meal last night. The arrangements with Jack and the supporting team. *What if they aren't available? Or Sally has her baby? What a mess.*

The stewardess walked past his row of seats and Amos beckoned to her. "A double bourbon, please, when you can, thank you."

"Certainly, sir, but if you don't mind waiting until we've taken off?"

Amos looked out of the plane again, this time just tarmac and palm trees waving at him… what a mess he'd made of the holiday. *Right, just gotta make the most of it. Yup, gotta do that; come on, Amos, pull yourself together and get into gear.*

He pulled out his laptop and decided to start editing Jack's report but it was difficult to take his thoughts off the events over the last twenty-four hours. He shut the lid and closed his eyes.

The plane took off and slowly pulled up and away from the island, the undercarriage now being raised and clunking into its housing.

"Right, I had better get started," he said to himself, opening up his laptop and waiting for it to power up. He looked out of the window again.

"Sir, your drink that you ordered. That's right, isn't it – a double bourbon?"

"Oh, yes, thank you, sorry, I've er… changed my mind."

"Well, I've twisted the cap and they're both open." She sounded put out as she had gone out of her way to be of assistance.

"OK, no problem, I'll take them anyway. I'll probably end up changing my mind again anyhow. Thank you. Sorry about that."

Amos called Jack's report up on the screen.

AJ INSPECTIONS Ltd
MONTROSE ALPHA PLATFORM
Block 22/17 b.130
Main Stanchions Inspection Report
4 May to 11 July ….
Published July ….
Signed………
Director………

Signed.........
Director.........

Right, well, that's the easy bit, he thought to himself. He then rubbed his hands together. "Here we go."

"Sir, I'm sorry to disturb you, but would you like any food? We have light refreshments available and snacks."

Amos rested his hands back from the keyboard, sat back in his chair and lifted up his glasses onto his forehead.

"Well, as it happens... yes," he replied with a level of annoyance in his voice at having been disturbed. "Please... what have you got that's hot?"

"Sorry, sir, this is only a short flight; we're only serving cold food like wraps and sandwiches, crisps and peanuts."

"I'll have a strong coffee, please, no milk, and that'll be fine, thanks... I'll get something to eat when we get to Miami."

With the space available on the plane, Amos could spread out and put his drinks on the fold-down table next to him.

"Thank you."

Amos started to edit the report. *Contents... introduction... where's the temperature section... good, that's in, and the maintenance section... Yeah... Good... Ecologically friendly products for barnacle removal... that's a good start, Jack. It should really be an easy edit as he's been doing the reports now for a few years.*

Amos used to prepare all the reports, but they found a better system was that Jack would draft and Amos would then do the final edit. It made for a much more robust report and recommendations with them both inputting.

Whether the oil or gas rig company paid any notice to their reports was another matter... ultimately, though, it was their problem to comply and face the consequences if they didn't. Like a small fine – pathetic, really. But the threat of closure would wake them up, although this rarely happened, which seemed to Amos to be a bit of a farce. *Why bother to undertake inspections and reports if the outcomes are rarely complied with or the penalties instigated are so trivial that they get ignored? The threat of closure needs to be better enforced.*

Maybe if the reports had to go to a third party, that would provide a wake-up call and the works recommended would be undertaken correctly and in a timely manner. Yeah, that would be good; I must make a note of that and mention it at the annual industry review in Houston to see how that could be implemented. The oil and gas companies won't like it, but it would benefit everyone in the long term.

Right, now... how are we doing here... temperatures... Oh... Can't see where he's... Nope, he's not got them in... Jack's not put in the historic temperatures, only the latest ones we've taken... that's strange, that's not like him, we agreed to get those in. I wonder why he hasn't done that? I'll have to give him a call from Miami.

Maintenance... past records and future, that's good... reference to the use of eco-friendly barnacle removal as per our recommendations and the company's change in product use below thirty metres... Mmm... it's not gonna go down well that we spotted that, but it's their own fault.

Amos sat back and took a mouthful of coffee and a brief glance out of the window.

Just because the product costs them more to use, that's not a reason to not use it... the industry's got so much money washing around to invest, it's literally a drop in the ocean. I just can't understand their logic of disrupting the ecosystems with extraction and yet not being prepared to even try to minimise the impact.

"Could I have another coffee, please, when you've got a moment?"

"Yes, sir," said the steward.

Amos returned to the screen and continued to read and edit the report. He was pleased to have this to do as it took his mind off the family problems he'd left back on Grand Cayman. But still his mind drifted back to them. *It'll be alright*, he said to himself looking out of the window. *Bernie will understand... but I've just gotta spend more time with the family. I'm also getting too old for this sort of thing; maybe the guy on the rig last week was right? Hey, what... I'm good at the moment.*

"Fasten your seatbelts for landing, please, and stow away any luggage in the overhead lockers or under the seat in front of you." Amos duly obliged and finished off his coffee before a bit of turbulence spilled it.

The plane landed smoothly, even through the rain shower moving across the runway, and parked up close to the terminal building. Amos disembarked and headed for the terminal building to check on his connecting flight.

Miami airport wasn't one of Amos's favourite airports. "Give me Aberdeen any day," he said to himself. They also sold a nice selection of whiskies, which was a nice memory jogger as he had two small bottles from the plane that he had kept in his pocket. He kept walking.

Miami airport was so big, it was like walking through the shopping malls of downtown Houston on a Saturday afternoon. *So many shops and people; where do they all come from and where do they go?* He didn't wander around for long although it was nice to be able to stretch his legs.

Amos grabbed a coffee and a hot patty and looked to find his way to the lounge and wait for his departure to London to be called up.

Looks like I've got another hour. That's good; gives me time to give Jack a call. What time is it over there? Mmm… Probably around 9.30 at night; yeah, that should be OK.

Brr… Brr… The phone was picked up straight away.

"Jack. Hi. Amos here; I'm in Miami."

"Amos, good to hear from you. Where did you say you were?"

"Miami, Miami airport, just waiting for the connection."

"We have the meeting set with them for 11.30 tomorrow morning. Are you going to get here on time?"

"Yeah, all fine – the flight's on time and leaves in fifty minutes, so will be at Heathrow for about 7.10 in the morning your time, so it's looking ok."

"Phew… thank goodness for that; I was worried it would just be me tomorrow. They want to see the whites of our eyes tomorrow – both of us."

Amos had a sudden close shark-eye flashback, and took a deep breath. He realised that he would need to get some therapy; *yeah, it was a close shave with death but I should be getting over it by now.*

"Amos? … Amos?"

"Yeah… Yeah, I'm fine. OK, I'm with you… How are we getting to their offices?"

"I'll pick you up at the airport, and we can go straight down to their offices in Guildford. It should only take about an hour so we'll have some time to collect our thoughts and look over the bid again."

"Jack, I've been checking through your draft report on the Montrose Alpha contract and it looks good except you've not got much on the salinity levels and temperature recordings we've taken compared to other data recorded… Why's that, as we wanted to make a point of it?"

"Well, Amos, there wasn't much data available. I did a thorough check on the internet for the organisations that carry out the data recording… and nothing. Don't know why."

"And the section about the rig maintenance looks a bit light… I thought we were going to make a point about that aspect in our report because they have been lax in doing what they should have done over the last year?"

"Well…" There was a pause from Jack. "Pete spoke to me just before we boarded the chopper and he asked us not to go too heavy with them on the maintenance as he was worried that the rig might be mothballed or even shut down completely. He even offered me some money to keep the report positive, but I refused."

"Jack, you know we can't do that," replied Amos crossly. "We're independent, remember, and supposed to be providing our report on facts and not influenced by others. How can anyone rely—"

"Sorry, Amos, I… I didn't think."

"Come on, Jack, you know that's not good enough. We're better than that. The last thing we want is our reputation tarnished. If we are seen to be influenced by others it will kick back where it hurts and then where will we be? All that hard work over the last eight years wasted."

"BA flight 742 to London Heathrow is now ready for boarding. Please proceed to gate sixty-eight," blasted out from the airport tannoy.

"OK, Jack, that's me. I'll catch up with you in the morning."

"Have a good flight."

"Yeah." *What was Jack thinking?* Amos said to himself. *Pete can't be expecting us to do him a favour on this... can he? And why? Particularly on something as important as this.*

"I need a drink," Amos said out loud, and pulled out one of the small bottles of bourbon he had kept from the plane, and finished it. *One spare,* he thought. Amos then got up and headed towards the gate with his luggage. He stopped at a bar on the way. He never liked drinking out of a bottle.

"A double bourbon, please, and quickly as I've got a plane to catch."

The barman obliged and Amos left a $10 bill on the bar, checking to make sure it was only $10.

"Whoa, that's good – I needed that." He placed the glass back on the bar. "Thank you, barman, just the job."

Amos got to the gate and was one of the last in the queue. He was never one to hurry onto the plane. *Drat,* he thought to himself, *I meant to give Bernie a call... too busy sorting out Jack and his report.*

"Passport and ticket, please, sir... Thank you, that's fine. We've already called your row so you can board straight away."

"Thank you," replied Amos. That suited him perfectly.

It was a short walk to the plane from the bottom of a set of stairs. Amos knew the route and procedure and felt he was doing it all in a dream.

He hadn't gotten much sleep the previous night after the discussion – or argument – with Bernie, which had understandably got a bit heated at times, then trying to book the flights and speak to the children and pack. He was glad he could now somehow get some shuteye.

"Good evening, sir," came the voice of a very perky stewardess for this time of the day.

"Let's hope it's a quiet flight," Amos said to the stewardess as he reached the top of the stairs boarding the plane. "I need to do some work and get some sleep."

Amos found his seat in the middle of the plane: no window, but at least an aisle seat so he could stretch his legs if he wanted to. The couple next to him seemed to have similar ideas and as soon as the plane had taken off, they pulled out their pillows and wrapped themselves in blankets. Amos rested his head back and took a deep breath. *Right, I suppose I'd better prepare for this interview.* He pulled out a pad and pen and started to make a few notes. His enthusiasm didn't last long, as he quickly went into a deep sleep, his hand slumped on the table.

A series of wobbles of the plane disturbed but didn't wake him; he drifted off again. He vaguely remembered someone saying "food", but kept his eyes closed and did not respond. It was not often that he managed that much sleep on a flight, but he obviously needed it.

***

"Any drinks, anyone?"

Amos stirred and opened his eyes a fraction.

"Ah, yeah," he said and moved himself into an upright position in the seat. "Yes please... and are you serving any food?"

"You've missed breakfast and your evening meal, sir; that was about five or six hours ago."

"Wow, did I sleep that long? I must have needed it."

"Sir, we didn't want to disturb you."

"Oh... That's fine, no problem... a coffee, please, and make it strong. And have you got a breakfast tray or something?"

"I'll see what I can do." She smiled at him and walked away from him down to the plane's kitchen area.

A breakfast tray arrived.

"Thank you," said Amos.

"You will need to finish that quickly, sir, as we are just over south-west England and will soon be starting our descent into

Heathrow and I'll shortly be collecting any outstanding trays and rubbish."

A bumpy landing caused by a gusting wind across the runway made a few people gasp and Amos could feel the relief from the passengers as the plane came under control and headed off the strip to park up.

"Welcome to London Heathrow. Would passengers please remain seated until the aircraft has come to a complete stop and the seatbelt sign is off. Thank you."

This didn't seem to make much difference to a number of people; Amos could hear the unclipping of safety belts and a number of passengers standing up and retrieving their luggage as they stopped at the gate. *What is it about people that blatantly ignore safety procedures? I just can't understand it.*

"Thank you for flying with BA today and we look forward to seeing you again soon."

Disembarking was efficient and the time taken to collect hold luggage, get through passport control and customs straightforward enough, which tended to follow with early flights mainly occupied by business people with a schedule to meet.

Walking out onto the arrivals concourse, Amos immediately saw Jack. No sign needed.

Jack pushed past a number of people to get through the crowd. "Hey, buddy, how you doing?"

"Great, thanks."

"Looks like you had a good flight, and on time?"

"Yeah, thanks, Jack, it was good... though I missed the evening meal... slept most of the way and only had a light breakfast, so to be honest I'm a bit peckish. How about you? Sally OK?"

"Yes, she's fine, all good, no problem. As the meeting's at 11.30, I suggest we just go straight away from here in case there are any hold-ups; we should have sufficient time to get a bite to eat close to their offices."

"Sure, let's do that," replied Amos. "Where are you parked?"

"Through there – short stay." Jack pointed up at the sign.

They were soon out of the car park and on the road. M25 then down the A3, to Guildford.

Having left the hustle and bustle of the airport, they now had the same on the roads. Rush hour. They had barely managed more than fifteen miles an hour since leaving the airport: stop, start... stop, start. Amos was getting agitated and concerned.

"Are we going to get out of this jam or what, Jack? You know we can't be late."

"Hey, Amos. Chill. It's always like this; once we get clear of the turn-off for the M3, it will be plain sailing, trust me. I live around these parts and it's just how the road system works over here."

"Are you sure about this, Jack? The freeways back home are always moving."

"Yeah, that's because they are six lanes wide, Amos! It'll clear shortly, don't worry; it's not like you to get impatient."

"Yeah, well, it's leaving Bernie and the kids on holiday." Amos continued to mumble to himself about it.

"Look, Amos, you've committed yourself to it now, so pull yourself together; we want to get the contract, right? Think about it... It's good for you and for the family's benefit, right?"

"Yeah, yeah, yeah..." Amos looked out of the car window.

Jack remained quiet as he knew that when his sister didn't get what she wanted, she made a big song and dance about it and Amos was probably still licking his wounds.

The traffic started to move more quickly and they sped through the Surrey countryside and were soon on the outskirts of Guildford.

"All the same, highways or motorways, whatever you call them over here, except we're on the wrong side of the road," said Amos.

Jack was pleased he had kept quiet, as it enabled Amos to pull his thoughts together and he was now returning to his normal self with his sense of humour. Jack just smiled across at Amos in the passenger seat.

"Looks like it's about half a mile from the next junction just coming up on the left," said Amos, reading from Google Maps on his phone.

They soon found the place, MPZ – not the most exciting of names – and parked up in the oil company's HQ building, which was just outside of the centre of town. Jack removed a briefcase from the rear seat of the car and locked up.

"Let's see if we can't find ourselves a coffee bar or something before we go in. We've got just under an hour to prepare. Have they given us an agenda, Jack?"

"No agenda, but that sounds like a good idea," he replied. "I've brought the project file with us, including our tender submission. They sent over the draft contracts to sign yesterday afternoon and I've printed them off... That's when I knew they were serious and had to call you. You remember, Amos, it was the bid where we had that legal guy check over the whole document and comment, particularly on the payment terms, which were pretty onerous. They've made all the changes that we suggested so it should be straightforward enough provided they like the look of us," said Jack as they were walking towards the town centre.

"There, across the road." Amos pointed with his phone. "There's a place... very appropriately named, too. The White House... this is a good omen. You know what? It feels like home with a name like that."

They found seats and a table in the conservatory area overlooking the Wey canal.

"Do we get served here or what?" said Amos to Jack. "As I need some food pretty quick."

"I'll go up to the bar and sort something out... what would you like?"

"A strong coffee and something to eat would be good." Amos stretched over to another table and picked up a menu.

Jack went up to the bar to order the drinks and whilst he was there, Amos stood up and called across to him.

"Jack, I'll have a steak sandwich... Hellfire... no I won't... Er, make that a tuna salad and some fries."

"OK."

Amos sat down at the table, looking out towards the water.

"Hey, Jack... Come and have a look at this... there's a barge making its way past on the river. This is really quaint; Bernie would really love this. Shit... I meant to call her... Argh... damn it...

what time is it anyway?" he said, looking at his watch and trying to work out the time.

Time difference... Four or five in the morning... there's no way I'm calling her now, I'm going to have to leave it till later, he thought, shaking his head from side to side.

"Let's have a look at what we sent them, Jack, and the emails after our bid went in just in case there's something in there we need to respond to. Could you get our tender out and we can remind ourselves what we've committed to."

They sat reading the paperwork, chatting and making notes.

"Did you speak with Mike the legal guy?"

"Yeah, I did, but as MPZ have agreed to all our amendments he said there was no need for him to be here."

"Just hope they don't bring up anything else, and if they do? Heck, we can worry about it when it happens."

Their food and drinks were brought to the table.

"Thank you," said Amos, tucking into his food straight away. "Why do you think they are so keen to want an immediate start?"

"They've sat on our tender for... must be three months now, maybe more? Could be that the price of a barrel of oil has gone up, making it viable, or maybe problems on another rig? Who knows."

"This tastes good," said Amos between mouthfuls. "Shame they didn't have this on the plane over, or maybe they did as I slept through... would you believe it, Jack, almost six hours' shuteye. Have we got the support team in place?"

"Yes, I spoke to Charles yesterday and he's ready to go as soon as we press the button... and knows it's an immediate start on the rig, but it will take a good few hours after the meeting to set it all in motion if they give us the go-ahead this afternoon."

"I wonder if maybe they've got problems on another rig? Are MPZ, or Zennor as they also seem to be called, new players?" said Amos, flicking through the papers.

"No, I've checked them out; they've been around for over ten years and, as you asked when we put our bid in, they are well backed financially by some billionaire out of Scandinavia."

"Right, that's me done," said Amos, wiping his mouth and

putting his serviette onto his plate.

"You were seriously hungry, Amos."

"Yeah, I could eat another but I don't think we've got enough time. Have you paid, Jack?"

"Yeah."

"OK, let's get going. We don't want to be late, particularly as it's only five minutes away."

Entering the reception of the building said it all... very palatial. Amos nodded to himself. High quality desk, wood panelling, brass fittings and smartly dressed receptionists.

"This is where the money is; let's hope when we deliver they give some to us."

Jack nodded back to Amos.

"Good morning, how may I help you?" came a voice from behind the reception desk from a particularly pleasantly spoken English woman, probably mid twenties and just out of university, having got her Masters in languages and couldn't get a job anywhere so ended up here.

"We're here to see a Mr Angus Bletchfold-Smith and a Peter Knowles, I believe, and booked in for 11.30, thank you."

"Oh yes, the Rosebank contract signing."

"Yeah, that's right." Amos raised his eyebrows, and turned his head slightly with a wry smile on his face as he looked towards Jack standing next to him at the desk. *The contract signing... It is serious. We must have got it, no messing.*

"If you would just like to wait here, Peter will be down shortly."

Jack and Amos turned to sit down.

"Would you like a drink while you're waiting?" came the voice of the receptionist.

"No, thank you, we're good. We just had a coffee."

The reception was a busy area and as they went to sit down, two men were standing and talking at the desk. Amos overheard the name Oliver Goldman and a reference to some new platform in Alaska.

"Jack," said Amos, joining him on the soft leather seating. "Jack. That's Oily they're talking about; he certainly gets around."

The lift doors pinged and the guy exiting looked towards the reception desk and the receptionist motioned over to where Amos and Jack were sitting. He came over with a big beaming smile on his face.

"Well, gentlemen, good to meet you. I'm Peter Knowles. You found us OK, then?"

Jack and Amos shook hands with him and introduced themselves and followed Peter into the lift.

He pressed the button for level three.

"You guys had far to come?"

"Well, I'm local," said Jack. "I'm this side of Woking but Amos here, he's—"

"I'm from Houston, Texas, and left my family on holiday to come and see you guys."

Jack closed his eyes and hoped Amos wouldn't say anything that would turn them off, as he could be quite blunt when it came to business matters, but fine once you got to know him.

They reached the third floor. "This way, gentlemen, if you would like to follow me."

Peter opened the door to the company's boardroom. It was as palatial as the reception area except there was a series of four glass chandeliers hanging from the ceiling and running the length of the table. There were seven people sitting at the table as they entered and they all started to stand up from their chairs at the table.

"Good morning," said Amos in a bold, forthright manner.

There then followed a series of hand-shaking and introductions. Angus Bletchfold-Smith, CEO; Julian Roberts, engineering and platform maintenance; Sarah Egan, contracts; Jonathan King, lawyer; David Keithe, lawyer; Lesley Smyth, solicitor; James Peters, planning. "And I'm Peter Knowles. We met a few moments ago; head of operations at MPZ."

Contracts and two lawyers... Hope you've got this one right, Jack, thought Amos, *otherwise we might be in a bit of trouble.*

"Nice to meet you all," said Jack.

"Please sit down," said Angus, the CEO.

There then followed the sorting of drinks and the coming and going of a secretary with what looked like the contracts being shuffled around at one end of the table with Sarah Egan.

Amos eyed the people in front of him and picked out the CEO, Angus Bletchfold-Smith. Another guy then entered the board room; he introduced himself as Ross Stewart, ops director. *Him and Peter Knowles are the key guys here...* But he still kept an eye on the others. Amos had an uncanny ability to read people's motives and agendas, which had proved well in the past and hopefully the future.

"Welcome, it's good you could come over at such short notice. Thank you. You do realise if you hadn't, we would have gone with someone else?" said the CEO with a wry smile on his face. "Is it just you two this morning? No lawyers?" he said, looking across the table at his, who were still moving papers around.

"Yeah," replied Amos. "We decided there was no need and an unnecessary expense in this instance, as our queries during the tendering period were all sorted out by email." Amos was shifting his position in his chair and realising that the inquisition sitting in front of him could start to get a bit heavy now.

"You put in a very good submission," said Angus.

"Thank you," replied Jack.

"But one thing that bothered us was: have you got the resources and manpower to deliver? As this rig needs an inspection clearance certificate urgently, and a good one."

Amos thought about the last point. *A good one... it will be what it will be,* Amos thought to himself. *Let's not respond to that just yet.*

"Yes, we've got the resources otherwise we wouldn't have submitted our tender," Amos responded, rather too bluntly for Jack's liking.

The last thing we want to do, thought Jack, *is to lose this after all the effort and sacrifice that's been put in. Come on, Amos, keep cool.*

"I like a man that's forthright and positive," said the CEO.

"So you're saying you can start right away?" added Peter Knowles.

"Yup, that's what your tender document called for and that's what we've allowed."

"And how long have you been working up in the North Sea?" asked the head of planning.

"This will be about our eighth year together," replied Jack, "and prior to that we both worked for bigger organisations."

"How do you deal with bad weather when it comes to the inspections?" The questions were coming fast now.

"We can't control the weather. If the conditions aren't good for diving, we won't risk our divers' safety," replied Amos rather bluntly again.

"That's good to hear," responded Angus.

"How can we be assured that you will be delivering our report on time?"

"Well, we have answered honestly in our submission to both resources and work rate requirements to complete the inspection, take samples and report. The timeline to undertake would not be any different from other organisations' submissions; perhaps the only difference is—" Amos was interrupted.

"Your rates for standing time seem rather high; why's that?"

Amos thought that this guy must be kidding; he knew what the big companies would be charging. *The guy's trying to con us into reducing our rates...*

"Our rates are reflective of actual costs we would be incurring with a small additional margin for overheads, but not profit, as it wouldn't be fair on you guys."

The CEO and the guy, Ross, looked at one another and both gave the look of... *Good answer.*

"We have, as you would have seen from the email correspondence, amended the contract so that it addresses all your comments and proposed amendments you made with your tender submission."

Jack nodded in response as he had checked the ones they had sent through yesterday. Amos still had an eye on this Ross character, whom he felt was untrustworthy.

"I would just like to ask one final question. What would be your actions if you found a problem in the rig support system?"

"It's our job to identify and record what we see. If we discover a problem or anomaly, we will ensure this is thoroughly covered with attached survey information, analysis and the appropriate data in our report."

"Thank you." The people from MPZ around the table then looked to seek approval from one another, acknowledging and nodding.

"Any other questions from you guys?" asked Amos.

Oh no, thought Jack, *here we go.*

"How come you want to use us and not some of the bigger players?"

The palms of Jack's hands, which he held together below the table, started to sweat profusely and through the tension of his clenched teeth he tried to keep smiling.

"To be honest with you," said the CEO, "we did, but having discussed it internally and checked out the references in your submission and other industry connections, we decided to go with AJ Inspections."

"If you don't mind my asking, who were these other contacts or sources? As it helps with our making other bids and submissions."

Ross replied, "A senior guy from Seline Oil, Oliver Goldman – you've heard of him?"

"Yeah, I've known him for years," said Amos.

"You come highly recommended," said Angus.

Well, well, well, thought Amos, *what a piece of luck bumping into Oily on the plane and giving him the business card.*

"That's us finished with our questions; can we get on with signing the contracts, unless you have anything further?" asked Angus.

"Yeah," said Amos, "just one more... the contract states that there is certain equipment available for the inspections already up on the rig?"

"Yes, that's correct and you are free to use it at no cost to you."

"Has the equipment been maintained and are the records available? As we don't want to be wasting anyone's time here."

Angus looked across the table.

"Yes, the records are up to date," said Peter.

"From memory, you advised in your tender invitation documents that you've got a Dräger two-man saturation and a three-man OME. I thought the OME built in 1984 was obsolete?"

"We purchased them seven years ago and move them from rig to rig when required," replied Peter.

"Makes economic sense," interjected Ross from the other side of Angus.

"As I said, we've got all the maintenance records if you want to see them and all the servicing costs are paid by us."

"Can we just have a couple of moments, please?" said Amos.

Jack and he left the table and walked away to a corner of the room.

"You know why it's us getting this job? It's the age of the equipment they've got and there aren't many organisations capable of using it."

"Maybe," said Jack, "but the equipment is in good condition and maintained; that's what they have said, and it clearly states that in the tender invitation documentation."

They returned to the table.

"Could we see the maintenance records, please, as you appreciate it's our lives and our team's lives at stake here and not yours."

Ross stood up and glared across the table as if to say, *You don't trust me do you?*, and left the room. He returned shortly with six lever arch files with *Alpha 12* on the side, and dropped them rather heavily onto the table.

Amos and Jack thumbed through the files.

"Well, they all look up to date and the certificates are all signed off by the HSE, thank you." They handed the files back across the table.

"The originals are all up on the rig," said Peter.

"Thank you. One final point."

No, Amos, please no… You're pushing them too far, Jack said to himself.

"The monthly payment schedule will be made on time, won't it, as we've had some not very satisfactory situations of late?"

"You've probably already checked us out," said Angus. "We have a strong balance sheet and treat our contractors and subcontractors well."

"Anything further?" asked Ross with a sharpness in his tongue, which the CEO detected. Angus looked at him with piercing eyes.

"No, no, it's all fine at the moment. We just want to clarify the ground rules so that we all know where we are."

"Well, unless there are any other questions," said Angus, looking around the table, "let's get the contracts signed. The sooner we do, the sooner we get our report."

Amos and Jack looked at each other and both shook their heads. "No more questions, thank you," replied Jack.

Amos and the CEO stood up and leant over and shook hands across the table.

"Good to do business with you," said Angus, who then shook Jack's hand.

"You too," replied Amos.

"You know we need this report to get carried out and issued quickly to enable the gas to flow again and the sooner it's done the better for all of us."

"Jack, you got a pen?" said Amos, rubbing his hands together.

Jack passed over the pen he had been using to make notes, wishing Amos didn't do that rubbing of hands – it always made him feel uncomfortable – but knowing it was only to warm up his hands for all the signing and initialling of the contracts.

"Right, let's get this show on the road and get these contracts signed. We've got some orders to place and work to do."

Amos and Angus moved to the head of the table where the contracts were spread out.

One of the legal assistants then pointed to where Amos needed to sign or initial.

"You just need to sign where the yellow tags are, and initial where the blue tags are – you will see as you go through the documents. You'll also notice green tags; these are for MPZ, and red tags are where the second director, Jack, needs to sign, and you will also need to date where shown by the white tags. Once you've done that, please then pass across to Mr Bletchfold-Smith for him to complete. There's three sets, one for AJ Inspections, one for MPZ and we'll retain the third set. You look like you've been on holiday?"

"Well, yeah, I started having a holiday but it only lasted for just a few days; it was then cut short. Hopefully I'll be able to get back there soon, once this contract is well underway," replied Amos.

Amos signed and initialled where required and stood up to let Jack sign and complete his sections. He couldn't help but look across to where the contract sum was written to remind himself that he wasn't dreaming: £1,663,457.89.

Amos and Angus chatted briefly away from the others.

"Do you realise we've got another seven or so of these over the next three years, and if you play your cards right and deliver to the programme, they're yours."

Amos was aghast and didn't quite know what to say other than a very restrained, "Thank you, we will bear that in mind." He had had false promises before… the sprat to catch the mackerel… but felt in his bones that there was substance in what Angus had said to him.

"OK," said Angus, "that looks like the three sets are all completed. Well, good to meet you, Amos, and you, Jack; I'm sure we will meet again soon. Unfortunately we've got back to back meetings and we'd better let you sort yourselves out and get things underway. You know the main points of contact if there are any problems: Ross and Peter here."

Jack was given the second set of the contracts and he put them into his bag.

"Yeah, we're used to that," said Amos.

They finished saying their goodbyes and were led out of the board room by Peter, who escorted them to the lift.

"Good to meet you both, and welcome on board. I may be up at the rig next week to see how you're getting on; just keep me informed of progress. You've got my email address."

"OK, we will look forward to it," replied Jack. Amos was wary of people that interfered with his work and was hoping that Peter was not one of those.

The lift doors closed. Jack and Amos then congratulated themselves.

"Amos, I can't believe it," said Jack, who then had to contain his joy as the lift doors opened to let someone in from the second floor. They waited to continue their conversation until they were well outside the building.

"This is unbelievable, Amos, I still can't get my head around it."

"I think we've got Oily to thank. Anyhow, how did we get to eighty-nine pence in our tender?"

"You might remember, Amos," said Jack, "that after we finished the tender submission calculations it was at about two in the morning, from what I can remember. We sat down to a bourbon or two, listening to the Blues Brothers in the background... Yes?"

"Oh yeah... six three four five seven eight nine." Amos chuckled. "Must make sure we do that with every tender."

"Did you realise, Amos, that the deal's in pounds, not dollars... I thought we'd get a bit of contingency in, incase of any problems."

"Yeah, I saw that... You old rascal, Jack," said Amos, shoving him in the shoulder.

"OK, let's get this show on the road."

They walked back to The White House and found a table tucked away in a corner. They sat staring at each other, neither saying anything, not knowing whether to celebrate or cry. This was a huge contract for them, the Big One, and so important for the future of the business and to them personally.

"Jack, as my breakfast was rather rushed, I'm going to order my food now. We can sort Charles and his team, the equipment and flights out later."

The waiter attended to them straight away and Amos ordered the vegetarian option and a coffee.

Jack ordered the same, much to Amos's surprise.

"Bernie's been having a go at you too, has she?" said Amos.

"No, far from it – I've been meaning to give it a go and the description on the menu looked good."

"Bernie – I must give her a call... mmm, still too early," he said, looking at his watch. "I'll give her a call once we've got everything organised later this afternoon."

Laptops open, they spent the next two hours, in between taking bites of their meals, notifying their team, organising aspects of equipment that were down to them to sort, and their flights.

"How's Sally with all of this?" asked Amos, settling back in his seat, relieved that they were making progress.

"She's fine with it all," replied Jack, "Her mother and father are coming up from the West Country in a week's time to stay over until the baby's born. They're only a couple of hours or so away but it's worth having them at home in case I'm not around, and she's got a good friend and neighbour who is also pregnant but about three months behind, so she's good. That's all reassuring for me, just in case we hit some bad weather or some piece of equipment breaks down and the job gets delayed." Jack looked up from his laptop. "Hey, Charles has just confirmed he's OK to be up there tomorrow with his team, all four of them."

They gave each other a high five.

"He's had his team on standby since we put our tender in, and they are raring to go. Did you know they've been out of work for over four months now, ever since the fire on that rig over in the Forties field – did you hear about that?"

Amos shook his head.

"Nothing to do with him and his team, but work just stopped on the rig overnight."

"He's essential… if he lets us down, we are in the shit."

"He won't, Amos, you know that, we've all worked together before… stop worrying."

"That looks like we're all sorted then. What time did you arrange the flights for?" said Amos.

"Er…" Jack checked on his screen. "16.45 from Heathrow, so we are back up the A3 again and then the M25. We will need to leave in the next fifteen to twenty minutes…"

"Why the rush?"

"Traffic on the roads can be unpredictable at times and the later flights were all fully booked so we'll get up to Aberdeen when it's still light."

"Back to grey, grey and more grey and when it's not grey... rain and grey. How do you all cope with the weather here?"

"Get used to it, I suppose, and look forward to holidays where the sun shines."

"Hey, you need to come over to us when this job is over and Sally's settled down after the baby's born."

"Yeah, sure, Amos."

"Bring Sally's mom and dad if you want – we've got plenty of space."

"Talking of flights, Jack... Waiter? Waiter, a double bourbon, please, thank you. Jack, do you want anything?"

"I'll just have another coffee, please, a latte – I've got to drive, remember, otherwise I would, thanks."

***

The journey back up to Heathrow and then on to Aberdeen went smoothly, other than Amos's frustration at not being able to speak with Bernie. All he managed to do was leave a message in reception to say they had signed the contracts and that he would speak with her later.

At the hotel in Aberdeen, they spent the evening finalising their report from the last contract, before heading off on the morning helicopter flight to Alpha 12 Rosebank.

"Pete's not gonna like this," said Amos. "It's reflective of everything we inspected and the samples are the samples... You can't change those."

"You know there's a big risk now that they'll close the platform. The repairs are gonna cost them a fortune."

"Well, perhaps if they had undertaken our advice on the repairs and protection materials we recommended last time, they wouldn't have to spend so much now... Just lack of regular maintenance, that's basically all it calls for, plus a commitment by all in the extraction industry to the environment, i.e. use the environmentally friendly stuff and to do it properly... make it a mandatory requirement."

"Good, that's good, excellent timing, finished our report before starting the next project."

"Glad we managed to recall our data of temperatures and salinity levels, and with that the discovery of those warm-water barnacles."

"I wonder how many other rigs have got them or if it's just isolated? Could do with mapping them out to see the spread of them – that's if they are on other platforms. What do you think, Jack?"

"I don't know how it compares with other data analysis and recordings but at least we can now keep a record going forward with all our future reporting."

"Yeah," replied Amos.

Jack pressed the send button.

"That's it… It's gone." He closed his laptop. "Good luck, Pete, and that's me done; I'm heading for bed. We're on the 7.15 out of the heliport… And I'm gonna get breakfast on the rig," said Jack. "You know: me, helicopters." He put his hand to his stomach and finger in his mouth.

"Night, Jack, I'm gonna give Bernie another call. Anything you wanna say?"

"No, it's fine, thanks, other than to give her my love and tell her Sally's doing fine."

"Yeah, sure."

The door to Amos's room shut and he sat down on the bed and gave Bernie a call from his mobile.

Brr… brr… brr… brr

"Good afternoon, Grand Cayman Marriott, how can I help you?"

"Hi, this is Amos."

"Oh, hello, Mr Amos, how are you today? We are missing you here and—"

"Yeah, yeah… me too. Could you please put me through to room 216? Thank you."

"Oh yes, Mrs Bernie… I saw her with the children a few moments ago."

"Oh great. Could I speak with her, please?"

"Oh, no. Sorry. no."

"But you just said you'd seen her."

"Yes, sir, Mr Amos, but she is not here now... she's gone with her children to Stingray City – you know, where they can go snorkelling and see the fish."

Drat, that's what I wanted to do with them, and heck, they're my children as well... well, they'll just have to do it again when I get back over there.

"OK, could I leave a message to... to tell her I'll call later. When is she back?"

"I don't know, Mr Amos, but I would say maybe sometime this afternoon, so that's about two, maybe three or four hours' time."

That's gonna be too late, thought Amos. "OK, thanks. That sounds like Caribbean time, so... that's gonna be any time in the afternoon?"

"Yes, sir."

Amos finished the call, disappointed.

Well, at least she's getting out and about with the kids. I wonder if she will dip her toe in the water with those stingrays? That would have been great to do with her and the kids... will have to take them on another visit when I get back. Just need to get this contract rolling.

He turned the side light off. He needed the sleep.

***

It felt like no sooner had he fallen asleep than there was a knock on the door.

Amos opened the door.

"Argh, you're already dressed, Amos?"

"Well, sort of," said Amos, rubbing his face and scratching his head. "I really do need to get a good night's sleep; all this travelling is messing up my sleep patterns."

"Cab's here in fifteen, Amos."

"OK, I'll see you in reception; I'm just gonna take a quick shower to wake up."

Amos opened the curtains to a damp, overcast morning, lights flickering through the early morning mist and street lights periodically extinguishing themselves. Amos knew he had to leave his family in Grand Cayman as this was a once in a lifetime opportunity... *I'm sure Bernie will come round as it is to the benefit of all of us,* he thought, but he hadn't seen her as upset as this for a long time.

The Bristow Helicopters courtesy car duly arrived at the entrance to the Ibis Quayside and took them to the heliport. Whilst making their way through passport control, there was the same customs guy as last week.

"Ah, I knew you guys couldn't keep away. Why haven't you brought some of that warm and sunny weather with you?"

"Well, if you'd like to know," replied Amos, "this isn't really my decision. Client wants work done so we do it, but I'm gonna make the most of it and get back to the sunshine as soon as I can, so on that basis, I'll see you soon, buddy." Amos retrieved his passport.

The 07.15 was on time and they were soon up off the ground, heading towards the platform. Jack was tucked into his usual position, huddled up close to the window with his eyes shut and hoodie over his head. The chopper was full of the usual guys who had had a long weekend off the rig and were recovering from too many beers the night before. So, other than the noise of the chopper, it was a very quiet trip. They passed over a group of shipping vessels, and then nothing until they got close to the fields.

"Alpha 12, ten minutes till landing, over," said their pilot.

"OK, that's good... light wind coming in from the west... other than that, you're clear, no other traffic, over."

Amos worked out that it was probably around twelve at night over in Grand Cayman, so he would arrange to call later in the afternoon.

On landing, Amos and Jack decided to go straight over to see Chris, the platform director. No sooner had they got off the helicopter than it was up and away back to Aberdeen.

They made their way from the helipad down to Chris's office. He had been forewarned of their arrival and told to ensure that everything that Amos and his team needed was provided for them. They found the office. A knock on the door and they entered. Amos and Jack introduced themselves and sat down opposite Chris at his desk.

"How long have you been in charge up here?" asked Amos.

"This is my first rig director position; I've been here about three weeks, so just getting to know the ropes."

"But you've done this before, haven't you?"

"Yes, been over in Forties on two platforms for BP and Exxon for three years, and then Peter and Ross called me up a couple of months ago and said they wanted to give me a chance as a rig director, so here I am. I've been told my priority is to get the rig up and running again."

And probably on a much better salary, thought Amos.

"So looks like we might be helping you out quite a bit whilst we're here?"

"Yes, we're going to have to work closely together," replied Chris, slightly taken aback by Amos's brusqueness.

"Chris, we're going to need to see the rig's maintenance records, please, for all the diving equipment. I want to see them all within the hour back here… I'm now gonna find myself some breakfast."

"Sure, I'll get those for you. Nice to meet you both," replied Chris. "And the canteen is down the stairs on the right and then follow the signs."

Amos got up and left the office, followed shortly afterwards by Jack, who had a quick conversation with Chris, apologising for Amos's sharpness but explaining that it was probably because he wanted to be with his family on holiday and he hadn't had breakfast yet. Jack then left to catch up with Amos.

"Jack, I can see we're gonna have a few issues on this one; that Chris is way too young to be in charge, not enough experience and with those suits coming up from their London office, probably just interfering, he's just a puppet."

Amos opened the door to the canteen and the shutter was about to be pulled down. "Hey, hey, wait a moment, can you do us some breakfast?"

"We're closed... and I need my breakfast."

"Argh, come on, we've only just got here. How about if we join you for breakfast, then there's no hassle?"

Jack chuckled. Amos had a way of making things work.

After a moment of thought, the chef responded, "Yeah, why not, be good to meet the new boys on the rig." He lifted the shutter back up. "There's not much left, I'm afraid, but I can do you a few eggs if that's any good."

"Yeah, that would be perfect, and as much brown toast as you've got."

"I'll keep it simple... make that two," said Jack.

They made themselves drinks from the self-serve coffee machine, whilst the chef prepared their breakfasts.

"All seems very quiet here," said Jack. "Almost spooky, like a ghost rig."

"Probably because they've got to get our bit out of the way first."

"How long you guys working here?" came the chef's voice from the kitchen.

"Probably around six to eight weeks, all being well. Our work is very much weather dependent; we're inspecting the rig below sea level to see if there are any problems and get you guys certified to operate again."

"I've always wanted to be a diver but got stuck in the kitchen and never moved out."

"How old are you – thirty... thirty-five?" asked Amos.

"Actually, I'm thirty-three. No house, no wife, no ambition, just stuck out here making scrambled eggs, fried eggs, boiled eggs and toast, brown, white... burnt, you name it."

"Well, if you really wanna do something different," replied Amos, "you've gotta set your mind on it and work to achieve that goal one step at a time. It took me a while to get my head around it. I quit college after the first year; that was probably one of the trickiest decisions of my life, but I've been happy with it... I'm my own boss, working outside most of the time and doing what I love, under my control most of the time."

The chef flipped the eggs in the pan and the toast jumped out of the toaster.

"What's your name?" asked Jack.

"Alan."

"I'm Jack and this is Amos; good to meet you."

"I'll bring it out on the table, just give me a few minutes. Are you sure you don't want anything else with your eggs? I can do you some tomatoes and mushrooms."

"Yeah, a couple of tomatoes would go down well, thank you," replied Amos. They went to sit at a table.

"Seems like a nice guy," said Jack." Always good to be friendly to the guy that feeds you," he added as they sat down at the table with their drinks.

"Have you had any response yet from Charles? Did he say when he is planning on getting here?"

"He's due in late this afternoon, so we will have time to brief him and start checking the equipment."

"There you go, gents," said Alan, laying the plates on the table, a dish of fried tomatoes, a pile of toast and a bowl of mushrooms.

"Thank you, Alan, are you gonna join us?" said Amos, winking over to Jack.

"Yeah, just give me a minute."

They were nicely sized portions: just what they needed to set them up for the day. They tucked in straight away, Alan joining them after he had closed the shutter to the servery.

"You know it's not often I get a chance to speak to many people up here. They all tell me to do this and that: 'When's the food ready?', 'Can I have more chips?', 'What have we got for an evening meal?' Then I've got the prep and clearing up to do... It's non-stop."

"Well, I suggest you start thinking about your diving career," said Jack.

"Yeah... and when those suits come up from London it's all about 'Here's your budget and don't overspend otherwise it will come out of your salary'. They've got no idea how much food you need to feed guys working on the rigs; they burn off so many calories up here, and they turn up and..."

"Who are these city boys, then?"

"Head office people bossing you around. They've got no idea what goes on on a rig, just pen-pushers and bean-counters; they need to get their hands dirty to really understand and appreciate what it's like up here."

"Would these suits be called Peter and Ross?" asked Amos.

"Yeah, that's them; evil bastards, in my mind."

Amos and Jack looked at each other and carried on eating. Eventually Jack said what Amos was thinking, but he was too busy eating. "Why's that?"

"Basically because of what I just said. I don't like them; there's something about when they arrive here that makes everyone uneasy, like you're waiting to get a tap on your shoulder at work and turn round and it's the boss and he's got a brown envelope in his hand and says, 'You're fired', it's that edgy up here. I think they just come up to try to show who's boss and to go into Aberdeen to have a night away from the office and away from their wives and girlfriends… you know what I mean?"

They didn't respond. Alan's rant had obviously been building up for a while and he'd needed to get it off his chest. Amos and Jack both finished their meals. Alan hadn't really started.

"Alan, thank you, that's been real good chatting with you, and we'll see you later for lunch. We've got the rest of our team turning up around one-ish so if you're able to provide them with something, I'm sure they will appreciate it, and remember about the diving; go for it if that's what you particularly want to do. If you find you don't like it, at least you've given it a go. We've got to go, Alan, sorry."

"We'll see you later," said Jack.

Outside the canteen, Amos said, "That boy really is pent-up about his life and working up here."

"That's always been a problem with the food industry and he probably needs another person helping him in the kitchen. He would be in a better place with someone to talk to whilst working – otherwise he's gonna get lonely and overthinking stuff, you know what I mean?" said Jack.

"Yeah," replied Amos. "Interesting what he said about those

two guys we met yesterday, Ross and Peter. You know they said they were coming up so we'd better get our ship in order."

They made their way back to the director's office, knocked on the door and walked in. There was a colleague of Chris's looking through the lever arch files.

"Hello, Amos, Jack. We've got all the files together for you as you asked and if you've got any problems or if anything is missing you can ask Peter or Ross."

But you should know, thought Amos. The two of them sat down at the table and opened the first of the lever arch files... it appeared in order. "Check the dates on the test certificates, Jack, that's the important piece of paper."

"They're here this afternoon," said Chris.

"Who?"

"Head office," replied Chris.

Amos and Jack looked at each other; it felt like the police were checking on them already and they hadn't even started.

"The test certificates all look OK... Chris, could you and your guys have ready for us to inspect the following equipment?" Jack started to list the equipment.

"We've already done that... it's ready for you. Head office emailed us yesterday and said to get it ready for you; there's one piece of gear that needs replacing on the Dräger and that's on its way over later this morning. It's one of the light switches that snapped off a few weeks ago."

"Very efficient, Chris, thank you," replied Amos, moving his head slightly to one side and raising his eyebrows. "Let's see what it all looks like, then."

They left the office, Chris leading the way down to the open deck area where the equipment was all laid out.

"Jack, could you check over this lot over here and then when Charles arrives later he can do a second run-through. I've never really been happy using other people's equipment. And I'll go and take a look at the Dräger 2 and the OME."

"That sounds good."

"Follow me down this way," said Chris to Amos, "and put this on." A site hat.

Give them their due, thought Amos to himself, *they have the rig pretty damn tidy and I suppose there's no harm in a strict regime on a rig as long as it doesn't result in being overly controlling.*

"Watch your head as you climb down the ladder, Amos, it's caught a few people out in the past."

"And will again by the look of things," replied Amos as he carefully manoeuvred around the steel beam.

"The Dräger is up there and the OME…"

"Yeah, thank you, I know what they look like, thanks, Chris." Amos was focused on the OME, as that was the piece of gear that he had particular concerns about.

"I'll leave you to it, then." Chris realised he had nothing further he could help with and was worried that he might be asked about something that he didn't know the answer to, but should, and that Amos was now in another world, one in which he needed to become more knowledgeable about and quickly.

"Yeah, thanks, could you send Jack down when he's done up there, thanks."

Amos knew what he needed to look for, having used the OMEs many times, but something nagged at him that he felt needed careful checking… *seals, controls, power, lighting, closing handles, compression… mmm, all looking good so far*, he thought. *Looks very well maintained.*

"Amos, you wanted me?"

"Yeah, Jack, over here. How was the equipment inspection?"

"All fine, it's all there. What about the OME? How's it looking?"

"Well, it may surprise you, it darn surprised me, but it all looks very well maintained, which to be fair is how it should be. Take a look around as you may see something, and I'll go and take a look at the Dräger."

Jack was as thorough as Amos, but two pairs of eyes are better than one. *All looks good*, thought Jack to himself. *Lifting gear… yeah… thank goodness for that; we'll put them through their paces later when the team arrives.* Jack exited the OME and went to check on Amos.

"The Dräger is good as well... looks like we're underway, but let's get Charles to do a final once-over when he gets here, particularly the oxygen lines. Anyway, it should only be another half hour or so before he arrives."

"Yeah, good idea," said Jack, taking a final check on something in the manuals. "It's all up to date."

They returned to Chris's office and handed over the lever arch files to him.

"Thanks. I'll keep them over there on the table if you need to refer to them again at any time," said Chris.

"Well, we've had a good look at it all, thank you, and all looking good, Chris. The equipment looks well maintained. Who does it for you?"

"We've got a planned maintenance programme in place and they are here regular as clockwork."

"What time is the chopper in with the rest of our team?"

Chris looked down at his PC and pressed a few keys, still worried whether they would ask him a question that he couldn't answer. "They're on their way and... it looks like they'll be in slightly early, so they should be here around 12.50, 12.55, spot on for lunch."

"Great, thanks. We're gonna head up to the canteen. See you later. Oh, and Chris?"

"Yeah."

"Could you send Charles up here when he arrives? Thanks." Amos shook Chris's hand and they left the director's room.

"So far so good," said Jack. "I see you're giving Chris a bit of a runaround with all those requests and instructions."

"Yeah, it'll be good for him and help him understand how things work on a rig. Let's see what Alan's coffee's like at lunch time."

The canteen was already buzzing when they entered with the expectation of food. Looking around, they didn't recognise anyone, but there were a few nice welcomes and "good to meet you", with explanations as to what they were doing on the rig, which was reassuring for them both.

"Jack, before I forget I'm gonna give Bernie a call as when

Charles arrives we're gonna be busy. So I'm gonna find a quiet spot away from here. It should be about eight-ish in the morning over there… she should be up. I'll see you back here in about twenty minutes when Charles and his team have arrived and we can eat together."

"Sure."

Amos took his coffee with him and went back to his sleeping quarters.

Brr, brr, brr…

"Hello, Grand Cayman Marriott, Melany speaking, how may I help you this morning?"

"Yes, hi there, we've not spoken before – is Dudley there?"

"No, sorry, sir, he's not working today."

"Oh, right, OK, I'm Amos and—"

"Oh my… Yes, Dudley mentioned that you might ring; would you like to speak to Mrs Amos?"

"Yes please." *At last*, thought Amos.

Brr, brr… Brr, brr… Brr, brr… Brr, brr…

"I'm sorry, sir, but there's no reply. It could be that the phone is off."

"Can you try again, please?"

Brr, brr… Brr, brr… Brr, brr… Brr, brr…

"I'm sorry, sir, maybe she's out walking. It's a beautiful morning again here, or she's at the exercise class or swimming; there's lots to do here…"

"Ah, heck… Not again. Have you seen her this morning?"

"I haven't, but you know it's still early. Would you like to leave a message?"

"Yeah, tell her that I called, thank you, and that I'll try and call her later."

"Yes, sir, thank you. Have a good day." *Click*; the call ended.

This is getting frustrating. Maybe she's giving me the cold shoulder treatment. I don't blame her, though, when you come to think about it. He made his way back to the canteen. The sound of a helicopter coming in drowned any further thoughts he could pull together. It was deafening. *Glad there aren't any night flights.*

That will be Charles, thought Amos. *I'll meet him up at the helideck.* Chris was already there, as well as a number of other people, and he gave Amos a hand acknowledgment as it was tricky to speak or hear anything.

With the helicopter engines and blades winding down, Charles and his team exited the chopper. On seeing Amos, they made their way over to him. There were also a few other recognisable faces exiting the chopper... the suits from HQ.

"Charles, hey, good to see you. You've made really good time and that's appreciated." They shook hands and Charles introduced the other three in the team.

"Like you, Amos, we're here to do a job and get off the rig back to our families. Hey, Jack," called out Charles.

Jack ran over and gave Charles a bear hug embrace. They went back a long way and had known each other longer than Amos had known Jack.

"Great to see you, Charles. Good flight?"

"Yeah, but starving – what's the canteen like?"

"We'll take you over once you've signed in and sorted your gear out in the sleeping quarters."

Chris made his way over. "Chris, this is Charles and the rest of the team. Charles, this is the rig director."

"Pleased to meet you all," said Chris. "Pleasant flight?"

"Yeah, thank you," replied Charles.

"I've got some other people to meet so I will see you later."

"Sure." He whispered to Jack and Amos, "He's a bit young, isn't he?"

Jack nodded back.

"Chris, hi," came a shout from one of the suits.

"Excuse me," replied Chris.

Amos looked across at them and they gave Chris a small package that must have been the switch, and gave them a wave. Ross strolled over to Amos.

"I'll leave you to it, Amos. Come on, Charles, I'll show you and the guys around," said Jack, "and then we'll get some lunch in the canteen."

"Good to see you, Amos," said Ross with a sly grin on his face. "I see you're making yourselves at home already. I had a good chat with Charles on the way over and he said that he was sub-contracting to you."

"Yeah, that's right, nothing wrong with that. Why do you ask?" replied Amos.

"You never said that yesterday at the interview in Guildford."

"You didn't ask," replied Amos sharply, realising that the inquisition had started already, "and it wasn't an interview yesterday, it was a contract award meeting. Anyhow, it's all in our tender; perhaps you should read it sometime... you'll find out exactly what we do." Amos walked away from him.

Jack looked across at them and saw that the conversation wasn't as friendly as you would hope at the start of a contract.

Ross called after him, "Look, Amos, I don't want to get on the wrong footing on this contract but—"

Amos interrupted him. "Well let's get this straight: we will get on with our job and you get on with yours and we'll all be happy."

Amos turned and continued to walk away from Ross, back towards Jack and Charles, who had been intercepted by Peter.

"OK, Charles, Jack," said Amos, "let's go and get some lunch and we can brief you and the team on the plan for the rest of the day. And Peter, thanks for bringing over the part for the Dräger."

"Yeah, no problem," replied Peter, rather taken aback by the sharpness of Amos's tone. He then walked away to meet up with Chris, who had been joined by Ross.

"What happened over there?" asked Jack.

"He was interfering in our work and I basically told him to read our tender rather than try to catch us out and to stay out of stuff he doesn't know anything about and we'll all get along fine."

***

Jack introduced Charles and the team to Alan in the canteen. He had obviously enjoyed the chat earlier this morning and was in a conversational mood. This boded well for the size of the portions he was dishing out, as they were more than sufficient for the team, who would be involved with a lot of the heavy lifting work.

"This is really good food," said Charles, tucking into his steak and kidney pie, two veg and chips, "and so much of it."

"Yeah, we've only had one breakfast here. The chef's a good guy." Jack acknowledged him by lifting his hand up to Alan behind the serving hatch.

"All good?" called out Alan.

"Yeah, just the job, thanks," replied Jack.

The canteen door opened and Chris entered followed by the suits. The level of conversation became subdued. The entourage made their way over to the servery, picked up their trays and were served by Alan. As they turned away from the servery hatch, Peter looked up and spotted Jack and headed towards their table.

"Do you mind if we sit here?" asked Peter.

"Yeah, that's fine," said Jack.

Amos didn't join in any of the shared conversation with them; he was still seething from his discussions with Ross. He did, however, glance across to see what they were eating and noticed a marked reduction in the size of their portions. *Very appropriate, thank you, Alan,* he thought to himself smugly.

Amos ignored them and finished his lunch quickly, mindful of time constraints as well as the additional company watching them.

"Charles, Jack, we'll meet in the briefing room in fifteen minutes, please."

"Right, Amos," replied Charles.

Amos returned to his sleeping quarters and pulled out the papers he needed to present to the team, then went up to Chris's office to retrieve the maintenance information held in the lever arch file. With everything he needed he set off to the briefing room, sat himself down and readied himself to present.

The team joined him promptly at two and took their seats around the table.

Once they were all settled, Amos stood up. "Thanks for joining me, and Charles in particular for organising the team at such short notice. Now you all know the timescale for this one but I'm gonna go through it again anyway so we are—"

There was a knock on the door.

A head poked around. "Hi. Are we OK to join you?" It was Peter.

"Er, er..." Amos was really put on the spot; he hadn't been expecting the police to join him. "Er, yeah, take a seat."

Amos regained his composure. "Right, where was I before I was..."

Jack closed his eyes, hoping Amos wouldn't have a go at the suits again.

"Ah yes... the timescale for this is very important as our... friends Peter and, er... Ross, who have just joined us at the back, keep reminding us of. Now you've all read the programme in the tender documentation: six weeks from first dive, weather permitting."

As Amos looked towards the men sitting in the corner at the back, he realised that this was an opportunity to set the ground rules. "And the safety briefing by Jack will follow immediately after my presentation. After the safety briefing, I want Charles to check over the OME and then set it up for a trial dive, paying particular attention, please, to the oxygen lines. We'll then move on to the Dräger... That should see us through for the rest of the afternoon. Assuming all the equipment is sound and in good order, we will start our programme in the morning. Jack, did you get a chance to check on the weather?"

"Yes, Chris gave me a printout of the forecast over the next three to four days and it looks pretty much ideal except for a squall or two coming in on day three, which we will have to keep an eye on, and we'll obviously keep everyone informed of any changes on the basis of a rolling forecast."

"Thanks, Jack. Now remember, we will have a briefing first thing each morning here at seven and then a review at the close of diving each day, and remember safety first at all times. I know that Jack will remind you about this later but if you have any doubt about what you are doing or the circumstances surrounding a colleague then tell someone immediately; your health and safety is the most important thing... *not* the programme." He looked towards the suits at the back. They moved uneasily in their seats and said something to one another and then stood up and left without a word.

"OK, that's me done for the time being. Jack, over to you and the health and safety guy from the rig... It's Jason, isn't it?"

"Yeah. Good morning, everyone. I'm Jason and I'm in charge of health and safety on the rig. Firstly I would like to welcome you all as you've come to get the rig ready again for production, and as new boys, please pay attention. Here's a manual about the rig for each of you to read. Study it well, if you excuse the joke" – no one laughed as they didn't understand the funny side of what he'd said – "as it may save your or someone else's life. I will give you any updates whilst you're here on the rig and you can insert into the manual..." His drawl continued, with Amos not really listening; he would have a better look at the manual later in his room.

Amos knew he had touched a nerve with Ross and that Peter was the one that they should keep fully informed as Amos was likely to bust a fuse if he spoke to Ross again. And if that was proving problematic, he could then get back to Angus the CEO; *let's hope it doesn't come to that as we want to get appointed on some more of these.*

Amos's mind was then back in the meeting, with Jason describing this rig. Each one is different, with safety routes, muster points and particular nuances like the steel across the stair on the ladder down to the OME to be aware of.

His mind drifted off again to Bernie and her health and safety presentation years ago... But not for long.

"Amos... Amos?"

"Er, yeah, sorry."

"What's the position with the safety certificates on the Dräger and OME?"

"I have checked them and Jack too, they are all in order, but it would be good if Charles could double check. I'm sure we've not missed anything but another pair of independent eyes will be reassuring. Thank you."

***

The afternoon trial dives went to plan with no issues and the evening's food in the canteen was much to the team's satisfaction. After the meal Amos left them to enjoy the evening's films in the mess and went back to his room, wanting to check over the plans of the stanchions again and the previous inspection records, as well as hope that Bernie would call him.

"Amos? Are you OK?" Jack opened the door to his room an hour or so later.

"Yeah, all fine, thanks, Jack. Just looking over the plans for tomorrow's dives and the previous inspection reports. You know, looking through the previous inspection reports – they're nowhere near as good as ours." He flicked the handful of papers and then dumped them on the table.

"Well perhaps that's why these guys wanted us," replied Jack. "Oh and by the way, there was a previous outfit appointed for this job, Reid and Merlin. We were second on the tender return."

"Well, I'll be… no one mentioned that to us either. Maybe they walked away from it… I wouldn't blame them. How did you find that out? That's why they are under so much time pressure and that's probably why Ross has been so nosey…"

"Yes, you could be right, Amos. Apparently, Charles overheard, on the way over on the chopper, part of a conversation between Ross and Peter that they hoped we would be able to deliver the job as they would be in deep trouble as the previous firm went bust without even starting."

"Perhaps I'm being a little unfair on those two guys… they've been let down and it's probably their jobs on the line if the programme isn't met."

"I did a bit of asking around, Amos, and Reid and Merlin had apparently been carrying out the maintenance on the rig for over three years and then with the change of ownership didn't like the management arrangements."

"Or perhaps didn't get paid?"

"Anyhow. Night, Amos, I'm just gonna give Sally a call."

"OK, thanks. Night, Jack, see you in the morning."

Amos decided not to call Bernie and the children; he had called them often enough over the last few days since he'd left them, and left messages, and he needed a good night's sleep, not a sleepless night reflecting on an argument.

***

Amos woke refreshed, ready for the day. A shower and up to the canteen for breakfast and then the morning briefing. The suits didn't attend the briefing, which pleased him, and were nowhere to be seen – probably sleeping in and couldn't cope with the early mornings, he thought.

Day one. The morning operations went to plan. They started with the north-west corner, deciding to get one of the difficult stanchions out of the way first as that part of the rig received the brunt of the Arctic storms. The maintenance records showed a lot of repair work particularly on stanchion three in the past; tackling this one first would also mean that they could address any problems early in their programme rather than having to sort them out late on and then face the potential knock-on effect. They had to complete on time. The risk of incurring financial penalty for noncompletion, Amos did not want to think about. The penalty clauses were onerous on this contract, and were very high, hence the need to invest in a strong back-up team.

Chris joined them for lunch in the canteen.

"Hey, Chris, where are the suits?" asked Amos. "Are they still in bed?" He chuckled.

"No, they returned to Aberdeen on the morning chopper; apparently they had meetings to attend in Aberdeen."

"That's good; now we can get on with our job without petty interruptions," replied Amos.

"How were your morning dives?" asked Chris.

"All went to plan, thanks… But let's get the north-west corner out of the way. Once we've got the first couple of days under our belt we'll know better how we're doing."

"Hey, here's the latest weather update for you, Jack." Chris handed over a sheet of paper.

Jack took a close look at it. "Looks like a bit of a breeze coming in from the north-east and a cold spell in a few days, sleet and even fog, which is a bit of a surprise at this time of year. Fog's not a problem for us; we'll be under the sea anyway, and the temperature's a lot warmer down there anyway," said Jack with a chuckle.

"Thanks for the update; appreciated, Chris, thank you," added Amos.

They had finished their lunch and stood up to leave. "Alan, thanks for a great lunch," said Jack, "and, I just wanted to ask: why is it called JT's Canteen?"

"It's not a long story but JT was the previous chef; he went back home to Hong Kong shortly after the change in management. Apparently he was into Asian food, which could get a bit too spicy for the men and the management at times."

"Well, why not give it a go? I'm sure the lads would enjoy a curry special on the menu once in a while – I know I would," said Jack.

"OK, you guys, let's finish up now; afternoon preparation and dive procedure to start in ten minutes – you got that? Ten minutes. I know you like the food here, for which we've got Alan to thank, but we've got a job to do," said Amos.

Jack gave a broad smile towards Alan. Amos was good at the state of the nation speech when they started a contract. It helped to motivate the troops; some viewed it as harassment, but inside they appreciated the leadership and structure that Amos was able to give them.

The afternoon programme worked like clockwork. The team were working well together and starting to gel; there was a good atmosphere in the mess later that afternoon when it came to the review of their day's work. So much so that Amos told them that he might even give them a weekend off in Aberdeen at his expense if they carried on like this, and assuming that the weather held. Jack considered what Amos had said and felt that it was much too soon to be giving promises, but to be fair to Amos it did provide the team with motivation and something to think about when standing on the rig, cold, wet and being blown around. Amos was a good leader and team player.

The evening routine was one of cleaning the equipment, reviewing the day's work and anticipating the following morning's plan of action; a shower, evening meal and film was the norm. Some of the crew would play cards; others would sit away from the hubbub and read a book. Amos undertook the required social interaction and had a short game of cards and then retreated to his own space.

It was 21.30 with an early start tomorrow. His mind was now starting to play with him. *I wonder if she's not answering deliberately; maybe she's so upset she wants a divorce, then all this is for nothing,* he said to himself.

He dialled.

Brr, brr... Brr brr...

"Marriott Grand Cayman, good afternoon; can I help you? Dudley speaking."

"Hey, Dudley, how are you? It's Amos here."

"Hello, hello, Mr Amos, I've given your message to your wife from yesterday – I can try and see if she is in?"

"Please," came the sharp reply.

Brr brr... Brr brr... Brr brr... Brr brr... "Mr Amos, I am sorry – there is no reply again. I know that the children enjoyed Stingray City as they came to talk to me about it and then they went out again straight after lunch, but I don't know where to."

"OK, fine. Just leave another message to say that I rang, again. Thank you, Dudley."

"Sure, Mr Amos."

Amos put the phone down and sighed. *Well, as long as they are OK and all enjoying themselves. Heck... it's only been a couple of days now; seems like ages.*

He changed out of his work gear and tuned into the shipping forecast.

"*Dogger 3 rising to 4, Iceland 4 rising to 6.*"

To 6, thought Amos. *That's a big rise. We'll have to keep an eye on that.* He pulled out the bundle of drawings and records for the remainder of stanchion three. *It does go down a long way and there's a whole series of interesting additional projecting supports. What are they for? I wonder if they were the repairs? We'll need to get plenty of samples from those junctions – that'll be where the worst of any degradation will be,* he thought, then put the drawing aside, turned the light off and went to sleep.

***

An alarm went off at 5.45; it wasn't quite what Amos wanted to hear, as it woke him with a start. He lifted his head to look at the clock and then slumped back on the pillow. He couldn't quite get his bearings; *where am I? Rig, hotel, holiday or home…?*

He checked his phone and there was a message. *At last,* thought Amos, and sat up and pressed the button for voicemail.

"It's me. Why are you never around when I need you? Anyhow, kids are alright now and I hope you're not enjoying yourself – because we are."

End of message.

Ouch. That's not really what I wanted to hear. He threw his phone onto the bed.

He showered and dressed for a 6.15 breakfast.

"Morning, Alan, how you doing?"

"Great thanks, Amos. I hear you had a good day in the office yesterday."

"How do you mean… with the diving?" replied Amos.

"Yeah, and telling those suits a thing or two – give me five."

Amos obliged. "I'll have the full English breakfast – veggie version, please."

"Coming right up. What is it with meat, Amos? It's good for you?"

"Well, I prefer a plant-based diet now. Don't get me wrong, I will have the occasional turkey or meat, say at Thanksgiving or Christmas, and then when we do, we buy ethically sourced meat."

"What's that?" said Alan as he was turning Amos's eggs over in the pan.

"Well, in basic terms, Alan, it's food that is not detrimental to the planet; that's the simplest way I can explain it. But that's just me – you should try it sometime. You never know, you might like it."

"Very difficult for me," replied Alan, "with all this food in front of you all day. Hence..." He pointed to his rather large, rounded stomach.

"You could get rid of that if you want to, you know that... and if you wanna do some diving, which Jack tells me you're keen on, you'd do best to lose a couple of stone. It sounds a lot, but you'll be surprised how quickly it drops off if you eat the right food."

"Thanks, Amos, I'll think about that." Alan handed over Amos's breakfast.

Other members of the team started entering the canteen.

"Morning, Amos."

"Morning, Steve, Barry... Mike, how's it going?"

"Great, thanks; a good start yesterday and a great way to get going with the food here. It's one of the best I've been to."

Amos asked him to repeat it a bit louder this time, which he did.

"Cheers," said Alan and waved a serving spoon and tongs in the air to acknowledge and then went back to turn the sausages.

"Oh seven hundred hours in the briefing room, please, everyone – you all got that? Oh seven hundred."

There were varying degrees of "yes", "yeah", nods, and "OK" from the tables as they were tucking into a hearty breakfast.

***

Amos and Jack met in the briefing room before the others joined them so as to go over the itinerary for the day's dives. The others joined them promptly at seven.

When they had all settled in their seats, "Gents," said Amos, standing up. "We had a good day yesterday. Let's keep it up. We're gonna see how we get on with getting to grips with stanchion three. It'll be a full-on day, so lunch will have to be a quick turnaround;

you got that? And hopefully we'll finish early. We've had a weather update from Chris this morning and it's gonna be a strong swell building up late morning and cold out there, so make sure you're prepared as I don't want anyone walking off to get a pair of gloves or to have to put on an extra pair of underpants to keep your balls warm." Laughter from the floor. "I know we have only just started but we need to keep momentum going... but remember safety first at all times. Have a good day, everyone." Amos motioned to Charles to come and have a word with him.

The scraping of chairs on the floor signalled the end of the briefing and the hubbub of voices slowly disappeared out the door, leaving Amos, Jack and Charles together.

"Charles," said Amos. "Thanks for a good day's work yesterday."

Charles acknowledged, "It's what you are paying us for."

"Your lads did a good job, thank you, are they gonna keep it up?"

"Yeah, sure, you are paying us good money and they want to deliver on time as much as you do."

"Thanks, Charles, we really appreciate that, and you might like to know that there may be a series of these coming up if we hit the programme requirements. OK, let's head out and join the others."

Amos and Jack went to the lower deck where their equipment was stored and got themselves ready; they were joined by Steve. They would take the tricky north side of stanchion three whilst Charles, Mike and Barry would deal with the southern side.

Amos was kitted out and ready to dive, but the wind had got up and was seriously biting and they could already sense and feel the swell building up. "Jack. You know the sequence: five, eight, ten metres, and then take me down to fifteen metres, please, and if it's starting to look too dangerous up here, i.e. when it gets to a 3 or 4, then you guys send me a message and pull me out – you got that?"

"Yeah, sure, Amos, I know the routine."

"And mention the same to Charles, please; we can't afford any accidents to anyone, particularly so early in the contract." He gave a thumbs up and put on his mask.

Amos lowered himself into the water with Steve and Jack's

assistance.

Once Amos was underwater, everything was calm; just bubbles, breathing and the occasional interruption on the intercom.

His view moving slowly down was never very exciting in the North Sea: green, greeny-grey and then more green floating around and waving at him from the steel supports. The trickiest part of the work was trying to get close enough to the stanchion steels through the seaweed and growths to take samples, and with this morning's strength in the sea he was aware that it may cause them some problems.

"Jack. The current is much stronger today; you're gonna have to be careful when you go down later."

"Thanks, Amos," replied Jack through the intercom.

The five-metre depth sampling was finished quickly. Amos knew that the deeper they went the longer it would take with each set of samples. "Sample bag closed and ready to go to eight," called Amos over the intercom to Jack. Amos was held at eight metres for the second set of samples, which was slightly awkward as he had to cut through clumps of seaweed to access the steel. He then scraped off the coating on the steel and placed it in his sample bag.

"Down to ten metres, please, Jack."

"OK, buddy."

Amos was lowered down further and could now see the particular junction of the steels that he felt would need additional samples. He slowly moved across to the area and started to pull away the seaweed and got a surprise when a handful came away so quickly that he fell back away from the steels. Making his way back, he could now get a closer look, and could see the considerable degradation around a plate connection; the bolts were also going to need sampling by the look of things.

"It's pretty bad down here, Jack," he shouted down the intercom. "And it's going to take a bit of time; I'm right on the junction that we looked at earlier on the plans, remember? I'm going to see if I can... lever... a bolt head..." Amos set to work with his tools. Jack could hear Amos straining. "... off," came bellowing down the intercom. The bolt head came away with a sharp unexpected jolt; he fell back, hitting his head against one of the additional steel supports that he had seen on the drawing last night. *Damn it,* he thought, his shoulder then scraping against another steel as the current pushed him up against the edge of a bracing support.

Amos knew immediately that something was wrong; his senses were slipping away and could see blood streaming from his arm and floating away in the water…

"Jack, Jack, get me up," he blurted out on the intercom.

Jack knew the routine, and with Steve they carefully lifted Amos up and out of the water, and onto the seating area of the platform. Jack called Charles to come over and help as Amos was semi-conscious and not in the best of places. They dragged him out of the water, sleet swirling all around them, blood dripping from the sleeve of one of Amos's arms.

"Amos, what happened? Amos?"

His head was lolling and he was barely able to speak.

"I dunno… one minute I'm levering the bolt head on the plate and the next thing the darn thing comes away… Ow, my head." He was slurring his speech, and trying to rub the back of his head.

"And your arm," said Charles. "We need to get that sorted out straight away; that looks pretty deep and messy."

They helped Amos up onto his feet and took him straight to the first aid room – basically the mess room with a first aid cupboard. Steve and Mike carefully taking off his top revealed a very deep six-inch gash in his arm and it was bleeding profusely.

"Jack, can you speak to Chris and get him to call in a chopper to take him to the nearest hospital?"

"Sure."

"Amos, you're going to need to get this stitched up properly; we're not going to be able to do that here."

Jack cut strips of plaster and wrapped them around Amos's arm.

"Hold your hand up, Amos."

"I can't; it's too painful."

"You gotta, Amos; it'll help stop you leaking blood, buddy."

"Argh." Amos passed out for a few seconds, his head lolling to one side, and then returned to the room.

"Let's get you changed and out of this gear, Amos."

"My head hurts. You know what? It was that bloody stanchion that I noticed on the drawings last night and I damn well forgot about it when I was trying to clear the seaweed to get at the bolt-head sample."

"Your head, Amos – it's not bleeding," said Jack, taking a look under his hair, but he didn't touch it as a big swelling was forming. "I'll get some ice on that as soon as we get you changed and into dry gear," said Jack.

Chris walked into the room. "Wow, you look in a bad way, Amos; what happened?"

"Nothing really," said Amos. "Just cut my arm, which will need some stitches, and then I'll be back." Blood was still dripping profusely off his arm and onto the floor.

"Yeah, the chopper's on its way from Faroe – it's the nearest hospital – and will be here in about fifteen minutes."

"Charles, could you finish off getting Amos dried and into dry clothes, thanks, and keep his arm up... even if he complains. I'll go and sort out an overnight bag for him in case he has to stay over."

"Sure."

"Can you get me some water, Charles? I'm really thirsty. Thanks."

"I'll get it," said Chris.

"What a stupid, stupid thing to do... It would have been alright but for that darn steel beam... what the hell is it for, anyway?"

"Let's just ease your arm in here," said Charles. "That's good... nice and easy now." Charles could see the blood already seeping out of the dressing. "You're gonna have a fair number of stitches in that one, Amos."

"Yeah, I'll be back in the morning."

"Here's your water, Amos, and a pack of frozen peas for your head, courtesy of Alan in the kitchen."

"Thanks, Chris."

"We're going to have to get you up to the heliport landing area, and that's going to take a bit of time. So we had better get going now... Chris, can you wrap that coat around him? Thanks," said

Charles.

Jack returned to the room. "Sorted your bag out, Amos, so you're all set to go."

Amos stood up and they helped him up to the helideck.

"You guys just carry on, right… I'll be back in the morning… Charles and Jack, you take over the briefing sessions, OK, and remember to keep Chris informed of progress. Chris, you've done a good job on keeping us informed about the weather, thank you, so if you could keep that going that would be great. What a stupid thing to do; I'm a bloody idiot, literally. I should have followed the procedure, then this wouldn't have happened… that's what comes from trying to rush the job – my own fault."

"It's easily done, Amos, don't worry yourself about it," replied Charles. "We've all done it and unfortunately there's occasion when a shortcut doesn't quite work out as planned."

They helped Amos up and supported him whilst he walked gingerly up to the helideck. The sleet started to settle on his coat and head. "That's handy; the sleet will cool my head down."

"Well," said Jack, "you haven't lost your sense of humour, which is always a good sign when you get a bang on your head."

"It's just a scratch and a bump; nothing to worry about, Jack."

"I think we'll just let the hospital decide that, Amos," said Chris.

They reached the helideck and could hear and then see the chopper coming in from the west. It circled and then came in to land when the gusts eased off a bit and were a little more reasonable for landing.

"Good landing," said Amos. "That gives me confidence."

The blades slowly came to a halt and the pilot got out and ran towards the group standing on the edge of the helipad.

"Hi, Bill, good to see you," said Chris. "Thanks for coming over at such short notice."

"No problem, that's my job; I'm used to it. This trip was an easy one, but the journey back might be more of a challenge. OK, let's help the injured soldier up into the cab and we'll get him fixed up in no time."

"It's Amos, by the way."

"What's the problem, so I can speak to the hospital before we land?"

"Head injury to the back of the head and a deep slash across the top of the arm sustained underwater – probably rusty iron, and it's been bleeding quite badly, definitely a lot of stitches. Make sure you get Amos to keep his arm up at all times as it will help stem the bleeding."

Charles and Jack tried to help Amos get belted up.

"I'm fine, you guys, stop fussing and just let me sort it," snapped a frustrated Amos.

"Stubborn to the last." But he needed help with his seat belt; Charles obliged and Jack put Amos's bag behind his seat.

"Give us a call in the morning, Amos," shouted Jack as the engines started up.

"Will do, and try to keep on programme," replied Amos.

"OK, can someone close the door so we can get on our way," shouted Bill. "We need to get going before the light fades and we get a white-out as there are a lot of sleet and snow showers around."

Chris obliged and Bill started up the blades of the chopper.

The helicopter was soon up to speed and it lifted off the deck and away.

CHAPTER 8: TÓRSHAVN, FAROE

"Where's the hospital you're taking me to?"

"Tórshavn," replied Bill the pilot. "And keep your arm up."

"Where on earth is that?"

"Faroe; it's about forty minutes away. Have you not been there before? Then you haven't lived. There's no place quite like it. Danes, Icelanders, Norwegians, Scots and even a few English and Germans, and that's on top of the locals."

"Ha ha."

"The landscape is really quite something… I don't think we've got any Americans on the islands. You could be the first?"

"That's not a problem, Bill, as I'm not intending to stay long," replied Amos. "How long have you lived on the Faroe Islands?" His speech was starting to slur again.

"Almost twenty years now on Faroe. My parents moved up here from Fort William in Scotland to retire and I was out of a job, so I followed them shortly after – I was a failed helicopter pilot in the navy – and had nothing else to do so I joined the rescue service up here. Best thing I did. Don't worry, I've passed all the exams since with flying colours and am fully qualified, with distinction I might add. A lot of people worry when I say I am a failed pilot."

"Yeah, I'm not surprised," said Amos with slight dismay in his voice.

"I did a few years' taxi service on the islands first, mind you, and then a job came up at the hospital as part of the helicopter rescue unit and the rest is history."

"Gee, my feet are so cold. Haven't you got any heating up here?"

"It's on full blast, Amos; just try to keep them moving. We'll be at the hospital shortly."

Sitting at the front, Amos could see what was showing on the control panel.

"What are those shaded areas on that dial?"

"Showers sweeping across, probably a mix of rain and sleet at the moment – it's cold out there."

"And those darker shaded areas?"

"Fog!" replied Bill.

"Fog?" replied Amos with a surprised look on his face.

"Right."

"That's gonna be a problem, isn't it? How do you land?"

"You don't. If it's too thick or risky, we—"

There was a crackle on the radio and a voice blurted out, "Victor One, Victor One, can you read me, over."

"Victor One here, I read you, over."

"Victor One, you've probably already seen on the radar… it's a bit foggy in Tórshavn. We'll give you an update in a few minutes. If it gets any thicker we'll need to redirect you, over."

"OK, over."

"What does that all mean?" said Amos.

"It means that what we saw on the radar was fog and we might be sent somewhere where it's not so foggy. I will not be able to land if I can't see where I'm going… So I'm afraid I could be taking you back to the rig! And that's assuming they are not fog-bound."

"What, are you actually serious about that?"

"Yeah, it happens regularly at certain times of the year. It can't be helped… It's called weather, Amos. Some things can continue, like your diving for example, but other things have to stop… or in our case be diverted if it's that bad. We get called out and one minute it's clear and the next change. The weather changes so quickly up here, you really need to keep your wits about you."

They both kept their eyes on the radar screen, watching the changing patterns of the sleet, snow and particularly the fog… and it wasn't clearing around Tórshavn. The wipers on the cab continued to clear the view – what there was of it through the screen.

"They are gonna redirect us… aren't they?" said Amos, seeing a large patch on the radar screen growing over the town.

"Could well do, could well do," replied Bill with a concerned, contemplative tone to his voice, trying to work out where they would likely send them.

"Victor One, Victor One, do you read me, over."

"Victor One, I hear you, over."

"You've probably already worked it out yourself, Bill, from looking at your instrument panel. We've got fog blowing in and it's pretty dense so you're gonna be redirected to Klaksvík. You need to head there straight away as there's a series of thick banks of fog sweeping in and likely to cover the whole of the islands within the hour. We'll call them and tell them to expect you, over."

"OK, over."

There was then a sudden change and feel about the helicopter in the *rattatata ratta rattatata ratta* of the engines as Bill changed course.

"I struggled with Tórshavn, but where the hell is Klaksvík? It sounds like a town in a Batman movie."

"Yeah, I never thought of that; ha ha, it does a bit. It's another town on Faroe slightly further north, on the island of Borðoy. Looking at the radar, the area is clear at the moment although you can see" – Bill pointed at the screen – "the fog rolling in from the north-west, but we'll be fine; we've got plenty of time."

Amos noticed that it was getting dark and gloomy outside the helicopter cabin and started to get a little concerned.

"We got enough fuel?" Amos suddenly blurted out to Bill.

"More than enough... hold your arm up, I can't do it for you... as I said, the worst scenario is we have to head back to the rig, but don't worry, we've got the fuel and we won't be doing that today. If you look down to the left you'll see a few fishing boats and then up ahead the lights of the town. We'll be landing close to the hospital. It's not as big as at Tórshavn but has all the facilities. You'll also have a nice bonus," Bill said, smiling and looking across at Amos.

"And what's that?" said Amos, shaking his head.

"There's a really nice Danish doctor there; if she looks after you, I tell you, you won't wanna go back to the rig."

"You might like to know I've got three kids and I'm happily married," said Amos. *Well, I was until a few days ago*, he thought to himself.

Bill winked at Amos and they didn't say any more about the doctor.

They both kept their eyes on the instrument panel, in particular the radar, and could see the fog rolling in towards their destination.

"Looks like we're just gonna make it in," said Bill.

"Victor One, Victor One, can you read me, over."

"Victor One reading you. Yeah, we're coming into Klaksvík; we'll be landing in the next three to four minutes, over."

"That's good to hear, Victor One, as the fog is closing in rapidly."

The lights of the town were blurred by the fog as the helicopter started to make its descent. They landed in what appeared to Amos to be just an overgrown school playing field.

"Welcome to Klaksvík."

"Thanks, Bill. Looks like we made it by the skin of our teeth. There doesn't appear to be much life here?"

"Perhaps another five minutes or so; I've had closer calls. The guys from the hospital will be over shortly. By the way, the hospital's full name is Klaksvíkar Sjúkráhás and we've parked up as close as we can to it."

Bill was closing down the helicopter as the blades came to a halt. Two people came running over to the helicopter and the passenger side door opened.

"Gee, it's so cold," said Amos as a rush of cold air hit him in the face.

"Hello, Bill, you did well to get in." Two people helped Amos out of the helicopter, supporting him on both sides as he stood up.

"Yeah, I was a bit worried we might be up there all night... only joking with you, Amos. Ha ha."

"That arm looks bad; we'll get that looked at. How are you feeling?"

"I've felt better, thank you." He stumbled slightly on the footpath as they made their way from the helicopter to the school car park where there was an ambulance waiting.

"It's only a short journey from here, but it's better than walking and I've rung ahead so they're expecting us. You will be seen straight away."

The short drive seemed like an age to Amos. He looked out of the vehicle's windows; it was very dull and gloomy. Looking around inside, it was more reminiscent of a Transit van with a few windows punched in the sides than an ambulance. At least it had a bed that patients could lie on if they needed to. Their journey slowed as they entered the main entrance to the hospital. The fog was now very dense; you could hardly see your hand in front of you, let alone drive.

"OK, we're here," said the driver, pulling hard on the hand brake. "As I said earlier, they're expecting you and the doctor will see you straight away as there aren't many patients in at the moment."

"Thanks. How big is the hospital?"

"It can take upwards of thirty-five to forty patients, but my guess is we only have perhaps a dozen or so patients at the moment, so it's pretty quiet."

Amos was helped out by a person who had come running from the hospital entrance as well as the nurse who had travelled with them. Walking up the steps, through the sliding doors and into reception, Amos was glad of the warmth.

"Aw yeah, poor wee laddie," came a voice from the direction of the reception desk. She stood up and continued to ramble on about his injury; she had obviously been well briefed. Amos wasn't quite taking it all in with the knock on his head, and was still slightly unsure on his feet. She was a full, rosy-cheeked lady and probably in her early sixties with an odd mixture of a Scottish and Danish accent, and he couldn't quite catch part of what she was saying.

"Mrs McKinnon, here's your patient; patch him up quickly now, he wants to go back to work."

"We'll sort you out, laddie, you've nothing to worry about now."

"Right, I'll be off then and leave you in capable hands," said Bill to Mrs McKinnon. "I can't be of any more help here."

"Thanks, Bill, you've been of great help," said Amos.

"Oh yes, thanks, Bill, you've done wonders getting him here," said Mrs McKinnon.

"I'm flying back to Tórshavn in the morning, fog permitting; I can't see myself getting there this evening... You never know, it might be me taking you back to the rig."

"All in good time," said Mrs McKinnon. "The doctor will decide that and will be with you shortly; now, the nurse here will get you some warm blankets, come this way and sit yourself down." Mrs McKinnon took Amos's good arm and helped him to a chair next to a radiator.

He had only just sat down when the nurse walked back into the reception.

"You must be the man who's had the accident on the rig," came the soft, singing, Scandinavian-sounding voice.

"Yeah, that's right, I've just arrived."

"Let's take you through this way," said the nurse, helping him up onto his feet and wrapping a blanket around his shoulders. "The doctor will be with you shortly."

The front entrance doors opened; Amos glanced around and the person pulled their hood back, unbuckled their coat and started to stamp their feet, shaking the snow off their coat.

They reached a patient cubicle and the nurse pulled across the curtains as Amos sat on the bed.

"OK, now, let's remove the blanket and see if we can carefully take off your coat and have a look and see what we've got here..."

"Ahh, ahh," was Amos's immediate response after lifting his arm, allowing his coat to drop to the floor.

The nurse took a closer look. "That doesn't look very nice but I've seen a lot worse. How did you do that?"

"Well, I was diving earlier this afternoon and—"

The screen curtains drew apart in a dramatic way.

"Thank you, Nurse. I'm Dr Svensen and you are Amos, yes?"

Amos was taken aback and didn't reply.

"Ah, Doctor, it's good to see you; you made it back. Here's your patient – he's off the rigs... they never can look after them there, can they."

"Thank you, Rosa," said the doctor, now walking up to Amos to inspect the wound.

Bill was right; crikey, you're not gonna forget her. He remembered Bill's words to him earlier. Amos tried not to stare, but he couldn't help it. She was blonde with a mass of hair down to her shoulders, very slight, maybe five foot four or five foot five, and yes… quite beautiful… Was he dreaming?

"Amos, isn't it… Amos, you've had an accident on an oil rig."

"Er, yes, sorry…" He kept trying to look away but he found it very difficult.

The nurse attending to him gave a wry smile of acknowledgement. *Another one taken,* she thought.

"I'll be your doctor while you're here; now please explain exactly to me what's happened to you with your accident?"

Amos started to reply as the nurse was trying to take off his jumper. She decided that it would be better to just cut the arm off his jumper with a pair of scissors as the blood was dry and his wound stuck to the clothing.

"I was underwater, about ten to twelve metres below, as I was inspecting oil rig supports… and before I knew it I had a bang on the head and tore my arm."

Dr Svensen saw what the nurse had left. "I think you must now take the shirt away from him, Rosa… that's better."

The wound started to seep.

"Thank you, Rosa." The nurse moved away from Amos and the doctor started to take a closer look at the bloodied material and bandages still strapped and stuck to the wound.

"So tell me again, how do you bang your head when you are underwater? Your arm, it's in a very big mess, you know that." She spoke with a distinctly Scandinavian accent and her English was… nicely intriguing.

The nurse left the cubicle and came back with a stainless-steel bowl with a needle in it.

The doctor then stood in front of Amos and held his head between her hands. "Look at me now. Eyes to the right… good, and eyes to the left, and down… and up." She then felt the bruise at the back of his head. "Ow, that hurt," Amos blurted out, moving his head away.

"That is big."

Now that the doctor was closer to him, he could clearly see the name tag: Dr Ingrid Svensen.

"You have a concussion, maybe just mild but you're going to need a... Have you been dizzy or feeling blurred vision and headache?"

"Yeah, yeah, and yeah," said Amos very reluctantly.

"Well, you will need an MRI for you in the morning and we will see what that shows." The doctor stared at Amos's scar on the side of his body. "What is that?"

"What?"

"That, on the side of you," she said, pointing at the scars.

Amos had an instant two to three-second shark flashback and shivered, his mind racing with the event two years ago and the pain of the teeth sinking in and ripping. He managed to control his response but started to perspire.

"Got attacked in the Gulf a few years ago; part of the territory when you're diving. You see them quite regularly there but this one must have been hungry because he didn't go away and kept pestering us and the next thing I know... I've got this." He pointed at his side.

"Oh."

"I thought I'd like to tell you that I don't like needles either," said Amos, looking up at her with sheepish eyes.

"That is also good as neither do I," replied the doctor.

Amos looked away and the nurse injected Amos in the arm above the wound and then below.

"How long am I going to be kept here? As I need to get back to work."

"You stay definitely tonight, and tomorrow we'll see – maybe more, depending on the MRI results in the morning."

"I can't afford that," Amos replied with dismay.

The doctor slowly peeled back the remains of the shirt and bandage.

"Nurse, we will need some clamps." The wound started leaking quickly now.

The nurse returned and gave the clamps to the doctor and continued cleaning around the wound, and as she did so the doctor removed the remains of the material as best she could with tweezers. Amos looked away.

Doctor Svensen signalled to the nurse and in went another needle.

"Ahh... how many more? I hate injections."

"That's it... for the time. Now we can clean out the wound and stitch you up."

Amos did not dare move whilst needles were around his wound, the nurse continually dabbing and relocating the clamp.

Twenty minutes later, he had a neatly sewn arm.

"Good, now that is all done. Now I go and see you tomorrow; Rosa here will bandage and finish off." And she went to exit the cubicle.

"What about me?"

The doctor turned around. "Yes. You must stay in bed and rest until the morning." She took a final look at Amos and left the cubicle.

"But I will need to get back to work tomorrow," Amos called out, now getting uptight about being away from the rig.

"Just rest now," said Rosa, putting a hand on his good shoulder to calm him down. "We'll sort out some night clothing if you need them and some food for you shortly; I'll take you to your bed on the ward. The duty doctor will be here later for the ward round and will take a look at you. Remember you've had a bang on the head. Dr Svensen only came in to see you as it was an emergency. She was not working this afternoon and had to come in for you as the other doctors were in theatre."

"Oh... OK... right, thank you... I didn't realise that."

Amos now felt slightly embarrassed as the doctor had put herself out for him and he hadn't appreciated it at the time. He had a slight dizzy spell and decided to settle down on the bed, realising that this was the right thing to do and place to be, especially as his head was aching again.

The nurse, Rosa, returned with the night bag that Jack had packed for him. Inside was a shirt and jumper which she helped him put on. He rested his head on the pillow and fell asleep. .

***

Amos woke the following morning, he vaguely remembered being spoken to by a nurse and doctor the evening before. He realised that he had had a surprisingly good night's sleep, though he could feel the throbbing and swelling in his arm and his head was still thumping, but nowhere near as bad as yesterday evening. He looked across at the clock above the double doors as you came into the ward. It said 6.30. *Just like on the rigs*, he thought, so he very tentatively got up, showered and dressed and headed off to the canteen.

Canteen closed till 07.30, said the sign on the door. There was, however, a vending machine outside the doors.

Let's see… what does it serve… coffee white, coffee black, and tea with or without milk. Mmm, not the greatest of selections but at least it's something wet and hot, he thought.

He placed a cup under the nozzle and pressed the button for coffee black. After a series of slurping noises, the machine started to produce a black liquid dropping into the cup.

"Now then, let's see what we've got here," he said out loud.

Amos picked up the cup, looked at it, lifted it up to his nose and smelt it and then tasted it… and wished he hadn't.

"Ah, so bitter… this will make people ill. You're supposed to come to hospital to get better, not worse." He put the cup back down and decided he would follow signs to the reception where hopefully he would find someone who could get him a proper cup of coffee.

"Morning, and how are you this morning? How's that head of yours?" It was the receptionist from last night, sitting behind the desk.

"Oh thank you, good morning. You were here last night, weren't you?"

"Yes, laddie, I was and you were in a pretty bad way. How was your first night?"

"Yes, it was very comfortable, thank you, and hopefully my last night. Is there anywhere you can get a decent cup of coffee round here, as I've tried the vending machine and…?"

"Auch, so you've tasted the vending machine… that's really only there for emergencies, you know."

"Now you tell me."

"I'll get you one of my special brews as the canteen is not due to open for a wee while yet."

Amos spotted the name board on the desk – *Mrs Mary McKinnon* – as she disappeared into the staff room behind reception. She was still speaking.

"You've got a nice hospital here," said Amos.

"Thank you. I've lived and worked here for almost twenty-seven years, and seen a lot of changes in the town. Not so many fishing boats in the harbour, but a lot more of those city business people – you know what I mean. They walk around thinking they own the place; black gold is all they are after and if not oil then gas. But what's it all doing to the sea, the poor wee fish that we end up eating and then in the air we breathe? Heaven knows what they are going to do about all the pollution." Mrs McKinnon returned with a tray, with two mugs of coffee and, separately, milk and sugar.

"There you are, and some homemade biscuits before the canteen opens. But if you're that hungry I can get you in there earlier if you want to."

Amos's eyes popped out, looking at the biscuits. *Yum*, he thought to himself. He was partial to a biscuit or two.

"No, that's fine, thank you, Mrs McKinnon, and yeah, I know what you mean. Men in suits; I had them stalking me up on the rig I was working on, but we managed to get rid of them for a while. Which reminds me, er… can I please make use of a phone, as my cell phone is dead and I need to speak with someone on the rig."

"I shouldn't really, but quickly come round this side and you can use mine; the pay phone's never reliable and costs a fortune to use. It's nine to dial out."

"Thanks."

Amos dialled. *Brr, brr... brr, brr...*

"Hi, who's that?"

"Jack, it's Amos."

"Amos, I tried your phone but it was dead; how are you? Are you all stitched up now?"

"Yeah, all good, just got an MRI later this morning. It should be fine; how did you get on yesterday after I left on the helicopter?"

"Well, after we saw you off, we didn't get much done. It threw all of us a bit so we are behind but at the team meeting this morning, we spoke of putting a system in place that should see us back on the programme in about six to seven days, which is pretty good. Just hope we get a good response from Charles and his boys to this."

"Hey, that's great, thank goodness we've got him and his team on board with us... Anyhow, I should be back later but it's really bad fog-wise here at the moment. What's it like with you... Jack, Jack?" The phone line went dead.

"Argh, heck." Amos put the phone down. "It's gone dead."

"Did you manage to get through?"

"Yeah."

"And everything's OK?"

"Yeah... thank you, Mrs McKinnon, that's kind of you, and thanks for letting me use your phone, I appreciate that."

"Call me Mary, Amos; it's a lot easier."

"Right. Mary it is then, thank you."

Amos picked up his drink and another biscuit, and slowly made his way back to the ward, admiring the views of the sea wildlife and landscapes on paintings on the corridor walls, as he could only see grey through the windows. As Amos was making his way back to the ward, he heard the main entrance doors open; he turned his head round to look. A howling gale and flurry of snow blew into the lobby. The person who came in stood shaking their coat and stamping their boots, removing their hood and sweeping their hair back into place. He then remembered; it wasn't a dream.

"Morning, Mrs McKinnon, and how are you this morning?"

"Morning, Dr Svensen. What a terrible, terrible morning; so much bad weather at the moment. Glad you made it in safely with the fog and low cloud. They say it's going to be with us for the next week, followed by snow and gales, and my allotment has been a real struggle this year with the amount of cold we've had; I cannae see myself getting nowt from it this year."

Mrs McKinnon would have continued her rendition about the weather and her allotment but Dr Svensen put her hand up, signalling her to stop.

"Anything to report overnight?" she said in a regimental fashion.

"No. No new patients other than Amos from the rig who you saw yesterday late afternoon. He's been up already, looking for the canteen so I made him a coffee. He's expecting to go back to work later today."

"Thank you. I'll check on him during the ward round as usual at eight. Morning, Sister."

"Morning, Dr Svensen." The sister picked up some folders from a table behind the reception and they walked away from the direction that Amos was standing looking at them.

Amos walked back to reception and leant over to Mary and whispered to her as the reception area was getting busier.

"Mary, was that Dr Svensen?" he asked in a low voice within close proximity to her.

"Yes, the doctor that saw to you last night and put your arm back together."

"You know... I can't quite remember," replied Amos.

"Oh, laddie, as I told you earlier, you were in a bad way; you might not think so. Anyway, you'll never forget the doctor. She's a real pretty lass."

Amos stood back upright, his coffee in his hand. "Yeah, she's real pretty, that one, real pretty," he said, and, turning around, he almost spilt his drink as he faced her.

The doctor had returned to the desk to collect some patient notes, much to Amos's surprise and embarrassment as she was standing behind him.

"I'll see you at the end of my ward round at about 8.30, so you have time to get yourself some breakfast."

Neither said anything more and Mary smiled at Amos as he walked off in the direction of the canteen with his drink.

On reaching the canteen he carefully eyed the food being presented, and felt the safest was the scrambled eggs with some salad.

After he had had his breakfast, he came back onto the ward, sat on his bed and looked around; 8.30 couldn't come soon enough for Amos. There were three other patients on the ward lying on their beds. An elderly man that hadn't seemed to move whilst he was there, a young boy who looked like he had a broken arm – *but I'm sure they wouldn't have kept him in if that's all that was wrong with him* – and a middle-aged man in a bed in the corner, coughing a lot. *I'd better keep away from him*, Amos thought. *Can't risk a chest infection; it might prevent me from diving.*

The sister he'd seen earlier at reception walked onto the ward followed shortly afterwards by Dr Svensen. They started their round at the far end of the ward and were slowly working their way down to him.

When they got to Amos, he was sitting up on his bed. "Sorry about the delay," said Dr Svensen. "We have some difficulties with a patient." She picked up the clipboard at the end of Amos's bed.

"No problem," said Amos, still feeling slightly embarrassed about what she had overheard him saying.

"That's for me to say, not you. Let's see you scanned first, yes, and then we have a look at that arm." The doctor and sister stood chatting to each other at the end of Amos's bed; Amos was listening intently but couldn't quite hear what they were saying.

They came back to the side of the bed, next to Amos. "Right, now, let us get you into the MRI suite and sorted. Are you OK to follow us or would you like helps?"

"Yeah, I'm fine; I just wanna get back to work."

It all seemed so straightforward: no waiting around in this hospital. *The system for dealing with patients is better than we've got over in the States*, thought Amos as he followed them, *or perhaps it's the lack of patients? She seems to be a very organised person, almost regimental and robotic; maybe that's the approach you have to take being a doctor and being able to deal with life-and-death situations in your own way.*

After a period of about thirty minutes, Amos came out of the MRI suite and was led back to his bed on the ward by one of the nurses who had been supervising the scanning. He waited. It was so quiet other than the occasional visitor to the young patient in the far corner, a bleep or two going off in the distance, doors opening and squeaking closed as nurses and porters went about their business. He lifted his bag up onto the bed.

"Good old Jack," said Amos to himself. He pulled out the book he had been reading with the bookmark still on page seven... he had a long way to go. *I might need this to keep me sane if I'm here longer than a few days; hopefully not*, he thought, and put his reading glasses on. "Now where was I... Ah yes..."

Dr Svensen returned to the ward, as she'd said she would, late morning with the sister and they walked up to his bed.

"How are the results, ladies?" said Amos enthusiastically before they could say anything. "As I need to get back to work."

"With the fogs outside, you will not be going back at the moment; you look out of the windows. Anyway, you are going to have to wait for a few hours yet, I'm afraid. The images, they have to go to the neurosurgeon in Glasgow in Scotland to check and comment and depending on his availability we then find out."

Dr Svensen then asked Amos to stand up and remain still. Amos did as he was told and got a waft of what he could only describe as angel perfume.

"Now, you pay attention, please. Looks straight... now look to the right and... the left... not your head, just your eyes... and now straights." Amos noticed how smooth and silky her complexion was, the depth of her blue-grey eyes and neatness of her eyebrows, and the carefreeness of her hair, yet in a funny sort of way neat and tidy.

"OK, now let's see to this arm, please. Off the bed and follow."

The nurse led him to the examination room off the ward and

he sat on a bench.

"Now please rolls up your sleeve… ahh… that's no good. Please removes your shirt from the arm."

The nurse helped Amos as his arm was stiff and tightly bandaged.

He looked at his bandaged arm and could see blood had been seeping through overnight.

"Nurse, please remove the bandages and I will be back shortly." Dr Svensen drew the curtains back and left the examination room, leaving Amos with the nurse.

The nurse started to unwind the bandage.

"We get a lot of divers now. Ever since the oil and gas fields opened up closer to us than to Norway." She started to cut away the bandages with a pair of scissors. "That's a very nasty scar you have there?" The nurse was trying to distract Amos whilst she was removing the bandages as she knew he wasn't best happy with blood, but it just reminded Amos of his close encounter with a deadly fish. "How did this happen?" asked the nurse, looking at the scars on the side of Amos's body.

Amos hadn't realised she was talking about his scars and thought it was the accident he had yesterday.

"Oh. Here. I thought… Err… Yes, that was when I was in the Gulf of Mexico." Amos had a flashback image of a shark close up about to sink his teeth into him. "And— Awwee, gee, that hurt!"

"Sorry. It's difficult when blood has dried and hair gets stuck…"

"No problem. It just felt like you were digging into the wound with your nails."

Dr Svensen returned to the room. "I thought I heard a child scream?" She had a smile on her face. "Let us please take a look now." She started to prod and squeeze. "It's septic… we need to clear the dirt and pus and before then we must—"

"Don't tell me… another."

"Yes, I'm afraid so. You still have dirt and maybe metals in there, perhaps some rust, so we must get it out to make your arm better."

The nurse left the room and returned with what was becoming the standard bowl and needle.

Amos looked away and tensed up.

"Relax now. It's for your good." The doctor gave him the injection this time. It was clearly a Danish accent with a bit of English thrown in, and definitely a touch of a Scottish accent on certain words.

The nurse and the doctor then set to work to clear the wound of infection. With a pair of tweezers, antiseptic and cotton wool, they worked their way along the edges of the wound and then rebandaged his arm. The doctor then showed him the tweezers and what she had just pulled out of the wound. A clink of metal landed in the stainless-steel pan.

"Wowee… no wonder my arm hurt. Thank you."

"That was a nasty piece and let us hope that is the last. I've taken out what I can; now you must lie backwards and the nurse will bandage your arm again."

The doctor left the room. As the nurse was bandaging his arm, he could see through the gap in the door and the doctor putting her coat on. She then walked back into the consulting room.

"Now you must rest for a while as I have other works to do and I will see you later this afternoon when I come back."

"But I might not be here," replied Amos with an astonished look on his face of *I'm going back to the rig.*

"You must be staying here, as we have the scan results to be checked later."

"What am I supposed to do? I've got work to—"

"Yes, I know, and you must be fit for work, yes?" She said goodbye and left.

"Now what am I supposed to do?" said Amos to the nurse, who was finishing off the bandaging.

"You're going to have to wait until the doctor gets back… The doctor has asked to be called as soon as the scan results are in; she wouldn't normally but said to Mrs McKinnon on reception to notify her as she knows it's important to you."

"Gee, can't ask for more than that." It gave Amos the reassurance he needed. He sat up when the nurse had finished and heard a voice that he recognised. Bill put his head round the curtain to the cubicle.

"Bill, are you still here?"

"Yes, still here. Fog-bound like everyone else. Anyhow, it gives me a chance to do some maintenance on the chopper. How are you doing, Amos?" He stepped into the compartment.

"I'm good, thanks; should be out of here this afternoon when the doctor returns. Just waiting on the results of my scan." He motioned his hand towards his head.

"Maybe, Amos, but there's no transport at the moment... anyhow, what do you think of her?" said Bill with a twinkle in his eye.

"Who?" replied Amos.

"Ingrid – Dr Svensen."

The nurse was finishing tidying up and smiled back at the two of them, well aware of the topic of conversation.

"You'd both be lucky; her first love is the environment, then being a doctor. So you'd both be a long way down the list."

Bill and Amos chuckled as the nurse left the room and nodded in agreement.

"Yeah, well, she should be married to someone by now; she is a real stunner."

"As you're still around and I presume not doing anything later, do you fancy visiting a local hostelry?" said Bill.

"A what?"

"A pub."

"Yeah, why not. There's nothing else to do around here."

"OK, Amos, I'll see you around 6.30 and be careful of the canteen food here; it's not all that it's made out to be, so we'll get a bite to eat when we're out."

"Yeah, Mrs McKinnon on reception warned me earlier, and definitely no coffee from the machine."

"See you later, buddy." Bill left the cubicle as the nurse returned.

Amos made his way back to his bed on the ward and carefully rolled onto his back as his arm was very sore from the treatment he had been given. He made himself comfortable, picked up his book and put his glasses on. *Change Your Thoughts, Change Your Life* by

Dr Wayne Dyer. Amos had got to Verse 3, Living Contentment, and had concluded that gratitude was his conclusion from that particular verse of the Tao. *Only seventy-eight to go*, he thought. *I'm going to read no more than three a day; that way it will give me something to think about, reflect and focus on.*

Amos was so engrossed he didn't hear or see that the doctor had returned and was standing at the end of his bed.

"What is that you are reading?"

"Oh sorry, I didn't see you there. It's a philosophical book about the Tao." Amos lifted his glasses to his forehead and moved himself up onto his good elbow with a wince of pain.

"Yes, a good book. I have read, you know. We have had a response from the neurosurgeon. So please listen, this is not me, but him. You cannot go to works for another three days so you must be staying here."

"Argh, no… you can't be serious." Amos closed his book with annoyance.

"As I said it was the neurosurgeon saying this; this doctor, who is the expert, he has said this, not me, so you must stay."

"Can I go out or am I stuck in this godforsaken building?"

"It is a hospital, and yes, you can, but not late at night; you must be back by nine, please, at the latest."

"Can I have a drink?" Amos realised that he was pushing things a bit here.

"Strictly no drink," came a sharp reply. "You must rest your mind and your body. Read your book; it tells you. Have a good night and I will see you tomorrow morning on my round."

She left Amos to ponder her comments. *Three days; how is Jack going to deal with the work with one man down?*

Amos stood up and took a walk to the canteen but didn't buy anything. Mrs McKinnon kindly made him another coffee.

Jack; I need to speak with Jack.

"Thank you, Mary. Er, Mary… am I okay to call the rig again? I need to speak to my business partner."

"Yer know, Amos, I shouldn't, but maybe in an hour or so when it's quietened down here."

"OK, thank you."

Amos found a seat in the day room and settled down to read his book. Shortly before Bill was due, he thought he would try Jack again. On walking into the reception area, he approached Mary and said, "Is it OK if…"

"Go on now, and be quick, laddie, before I get told off."

"Thank you." Amos dialled Jack at the rig but there was no response from Jack so he just left a message saying that he had called. As Mary was busy talking with a nurse and a new patient, he also decided to give Bernie a call. It was about lunch time so they should be around, he thought.

Brr, brr…

"Hello, Marriott Grand Cayman, how may I help you?"

"Could you put me through to—"

"Hello there, is that Mr Amos?"

"Er… yeah."

"Oh, how nice to speak with you, Mr Amos. It's Daphne here; do you remember me?"

"Yeah. Hi. May I speak to my wife please…"

"I have not seen her."

"Well, could you just tell her that I called… bye." Amos had to keep it short as he saw the staff nurse making her way over to reception and realised that it would not be good for Mary if he was seen using her phone.

"Mary, if Bill arrives do you mind telling him that I'll be back in reception shortly? I'm just going to get my coat and" – he glanced across at the phone – "oh, and thank you again."

"Yes, Mr Amos, I will." Mary was short with her response as she needed to concentrate on dealing with the staff who seemed to have appeared en masse.

Amos grabbed his coat from the ward and returned in good time. Waiting in the reception area, he picked a leaflet up off the table that read *Your Planet Needs You*, with a finger pointing towards the reader, followed by *You must help to heal OUR planet*. He flipped the leaflet over and started to read about whaling and fishing. The outside doors to the reception opened and Bill walked in, clapping his gloved hands together.

"Are you ready, Amos?"

Amos stood up from the sofa in the reception area. "Not quite, I just need to get my arm into my coat. Argh. I've also had the results through on my scan, and not good, I'm stuck here for three more days."

"Well… I can think of worse places to be. How's the doctor by the way?"

"She's fine and she's very strict."

"Yeah, needs to be; doesn't want you to be getting any ideas. Ha ha."

"Where's the place we're going to? I hope it's close as I'm absolutely starving," said Amos, trying without success to pull on his coat. Bill helped him with it and they made their way past reception.

"Now where are you two off to?" came a voice from behind the reception desk.

"Hello, Mary, and how are you? We're going to get a bite to eat. The doctor said it was OK and Amos here hasn't had any lunch."

"Mind you take care of him and do as she asks you to," said Mary. "You know she's a stickler for detail."

"OK, we will. Good night, Mrs Mc," replied Bill, waving to Mary and helping Amos through the doors.

"Is she always like a mother hen?"

"Yup, always," said Bill. "Mary, she runs the place. Without her the hospital would shut down."

"Good night, both of you. And Bill, look after him now." She put her finger up in front of her face towards Bill, telling him off before they had even left the building.

They exited the hospital into flurries of sleet that the cold of the night was throwing at them. Vision was limited; they couldn't see more than a few metres in front of them, Amos sticking close to Bill.

"I hope you know where you're going, Bill, and please keep close otherwise you're gonna lose me!" Amos could hear the lapping of water against the shoreline and the dim street lighting showing through the fog made it quite eerie.

"It's not far from here, perhaps a five-minute walk, Amos, and it's not difficult to find, slightly up away from the harbour."

"And before I forget," added Amos, "thanks for entertaining me tonight. It's much appreciated; I was getting so bored there. Don't get me wrong, the people are nice but there's nothing to do."

"It's nothing, Amos, honestly, I was looking forward to spending some time with you when we were chatting yesterday in the helicopter on the way over but you weren't quite with it so we've got this evening."

Amos was very careful walking; the last thing he wanted was to slip and hurt himself. He could just make out the sound of music in the distance and wondered if that was where they were going. The buildings around them as they walked looked very stark and industrial. *Is there really a restaurant around here?* he thought.

"This is it, Amos. I told you it was only a short distance; it's just up here on the right, and be careful of the steps – there's five of them leading up to the door and the fourth step is a short step, not the same as the others."

The inn was tucked behind what looked like a series of rundown buildings and workshops.

"A lot of these buildings are the drying sheds for fish if you're wondering why there's a bit of a smell around here." They followed the footpath up an alleyway to the set of stone steps Bill had warned Amos about. Amos took them carefully. Bill pushed the door open.

"Mind your head, Amos; the sooner we get you inside the safer it will be for you."

The strength of the open fire sent a wave of warmth towards them as they entered and with the low ceilings the need to find a place to sit down was essential. Bill initially made his way towards the bar.

"Two Okkara Gulls, please," said Bill to the lady behind the bar and then motioned with his head to Amos to grab a table, pointing towards an empty one by the fire.

Stamping his feet and carefully shaking the snow off his coat, he made his way to the table Bill had pointed out, slowly managing to take his coat off, by which time Bill arrived at the table with the beers and a menu in his mouth.

"Thought you might like to take a look at the menu."

"Thanks... I need some food inside me. Hey, that's a lot of beer in there, Bill." Amos pointed at the two glasses.

"*Skål*," said Bill, raising his glass towards Amos.

"Yeah, cheers, good health and thanks again," replied Amos; their glasses clinked. "You know I would have gone for a smaller one as the doctor said..."

"This is a small one, Amos. Look at the other drinkers' glasses." Sure enough, Bill was right; there were some much larger glasses out there.

"This is a lovely drop of beer; what did you call it again?"

"Okkara Gull."

"I must remember that. It tastes good; not sure we would get this back home, mind."

"I've been coming here for years on a Thursday evening. It's a great way to start the weekend." Bill took another mouthful of beer and wiped his lips with the back of his hand.

Looking around, Amos thought that the pub would go down a treat back home, other than the fact that it was probably a bit too warm inside and it would be a waste of all that heat from the fire, which continued to roar. Amos took another sip of beer, Bill a gulp. Not having to fly meant he could enjoy a beer or two when he could fit it in.

Bill's glass, empty, landed on the table.

"Sorry, Amos, it's the first one: never lasts long, and is always the best. If you're thinking about food then I suggest the peppered salmon – you'll not taste anything better."

"OK, that sounds a good choice as I can't read the menu anyway; it's all double Dutch."

Bill got up from the table and walked towards the bar to order the food and another beer.

"Evening, Elka."

"Bill. How are you?"

"Fine thanks. Two salmon and another Okkara please, and make that a large one, thank you."

"On its way, Bill. Who's the man with you?" said Elka, behind the bar, whilst pouring the drink.

"He's off the rigs; picked him up yesterday afternoon. Banged his head quite badly and stitches in his arm – likely to be here a couple more days, longer if the fog hangs around. We were lucky to get in yesterday."

Amos looked towards Bill at the bar and could see that there was another pair of eyes looking across the room at him. A waitress then put a knife and fork onto the table and he had to do a double take, realising that she must be the daughter of the lady at the bar as they both had mousey-coloured hair and similar-shaped faces and smiles.

"Hello."

"Er, yeah. Hello… Er… thank you," replied Amos.

Bill returned to the table with his glass refilled. "Chatting up the locals already, Amos?"

"No, no, not at all."

She walked away with a smile at Amos and Bill and went to clear another table.

"I just noticed that the two ladies look very similar."

"Yes, you're right – mother and daughter. You've probably noticed that there are a lot of beautiful Scandinavian women up here."

"Tell me about it… the doctor, she—"

"Argh, yes, of course," interrupted Bill. "The doctor; how are you two getting along?"

"Well, she's very… very, er, efficient and doesn't seem to have much of a sense of humour and is very work-like."

"She has always been that way, particularly with strangers; she's fine when you get to know her. You know she's only part time at the hospital and—"

The landlady's daughter brought over the food. "There you are, Bill, your favourite."

"Thank you, Karina."

"I've only added the extra pepper to yours, Bill, as it might be too hot for your friend to handle."

"Yes, you could be right there," said Bill, looking towards Amos and noticing that Amos had taken an interest in Karina. "Oh yes and by the way, Karina, I should have introduced you – this is Amos. He's staying here for a few days whilst he recovers from an injury; he works up on the rigs."

"Well, I hope you enjoy your meal." She turned and walked back to the bar, having a jovial chat with a couple on the way and then dropping her towel on the bar.

"She seems to be quite a livewire, that one," said Amos.

"You're right there," said Bill, "but she's got a temper on her even for a Viking goddess."

"You sound besotted, Bill."

"Yes, you're probably right. *Skål*... But I'm too old and have a lovely family to look after."

"Me likewise," replied Amos. It reminded Amos of what he had left behind. *I must call them when I get back to the hospital.*

"Well, I'm starved." Bill and Amos tucked into the salmon, which Bill explained had been freshly caught and was one of his favourite meals. A very tasty, good choice in Amos's eyes and stomach.

The two of them worked their way through the big plates of food, discussing Bill's job, his family and life on the islands and Amos explaining his work on the rigs and his discovery of a species of barnacle that he hadn't seen before up in the North Sea and the potential impact of warmer waters and changes in the salt content of seawater.

"My turn to get you a drink... What did you call it?"

"Okkara Gull."

Amos made his way through the throng of people up at the bar. "Two small Okkara Gulls, please, thank you." He looked around to see if he could see Karina again but she was nowhere to be seen. The landlady, Elka, said she would bring them over.

"Nice pub, this, Bill," said Amos as he returned to the table. "Very friendly and a nice cosy feel to it."

"Yeah, the people here are very nice."

Elka brought the beers over to their table, not soon enough for Bill as he immediately took a big mouthful.

"It's a very close community here. If there's a problem then there's always someone who will try to help you out. There was a fishing boat last year that came aground over on the west coast, trying to shelter from a storm, and all the men from the village came out at high tide the following day to pull it out to sea again. It's part of the island life and community make-up."

"Wow, is that time already? 9.25... I'm supposed to be back by nine."

"Who said that?"

"The doctor."

"Argh, you'd better get back then otherwise there'll be some harsh words." Bill finished his drink.

Amos took another sip then left the rest of his drink; it really was a big small glass of beer. They made their way to the exit, saying their goodbyes. Amos made to put his coat on and the landlady could see he was having difficulties and came over and helped him. *Very friendly people here*, he thought.

"Thank you." The landlady stood back and folded her arms. "You are welcomes." Amos gave a wince as he shifted his shoulders up under his coat. Bill and Amos exited the pub.

They made their way back through a biting cold, whistling wind with sleet stinging on their faces. *This one's definitely straight off the pole. Bit early for that, mind*, thought Bill to himself.

"Thanks for the night out and entertaining me, Bill. The food was excellent. If I'm still here tomorrow, perhaps we can do it again."

Bill left Amos at the entrance to the hospital and went back to his lodgings. Amos entered the hospital and was greeted by Mary on reception.

"Where have you been, laddie? I was about to send out search parties for you. I've already had a call from Dr Svensen checking on her patients and I said you were OK the last time I saw you. Fortunately for you she didn't ask when that was. Now get off to bed, will yer now, and I'll see you in the morning. I've been waiting for yer. I'll get you a wee brew and then I'm off home."

"Thank you," said Amos, feeling it was like being told off by his mother for getting home late and being scolded for it and sent to bed.

Amos cringed with pain as he took off his jacket and sat on the bed in the ward. There were now only two other people in the ward, one still reading by a night light and the other asleep.

"There you are now, laddie," said Mary, delivering the hot drink to his bedside, and she went on her way.

"Thank you."

Amos leant across the bed, wincing with pain in his arm and shoulder, and took a sip of the drink. There was definitely something special in that drink… A definite taste of a strong whisky!

He took another mouthful to finish off the drink – it tasted good – and replaced the cup on the side table by his bed, lay back on the pillow and fell asleep.

CHAPTER 9: HLAKSVÍK TOWN

Amos woke from a second night in the hospital with itchy feet at the bottom of the bed and wanted to be doing something or to leave the hospital and get back to the rig.

Amos was still in bed and hadn't had time to get up before the morning ward round began. Dr Svensen arrived at his bed with the nurse that looked after him yesterday. The doctor was quick to point out that it didn't look like he had got up yet. Probably just as well as, other than his shoes, he hadn't changed since getting back last night.

"Mrs McKinnon tells me you went out last evening with Bill. How was your evening?"

"Er, yeah, Doctor… it was very enjoyable, thank you, Doctor." Amos was waiting with the expectation of being asked about whether he had had any alcohol, but thankfully she didn't ask; perhaps she already knew he had had a drink.

"I see you have a drinking mug here from the staff room."

"Yes, Mrs McKinnon, er… kindly made me a drink last night… yes."

"Looking at it, I would say that it was probably very nice for you as Mary makes good evening drinks, so I am told."

I'm sure she knows that Mrs McKinnon looks after the patients in a very motherly way. Perhaps the doctor has got a sense of humour after all.

"Can you tell me please when I can go?"

She took a deep breath. "Amos, you must realise that no one is going anywhere at the moment… look outside. We are still with the fog and also the snow. But I will check your wound again now for you. Nurse. Nurse. Please, I will come back in a few moments."

This gave Amos time to change his top to a tee shirt and take his socks off! The nurse drew the curtains around the bed just as he had thrown his top under the bed.

"Morning, Amos, let's see how this is mending."

It took the nurse quite a while to unravel the bandages again and finally with a pair of scissors take the final strips away. It had been weeping again.

"How's it looking?" asked Amos, daring to take a brief look and then looking away again.

"I can't see yet," she said. "Please stop being so impatient and just wait for me to finish. Thank you."

The doctor then came in and straight over to the nurse and pulled the last of the bandages away to inspect the wound and stitches. "That is looking better; there are still a few areas where it is pus-y and inflamed but that will go away." She pointed and prodded his arm around the wound.

"So I can leave, then?"

"But you cannot go yet or have you lost your memory also? Your MRI report from the specialist said you have two more days, then we check again. Only then we will make a decision."

Amos was not happy and looked away, shaking his head.

The doctor left and the nurse rebandaged his arm.

"Well, at least your arm is getting better," said the nurse. "I will check it again in the morning, but it does look well on the mend." The nurse left him in bed.

"Yeah, thank you," came a disappointed and mumbled response from Amos.

Amos got up and washed as best he could and then headed for the main reception.

"Mary. Good morning, how are you today?"

"Well, I got home late last night, no thanks to you, laddie, and my husband had decided he would start trying to cook the meal. That wasn't good; it wasn't good at all. But," she said with a sigh, "I managed to rescue the situation and sort out the mess he had created, and yes, thank you, I had a nice evening."

"Oh, I'm so sorry that was me holding you up; I didn't realise that you were waiting on me."

"Don't worry, laddie, mind you don't do it again now," she said with a wee smile on her face. "Just think of the impact your actions have on others."

"Mary, I was wondering if I, er… could ask you a favour. Would it be possible to…"

"You want to use the phone? Now be quick with yer, I'm busy this morning and we've got the big boss around this morning."

"That's very kind, thank you, thank you." Amos quickly came around to the other side of the reception desk and sat down by the phone.

"Remember, you dial nine first."

"Yeah, yeah, thank you." Amos kept himself low behind the reception desk to minimise anyone seeing him and getting Mary into trouble.

"Jack, Jack, hi… it's me, Amos."

Jack updated Amos on their progress at the rig. Although they were still behind schedule, the team should be able to catch up by the weekend. Jack had managed to agree with Charles and the team a satisfactory overtime payment arrangement and they would be back on programme provided they worked a full day on both the Saturday and Sunday. This was understandably reassuring for Amos. The telephone line started to crackle and they both struggled to hear each other. Jack also advised that he had managed a brief chat with Bernie and that she blamed Amos for getting injured doing too much work. "She also said—" The line cut out.

"Argh, gee, it's gone again; what is it about communications around here?" said Amos, holding the phone away from his ear and then putting it down. "Are the communications always this bad?"

"You'll just have to get used to it, Amos, if you're staying here a while; it's all part of island life. It'll slow you down a bit and we all need that from time to time."

Amos, although frustrated, didn't call Jack back again.

"I think I'm gonna see what there is for breakfast."

"Try some of the tatties, Amos, they are really very, very nice this morning," said Mary.

"What are tatties?"

"They're what you call a fried onion and potato cake – one of my favourites to start the morning with after I've had my bowl of porridge."

"OK... mmm, sounds nice. I'll give them a try... thank you." Amos left the reception and headed straight for the canteen.

***

On returning from breakfast, he caught a glimpse of the doctor at the reception desk, signing off what looked to be paperwork. She then left the reception area with a posted note given to her by Mary. Amos overheard the word "professor". Amos walked over to the desk.

"Mary, might I ask you, er..."

"No, Amos, you cannot use the phone, not right now. Please, Amos, I'm sorry, I'm so busy." She was getting flustered with there being so many people arriving.

"It's OK, thank you. I wasn't going to ask about that..."

"Oh, what is it then? And be quick, you can see I'm busy here and I've got my work to do."

"Well, I was going to ask about Dr Svensen."

"Did you not know? The doctor's only part time here at the hospital, three days a week here as a doctor, sometimes full and sometimes half days, and then on her other days she works for the Norwegian Oceanic Organisation; she's got a degree in environmental studies."

"Wow, I didn't know that; she keeps herself busy. Must be a very dedicated person with the demands of the hospital as well."

"Aye, laddie, Ingrid does that, and is very passionate about both her jobs. She'll make a fine bonny wife for someone one day, that one will. Now I really do need to get on if you could excuse me. Yes, hello there. Good morning, can I help you?" Mary was now busy talking to a new person entering the hospital reception.

Amos decided to go back to his bed on the ward and tried to

start reading his book. Chapter 5, Living Impartially. He put his glasses up on his forehead and closed the book. *I need to get out of here somehow*, he thought, looking out at the view of mist and fog from the ward windows.

The late morning ward round arrived, but not quick enough for Amos. He was bored and seriously fed up.

"Excuse me… excuse me. Nurse," he called out across the ward from his bed. "Is there anything to do around here other than lie in bed? As I am seriously bored. What does everyone else do?"

"We'll be coming round to see you shortly, sir, just wait a little while and we will be with you."

Dr Svensen overheard the conversation and motioned over to the nurse to see Amos next.

"Good morning, and how have you been feeling? Any better than last night?"

Amos realised it was another reference to being out late last night without her saying it outright and directly to him.

"Yeah, yeah, I'm fine but I'm stuck here and there's nothing to do. I need to get back to work as my livelihood is at stake."

"Well. I am sorry, but your health is at stake also if you go back too soon. You have a book, and people on the ward to talk to and you can walk around the town. You have been out, yes?"

Amos had a good moan to himself, shaking his head from side to side as the doctor and nurse moved on to the last patient. At the end of the ward round he looked up from his book, which he had decided to read, and saw the nurse and the doctor chatting at the exit doors. He settled down and continued to read. He suddenly heard a voice.

"Hello."

Amos stirred from his book with a start and looked up. It was the doctor. He removed his glasses.

"Hello. I have no work here this afternoon and I must do my other work elsewhere on the island for the Norwegian Oceanographic Organisation. Would you like to join me?"

Amos was taken aback and initially couldn't decide how to respond.

"It is only to visit the weather station that I have to do as part of my work, and you can see maybe some of the island if you like?"

"Well, er… yes, I suppose so. Yeah, I would like to, er… yeah… you must have heard me talking earlier to the nurse?"

"Yes, and to Mary, and to most of the other people here at the hospital… I will see you at twelve o'clock in the reception." Dr Svensen made her way out of the ward.

Amos wasn't able to settle back to his book after their conversation and stared out of the window for a while, reflecting on the last two days, and was thankful that he had Jack as a reliable partner. The fog did seem to be lifting a bit, looking out of one of the windows. He continued to read his book for a while, then as time got closer to noon he got himself ready and waited in the reception area.

"Now, you make sure you look after yourself, Amos," said Mary when he went to sit down.

"Well, I'll have the doctor with me so I'm sure I will, thank you, Mary."

"Right, we are ready, yes?" came a voice from the front doors of the hospital as Amos was flicking through a magazine and daydreaming again. "I get my car and we go, yes? We come back at about four o'clock, Mary. I must visit one of the weather stations and I can show Amos some of the islands."

Mary must have known the routine as she didn't respond and carried on at her desk, busy with a new patient. Amos and Dr Svensen exited the hospital reception.

Although it was still very cold outside, the fog was definitely lifting, but there were still snow flurries in the air. The doctor walked towards a light blue Fiat 500 in the car park and Amos followed.

As they got to the car, Amos noticed a number of dents and scratches along the near side wing.

Dr Svensen noticed that Amos was looking at the damage to her car. "That was not me; I am a careful driver, and the car, it is a light colour so you have no need to worry."

Amos's eyebrows lifted and he chuckled to himself. He wasn't able to get into the car immediately as Ingrid was leaning across from the driver's seat, moving bags and a handful of papers onto the back seat.

"Do you need any help with moving the stuff from the front?"

"No, it's fine, it's papers from my last visit that I have to keep for the professor at the society. I normally sort them out on the day of my visits but I have been so busy lately. Normally I cycle to work but as today we must go into the countryside it is better by car. You may get in... At last!"

"Thank you, er... Doctor." Amos sat down in the passenger seat and awkwardly closed the car door.

"We are not at works now, so you can call me Ingrid. When we are in the hospital it must be 'Doctor.'" She started the car engine and gave it a few revs before accelerating off at speed. "Please, you must put on your belt."

She had driven off so quickly that Amos hadn't had the time to put it on and it was also tricky for him with the injury to his arm, so Ingrid stopped the car, rather abruptly, and leant across Amos quickly and clipped it in.

"There, now we are ready." Amos was a little surprised by her closeness.

She crashed the engine into first gear and they were off again. Amos's immediate thoughts at the start of the journey were: *Is Ingrid sure the accident she had wasn't her fault, as she was driving very fast away from the hospital and again now.*

"We go into the town first as I must pick up a parcel from the post office and then we can go. You can wait here in the car."

They soon drove into what Amos thought must be Klaksvík main town and, to be fair on Ingrid, she did slow down and was much more careful than the first couple of minutes. Maybe it was the feel of freedom that made her drive so powerfully away from the hospital.

She parked up. "Wait here; I will only be a few moments." She got out and slammed the door shut.

Amos looked around. The surroundings were all so drab and grey, interspersed with a few buildings with red or yellow walls, brown and green roofs, which looked so out of keeping with what was basically a town built around a harbour. On one side was the centre of town and on the other, the sea. *They must have a big fishing industry here.* There were a lot of boats in the harbour.

The car door opened abruptly and startled Amos.

"All done." The parcels she had picked up from the post office were thrown onto the rear seats of the car. "You don't have to worries; it's from my parents and I know what is inside. Now we go. It's about maybe twenty minutes in the car and we can hopefully see the beauty here."

Amos looked across at her and then out of the side window as they got going… and agreed with her. They were soon out of the main town and onto the country roads. Amos could make out what he thought was a steep cliff or hillside to his right, and hoped that Ingrid was paying full attention to the road.

"We go to the island of Eysturoy. It is basically south from Klaksvík. Did you see the bridge?"

Amos didn't respond. He hadn't seen it.

"Then we go to a village of Æðuvík; it is not very far. You tell me when you see signs for a camp site, then we are there."

"Is that a mountainside that I can see over there?"

"Yes, all around you will see when the weather clears it is very beautiful." They drove up a steep hill and reached the snow line.

"Already snow."

"Yes, and it is low and yes, it is early this year. We are used to snow here. The weather changes so quickly you just have to be prepared. That's why I have the shovel in the back and wheel chains. You cannot drive here when there is lots of snow without them."

The car moved back into second gear and the road climbed steeply and turned sharply to the left.

"Wow, look at that," said Amos.

An opening in the low cloud left a viewing window for him to gain a glimpse of the scenery.

"It is good, yes?"

"Yeah. Fantastic… How long have you been on the island?"

"About seven years now, since I qualified as a doctor, and then I works in Copenhagen where my parents live for two years, but I didn't like it as I wanted to be more outside and with nature. Then an opportunity to work here came up at three days a week which was so perfect for me that I didn't hesitate and it meant that I could then study and research for my oceanic and environmental degree. My dissertation is the impact of climate change on the food chain."

"Well, a few changes in temperature here and there won't make any difference," said Amos rather flippantly.

There was a sharp response from Ingrid. "You are wrong, very wrong there. The planet's average temperature has hardly altered in the last ten thousand years, and now in the last hundred years it increases by 1 per cent and the speed of increase has doubled in the last fifty years. 2021 was the warmest on record since global records began in 1880 and the last four hundred and twenty-one months have been warmer than average, caused by skyrocketing carbon emissions. In Oslo, Norway in January 2020, they have no snow and no temperature below zero degrees Celsius. It is the first time ever. Do you know that a one-degree increase in global temperatures will cause a two to three-metre increase in sea level?" Amos realised that he was out of his depth and had hit a sore point as her response snapped back at him, and he bit his tongue.

"You are just like everyone else, not opening your eyes to everything happening around you and doing nothing. One of the key problems we have now will be the seasons. We won't have any; they will disappear. It will be… how do you call it…err, a pea soup. No structure to the weather and plants will not know when to blossom and then how do the bees know? Hey? We are disturbing the earth's natural rhythms," she said very forcefully. Amos was hoping that she was keeping her eyes on the road.

"OK, OK, I'm sorry. I didn't mean to upset you. It's just that, where I'm from, it's hot all the time, not two or three days in the year."

Ingrid gave Amos a rather stern glance from the driver's seat that looked like it was saying, *That's no excuse.* There was a lack of conversation for a few miles in the car.

"You seem agitated. Is it something I've done or said?"

"I am anxious, very anxious about the environment. Many peoples are. What we are doing or what we are *not* doing." She paused for a while, her eyes flitting between Amos and the road, her hands gesticulating. "Do you know that peoples in the world make forty billion tons of carbon dioxide every year and that it is mostly from fossil fuels? And that over the last hundred years the amount we produce has exploded? Oceans absorb about half of what we produce… but here is now the problem. As waters warm they are less able to absorb carbon dioxide and our warming is greater than the earth's natural cycle of warming and cold. Result: a warmer climate and no ice sheets, rising sea levels and we now cuts down all the trees… It is ridiculous, we destroy the things that feed us oxygen. Without it we have nothing. Did you know that the rainforests produce over 20 per cent of the earth's oxygen and the deforestation that is taking place is producing 20 per cent of carbon emissions? Well?"

She paused, but Amos didn't get a chance to respond.

"In 2020 and 2021, over three and a half million hectares of the Amazon rainforest were destroyed each year; it is not sustainable and we lose biodiversity and kill animals. It is very simple; we benefit in two ways to stop this, yes? We have the earth's natural rhythms when the sun is not so hot, like the sunspots cycle in 2020… it will cool for a little and we then thinks we have solved the problem… We have not. When it is cooler, what do we do? We burn fossil fuels to keep warm, more carbon pollution. The sun gets stronger again and then it is very hot and our chance has gone… We are then past the tipping point." Ingrid took a deep breath, which felt like anger was building up inside her. "We are burning oil and coal and blasé and ignorant and stupid. The carbon parts per million in the air have risen over 50 per cent in the last one hundred years."

She paused for a few minutes, allowing Amos a chance to take it all in. He was listening.

"We only have the earth. There is nowhere else to go, and we are poisoning us, our planet. Our food is also running out and we have too many peoples. Do you know that in the last one hundred years the planet's population has more than trebled? So I decide I will not have any children. I make that decision many years ago." There was another pause in Ingrid's "lecturing", which Amos felt it had been, and it gave him a chance to take all the information and statistics in.

"Wow, that was all very, very interesting, Ingrid. Where did you learn all that from?"

"My university studies, and now it is part of my lifestyle," she replied buoyantly, feeling pleased with herself having been complimented on her knowledge. "I love the outdoors, the rain on my face, the bushes and trees waving; and here the air is so crisp and clean and there are so many lovely walks and views, bays and cliffs with birds of all types; you will see."

Amos smiled to himself and was happy listening. He felt that that was the best policy, as she might go off the handle again if he said anything else. He thought for a while. *She needs another compliment.* Ingrid continued driving.

"You seem very enthusiastic about the environment... and with the extra studying on top of working as a doctor, it must be—"

"The environment, it is *so, so* important," she interrupted him. "You must realise this... yes? With the long winter nights here there is not much else to do other than keep warm so I make best use of my time and study and do my research. You might think that there is isolation here, but there is so much also with a warmth and closeness of the community. We are lucky here in Faroe... we also have a mother and father close by to keep an eye on us... as well as an uncle and auntie."

"What do you mean?" replied Amos with a very questioning expression on his face.

"We have Iceland and Norway, and then Denmark and Scotland, all able to help when we need and keep us warm. What about you?"

Amos was slightly taken aback; suddenly he was in the spotlight.

"Well, that's a long story. I started at college, a course that I really shouldn't have started; it was just all my friends from school were going. It was so dull, and then I drifted away from that to learn how to dive, not much money in social diving so I then became a qualified instructor. Went down to Houston in Texas where I got myself a job in the Gulf, which then led to inspecting oil rigs below sea level… Oil's where the money is."

"There you are again, the oil industry. But life is not just about money. Is that all you value, money? You…" She stopped talking and was concentrating on the road ahead.

Ingrid wasn't really paying attention to the conversation now as she was navigating the car around a snow drift and then down towards what looked like a small holding or hamlet.

"We speak more later; I must concentrate on where we are going." They continued their journey at a slightly slower pace, which pleased Amos. He thought that they must be nearing their destination.

"Ah, look, is that the sign for the campsite that you mentioned?" said Amos, motioning to the left.

"Good. Yes. Sorry… we are almost there. Yes, there we are. The small building just past the farm sheds, you will see?" She pointed out through the windscreen up on the slope just below the snow line.

Amos thought he could make out a few buildings that Ingrid was referring to but to be honest he thought it was just a load of grey.

She parked up.

"Good, at last we are here. We shall first see what data we have to keep the professor happy and then we go to the Hanusarstova restaurant. You saw on the way here, yes? I don't think we can go to walk anywhere today as it would be dangerous, with so much cloud and fog and snow on the ground."

"Yeah, food sounds good."

On reaching the cottage, Ingrid walked past the front door and lifted a loose stone off the paving and returned with a key to unlock the front door. She opened the door and then reached up to a small cupboard behind the door and flicked a switch. The lights came on.

"Ah, that is good, the electricity. It is working. Sometimes when

I am here we have none and then I just walk along the cliffs or go back to the town."

"Gee, it's pretty damp and cold in here," said Amos, looking around the entrance and noticing the yellowed paint peeling off the door frames.

"I've not been here for maybe three weeks now. I have four other weather stations that I look after here on Faroe and collect data for the professor at the university... I think if they build it now it would be in one centre, not five, as technology has moved on so much since these were built over thirty years ago. Amos, can you fetch me some logs, please? They are under cover around the corner at the side of the house." She signalled with her arm.

"Yeah. Sure, er, how many do you want?"

"This many," she said, holding her hands out, "so maybe twelve or fifteen, as we will light the fire and then only be staying here for a few hours."

Amos left the house and had a more considered view of their surroundings, the wind biting his face. *I know what it is; there is so little tree cover and mainly shrubs and gorse flowering with tinges of yellow and orange, and drystone walls. An escape from the hustle and bustle of life. Back to nature.*

He returned to the cottage and Ingrid had already got the fire going with some smaller dried pieces of wood. "Now be careful you don't put too much on at once; you need to slowly feed the fire, OK?"

"Yeah."

Amos set the logs down close to the fire and settled down to feed it.

"I will make a special Danish drink for us shortly. I think you will like it; it is like the one that Mary made for you yesterday... is that alright for you?"

"Yeah, that's good."

Amos tended to the fire. He then heard the front door open and close. He didn't think anything of it until it opened and closed again.

"Oh, that was nice and good; here I am thankfully at one with nature. I do my stretching exercise and meditate outside for a while. It is so good."

The kettle had boiled so Ingrid started to make the drinks. Amos stood up from the fire and walked towards the kitchen; he glanced across at a room with the door partially open.

"Is that where the computers are?"

Ingrid poked her head out of the kitchen doorway. "Yes, that is right; I will come through in a minute."

"Do you mind if I go through?"

"No, that is fine, please."

Amos pushed open the door and saw various computer screens and monitors on desks around the room. The room looked like it had been held in a time warp, with dust on surfaces and cobwebs in places drooping from the ceiling, some lights flashing on and off and the occasional beep of a machine. The telephone flashed red, indicating messages waiting. But what was particularly surprising for Amos was seeing computer paper and printouts strewn all over the floor. Ingrid joined him in the room.

"Oh, I must tidy up. This happens when I have not visited for a while: the paper overflows on the floor and then the printer runs out of paper." Ingrid opened up a cupboard door and pulled out a box full of reams of printer paper.

"Right, that should be enough." She refreshed three printers' paper feeds and on pressing the restart buttons they began whirring into action and producing more data and paper.

"Those pieces of... equipment... they're ancient, yet they look very busy and there's still lights flashing on two of them."

"That is OK. It is because I just put the paper in and they wake up and they start again. They are very old and I think that's why they make so much noise and produce so much paper. I must collect these papers now from here before they are muddled and put them together so I will sort them out later when I get back."

"Do you want me to help?" he asked as he bent down.

"No. No, thank you. I know which orders they come from."

Amos stood up and left her to pick up the printouts. He noticed her shapely figure and then looked away and glanced around the room and spotted calendars from various oil companies. *That's strange*, he thought to himself. *Oil companies supporting a weather station data centre?*

"How come you have calendars from this company?" asked Amos, pointing to one with landscape views of the sea and platforms on the horizon.

"Oh... that one... they help with funding; the professor that I have to speak with, he has some connections there, which is good for us."

Amos took another look at one of the screens and saw a series of dots, some flashing red and others amber in various places on the screen.

"What's all this do?"

Ingrid stood up and looked at the screen whilst collating printouts. "Oh... It's basic information and once an hour the computer sends a message to print out what's on the screen. That way we always have a hard copy in case the computer breaks down."

"Who reads all of this stuff? There's so much of it."

"Well, the professor at the Norwegian Oceanographic Organisation, NOO for short. He asks for it and I send it to him once a month from here to his office in Oslo, Norway or when he works in London. All very simple. But sometimes I look at the information; there is so much that it is really to me a lot of numbers on pieces of paper and lots of them. I would need to spend much time looking and studying them to see what it means and I do not have the time."

"So what do the printouts check or show?" Amos pointed at a screen.

"Well, it's things like water temperature from buoys at various depths in the sea, sea level, storms, shipping movements, that sort of thing, so the professor tells me. You see, I press this button for various depths of temperature and this one for lower. Are you interested in oceanography?"

"Er... um... well I suppose I am, in that it affects if I can dive or not. What's this flashing light on this screen mean?"

Ingrid looked at it and thought for a while before replying, after collecting some papers and bundling them together.

"Oh. Yes. I remember, that is the recording beacons. We had the same lights flashing a few months ago and the professor told me to ignore it, probably old machines, so I turned the computer off and then back on again to reboot it, and here you see it still comes up. Anyway, I am not worried as we have seen it before."

"Oh... I forget." She handed Amos his drink. "And, oh. Here are some *pepparkakor*; I make them myself. I think you call them gingersnaps." She handed the plate to Amos, who picked one out.

Ingrid took another brief look at the screen and reminded herself to check sometime, but not now as she had company. Amos crunched a bite out of a gingersnap.

"Thank you, these are nice. Hey, this smells good as well. What is it?"

"A Danish favourite of mine. It is called *glögg*... and then down at the bottom you will see some almonds and raisins. You can mix it around with the spoon. It is not strong, but very warming inside you when it's cold."

"Woo, that has a nice taste to it. I thought you said it's not strong?" Amos reflected back on the concoction that Mary had given him. Ingrid smiled at Amos and then took a look outside through a window.

"It is only some small brandy. Mmm... I think maybe we can walk for a little while, as the cloud is lifting. Finish your drink now and we go. Please put some logs on the fire."

Amos saw and then looked more closely at a series of pictures on the walls as they left the data room.

"Yes. That is me when I was sixteen. I had just been in a yacht race and here, this one is off the coast of Denmark. Esbjerg – have you heard of it?"

"No, and that's you with a trophy?" Amos pointed at the photo.

"Yes. Me again with my father... very happy days for me and my family."

They wrapped up warm with their coats and scarves and left the fire roaring. The footpath from the cottage took them towards the cliff edge and a series of rocks led them down towards the shoreline.

As they descended the narrow path they stopped to admire the views and looked down onto a cove with the sea spray drifting in gusts towards them.

They saw all varieties of bird life, from puffins to cormorants.

"So much movement to see. Yes?"

Amos nodded back, turning his head from side to side. "The views here are absolutely amazing. You've really escaped from civilisation, haven't you."

Stunning scenery, but a biting cold wind was spoiling it for Amos.

"I think we must return now," said Ingrid.

The snow flurries were getting more frequent and it was becoming darker as fog was rolling in again.

Back at the cottage, she said, "That was good, yes?"

"Wonderful, truly amazing, thank you for bringing me here. Much better than being stuck in that hospital ward."

"So we must go back now before it is too dark. Can you collect the papers from the computer room and put them in the car, please, Amos? Thank you, and I will close up."

Amos picked up the two bundles from the table with his good arm and took another look at the screen. A flashing red light was joined by two orange ones either side of it. He shrugged his shoulders and shook his head and left the room to load up the car.

"All finished?"

"Yeah. I've put them in the back with the other bundles."

Ingrid picked up her backpack, threw the electrical switch and locked up.

"Why is all the data collected like this? Surely with the technology we have we can pick it up from space?"

"Yes, you are right. We can get some information from space but it's not as detailed or as accurate as from here, where we know straight away the temperatures," replied Ingrid as she got the car going.

Yeah, if you can find the right piece of paper, thought Amos to himself.

They drove, as promised by Ingrid earlier, to the Hanusarstova restaurant for some food, only to find that it was closed for meals. *Drinks only*, read the sign on the door.

"That is a shame; it's one of my favourite spots to eat. Well, I think we should go back if there's no food as the late afternoon light is fading."

"Yeah, the visibility is not good. How often do you have to come up to these stations?" he added.

"Maybe once every two weeks, sometimes, as I said earlier, maybe once each month depending on what the professor wants, but to be honest I like to come up here as often as I can. Well, I hope you enjoyed the walk. I am so sorry it was so brief but at least you have seen some of the islands, if only through the cloud and mists."

"Thank you, yes, that was a great experience to see all those sea birds swooping into the cliffs – it looks so haphazard." Amos then paused for a while, whilst Ingrid was navigating the car rather quickly around a series of bends in the road.

"So… is there, er… no Mr Svensen?" Amos was and then was not sure if he should have asked the question as there was initially no response from Ingrid.

"No… I had a boyfriend for many years in Copenhagen but he was too interested in money, money all the time and no time for us together, you know."

Amos pondered her comment and reflected on his relationship with Bernie and his family.

"So when the chance came to come here, I took it and have never looked back. It has everything for me: my work, my environmental studies, the wildlife, the peace, the freshness. I live by myself on the other side of the town where there are no boats or harbour. I can see the mountains and the sea. It is good. But maybe perhaps sometimes I'm a little lonely, but as I said earlier the people here are all friendly, most of the time."

"What do you mean, 'most of the time'?"

"Well, they have traditions here that are not nice and I tell them not to."

"How do you mean?"

"Well, they have what is called Grindadráp, or the annual grind. Do you know what that is?"

"No, I've never heard of it."

"They catch fish and kill them… for fun! And they are not the small fish but big whales and porpoises. There can be hundreds of them and the sea is red with their blood. It is terrible and I try to stop it every year that I have been here and they carry on. I think the women are starting to understand, but the men… It's as if they return to being a Viking and… what do you call it… sauvage… No… savge…"

"Ahh, do you mean 'savage'?"

"Yes. Yes, that is right. It is a horrible spectacle and such a waste. It makes me very sad just to speak of it."

Amos looked across at Ingrid driving and could see a tear welling in her eye. *Crikey, she really is passionate about it.*

"And what about you Amos?"

"Well, I'm fifty-seven, married and got three kids back in Houston. I started diving when I was about thirteen, it gave me the confidence boost that I needed as I didn't have the best of times at school." Amos had a flashback to when he was at school. He was being bullied, locked in a school sports equipment cupboard and not let out until the school caretaker did his end-of-the-day inspections after the school closed. His knuckles turned white as he gripped the door handle.

"Are you OK? You've suddenly stopped."

"Yeah, I'm fine, thanks, just a past experience when I was at school locked in a confined space, that occasionally makes me apprehensive, and then at college when I thumped someone who was trying to do the same." Amos paused and then continued. "I managed one year at college, too many distractions, you know, drinking and girlfriends and lost my way a bit. Then at twenty-four I got back to my diving and managed to get a job working on a rig. Started my own business about eight years ago."

"Why do you come up here to work when it is so cold?"

"Well, it's a long story but it's basically about…" He paused and didn't want to say the word "money" as it had thrown her earlier when she was talking about her ex-boyfriend. So he said, "We needed to pay off a few debts." Which was true enough, as he and Jack as well as his family had stretched themselves financially.

"And your family?"

"Yes, my wife, she is from Scotland and my kids are all doing well since the last time I saw them."

"Do you like it here?"

"Well, I must admit at first when I got here, this was the last place I would want to visit, but I must confess the islands are growing on me and seem to have a lot going for them."

They approached Klaksvík quicker than both of them wanted to as they both enjoyed the open conversation.

"OK, so here we are back at the hospital."

"Thank you again," said Amos.

Amos got out of the car and before he closed the door he suggested to Ingrid that as they'd missed lunch, perhaps she would like to join him for an evening meal.

"Yes," Ingrid replied immediately. "Why not. I come back here at 6.30 to collect you, then we go. I will choose."

Amos closed the door and she drove off at pace. Amos watched as the car sped off and disappeared in the distance.

He returned to the ward, showered and got dressed so that he was ready by the time Ingrid returned. He tried to pick his book up again, but found it difficult to settle and decided to give Bernie a call and then Jack, from reception. It wasn't Mary on reception, but the lady had previously seen Amos using the phone. She said for Amos to be quick. He could only let the call ring for a few moments each time and leave a voicemail with each of them. *I must get a charger for my phone in the morning if they have anything like this up here.* He concluded that Bernie was probably out with the children, and Jack working or at a dive review meeting. *Just hope it's going well; we can't afford any more hiccups on this one, there's too much at stake.*

6.30 didn't arrive soon enough for Amos, or Ingrid for that matter, as they were both hungry having missed lunch.

Amos sat down and waited in the reception area and started looking at the leaflet he picked up yesterday, *Your Planet Needs You,* and moved on to some old magazines from the table: *Deep Sea Fishing* dated August 1996, 1987, 1988. *That's almost before I was born!* he joked to himself. *Scottish Wildlife,* March 2008; *Mmm... well, that's a bit more recent.* The picture on the cover showed a seal soaked in oil and the caption, *What are we going to do about it?*

Oil and Gas Journal, July 2019. Amos had read these before but never in much detail.

He threw the magazine back down on the table and picked up the *Scottish Wildlife* magazine to find out what it said about what we were going to do about it. *Page seventeen... Here we go... Mmm, interesting... Point one: no more oil extraction... not sure that would go down well in congress.*

"Hello."

"Oh... hi there," replied Amos.

"I see you are reading a wildlife magazine; have I converted you?"

"No, no, well, I just... well." He put the magazine down.

"It's OK... I joke. But you should think seriously about it. Let us go. I chose a pub close that we can walk to for about five minutes at most so that we can eat soons as I am very hungry."

"Yeah. Me too."

They wrapped themselves well in their coats, scarves, gloves and hats and exited the hospital.

As they left the hospital, heading for the pub, Amos noticed that Ingrid had made a lot of effort. She had put a slight bit of make-up on, although to be honest she didn't need to, and was dressed very smartly. *Puts me to shame, and... Wow... a subtle perfume... honey, perhaps?* Amos couldn't quite make it out, but it did smell nice.

"It's just a short walk now." Amos lost his footing slightly on the icy footpath and Ingrid grabbed his arm to steady him and then let go.

"Thanks, it's tricky in places along here."

He didn't say anything further but it suddenly dawned on him that they were going to where Bill had taken him last night. Ingrid pushed open the door to the pub and the level of conversation quietened for a while as they recognised who it was, and then picked up again. Amos noticed again the dank smell of peat on a fire and the extreme glow and warmth it gave off. He immediately saw one of the ladies at the bar from yesterday and she gave him a smile and nod.

"Hello, Ingrid, nice to see you. How are you?" said Karina, the barmaid that he recognised from yesterday. "I see you've brought our visitor back again; cannae keep you away, laddie, can we?" she joked. Ingrid glanced at Amos.

"I find a table and then we can order food. OK?"

"Yeah, yeah, that'll be perfect." They shuffled their way past the bar area.

"Here we are; here, this will be nice," said Ingrid. "I am going to drink a beer. Would you like one?"

"Yes please – Okkara Gull," replied Amos in a confident manner.

"Ah, of course you already know the beer."

"Well, I…" Amos was now extremely embarrassed at having been caught out.

"Of course you have a drink with Bill… against doctor's orders. But now, you may have a drink… on doctor's orders."

"Thank you," replied Amos rather sheepishly.

Amos removed his coat and Ingrid returned shortly with the menus.

"I already know what I have… the peppered salmon, but you might want differently?"

"Yeah, OK, I'm good with that. If that's what you are having, it must be good for you; my mouth's watering already."

She placed the food orders up at the bar and returned with two large beers.

"*Skål.*" She clunked glasses with Amos.

"Cheers."

They were looking around at the people in the pub. "Did you know that the peoples here are one of the biggest drinkers in the world? And my country Denmark has some of the highest levels of smoking?"

Amos looked around and, yes, the pub was very busy for a Wednesday evening, as it had been the previous evening with the number of people with large drinks in their hands and smoking.

"And did you know that both male and female cancer rates are some of the highest in the world here?"

"Er... No, I didn't," he said, taking a sip of beer. "This is very nice, thank you." There was silence in their conversation for a while. Ingrid broke the silence.

"Have you heard of David Attenborough? He is like the elder spokesman for our planet."

Amos nodded.

"And also Greta Thunberg, the young schoolgirl behind a lot of climate protests since 2019? She is awakening everyone and brave to speak out for someone so young. But is anyone listening to her?"

"I haven't heard of her, no."

Ingrid gave him a questioning look.

"So how did you manage to get the job for the NOO?"

"Well, I had started my distance learning degree and they needed someone to check the old weather stations... It was perfect for my dissertation."

"And you send the hard copies every day to the professor?"

"No, not every day, maybe weekly from the different stations. He asks that I send him only when there is a change so I check the printouts and highlight the changes. There are sometimes lots; it varies throughout the year with the different seasons. So then I send him a summary of changes and he does the rest."

"Which is?"

"I don't know if maybe he collates summaries or analysis; he has data from the other weather stations in Norway and Iceland."

"Surely they do all of this by computer and satellite?"

"Yes, but as I said before it is not accurate enough. Anyway, I must go to the bathroom, please excuse me." Ingrid got up and left the table.

Whilst waiting for Ingrid to return, Amos overheard a conversation behind him about Ingrid and her persistence with green and environmental issues and her interfering with local traditions.

The conversation was then directed to Amos. "Do you know she's interfering with our traditions and culture, trying to be an eco warrior… The yearly Grindadráp is for us and not to be interfered with. She is a pest, you know; we have been doing it for hundreds of years. The dolphins come back every year. What is the problem with her?" said the local.

Amos responded by saying he understood the man's comments so as not to make a scene. But actually he agreed with Ingrid. On Ingrid's return, the locals moved up to the bar, away from them both. Ingrid noticed and looked back at them to see them grinning and drinking. She turned back towards Amos.

"Everything OK?" she asked with a bemused look on her face and a glance back at the bar area, where the men raised their glasses to Ingrid.

"Yeah, fine."

"No food yet?"

"I've eaten it… Joke."

"Ha. In the bathroom, the soap, it is in plastic containers to push down; it is crazy. I have spoken to them here but still they use them. There are a lot of things that are wrong for the planet, like the constant production of plastic bottles… and why not reuse or use glass or plant-based containers. Encourage the return of bottles instead of a waste mountain; it is all so simple."

"Yeah, good point; you know what? I heard somewhere that scientists have discovered a bacterium that eats plastic."

"That is good… But what about the by-product? Do we know that? We must fight against plastic production as well as pollution. The sea is poisoned; we see bottles and plastic bags but the small pieces we don't see are also a very big problem. If a fish you eat and is caught in the sea has eaten small pieces of plastic, which it does, and then is cooked, then you are eating cooked plastic. Nice, yes? And… In 2020 we decide to try to clean up the sea; it is pathetic. A ship – yes, just one ship – is sent from San Francisco to collect plastic in the Pacific Ocean; nice thoughts. But it will need many, many, many boats to do it. In 2022 it will be a hundred years of

World Ocean Days on 8 June. We've just filled the sea with plastic and rubbish; no wonder sea level is rising. It's embarrassing. There are hundreds of square miles of floating plastic in the middle of our oceans; we have massive industrial trawlers catching fish – they should be used to collect plastic as well. We need a navy of these ships, and now."

"Yeah. You're right there as well."

"And with waste, we make so much of it. Why do countries send waste to other countries to dispose of it? It's ridiculous and stupid. It's very simple… each country must keep their own waste and dispose of it ethically and in a responsible way. All governments know the reality of what is happening but they choose to ignore it and the implications… like children in a playground that won't do what's required of them until it's too late and they have to experience it first. And then… it's too late for all of us."

Amos nodded and realised that he would have to be in listening mode this evening.

"Have you heard of the Citarum River? It's in Indonesia. It's the most polluted river on the planet… they dispose of nearly twenty thousand tonnes of waste and over two hundred and fifty thousand tonnes of water every day, with some two thousand industrial sites along its banks throwing in waste such as mercury, arsenic, lead, rubber and plastic by-products. We must as individuals and countries reduce our waste and carbon footprint and become carbon neutral. We must plant trees, lots and lots of them – they love carbon dioxide – and do not allow any trees to be cut down until we know we have better control… They are our lungs. How would you feel if you only have one lung when you are used to two lungs when running a marathon? Well?"

Mmm, thought Amos, *another valid point.* He nodded.

"Am I boring you?"

"No… no, it's all very interesting…"

"Do you know that the top twenty companies are behind upwards of 33 percent of all carbon emissions… that's 33 per cent… and guess what." She sat back in her chair. "The majority are oil firms."

"Mmm." Amos took another mouthful of beer and contemplated a response.

"Have you heard of A-68?" Ingrid leant forward again towards Amos.

"It's a road in England; I saw it on a map a couple of days ago and—" said Amos with a wry smile.

Ingrid sharply interrupted, "I am being serious... don't make fun of me."

"Hey, I'm sorry, I'm sorry." He lifted his hand slightly.

"The A-68... It's an iceberg in Antarctica, and you know? It is 2,239 square miles and upwards of six hundred feet thick. Its area is four times bigger than Greater London, than New York... four times! And floating in the sea, and now melting, all because we are greedy. And the Thwaites Glacier, or Doomsday Glacier as it is also called... it is the size of the UK, yes, and melting fast. We have big problems and peoples just ignore. The seawater temperatures have increased and are melting the underside of the big ice sheets and glaciers and they are melting faster than predicted. Since 1993 we have used satellites to check sea levels and they have increased on average by three point three millimetres per year, but the last five years the average is five millimetres per year. It is accelerating. Amos you work it out. Let me read you something..."

Her hand went into her bag and she pulled out a file and opened it out on the table. Amos took another sip of beer.

"You don't believe me? Hey? Well? Now you listen, please: successive reports by the Intergovernmental Panel on Climate Change have evaluated the causes of climate change and that the 1.5 per cent temperature increase over the last fifty years is almost entirely down to human behaviours and *not* due to natural causes. And for your information, El Niño and La Niña fall into the category of climate variability, *not* climate change. Natural increase and decrease in volcanic activity and solar radiation occurs every eleven or so years and this can vary the earth's global temperature by 0.2 per cent. Global temperatures are currently increasing by 0.2 per cent every ten years because of the increased concentration in greenhouse gases... the oceans are warming faster and expanding as they naturally absorb the extra heat, hence the steep decrease in Arctic summer sea ice. This in turn will cause flooding and affect the Arctic ecosystems. Multiple lines of evidence using different lines of scientific calculation show that the steep increases in carbon dioxide and methane are caused by humans... burning fossil fuel, cement production and usage, deforestation and cattle. Most of us from one day to the next, one month to the next, will not notice the difference. Key to minimising the impacts of climate hazards is climate adaption... But this is just another excuse and will not solve the problem. We are still accelerating the problem... *key* is actually reversing the trend before it's too late." Ingrid's fist hit the table.

"Two salmon?" Karina placed them in front of each of them.

"Thank you," replied Amos.

"Enjoy." She looked at Amos with an enquiring look, smiled and shook her head, which Amos read as a *Be careful; do you know what you are doing? You are playing with fire.*

"You have some very strong views, Ingrid, and so much knowledge, but I can't see how this reverse you talk about is gonna be achieved?"

"You can start, Amos, in all the things that you do." Ingrid continued, "And again, you know that the earth's thermostat for carbon dioxide concentrations in the atmosphere is now over four hundred and fifteen parts per million and rising by two to three parts per million every year... It might not mean anything to you, but we are now reaching levels in the atmosphere not experienced for over one million years! Some countries are trying very hard and in 2019 even small countries like the UK have gone weeks without burning any coal for energy. It is possible, and then they have 40 per cent of their electricity now from renewable sources... that is good, but you must then have to compare that with the amount of products the country imports. The UK emissions produced by imported goods are up by 36 per cent. This means we all have to work harder."

Ingrid sat back in her chair and paused for breath. Amos didn't respond to her and was distracted by laughter from the bar area.

"Even the biggest fossil fuel funder stated in a report that in 2020, climate change could end human life as we know it. We must stop using fossil fuels; we have our sun, wind and water. They all give us *clean* energy, and it is free energy. And then we have Amazon. Yes… one of the biggest companies in the world saying they will invest ten billion dollars into climate change initiatives. That means nothing; it really is the tip of the iceberg. When will they and how, when they continue to be delivering parcels wrapped up in two, three, five wrappings so that when the driver throws it onto someone's front garden it doesn't break? Prove it, Amazon. Companies say these things to keep their shareholders happy. All governments need to police these statements and have controls in place to achieve promises that they are making. There is listening happening but at least now some countries have woken up and are making statements and taking action."

"I think I'm gonna start, Ingrid." Amos picked up his knife and fork.

Ingrid continued. "We can do it if we all work together instead of as individual peoples and countries. We have done it before and we must do it again. The Montreal Protocol – you have heard of it?"

Amos shook his head as he had a mouthful of food.

"Well, it was an agreement in 1987 where all governments would work together to repair the gap in the ozone layer. You know, it protects us or, how you say, er… shields us from harmful rays from the sun. So what did they do? They banned the use of chlorofluorocarbons, CFCs to you… the liquid they used to use in refrigerators and, guess what? Since 2000, the ozone layer has started to repair itself and close up by between 1 per cent to 3 per cent each year… It is healing," Ingrid said with a satisfied smile on her face. "But we now have a similar problem with the ozone in the North Pole that scientists relate to the changing position of the winds, which are affected by warmer seas and oceans." She took a gulp of beer, but it didn't stop her talking. "And what is very interesting is that scientists have noticed that the jet stream that was slowly moving towards the South Pole is now slowly moving northwards again and it is related to the ozone healing. So this might mean that temperatures can come back down again in the South Pole and slow down the melting. So working together can be done."

Amos nodded again whilst eating his salmon.

Ingrid lifted her fork and took a piece of fish. She did like speaking with her mouth full; Amos was glad that at least it wasn't beer.

"Do you know the environmental impact of eating red meat? Well? You should."

Amos was gobsmacked by all these facts. He thought to himself, *And I'm eating fish, anyhow.*

"You should look it up," said Ingrid, taking another mouthful of beer. He realised that he would soon need another beer.

"At the G8 meeting in 2020 – eight supposedly leading and 'intelligent' industrialised nations – they meet to discuss global issues and agree on a timetable for implementing key measures to reduce global warming. And even now it's being ignored and people just sit and nod their heads at meetings. Where is the action? It is all so slow. New Zealand says it will be carbon neutral by 2025 and China says it will be carbon neutral by 2060. It is a big challenge for all of us, but it should be much, much sooner. Carbon neutral is just not good enough; we have to achieve better than that, as we need to recover and reduce our impact. Each year we have the United Nations COP meetings about the environment, they have been going on now for over twenty-five years and what are they doing? Hey? I hopes it is not just more words from these countries and they will make the actions needed and soon."

Ingrid's fork then lifted a piece of fish off her plate, but there it remained in mid-air, waving around as she spoke.

"Oh yes, and another thing... some peoples they think they can change the weather's air content by 'geo-engineering'... It's a crazy idea; we mess up the seasons. This is not an experiment in the classroom. This is real life and we have one chance and we are messing it up. The politicians of all countries need to stand up and be counted. What have each of them actually done?"

Amos realised she was getting very heated and tried to calm her down by lifting his hand off the table and facing his palm towards her.

"Hold on, and wait a little and calm down. I understand—"

"No, now you listen; we will all be tracked for carbon dioxide emissions in the very near future with everything we do and buy... It will be a very, very good thing... Even the beers you drink... Ha... That made you and all the people here think," said Ingrid, now laughing. "Most countries do not have realistic carbon dioxide targets. In Denmark we have food labelling that tells us the carbon impact of the product; we are already managing the change that must happen. Most companies or firms throughout the world have no carbon dioxide reduction targets... yet most of the bigger companies, over 80 per cent of them, see climate change as a big risk. And only one in three firms have climate goals set beyond 2025... Uber, you know."

Amos nodded.

"They say they will have zero emissions by maybe 2040 but why not now and only use electric vehicles? For some companies like Facebook and Google it is easy to say 'we are carbon neutral' – that's because their business is computers. Carbon neutral is the minimum that they should achieve, as I say before. All business and countries need to go beyond that and give something back as we have had fifty years of planet abuse. We now need fifty years of caring for our planet and giving back. It will hurt big business and countries but they and we need to do this. If only 0.5 per cent of GDP is allocated to achieving carbon neutral, we will have made progress. It is very little."

"Do you think, Ingrid, that all these firms and countries know something we don't? Does it all end in 2026 and New Zealand the only ones who made an effort?" replied Amos.

"You are in the oil industry, producing all this... all this... dirty energy. You think it's just oil you produce? Well, it's not... it's plastic bottles, plastic bags, plastic trays and plastic clothes everywhere and in the bottom of the ocean and in our food... what next? Plastic clothes are very bad. Just one fleece can release hundreds of thousands of microplastic fibres in the sea, and then guess what? It's on our plate and we eat it. What is sad for me is that Norway, one of our nearest countries, was just a few years ago voted the second most eco-friendly country in the world but what does it do in 2020? It has an eighty-seven-mile pipeline across the North Sea to the Johan Sverdrup oil field that will produce 0.5 per cent of all the world's oil. It is double standards. We all have a responsibility and shouldn't just shrug our shoulders and shy away from it." She sat back in her chair and ate the fish on the end of her fork, followed by a mouthful of beer.

"I think you are right, Ingrid, but—"

"I know I'm right and—"

"Hey, come on, let me speak now. I check oil rig and platform stanchions; I don't produce any oil."

"But you are part of it... wake up, Amos, and take a stand. Listen to me: you are part of it. Every individual and every company and country must think GREEN and not greed... There's only one letter difference but it makes such a massive difference. There are people out there," she said, pointing all around her, "that care and want to make a change. Have a look at some weekly reports and podcasts produced by enlightened people – like Curious Earth and Greenpeace – on the subject and then you will understand. It takes just five minutes... a reminder each day, each week. How do you get to work or buy your shopping?"

"I drive my car and—"

"Precisely. Why not cycle, walk, catch a train?"

"Yeah, you're probably right."

"I am right, Amos; it's easy. Just change your mindset and habits; everyone must change. As I say, 'Think green, not greed and make green the norm.' In Denmark the government has a cycle plan... for the whole country; yes, not just your local street – the complete area. We already have over seven thousand, five hundred miles of cycleways. We are also already planning for sea level increases as our country is quite low; we plant along our coastline to protect the land."

Amos felt he needed to try again to change the subject as this wasn't quite what he had expected from a quiet drink and meal with a pretty lady.

"Tell me something, Ingrid; I thought that Danish people were the happiest in the world."

Ingrid stopped her rant and the colour in her cheeks returned from red to a light pink.

After taking a deep breath and in a calm voice, she responded.

"Scandinavian or Nordic countries are consistently the happiest, most of the times, and I am generally happy. I have a good work-life-relax balance... and people who are happy are more efficient. My work for the NOO is free, it makes me feel good and I enjoy it. In the mornings I do tai chi whatever the weather. We Danes are happy people and try to live healthy lives... but what we are all doing in all countries to the environment must stop; we are slowly killing ourselves and the future of the planet. In Denmark we have a good open government and are trying very hard to help; we produce over 40 per cent of our energy from wind farms, simple, and will be reducing our carbon emissions by more than 40 per cent in 2020." She paused for a few moments.

"The earth is fighting back, you know... the Coronavirus, it means we all stay at home for a while and guess what... the air quality everywhere in the world is better. That says something, doesn't it. The people that have unfortunately died from the virus have helped countries realise the impacts we have on the environment; they have not died in vain, and this will help the planet start to breathe again and rejuvenate, as long as we recognise this and act on it. But we are playing at being ignorant... we need to have strict controls, at least until the carbon dioxide levels are under control at an acceptable and then reducing levels. But a problem now is that countries suspend 'environmental standards' in order to accelerate 'economic growth recovery'. We can't keep swapping from one to the other all the time when it suits us. Make carbon dioxide reduction the target in everything we do... Not just dollars all the time. Before World War Two, carbon dioxide levels were generally OK... there was a slight jump between 1940 to 1945 and then to the mid-1980s generally level, but since then the increase, it has been exponential. The earth's air temperature is increasing so rapidly it is affecting the land and melting the permafrost – do you know what that does?"

"No…" Amos continued to eat his meal – by himself.

"It is melting the permafrost, hundreds and hundreds of square miles of frozen ground, and it is releasing methane. Parts of the Siberian Sea are bubbling with methane… it is a vicious circle we are in now and scientists have calculated that a one degree increase in global temperature will result in a 20 per cent increase in methane emissions, and as a greenhouse gas it traps 23 per cent more heat than carbon dioxide. That is on top of the methane produced by cattle, which is 80 percent more dangerous to our climate than carbon dioxide. Did you know that methane levels reached an all-time high in 2020? It has to stop."

Ingrid took a deep breath and then a sip of drink and tried to calm herself down again, waving her hand in front of her face.

"And… I have to say this also… what will you do when all the ice on earth melts? Well…"

Ingrid took a breath. Amos was glad she did.

"Well? Sea level would rise by over sixty metres, yes… and the melting is accelerating and happening quicker and quicker and quicker every year. You know who I blame? The oil companies again, and so much burning of coal and gas when we all know it is wrong. The Western world, in particular the USA, Europe and Russia and China, all need to wake up… *now.*"

"Hey, hey, hey, come on now," said Amos, trying to calm Ingrid down. The locals were staring and laughing at the pair of them. "Don't start blaming until you know the facts…"

"These are the facts, Amos, what I have been telling you and others. You have not been listening… ice sheets melting, plastic everywhere, seas polluted, our air and food polluted, birds dying, fish stocks depleting, sea temperatures increasing and coral being bleached year after year. The issue is also not just climate change but also other things… like turtles now more female than males! Temperatures rising, with every one degree Celsius increase in temperatures, air holds an extra 7 per cent more moisture – yes,

7 per cent… and this explains why we have had the wettest last twelve months since records began. My studies have clearly shown that what will be the biggest problem will be not just a few degrees here and there and more rain, but as I say before, the seasons. We will not have any. We must wake up, Amos! You must wake up! We are now the sleeping ignorant dinosaurs, and look what happened to them… It will be a mess with all countries having floods or heat waves. When do you think crops can grow? There will be no spring, summer, autumn, winter… just weather and with no seasons, you are right: no food."

"I just think," said Amos, "that a lot of this is related to the natural earth's cycle of warming and cooling… The earth's natural rhythmic cycle."

Ingrid sat up sternly in her chair and folded her arms in astonishment. "This is your big excuse: blame it on something else, so that you don't have to do anything about it, blame our planet earth… you ignore your responsibilities to our planet; you have no environmental values, do you? I say again so you listen: you work in the oil industry and you are part of it and you are guilty."

"Hey, hey… I work in it to feed my family."

"Well, do something positive about it so your children can feed their children. We are now living in the warmest period of our planet for thousands of years, maybe four hundred thousand. The melting of the Greenland ice cap is happening faster and it is next door to us; we have experiences throughout the world of extreme weather, records being broken… the climate change impacts are already here and we are pretending to be blind."

Having hardly started her meal, Ingrid threw her knife and fork down onto the table. Amos realised he was now in deep water here. She continued.

"We are so intelligent but we have tunnel vision and have no environmental thoughts in what we do. We are inept." She stopped talking, exhausted and sat back in her chair.

A series of raucous laughter from up at the bar signified that the locals were enjoying the tirade.

"These people here are ignorant." Ingrid waved the back of her hand at them.

"But they have an opinion, just as you have," replied Amos; he couldn't help himself.

"But they are not listening; they just live from day to day... No thinking. You know that pollution from energy production is the biggest problem here; the facts are right in front of you and they and everyone are ignoring and saying things they don't mean. Doesn't the fact that over 10 per cent of the species on earth are at the risk of extinction say something to you? Thank you, human race." She stuffed the piece of fish that had got very cold and dry at the end of her fork into her mouth and sat back again in her chair. "Are you paying attention to all of this? I don't think you are."

Amos didn't know how to respond to the tirade of information and her frustration. He just looked back at Ingrid, chewing a mouthful of salmon. She threw her fork onto the plate in front of her.

"Argh... Am I just a theatre production that you can all laugh at? I am just talking to myself, aren't I, no one listening?" she said, gesticulating with her hands to the people around her.

Ingrid stood up abruptly, scraping her chair on the floor, put her coat and scarf roughly around her head and left to jeers from a group of men at the bar. Amos took a final mouthful of salmon, finished his beer, picked up his coat and followed her out to more banter from a group of locals drinking at the bar.

Amos caught up with her and they walked back in silence to the hospital with just a "good night" from Amos.

Amos entered the hospital and Ingrid drove away.

Amos was greeted by Mary on reception.

"Is the doctor with you, Amos?"

"No, Mary, she's gone. Why?"

"Well, she's had another call from a Professor Hargreaves in London – something about information needed urgently from a weather station."

"Oh yes, she did pick up some papers and Ingrid – I mean Dr Svensen – has them in her car."

"Oh good. Well, it will have to wait until tomorrow then. Amos, she may be very nice, laddie, the doctor, but you can't keep making a habit of getting in late, Mr Amos; I've got a home to get to as well, and I'm not going to be late again. Good night, Mr Amos." And she exited the hospital reception.

CHAPTER 10: FISHERMAN'S COTTAGE

The following morning, Amos woke in his hospital bed with a thumping headache. He wasn't sure if it was the result of the heated conversations with Ingrid yesterday evening at the pub, or the one and a half glasses of Okkara Gull. Perhaps it was his concussion kicking in. Whichever one it was, it was making his head hurt. You know, like one of those that thump every time you move your head and you try to keep your eyes closed to overcome it.

Amos caught a glimpse of a breakfast tray on a trolley being delivered to one of the patients on the ward. He decided to skip breakfast and take a shower. He got dressed and made his way towards the canteen past the reception. Mary was on reception duty again and saw that he was looking worse for wear.

"Morning, Amos, laddie, and how are you this morning? How was your meal out – what did you have? And how's that wee head of yours, as you are looking rather poorly this morning?"

Amos didn't want to respond to any of the questioning but felt he should out of courtesy to Mary.

"Thank you, Mary, yeah… I have a thumping headache… Not sure where it's from. I only had a few drinks."

"Well, I think it's all those late nights you've been having and you're not used to the drink. It can be a strong drop of beer, that one. I'd have a word with the doctor when she does her ward round later as it might be something more serious than just a hangover."

The phone at reception rang. "Good morning, Klaksvík Hospital, Mary speaking – how can I help you?"

Amos made his way round to the canteen and stood in front of the kitchen assistant trying to make his mind up as he needed something to eat.

"Toast looks OK; perhaps I'll have something after all, and a coffee, please, and make that a strong one, thank you."

He returned to the ward via reception, Mary acknowledging him but busy on the phone still. *Tough job when the phone keeps ringing and people come up to you all the time; never a moment's peace and you can't even get yourself a drink.*

Amos sat on the chair next to his bed and ate his toast and drank his coffee.

A nurse that he hadn't seen before entered the ward, followed shortly after by Ingrid. They came over to him first.

"Morning, Ingrid – I mean Dr Svensen, sorry."

"Good morning. How are you this morning and how's that arm of yours?"

"It feels good, thanks."

"Well, we're going to take another look just to make sure it's all holding together nicely and the infection has gone."

Amos, being used to the routine, removed his shirt and the nurse removed the bandages very efficiently. Amos was impressed. He saw her tag: *Student Nurse Agnes McTavish.* Ingrid took a look and prodded the wound in a few places.

"That is good now; Nurse, please redress the wound. Your head, how is this today? Mary tells me you have a headache."

"Er, yeah, I had a couple of words with her and..."

"Where does it hurt?"

"Mainly above my eyes; it's almost as if I've spent too long in front of a laptop and my eyes are sore and the pain has spread to my forehead."

Ingrid took a hold of his head and looked into his eyes.

"Looks left, right, down, up. That looks OK, but you must be careful and we have another scan for you tomorrow morning. Then we know if you can go."

Amos decided he was not going to moan and complain but to go with the flow; what will be will be.

The doctor moved on and left the nurse to complete the rebandaging.

"Thank you," said Amos.

"That's alright; it's only my second week on the wards," she replied in a quiet, whispery voice which took Amos by surprise. He was expecting a much sharper reply for some reason; maybe her name tag?

"Well, you're pretty good at the bandages, thank you."

Amos put his shirt back on, slightly less awkwardly than a few days ago. Amos settled down on his bed again to finish off his breakfast and then decided to read his book. He was disturbed moments after picking up his book by a voice.

"Hello." It was Ingrid. She was by herself and looking rather glum. "I am sorry about last evening. I lost my temper and with all the people looking at us I had to leave otherwise I would have screamed at them."

"Hey, that's fine, no problem, no apology needed and I understand your passion about life and taking care of the environment... there's no issue."

"Thank you," she said rather tentatively and went to leave the ward. She then stopped and stood still for a while, turned around and walked back to Amos.

"Perhaps maybe if you want to visit another part of the island it will stop your boredom. The professor at the university who keeps leaving messages, he wants me to collect and print out papers from another weather station. It's on one of the other islands called Viðoy. It's in the northernmost part of Faroe and about fifty minutes, maybe an hour depending on the weathers. I can't say if you will be able to see much as it's another cloudy, foggy day but we might be lucky to see somethings like—"

"Yes, I'd like that," Amos interrupted her. "Oh and by the way I informed Mary that you had picked up papers yesterday and that they were in your car as the professor had asked her where you were."

"Thank you. When I finish today, I can be available from maybe eleven o'clock. So perhaps..."

"Yeah, I'll be waiting in reception; I've nothing else to do."

Ingrid left the ward with an uplifted skip in her step, relieved she had been able to apologise for being rude to Amos yesterday evening.

Amos started to settle down on his bed to read, then realised he hadn't spoken to Jack, or Bernie for that matter. *Damn... I'm gonna get a telling-off... probably from both of them. Heck... It's what, six, seven-hour difference? Damn... can't ring Bernie and the kids; that'll have to wait. Jack, what's the time? 9.45 – damn, he's gonna be diving, weather permitting.* Amos stood up, now feeling guilty that he hadn't called either of them and made to go to reception when Mary came towards him.

"I have a message for you from someone called Jack?"

"Oh yes, thank you, Mary, that's what I needed; Jack's my business partner. He's up on the rig right now, where I got hurt."

"He left a voicemail message last night saying all OK and then the message machine rang off. I think it must have got full overnight as I've had an extremely busy morning. There were a lot of messages for Dr Svensen from a Professor Hargreaves in London that she works for; he must want something important if he's that insistent on ringing."

"Mary, that's kind of you, thank you very much. I was just on my way to see you and ask if I could give him a call. The professor must have left so many messages; that's why Jack couldn't finish his call. Oh well, at least he said it was all OK."

That's a relief, thought Amos, *and one problem out of the way for the time being. I just need to make sure I call Bernie this afternoon and to get off this island and back to work.*

Amos settled down on the ward to read his book. He very rarely read unless it was something to do with his work, but was finding this book an interesting read. The book had been given to him by Bernie's father for his birthday last May, and it had been on the living room bookshelf picking up dust until he decided to take it on holiday to Grand Cayman, thinking he might have some time to read it. *Wow, that seems such a long time ago. How long have I been on the rig? And now here?*

Chapter 7... Here we go again.

***

The alarm by Amos's bed went off at 10.45; he had been so engrossed with his book that he had forgotten about the arrangement he had made with Ingrid. Amos made his way to the reception, sat down and waited. He didn't recognise the receptionist; it must have been Mary's break. The reception was busy with school children for some reason – probably coming in for vaccinations or maybe work experience, who knows, thought Amos, other than it was very noisy.

A voice he recognised then interrupted the constant excited nattering of the children.

"I must go to Viðoy, so I will be back at about 4.30," she said to the receptionist. She turned towards Amos. "You are ready, yes? Then we go."

"Er... Yeah, coat, jacket, hat and scarf; looking forward to it," Amos replied, picking up his clothing, and stood up.

"I promise you I will be on my best behaviour." She then turned away from Amos and left the hospital reception. Amos followed at her heels.

They set off again, at speed, in Ingrid's blue Fiat, this time in the opposite direction to yesterday's journey. They drove past the harbour area and Ingrid pointed out a few landmarks and the seafood market. They stopped off at a bakery: a quaint corner shop with a vast selection of breads and cakes. Amos was amazed by the variety available.

They picked out their bread rolls for lunch and after much deliberation decided on their choice of *snegles*, and plenty of them. Ingrid admitted that it was one of her favourite pastimes to eat them with a strong coffee with her feet up in front of a roaring fire. Ingrid had her recycled mug for her coffee and bought one for Amos as a memento.

"A gift from Faroe, as I spoil your evening." Ingrid passed the coffee over to Amos.

"Gee, thanks. You needn't have, but that's real kind of you... Thank you."

They sat for a while in the car, looking at the people passing, whilst drinking their coffees.

"So we go now to Viðoy." Amos had just finished the last drops of his coffee and Ingrid accelerated away from the bakery. The bumpy road wasn't doing Amos's head much good but he wasn't going to complain; he was out of the hospital and in good company and he just needed to get out of the confinement.

More of the same rugged and barren scenery, thought Amos, looking out through the windscreen. The wipers moved intermittently to remove the sleet. Their journey then took them across a bridge, which Amos pointed out to Ingrid that he'd seen today as he had missed seeing a bridge yesterday that she had pointed out. Then the car ran parallel with the water's edge for a while. Just glimpses of the sea and the occasional bird through the mist and low cloud… beautiful landscapes and scenery. *So few trees*, observed Amos.

"You don't have many trees here, or are there trees elsewhere on the islands?"

"No, it is too windy here and those trees that were here many years ago have been cut down. We need to be replacing them again; it helps with protection and wildlife. So I have made a start here, on the island and I have a small piece of land that I buy. I plant trees, heathers and shrubs to help and grow my own vegetables," Ingrid replied with a contented smile. "I make a beehive to help pollination."

"That's impressive."

"You know for some colder countries it is cheaper and more environmentally friendly to import fruit and vegetables than to grow it for themselves because their energy costs are so high and they use fossil fuel or nuclear energy. And our soil, yes, it is so important and did you know that it can take five hundred years for just an inch of topsoil? And that one of the most efficient food producers in the world is the Netherlands."

"You know so much. Tell me, how come you always seem so happy? Except perhaps last night. How do you do that?"

"It is how I am, and lots of people here and in Denmark and Scandinavian countries… It's in our genes," she said with a broad smile. "Did you know we have a gene called 5-HTT that is nice and long and makes us very contented and we trys to balance our life with good food, exercises and sunshine."

"But there's no sun here. When does it ever come out?" added Amos.

"We have glorious long summer days here for six months every year and then when winter is here we find some sun when we can for a while elsewhere for a few weeks. I have a winter vitamin D sun lamp that helps me through the dark months. As do a closeness of friends… and hygge."

"What's that? You have a mind of information."

"It is basically staying in when it's dark and cold, and then keeping warm with friends and family. It is easy for us here."

"So how many islands have you got here in Faroe?"

"I think maybe there are about eighteen main islands and lots of small uninhabited islands and rocks. The island we go to now is Viðoy – it is one of the most northern – and Klaksvík, where we come from, is on Borðoy. We have a saying here: 'if you don't like the weather, wait ten minutes and it will change for you.'"

Amos reflected on her comment and thought, *Why then has it been so cold and foggy for the last few days?*

"I know English is widely spoken but is there a particular language that's spoken here?"

"We are part of Denmark so some people speak Danish but our main language here is Faroese. It is a mixture of Icelandic, Danish and Olde Norse. Yes, the Vikings."

They continued to run along the coast for a few more miles. "You know I say all these things that are a problem, but it is not all bad news; there are some peoples are making a big effort like Costa Rica. Their country was covered by over 75 per cent rainforest which they had cut down to only 25 per cent, but in twenty-five years now they have protected and planted trees and the country is covered by over 50 per cent rainforest. It is good, yes?"

Amos nodded, contemplating all Ingrid had said.

"New Zealand sustainably manages their coastline and oceans around them from industrialised overfishing and pollution; why can't other countries? We are getting close now, yes and we are soon here." Ingrid slowed the car and changed down a gear to turn into a small car park up on the right. Amos looked outside to the grey mist; *just like on the rig,* he thought to himself. There were a few houses he could just about make out scattered around toward the sea but nothing much else. They looked like smallholdings or shepherds' houses.

"So, we are here in Viðareiði. As I say before, it is not very exciting yet but we will see."

"No, that's fine; it's very different from what I am used to."

"We must now walk for some minutes so we wrap up well when we leave the car as it can be very cold up here. We follow the footpath and you can see in a minute over the brow of the hill the weather station. It used to be a fisherman's cottage as it is close to a small cove. You will see, maybe later."

With intermittent flurries of snow swirling around them, they reached the cottage. Ingrid unlocked and they entered, glad to get away from the bitterly cold wind.

"Ay ya ya ya ya," she said out loud. "It is cold in here; fire on straight away, please, or else we will freeze."

Ingrid threw the light switches and placed the grocery bag onto the kitchen table.

This is like the other place we went to yesterday, observed Amos, taking a look at the other rooms downstairs: a large sitting area in one, computers on tables and a lot of paper strewn on the floor in another and a small dining room off the kitchen.

"Yes, you have noticed, Amos. This cottage is similar to yesterday's but it also has school parties for climbing and sea adventures. They pay to use the facilities so it helps keep the place open and money is tight for us."

Amos saw climbing gear, rows of jackets hanging up, boots neatly arranged on shelves, dinghies, life jackets and ropes hanging up in the hall and piled up in all corners of both the sitting and computer rooms.

"You can get logs, please, from outside." Ingrid pointed to somewhere outside to the left of the front door. "And mind your head as there are some beams."

Amos searched outside and finally found the stack of logs partially covered by snow. He returned and placed them next to the fireplace to dry.

"You do realise, Ingrid, that there's not many logs left... I searched around and there were maybe only a couple more loads like this."

"We are only here for a short time, so those will be fine for this afternoon. The rest for my next visits." Ingrid got the fire going quickly.

"You are an expert at this," he said, admiring Ingrid's ability to get the fire going again so quickly.

"And you now must keep it going, please, Amos, as before. I get our *snegles* and drinks. Would you like a coffee or some of our local drinks? We have here an old Viking tea made from moss and birch leaves or a very red tea... it is called *rauðr*. They are all natural from here on the islands.'"

"Mmm. I think I will stick with what I know tastes good: the coffee, please, Ingrid. How often do you come up here? As it seems out in the wilderness."

"Maybe every two, possibly three weeks, average, to this weather station depending on the professor and also, as you have seen, the weather. This one is quite remote. Sometimes I come here for peace and quiet, relaxing and walking. You see outside the cloud is lifting a little. I think we walk before the views go. There is a cove that I will take you to. I show you. It will be beautiful down there with birds and flowers. It is maybe ten minutes' walk from here and is steep and narrow in places. You will need to choose some walking boots and a jacket. Then we go. I will get lunch together and you keep the logs on."

Amos did what he was told. Whilst Ingrid was in the kitchen, he strolled into the sitting area.

"This is just like the other station."

"Yes, yes, it is," came the reply from the kitchen.

Amos started to nose around, as he had done yesterday at the other weather station. Various monitors and equipment were sitting on a table, a light flashing on the telephone and a monitor beeping, printer trays desperate for paper and printouts littered on the floor. A coffee mug with the same oil company's logo on it that had been at the other weather station. Amos bent down and picked up a handful of papers and tried to shuffle them together into some sort of order.

After reading the headlines on a few of the sheets, he started to realise what they were showing... *Buoy 78 / 15m... Buoy 79 / 25m...* more of the same.

"Do you realise that you've got the same problem here as yesterday's weather station with printouts all over the place."

"Yes, yes, I know, I will attend to them later, so please leave them. But first we have our walk and then lunch as the weather is good for us."

Amos put the sheets he'd picked up off the floor back on the table nearest to the printer that he thought the paper had come from – guesswork from his perspective – and then went to pick out his walking gear.

Ingrid did like to speak loudly, thought Amos, maybe caused by her wanting to be heard. "So, I have made our lunch, now we can walk. Have you chosen your boots? Yes? Then you are ready. So we go." Ingrid grabbed a jacket from a peg close to the front door.

They left the cottage and followed a winding footpath that took them immediately down towards the coastline. The fog was still swirling around but it was definitely clearer.

"It is not far, but please, you must be careful; the cliffs here are dangerous."

Amos caught his first glimpse of the sea and part of the cove that they were heading towards. It was surrounded by towering cliffs with vertical faces that only sea birds would ever touch. The path became narrow, with rocks protruding across the footpath, making it hazardous to pass through.

"This is really quite dangerous," Amos called out, following Ingrid down the coastal path to the sea.

"Yes... look. Look, Amos, at the bird and its colours," called out Ingrid suddenly, pointing up to the right of Amos's shoulder.

Amos glanced up and only caught a brief glimpse as he stumbled and fell to the ground and slipped down the slope. Ingrid heard the thump on the ground and turned.

"Argh," came from Amos. He had stopped sliding down the slope. Motionless. He had landed awkwardly.

"Argh, that hurt." Amos rolled to one side, trying to carefully sit up.

"Stay still," came a cry from Ingrid lower down. She hurried back up the path to Amos and helped him sit up. She held him by the arm to support him up. Amos found his feet and noticed that when he was standing, she still held his arm… slightly longer than perhaps she ought to have and they looked into each other's eyes. They parted.

"You must be careful, Amos… it is not safe if you do not pay attention to look where you are going."

"Yeah, yeah, thank you, Ingrid, I got distracted looking for that bird. What was it? As I only caught a fleeting view; it was very colourful." Amos reflected on the brief moment their eyes connected.

"It was a puffin. We see lots of them. Now we only have a few more metres to go and the last section is very rocky and then we are down into the cove."

Amos clambered down through gaps in the rocks and onto the beach, the waves regularly climbing their way up the seashore – what there was of it. The sea was pushing into the cove and sea spray cascading off the cliff face to the right of where they were standing. Huge boulders that had fallen off the cliff face and into the sea were on the other side of the inlet.

"We are on the protected side of the prevailing sea and wind, but looking at the tide level we only have a short time here. Follow me quickly now, but be careful."

Amos followed and paid close attention. Ingrid walked towards a gap in the cliff face, turning her torch on; they squeezed through the gap. Once they were through, the space opened up into a high cavern.

"Wow, how did you find this? It's fantastic."

"When I came here first for my work and didn't know anyone. So I used to go for long walks. I met an elderly shepherd and he showed me along the cliffs and seashore. There are nooks and caves all along the coastline here. We also must be careful with the tides – they come in quickly."

"This is quite something." Amos looked around. The rocks and sand were strewn with pieces of wood and fishing line. In the far corner there were piles of wet seaweed, a sign that the sea entered the cave regularly.

"It is only a short time that we are here, but we go now to be careful." They turned and squeezed out of the cave and onto the shore of the cove. Ingrid was right, the sea was coming in quickly. They headed back up the cliff path, watching the fog rolling in again off the sea, their faces receiving a continuous cold buffeting of wind.

"We go back for our lunch," shouted Ingrid, "as it is getting not so good."

They made their way back up the path to the cottage, Amos treading carefully around the rock that tripped him earlier and thankful of reaching the safety and comfort of the cottage, the fire still going. Ingrid immediately added logs and then walked into the kitchen with a slight skip in her stride. She shortly returned with two plates of food, passing one to Amos.

"Now we sit and have our lunch." She sat in an easy chair and relaxed next to the fire.

"This tastes good. What's in it?" asked Amos.

"Cheese and an apple chutney that I make and with the brown breads we buy earlier. You know we have so many varieties it makes it difficult to make decisions as to which one to buy, but it is fun to have choices. This one is good to eat. Yes?"

Amos was still eating by the fire when Ingrid got up and took her plate into the kitchen, then made her way to the room where all the equipment was laid out.

"I will not be too long," she called out to Amos, who was still eating his way through his lunch. *She must have given me extra as it takes a while to chew through this, or it's probably that she is very hungry as she didn't eat much last night.*

Sitting down at the desk in the dining room, she started to deal with the flashing lights one at a time. "Right, which one first?" She decided on the phone first, with an answerphone full of messages. She listened to them one at a time; they were all from the professor in London asking for her to call him. Then she called out, "Remember the fire, Amos, keep it going, thank you."

Amos added a few more logs and gave the fire a rake and then went outside to replenish the log basket. On returning he then joined Ingrid in the computer room as she was calling the professor in London.

Brr, brr... Brr, brr... Click to answerphone. "Hello, this is Professor Hargreaves, please leave your message."

"Hello, Professor, it is Ingrid Svensen here from Faroe; please ask me for information that you need. I am at the fisherman's cottage on Viðoy now." And she put the phone down. "Well... now it is me that must wait for him so that is better, yes?"

"Is this the same equipment as the other weather station?" asked Amos, having watched Ingrid whilst she was on the phone and now looking around the room again and spotting the now familiar calendars.

"Yes, it is similar, but it also deals with our air temperatures, water temperatures both at different depths in the sea and heights in the air, wind direction and speed of currents with each of the buoys. These are probably our best computers. Look, I show you." Amos pulled up a chair and sat next to her. She moved her position slightly, glancing at him briefly, smiled and looked back at the screen. Now distracted from what she was doing.

"And all these dots..." Amos pointed at the big screen in front of Ingrid.

"Yes, they are the buoys. They are like mini weather stations spread across the sea. They are around Faroe to Iceland, across to Norway and south to the Orkney Islands."

Amos noticed that there were a number flashing to the north of Faroe. The telephone rang, and interrupted their closeness.

Ingrid stretched across Amos and picked up the phone.

"Ah, Professor, how—"

The professor interrupted her straight away. He wasn't interested in pleasantries.

Amos gathered that the professor was speaking very loudly. Ingrid moved the phone away from her ear, looked to the side of her and smiled at Amos, shaking her head from side to side.

"Sounds like he is trying to shout all the way from London," said Amos, listening to the noise from the phone which Ingrid held away from her ear. She waited until the voice calmed down.

"I have been up here and at the other stations," replied Ingrid, when she got her chance.

"But you haven't replied or contacted me," said the professor.

"You know that I am not paid and do this because I want to and to help you and the university."

"Just give me the information," he replied bluntly to Ingrid.

"What does he want?" asks Amos.

Ingrid put the phone on the table and shook her head again from side to side, stood up and walked round to another screen and turned it on.

She picked the phone up again. "The computer four... It is on now, Professor." She spoke with a loud, cross tone in her voice. Amos remembered it very well as it was similar to the tone in her voice that she had had at the pub last night.

"Come on, Ingrid!" shouted the professor.

"I am, Professor, be patient! Here, I have them... which area? ... Yes... fifty-six, seventy-three, eighty-five and one hundred and nine. Yes, here."

"About time. Tell me the readings."

Ingrid duly provided him with the information he had asked for.

"Thank you." The heated telephone conversation calmed down. "Now the other screen..."

"Which one?"

"Screen two."

"Oh yes, with all the buoys on and radar..."

"Yes, shipping movements – other than the buoys, there are

some vessels on the screen… Can you see them?"

Ingrid paused for a while. "I have them…"

The telephone line cut out mid-sentence.

"It's gone dead again." She put the phone down. "Oh well, he will ring back if it's important enough."

"What was he after?"

"Something about buoys and then shipping movements."

Amos went up to the screen where Ingrid was standing showing the buoys and they saw a number of them flashing just north of Faroe. Ingrid explained the reason for the flashing: it was that the detectors on the buoys either on the surface or at various depths under the sea at that particular point had gone out of the expected range of temperature or current direction.

"Can we check earlier readings?"

"Yes. We can."

They both noticed a trend, Amos pointing at the screen. "Here… and here's another… the buoy temperatures have gone down… but by how much? And is it on the surface or at what depth below sea level?"

"I look now." Ingrid sat down at the keyboard and tapped.

Amos went to replenish the fire and returned to the computer room.

The phone rang. This time the professor managed to say something to Ingrid before the line went dead again.

"What did he say?" asked Amos.

"Something about 'lost' and 'shipping' before the line cut out again."

Amos sat down next to Ingrid and with two screens in front of them they started to compare screens, each calling off the buoy numbers and temperatures.

Amos picked up a pattern developing; he reverted back to the screen showing the shipping and they saw shapes for ships and a huge area of misty grey on the screen.

"What's that?" asked Amos. Ingrid peered over his shoulder.

"Oh, that. That is the fog… maybe. That's what appears to be causing the fall in temperatures?"

"And what are these smaller dots on the screen here… they don't seem to be the buoys. Puzzling."

Ingrid called the professor back. "Hello, Professor. Professor? Hello… I have the shipping movements for you up on the screen and…" With the telephone line breaking up, Ingrid could only leave part of a garbled telephone message. "There is a vessel travelling from east to west about three to four miles north of Faroe – the light is there and then yesterday afternoon it is disappeared and now it is gone…" Because of the poor connection, she put the phone down. "Gone again. I will send an email – argh… but no… now the computer is flickering. We must get the oil lamps and candles out and boil water before the electricity is stopped."

"Surely the equipment must have some kind of back-up?" asked Amos.

"Yes, we have a battery back-up for the equipment but it doesn't last very long."

Amos took a look out of the window. "It is getting darker outside and the snow is definitely getting heavier… Take a look."

Ingrid left her desk and opened the front door. "I think yes, maybe we must stay," said Ingrid. "But it should be OK. We have food here for a few days and the hospital knows that, from when I've been here before, when the weather is bad I stay up here." They returned to the computer room.

With the two of them engrossed in what the computer screens were showing, they had let the fire go down and almost out. Amos noticed the room getting colder and left to get the fire going again. He needed more logs so put his boots and coat on, pulled his hood over his head and set out to collect some more whilst Ingrid, who had got fed up with the computers and the professor, had decided to prepare food for their evening meal before they lost power altogether.

Gathering the logs, he thought whilst looking through the swirling snow towards the car park that he could just make out the silhouette of people. Amos blinked repeatedly as the snow was falling heavier on his face. He stared for a short while but the image was lost, hidden by the swirling snow. He entered the cottage with a basket full of logs, stamped his feet and brushed the snow off his coat.

"Woo, it's blowing snow all over the place out there. You can hardly see anything... it's just as well we are staying," he said, slamming the door shut with his foot. He put down the logs in the lounge, hung his coat up in the hall, removed his boots and returned to the computer room where Ingrid was busily working between the screens and making notes. Amos blew on his hands to warm them up.

"Brrrr. It's good to be back inside. That smells good; what is it?"

"It is a soup we have. I have had enough of this professor. He is... he is... I could scream." Ingrid threw her pen onto the table. She stood up and walked to the kitchen leaving Amos looking at the computers.

Amos followed her out, picking up the second log basket he had left in the hall, putting it down next to the fireplace to dry out. "I have made a soup, it has salmon and parsnips and maybe sometimes I add – yes, we have some. I add radish and pepper. Do you like that? Or is that maybe too hot?" came Ingrid's voice from the kitchen.

Amos poked his head around the kitchen door.

"Yeah, that sounds good. If it tastes half as good as we had at the restaurant, that would be nice, thank you." He strolled back into the lounge to feed the fire.

"The soup it is very warming, you will see, and good for you and we have some different breads so that is fine for us also."

Amos had got the fire roaring again.

"I bring the soup through; are you ready to eat?"

"Yeah, all good in here." Amos looked into the flames of the fire and pondered the situation he was in. In a cottage, alone, with not just a woman, but a beautiful ... A noise from the kitchen interrupted his thoughts.

Amos looked up. Ingrid proudly emerged from the kitchen carrying two bowls of steaming soup and placed them on the small wooden coffee table. "We have lots more if you like." Returning to the kitchen, she then brought in a huge plateful of bread and sat down.

"This is very nice," she said, sitting herself down opposite Amos and lifting her spoon to start.

Amos followed her lead after putting his nose close to the soup. It looked and smelt very nice. He looked up towards Ingrid and was about to say something.

Ratta-tat-tat.

Their expressions changed from a warmth and closeness to the look of surprise and danger. Both looked up from their food and at each other. There followed a more urgent and louder...

Ratta-tat-tat.

"Is that what I think it is?" said Amos, rather startled.

"Yes, there is someone at the door. That is strange. We have not many people here but now when it snows someone comes to visit?"

Amos put his spoon back down by his soup bowl and stood up. Picking out a good-sized log from the basket as a weapon he headed for the door.

CHAPTER 11: HYGGE

Amos stood by the front door with a piece of firewood in his hand, ready to use it if he had to. Ingrid was by his shoulder.

"*Hvem er det?*" Ingrid called out loudly in Danish.

"Who is it?"

There was no reply. Even if there were, they couldn't hear because the wind was howling outside. Pausing for a few seconds, Amos decided that he had to open the door partially to start with; as he did so, a flurry of snow blew in from the porch.

He took a deep breath, and opened the door fully.

To his utter astonishment, standing in front of him… were his wife and three children.

He lowered his hand holding the log. "What the heck are you doing up here?"

"Daddy!"

"Dad!"

His two youngest children ran and hugged Amos as he moved forward and put a hand on Robert's shoulder, then stepped forward without hesitation to give Bernie a kiss on the cheek.

"We were so worried about you, Amos," said Bernie, so pleased to see him.

Ingrid shied away from the front door and the family reunion as it had become rather too crowded for her liking.

"How did you find me and what…"

"Mrs McKinnon, the receptionist at the hospital, directed us up here to the cottage," replied Bernie. "Can we come in? We're shivering out here."

"Come in, come in," said Ingrid boldly from behind Amos. "It is too cold to be out there and please close the door."

They all squeezed into the hall and took off their shoes and coats.

"Come through into the sitting area and warm up next to the fire – let me take your coats," said Ingrid.

Bernie gave Amos a few *stand back*-ish glances as she walked through into the lounge and then looked back towards Ingrid and then to Amos.

"Is there anyone else here, Amos? It's a very small place, isn't it?" enquired Bernie.

"Er, no… we, er…"

Bernie was starting to boil, her face turning a bright red; her anger was for all to see and she seemed about to explode.

"You mean that you… that you are here by yourselves?" whispered Bernie sharply into Amos's ear trying to contain her anger, folding her arms tightly; she was never one to mince her words.

Amos looked down at Bernie very sheepishly and was about to reply when…

"Come in, please, come in; it is warmer here in the lounge by the fire." Ingrid led Bernie through to the lounge; Amos followed reluctantly at a safe distance.

The timing of Ingrid's voice and invite was perfect from Amos's point of view, as it took the steam, for a few moments anyway, out of Bernie, who Amos did not want to be alone with at the moment. He needed a few minutes to gather his thoughts and explain to her, he knew it would be tricky.

"Please, please, you all come through and close the door and get warm."

Bernie moved into the sitting room, far from happy about the situation. Her mind raced. Amos here, with a… with a woman, and not just any woman, but a… very beautiful woman… and alone. Bernie's face was a picture of thunder. Taut lips, tightly folded arms. She sat down.

Ingrid came into the room. "We have some soup and breads if you would like?"

"Yes, please, Mommy," replied Elizabeth on behalf of the family.

"It's so cold here." Henry moved from standing next to Robert by the fire to sitting on his mother's lap, rubbing his hands together and then wrapping them around Bernie, trying to warm up.

Amos needed to say something,

"Er... how come you're all here?"

"Didn't Jack tell you?" came the snappy reply from Bernie.

"Tell me what?"

"That we were coming to visit you, as we wanted to spend some time with you whilst you were recuperating from your accident in the hospital."

"Well, no... he didn't but..."

"Well, he said he would, and anyhow, what are you doing up here? It's so isolated and there's so much snow out there. We just hoped that this was the place, otherwise I just don't know what we would have done. Robert here a few minutes ago saw someone who he thought was you and called out but you obviously didn't hear," said Bernie, shaking her head and looking away from Amos.

"Yeah, I saw a hood blow back and saw a head that looked like yours, Dad, and then thought that this must be the right place. I called out, but it was so noisy with the wind, so I went back to Mom in the car and we decided we had better try. So glad we found you, Dad; we were getting worried," said Robert.

"Yeah, me too," replied Amos, giving Robert a hug. Elizabeth was still holding on to Amos's leg; she was obviously cold and tired as well so he lifted her up and she hugged him around his neck.

"Dad, we were worried when we heard you had had an accident and when Jack rang and told us we all agreed we wanted to come to see you straight away and then when you get better we can go back to the island holiday together," said Elizabeth.

"I spoke to Jack, Amos. He must have said something to you?"

"No, nothing. Absolutely nothing. We have had a number of calls and he was halfway through saying something a few days ago about you on our last telephone conversation, but we got cut off. The communications up here are terrible."

"I don't care about the communications, Amos. What are you doing up here, Amos?"

"I left messages for you… you must have got them?" Amos now sounded rather desperate and needed some help here.

Bernie didn't reply. She had got the messages but had been in such a rage that Amos had gone off from their family holiday that she'd decided that she would give him some of his own medicine. That was until Jack rang and spoke to her about his accident, and now this, alone here with… with…

"Well, it's a long story and—" replied Amos.

"Well, it had better be good," interrupted Bernie.

"Here is food for everyone." Ingrid came into the room with a beaming smile on her face and a tray of steaming bowls of soup and placed them on the table, then returned a few moments later with a huge pile of bread rolls.

"I hope you like? It is from Faroe and a recipe I make, so… please." She motioned with her hand to all of them to help themselves..

"Please, it is hot, so slowly, please."

"Yummy," said Elizabeth, climbing down from Amos's hold. "It does smell good."

"Mmm, nice," replied Robert. Amos smiled at the happy children. He looked across the table towards Bernie; she didn't smile back, just glanced at him briefly then looked away.

Henry had half a thumb in his mouth but still managed to speak. "I'm hungry but don't want it." His thumb returned into his mouth and he held onto Bernie with his other arm.

"It is salmon and parsnips, my own recipe. I think you might like."

Elizabeth wasn't quite sure with her trying to be a vegetarian but she did occasionally have fish at home.

"What type of fish is it?" she asked Ingrid.

"Well, it's local wild sea salmon; I only eat this fish because it's fresh and natural."

"Oh that's good – it's local. That helps, doesn't it, and fish is OK to eat sometimes?" asked Elizabeth, looking across at Robert.

"Yes," replied Ingrid. "I am what you have heard is sometimes called a pescatarian, which is where I have only vegetables and fishes."

Henry produced a questioning face of *Do I really wanna eat something called pesca... pesto... pasta thing?*

"Pescatarian," said Ingrid.

"Come on, Henry, this lady has made it specially for us," said Bernie, giving Henry a gentle nudge.

"Please call me Ingrid," she said with one of those smiley expressions, thought Bernie, that you just can't get cross with.

"Thank you... Ingrid," said Bernie, moving Henry off her lap and towards the food.

"It's really nice, Henry," said Elizabeth, devouring another spoonful. "Come on and try some."

Henry took his thumb out of his mouth and headed to the seat next to Elizabeth and pulled himself up and onto a chair; he then reached across the table and took a roll.

"Dip it in, Henry," said Robert. "Look, like this."

"And then let it cool down before you eat," said Ingrid. Henry decided to trial the soup.

Amos felt it was a good time to put a few more logs onto the fire; as he did so, Bernie turned towards him and whispered sharply in his ear again.

"What's going on here, Amos? This isn't right; you know that."

"Well, she's er... actually she's my doctor."

"Your what?" came Bernie's sharp and loud reply, sitting back in her chair. Amos winced.

"Er, yeah, she's a part-time doctor at the hospital and then on the other days she's an environmentalist."

Elizabeth overheard their conversation.

"What type of environmentalist are you, Ingrid? As I am too," asked Elizabeth.

Ingrid realised that this was a good opportunity to calm the situation down and explain, particularly to the benefit of Bernie, what she did, and why they were there.

"I have three days in the week at the hospital and then the other days I work at the weather stations around Faroe and this is one of them. I help with the Norwegian Oceanic Organisation and their recording and collection of data and analysis to help them understand the oceans and what is happening to them."

"Wow, what a cool job," said Elizabeth. "Wait till I tell my teacher when we get back home. How did you get a job like that? I would like to do that when I grow up. My teacher is keen that we all look after the planet. She says that we've gotta stop using plastic and she says you only see some of the problem as there are minute particles of plastic that we are all now eating."

"Yes, Elizabeth, you are right. Microplastics is a bigger issue. We can pick up the bigger pieces but how do you filter the small pieces out of the water?"

Robert was enjoying his soup and rolls and decided not to join the conversation just yet. Henry was starting to enjoy his soup and Bernie… she was listening intently to find any flaw in Ingrid's story from what Amos had told her.

"I was first in Denmark where I was born and at the university to be a doctor and then for the last three years I have had a job here. It is really good for me as I love nature and the environment and so this is what I do. We all need nature. I don't know for how long I am here but it is good for me and I am happy here. The peoples here on the islands, I don't always get along with so I usually keep myself to myself and they are not very concerned about nature but mostly they are very kind and friendly."

Henry took a spoonful of soup. "Mmm, I quite like this, Mom." Bernie acknowledged Henry and although she was listening intently and understood what Ingrid was saying, she was looking to catch Amos out on the explanation from him earlier and was still very much on edge about the whole situation.

"So, when I am not working at the hospital I go to the weather stations whenever I can and then send the information to the professors from the Norwegian Oceanic Organisation and go walking and climbing and see the birds and when the weathers are good I collect rubbish on the sea shores; there is so much of it every day, sometimes I have to go twice with a bag and fill it."

"She talks funny," said Henry quietly to Robert after a spoonful of soup.

"Henry, she's from Denmark, that's why, silly."

"Oh." Henry took another mouthful of soup.

"Yes, my teacher tells us to collect rubbish from the street and back home we have field trips to the beach. We went for a school outing to East Beach near Galveston to collect rubbish and then to analyse the types of rubbish but we had to wear gloves and it's difficult when you walk along the shoreline and then there are rocks as you can't get all the plastic... and there are so many pieces of fishing net."

"Yes, yes, we have that problem here also in Faroe," replied Ingrid, beaming, with excitement in her voice at finding someone who also had a passion for the environment.

Robert had finished his soup and was sitting back in his chair.

"Would you like some more, Robert?" enquired Ingrid with a smile on her face, knowing the answer would be yes.

"Er, thank you. Yes please, if there is any going?"

Ingrid left the room to go to the kitchen and brought back the saucepan with the remains of the soup and placed it in the middle of the table. Robert helped himself.

Henry finished his soup. "Mom, I'm still hungry."

"Well, you liked it after all," said Elizabeth.

"There's no more bread rolls but we have some *snegles*," replied Ingrid.

"What are *snegles*?" asked Henry.

"They are like sweet breads or cakes with, er... what is it, er... *kanel* on the top... err what is it called... cinnamon, yes, that's it, or icing on top, usually in a whirl shape, like snails, you know. I get them, yes?"

"Mom?"

"Yes, Henry."

"She's very kind, isn't she, all this food she's giving us."

"Robert, have you had enough?"

"Thanks, Dad, yes."

Ingrid returned from the kitchen with a plate piled high with *snegles*.

"Wowee, there's so many," said Henry as Ingrid placed them on the table in front of him.

"You don't have to eat all of them, Henry," said Bernie. There was a bit of humour in Bernie's voice at last, much to Amos's relief.

"Can I have one? Please," asked Henry.

"Yes. Please, here. This one is cinnamon with raisins and this is no raisins; these ones are plain. And these with snow on the top." Ingrid pointed out the swirls of icing on the cakes.

Henry's hand stretched across and picked out one with raisins in it. "Why don't we have these at home, Mom?" Ingrid shared the plate around so they each had one.

"Well, we do sometimes, Henry, it's just that you all eat them so quickly."

"I like this one as well, Henry, the same as you." Ingrid picked one from the plate and took a bite, smiled and returned to the kitchen, thinking, *Well, that'll be most of the food gone; it would be good if there were some left for breakfast.*

Amos grabbed a *snegle* off the plate before they all disappeared and offered one to Bernie… but she wasn't interested and shook her head.

"When you've finished, children, could you take your plates through to the kitchen." Elizabeth was the keenest of the children and took them through to the kitchen where Ingrid was washing up.

"Thank you, Elizabeth, you are very helpful." Ingrid continued with the washing up.

"That's alright. What do you think is the biggest problem we have now, you know with the planet?" said Elizabeth.

"Well, that is a very very big question."

"My teacher says there are too many people and we make so much pollution and don't recycle or reuse enough and that it needs to change. She says that fishermen need to respect the sea and that even marine protected areas are still being dredged in some cases, up to 90 per cent of the areas. She says that farmers should respect nature every year by not tilling their fields and using locally produced compost, and we should buy locally produced food; it's very basic, I know. What do you think?"

"Well, I think your teacher is right, there is a lot we should do and can all do."

Robert brought through some more dishes.

"Thank you, Robert."

"That's OK." And he returned to the dining area.

"Why can't everything be reused or recycled? Like plastic bottles, take-out cups and containers. I think that would be a very good way to help and it's so simple." Elizabeth was now drying up and stacking the crockery on a table.

"I think you are again right and have a good teacher at school. Here and in most Scandinavian countries, Germany and Netherlands, they recycle bottles by getting people to return them with a deposit return scheme. Why can't we do this everywhere? We go to the supermarket to buy goods and food, so why can't we return the containers and packaging when we visit the shop? Companies that make the plastic bottles, bags and containers must be in some way accountable for its environmental impact. I blame our throwaway society and lack of respect and laziness. In 2002 a very poor country, Bangladesh, banned new plastic bags and then it takes countries in the Western world over ten years to react positively and charge for bags. Did you know that the average person in Europe is responsible for one plastic bag each week that ends up in the sea and in the USA it's almost three bags every week per person. At the rate of twelve million tonnes per year into the sea. Soon there will be more plastic in the sea than fish; we're killing ourselves."

Whilst Ingrid and Elizabeth continued their conversation in the kitchen, the boys, Bernie and Amos were making themselves comfortable around the fireplace, Amos keeping himself busy, feeding the fire again, the logs rapidly diminishing.

"So what did you do after I left Grand Cayman? As I've been trying to contact you."

"We decided to go to a place called Stingray City," said Robert. "It was really cool with so many colourful fish and you could see right to the bottom."

"Yeah, Dad, you should have been there. You could touch the

stingrays; they were so big. Robert held me up in the water for a while as it was too deep sometimes and I couldn't touch the bottom. They would come right up to you and, and... You have to be careful of their tail," said Henry, motioning where there was a sting.

Amos chuckled. "Yeah... I should have been there and maybe we can go again when I'm better."

"Oh yeah," said Henry, "can we go on the same boat? As the man let me sit at the front and steer."

"Sounds like you really enjoyed yourselves."

Bernie remained silent.

"The following day, we went up to the turtle farm and saw how they move the eggs away from the edge of the water so that when they hatch the seabirds don't get them. Then they bury the eggs in the sand, put a flag in the ground with a number on it and monitor the area for when they hatch. They are so big, Dad, I never realised up close that they were that big."

"And," interrupted Henry, "when we saw the stingrays we could see one swimming towards us."

"Yeah, it was a... leatherback, one of the biggest," replied Robert.

"Yeah, the turtle farm was cool. When they hatch they put some back when they've grown and some they keep like farming which I suppose is a good way to breed them for food. Did you know how many turtles die and don't grow big? Well, it's loads of them and some eat plastic in the sea because they smell it and think it's food."

"That's terrible," said Amos.

"In the evening we spoke to Jack when we got back and he said you were OK but hurt and in hospital. We stayed in at the hotel that evening and over the meal we decided to come and see you," said Bernie. "Robert here organised the flights and connections and made a really good job of it."

Ingrid and Elizabeth then came into the room.

"Mom, I've had a really nice talk with Ingrid about what she does here and she said we could come back any time during my school holidays and that she would show us around the islands and walk down to a secret cave on the beach."

Amos was about to say that he had been there, but decided better of it as Bernie would only make more of it than it actually was and be suspicious.

"Now we have just one room for sleeping, up the stairs, but I think it is better that we all stay here as it will be warmer and we have the fire; there is no fire up the stairs. I come back in a minute."

"Nice little place here, isn't it?" said Amos. He then wished he hadn't opened his mouth.

Bernie stared at him. "And how long were you going to stay up here, Amos?"

"Well, the weather turned, and with the snow, Ingrid, not me, decided it would be safer to stay up here; we had no intention of staying but…"

Bernie shook her head and folded her arms again, turned away from Amos and didn't reply.

They could hear a lot of rummaging from upstairs followed shortly after by a thumping sound of Ingrid making her way down the staircase. She came into the room with a huge box full of blankets and clothes and placed it in the middle of the room.

"Here we have some blankets and spare clothes that might make you warm, please, for you."

At which point the phone rang. *Brr, brr… Brr, brr…*

It startled everyone.

"Oh that is good, it works for us again." Ingrid went to pick up the phone. "Hello?"

"Ingrid, Ingrid, oh thank goodness I have got through to you." It was Mary, the receptionist at the hospital. "Are you okay Ingrid?"

"Yes, Mary."

"Oh thank goodness, thank goodness. I have been so worried since we were told as i …" The line started to crackle when she was speaking to Mary. All Ingrid could then hear was the words: "… off island as…" The line went dead. She replaced the telephone.

"It is so often that this happens that we get used to it. It is not a problem; we have the Calor gas for the cooking and candles for light. Have you helped yourselves to blankets and warm clothes? It is what we do here in Faroe and Denmark when it is winter and cold."

The lights flickered on and off. Ingrid left the room and returned with some matches.

"Robert, could you go round the rooms and light the candles, thank you, as I think that maybe the electricity may cut out completely. Not all of the candles but just one in each place so that we can then light another when it's finished in the same places."

Looking around the room was a strange sight. Elizabeth was wearing a yellow jumper far too big for her and an orange bobble hat. Bernie had a multicoloured scarf around her and the boys were digging to the bottom of the box, finding and trying on different hats. Amos saw Bernie smiling at the children and caught her eye. This time there was less of a steely stare and more of contentment and satisfaction. Amos was relieved.

"This is like the fancy dress party we went to over at Ben's house, do you remember?" said Elizabeth.

"This is fun," said Henry. "You dig down and find so many different things…" He pulled out a hat and put it on.

"You look like an elf in that hat," said Elizabeth. Then she looked across at Robert. "And you look like a goblin."

"Ha ha ha," they all laughed together.

"I'm gonna get some more logs. Robert, do you wanna come with me? Then you'll know where they are when we have to get some more."

"Yeah, sure, Dad."

They left the others still rummaging in the clothes box and put on their boots and coats and went outside with the log basket, Robert still with his goblin hat on.

"Where did you get all these clothes and blankets from?" asked Bernie, now taking more of an interest.

"Oh, it is over the years here, people visit and they forget their jumpers and hats, but the blankets I have bought." Bernie and Ingrid chatted amicably together whilst Henry and Elizabeth were enjoying themselves, getting dressed up and generally messing about. It was starting to get a bit raucous.

"OK, you two," said Bernie, pulling them apart. "That's enough of that, let's settle down now."

"Yeah, that was fun," said Elizabeth.

"Yeah, we need to get a clothes box like this at home," replied Henry.

"OK, you guys, now settle down." Bernie started to prepare one of the two sofas for them and wrapped blankets on and around the sofa and the two children.

"Here," added Ingrid. "Here are two thick blankets that are good to keep you warm." She handed them to Bernie. The two children hid under the covers whilst she was tucking them up.

"Hygge," said Ingrid.

"What's that?" replied Bernie.

"Hygge; that's what we call it here when it is cold and dark and we need to keep warm. We all have hot drinks and food and it's nice by the fire. Oh, I am sorry, I must go to check on the computers for the professor."

The front door opened. "Gee, it's still snowing heavily out there. You know, I think we did the right thing to stay up here. You can't see more than a few feet in front of you and we really would have struggled driving."

"Shh," said Bernie. Amos then realised that she was trying to settle the two youngest.

Robert and Amos removed their coats and stamped their feet as quietly as they could to remove the snow. Robert's hat was coated in snow so he shook it outside and then took it into the kitchen area to dry out and returned to the clothes box to find another hat.

"Hey, the electricity has come on again; that's good," said Robert, now blowing out the candles.

"Yes but maybe for not very long, so perhaps we keep some candles going, Robert."

Amos tended to the fire, looking down at Bernie snuggling up to the two children under the blankets.

"Hygge," said Bernie looking up with a smile on her face.

"What?" replied Amos.

"Hygge; it's when everyone keeps warm in winter over here."

"Oh… good," replied Amos, not quite sure what that was all

about, and left them to it whilst placing his coat on a clothes dryer in the kitchen.

"Ingrid was telling me earlier that she thinks we have less than ten, perhaps twelve years from now to prevent the worst of climate change," said Amos to Robert.

"Yeah, I was reading about that at school last term and we ran a number of computer simulations and one of the big issues that is coming up now is that with the ice sheets at the poles melting so fast, six times quicker than forty years ago, it will cause the earth to destabilise and cause the poles to shift... They've shifted before, the earth spinning randomly for a while resulting in huge temperature variations and no seasons until it settles down again. She then said that she might be wrong and the melting may be caused by the flow underneath the earth's crust of molten iron moving slowly from the centre of the earth and the different temperatures causing a regular or cyclical heating and cooling, every five to seven thousand years. If climate change occurs at the same time as a Milankovitch cycle, that we really are in trouble"

"A what? I've never heard that before," replied Amos, rubbing the stubble on his chin in a contemplative way.

"You should be at home more, Amos," said Bernie, who had overheard their conversation.

"I have also heard about that," added Ingrid. "I believe it is nature, but also that we are affecting nature by our actions much too quickly so that species do not have time to adapt like they have been able to in the past; and we abuse the earth's resources and will soon reach a tipping point... maybe we have already. If you think we only have an atmosphere around our planet eight to ten miles up from the surface with air and after that... nothing. It's such a thin layer of life for us to breathe, when you think of the circumference of the earth as twenty-five thousand miles. The layer is so thin and we are poisoning ourselves. We are stupid. We have to control carbon dioxide and methane and nitrogen dioxide emissions," she said, raising her voice. "Oh... I'm sorry." She put her hand to her mouth. "The childrens."

Bernie replied, "It's OK."

In a quieter voice, she said, "Every people and country must take responsibility."

"That's what Mr Anderson at school says," replied Robert.

"You've got another convert here, Ingrid," Amos said, pointing and smiling towards Robert.

With the electricity back on for a while, the printers started to reel off paper again.

Amos went into the computer room followed by Robert.

"Let's see what data we've got coming through these machines this evening," said Amos, sitting down in front of a screen.

"This is really old equipment, Dad," said Robert, sitting by another of the machines.

"Yes," replied Ingrid, walking into the room, "it is, but it works, which is the most important thing and it is for the information that the professor at the university wants."

Robert bent down to pick up a handful of printouts and placed them on the table.

"What are all these showing?" asked Robert.

"These on this screen show the weather... You can see the snow or fog and other things here." Ingrid then replenished the paper in one of the printers. "On the computer screen, there. This one shows the temperatures of water and when you press up or down over a particular buoy it tells you the temperature and current at the various depths."

This interested Robert so he started pressing the mouse over the various points on the screen.

"If you expand the screen you can see past Iceland and all the way to Greenland and Canada, you see?"

"Oh yeah, this is cool."

"The machine over there does the area towards Norway and the Arctic and these two computers towards Scotland."

Amos sat in front of a computer screen and followed what Robert was doing.

"Ingrid?"

"Yes."

"What do all these different colours mean – is there a code or something?"

"It's like a traffic light system, Dad; green is OK, orange is something that has changed and red I suppose is saying that there's a problem?"

Ingrid looked across at Robert and Amos and said, "Yes, he is right; we also have another weather station professor here with us this evening." She smiled at Robert.

"So what am I looking at?" said Amos, moving the mouse over the various buoys and then going deeper or down and then up again. "I've got red then a green and then another red... very odd."

"Ah, that is three lights: the first is temperature, the second is the speed of the current and the third is direction of current."

"So it's a lot of information, but what do you do with it all?"

"Dad, I think what you have to do is read it at different levels and then pull together an overall picture of what is happening rather than just individual buoys or areas."

"Robert, you are good at this; yes. You learn at school?" said Ingrid.

"Yeah, I enjoy computer studies and maths so yeah, this is really interesting."

"What did the professor ask you earlier, Ingrid– something about a ship going missing?" asked Amos.

"Yes but he has not asked for any more information since then. Maybe he has enough now."

"I think perhaps you should call him?"

"But it is late."

"I think you should. If he wants to speak with you, he will answer it; if not, you can leave a message."

Ingrid was unsure if it was the right thing to do, and after a short while pacing up and down, picked up the phone and called. There was no reply, which she was thankful for, so she left a message to say that a ship location indicator on screen three had disappeared at 11.25 on Tuesday 11 July.

"The buoys in one area on my screen all go red from about... yeah, from about ten metres down to the lowest depth, whatever that is," said Robert out loud.

"That's fifty metres," replied Ingrid.

"The lowest… and all are red."

"Yes. The first colour is red on all of them and then on some the second colour is orange, then a red, then a green; it's a right old mixture."

"Yes. That is what we have sometimes but mostly they are not so much different colours; maybe just the green and oranges."

"But we've got quite a few red ones here as well," said Amos with concern in his voice.

"I've got the same now," added Robert.

"Let me see, please." Ingrid got up and looked at what was on Robert's and then Amos's screens. As they moved the mouse, she followed the cursor on the screen. "That is strange but it is probably OK; the professor is not asking so it must be good."

"Looking at this, Ingrid" – Amos pointed at an area on the screen – "this group of buoys here, look, it's all red at ten metres down and spread generally in this direction north to south all the way down towards… Faroe." Amos stood up and went over to Robert's screen. "What's that you've got there?" There followed a flickering on the lights.

"We are OK, we have some UPS battery system that helps this equipment whenever the power goes but not the lighting or power or phones; the batteries last about five minutes."

"This area here, Dad, is to the left of yours… up towards Greenland, but…"

"Now try here," said Amos, pointing at the screen, "and then expand it a little, Robert, that's it."

"What do you look for?" asked Ingrid.

"How far back does the computer hold information for, Ingrid?"

"Well. We have the equipment here for maybe some for twenty-five to thirty years so the information should be stored here somewhere on the computer. I don't know where else it would go other than the hard copy prints that I send to the professor every month."

"Robert, the area that you are looking at… can you see what the data was saying yesterday?"

Robert pressed a few keys and then looked up at the computer screen.

"Yeah, that seems to come up."

"And… how about a week ago, same buoys?"

"Yeah," Robert replied after a short pause to retrieve the information.

"And what about, say, a month, a year, five years and however far back you can go?"

"Yeah… it looks like it's here, Dad, according to the dates coming up on the screen."

"This is the sort of information I have been trying to find and pull together for my reports on inspections I carry out on the rigs," said Amos. "We couldn't find anything on the internet last week when I was with Jack, so why is it here and not released? Robert," said Amos with a glint in his eye, "I wonder… I wonder…" He was thinking about what could be achieved with all the archive information available at his fingertips.

"Yeah… Dad?"

"What are you like at bringing past information together and running a timeline on the historic data, say back over the last month?"

"Yeah. That's easy… give me a few minutes, Dad."

Amos stood away from the screens and rubbed his hand over his mouth and chin. "I wonder…" He was talking to himself.

"I get us some drinks, yes?"

"Yeah, that's a very good idea, Ingrid. Thank you. Could you make it a strong one, like the ones Mary gives out as medication back at the hospital?" he said with a smile.

They left Robert to work his way through the historic data. Ingrid went to the kitchen to sort out the drinks, whilst Amos returned to the sitting room to see how Bernie and the children were.

He walked in to see Bernie with both children asleep on either side of her. Amos raised his eyebrows and smiled. Bernie returned the smile.

"Do you wanna drink honey?" he whispered and put a hand on

her shoulder.

"Yeah, a coffee, please, if there is any going."

He bent down and gave the fire a rake and put a handful of logs on.

"A coffee for Bernie, please, Ingrid," he said as he went into the kitchen.

"Any milks or sugars?"

"No. No thank you, just black and not too strong."

"Dad, I've done it," came Robert's voice from the computer room.

Amos returned to the computer room to see Robert swinging back in his chair and feeling pleased with himself. Ingrid followed him into the room with the drinks.

"Look, Dad... you see that dot moving across and what looks like fog or snow or something, and..."

"It's not unusual for us to have banks of thick fog and snow but it is strange at this time of year," came Ingrid's voice, as she placed the drinks onto the table.

"Yeah," replied Amos.

"Look, Dad... it's gone. It's as if it just disappeared." The heading on the screen was titled *Shipping movements over the last four weeks.*

"Look... and here's another... Water temperatures over the last four weeks. Generally no change over the different depths except there were a lot of orange and a number flashing red with a figure of 0.75 against it, whatever that means. And another... current direction this time... this one headed from Greenland past Iceland... and this one, it's coming straight down towards Faroe... south from the Arctic. Now the salinity levels..."

Amos then pressed a key on his keyboard for the speed of the current. "It looks fast... and the direction? Well, no wonder there have been a few shipping problems, but I've got nothing to compare it with."

Ingrid was standing between them, looking from one screen to the other, watching and listening intently to their conversation.

"Don't forget your drinks, Amos and Robert. I will just see to

Bernie's drink and then I will come back and look also."

"Robert, could you now try to go back to this time last year?" said Amos, looking across at the information showing on Robert's computer screen.

"Yeah… that's easy, I've set it all up now so that you just have to type in a date and it recalls the information pretty much straight away."

"OK, then let's try going back five years and see what we have."

Whilst the computer was retrieving the information, they both grabbed a mouthful of coffee. Amos's mug had a touch of Faroe hospitality in it.

"This is intriguing, the changes in current direction and speed and temperature swing," said Amos. Ingrid re-joined them and sat at one of the other computers. They were all now looking intensely at the screens.

"Yeah, that's what I noticed," said Robert. "On the last run-through there was a slight change in temperatures but the current direction turned sharply south-southeast."

"Yes, well that may be the seasons where the ocean currents change direction and speed, depth and temperature. It can be all very complicated," said Ingrid with her hands wrapped around her coffee, waiting for her computer to reboot.

"Let's see what we've got."

"OK… Here we go, I've been able to track back using previous recordings," said Robert, pressing keys on the keyboard.

Ingrid and Amos both moved from their seats either side of Robert and looked intently at the screen in front of Robert. There was a lot of information to take in as the movements and colours kept changing on the screen. The lights flickered and the power went down but the computers kept running.

"We only has a little time now with the power."

"Robert, we're gonna have to move quickly on this; could you run just the last year and slow the speed down a little as it was difficult to take in."

"Yeah, sure, Dad."

They looked up from the screen and at each other as the

timeline stopped.

"There's been a sharp drop in water temperatures to the north of Faroe over the last six to nine months; can you see that? Run it again, please, Robert."

As it stopped, Ingrid said, "Yes, that is a big change; but I thinks it is the change in seasons as the currents always are changing." Amos wasn't convinced and felt that there was more to it than Ingrid's conclusions.

"Robert, could you now run the program from as far back as you can from when the data started to be collected and we can see what that shows."

Amos stood up and started to walk around the room, looking at some of the other screens trying to make sense of it all. *It could be nothing*, he thought, *but what if... If with the melting ice sheets the salinity will change, direction changes of the current and temperature... All... and the barnacles that we found on the last rig?*

Ingrid interrupted the silence and the quiet whirring of the computer. "In Faroe we have much different weather all of the time. We have banks of fog and snow for the last days. But it's strange that a dot on a shipping movements chart should disappear? It could have been a submarine; that would be an easy explanation... Maybe, but I don't know enough about radar. I think perhaps we have the problem with the old equipments again. I have said to the professor that he must invest in some new ones. We have a better look at it further in the morning as it is already past 1 a.m."

"OK, I've got it," said Robert with excitement in his voice.

He ran the timelines at the different depths of the buoys and then with the combined historic data.

They all looked at each other, aghast. Ingrid's hand moved and covered her mouth.

"Robert, can you do that again, please, and instead of daily, slot it in monthly; it will be easier to see what's happening."

The timeline ran on the screen.

"If I am reading that right," said Amos, pointing at the screen, "the sea temperature has dropped. Can you run it this time yearly, Robert, thanks."

Looking intently at the screen, they couldn't believe what they saw. The changes in current direction, temperature and speed; it was as if...

"That explains the difference in salinity levels that me and Jack have been recording. The melting Arctic and Greenland ice sheets... So much freshwater now in the sea in such a short time; oh my God, the current direction and speed. Robert, the timeline for the current speed and direction – can you run that, please."

"Sure, just give me a moment."

"And then extrapolate for, say one year... Now for five... and now ten years. Oh my God... the current has slowed or even stopped. Shit, this is bad, really bad," said Amos, looking away from the screens and then back again.

"What is it, Dad?"

"The Gulf Stream," replied Amos. "Go back to the current direction, temperatures and speed and extrapolate into the future... assuming the continuing trends that we have had over the last twenty-five years of data. Thanks. Shit... am I reading this right, that there is the Gulf Stream? Yeah." He pointed at the screen.

Robert and Ingrid both nodded.

"And it is slowing... It's slowed so fast over the last twenty-five years, we've got high sea and air temperatures melting the ice, diluting the seawater, changing the temperatures and direction of the currents so that it will then get colder really quickly. We rely on the warmth of the Gulf Stream."

"Extrapolating the slow-down for you now, Dad, for the next...?"

There was a motionless silence in the room.

A figure of 8.75 came up on the screen.

"What does that mean, Robert?" said Amos in an extremely concerned voice.

"8.75 years' time, Dad."

"What?"

"The Gulf Stream just stops up here in Faroe. Look. There's no movement. Nothing."

Amos slumped down in his chair, looking aghast and exhausted.

Ingrid's hands went to her face. She turned white in a matter of seconds and looked like she was going to scream. But she couldn't; it was as if her whole body was paralysed. She just stood there like a statue, motionless except for her eyes looking from one screen to another.

"This is mind-blowing. That can't be right, that just… can't be. Are you sure you've plugged in the right data and information?"

"I'll check it again, Dad, but I'm pretty sure that I inputted the correct historic data to extrapolate the trends; the machinery may look old but it's working OK."

"This is just… unbelievable," said Amos.

"I think we now have proof of the impact of man and global warming and then this… cooling… all so very quickly," added Ingrid.

The computers died… the battery back-up had run out of power. Ingrid quickly lit candles.

"So the professor has all of this information?" asked Amos.

"Yes, all of it."

"So why, why, why hasn't he done anything with it or reported it? Or are they just scared of the implications? They just need to get this out there so that we can all prepare ourselves… it's just… It's just incredible… unbelievable. And this is probably the tip of the iceberg because on top of this it must be happening in oceans and seas throughout the world."

It was now very late. They made their way to the warmest room in the cottage, the lounge. Bernie, Elizabeth and Henry were all asleep. Amos quietly placed a few more logs on the fire. They all grabbed handfuls of blankets and settled down for the night, Amos on the sofa next to Bernie, Robert on the floor leaning against the wall and Ingrid in a single-seater sofa next to the fire. Hygge.

CHAPTER 12: MORNING

Amos shivered. He was the first to stir in the morning.

He hadn't slept well, his mind thinking and then overthinking about the computer timelines that they had run last night and what the implications might be.

Had they done the calculations correctly? They would definitely need checking, not what Robert had done, but perhaps the data that had been saved on the computers. Was it correct? Were the old computers producing reliable data?

He drew chilled air into his lungs and rose slowly from the deep sofa with difficulty, his injured arm aching, trying not to disturb Bernie and the children, who were still asleep close to him.

Henry and Elizabeth were on the sofa somewhere beneath pillows and blankets. Trying not to disturb any of the others, he quietly tended to the fire, hoping to get it going again with the last of the night's embers. The fire soon took hold. *The basket's now empty; gonna need another trip to the log shed*, he thought to himself. *I think I'll get the kettle on first.* He blew out the final flickers of light from the candles.

Amos set the kettle up on the cooker as quietly as he could and turned the gas dial and lit the oven. He looked through the kitchen window and spent a few moments in quiet thought about his last few days on Faroe. The birds and flora he had seen and the conversations with Ingrid. There was so much in what she was saying that was starting to make sense. *The quiet outside when we take the time to stand and listen to it. We need to change our values from dollars all the time to a quality of life that puts the environment, nature and love at the top of the list of priorities.* His thoughts were suddenly interrupted.

"Hello," came a sleepy and subdued voice from behind him.

He turned and saw it was Bernie. She gave him a big hug.

"I'm so sorry about yesterday, honey, but we were all so worried about you with your accident and that you were not in the hospital and all of this. We didn't know if we were going to find you, and, and you up here with… I just couldn't get my head round it all."

"Honey, that's fine. I understand and I'm sorry if I caused you any grief."

The kettle started to boil.

"I'm just so glad you are OK," said Bernie, pulling away from Amos and wiping a tear from her eye with her sleeve.

"Yeah."

"I think we should give Jack a call if we can get through to him and tell him we're OK as he might be worried about us," said Bernie.

"OK, yeah, that's a good idea, and I can have a word with him after, about the work on the rig." *That's assuming*, he thought to himself, *that we have some electricity, unless there is a cell phone*. Amos took the kettle off the boil and made coffee for both of them. "It's gonna be mainly black, Bernie; we're gonna need to save what's left of the milk for the kids."

"I think it's only Elizabeth's phone that has any battery left… I'll try and get it." Bernie returned to the lounge area whilst Amos made the drinks.

In the meantime, Ingrid had got up and made her way upstairs to the bathroom. Bernie gave a quiet "hi" and a wave as they passed in the hall; she didn't want to wake the children.

Bernie carefully lifted one of the blankets to find Elizabeth and Henry still cuddled up together, and saw Elizabeth's phone in the corner of the sofa. She carefully took it and returned the covers back to where they were and tiptoed back into the kitchen.

"Got it, but there's not much left in the battery."

"Robert's good with computers, isn't he," said Amos.

"Yeah. He was in the top grade at school last term and his teacher said he was well advanced for his age." Bernie was now dialling Jack.

"Not sure where he got that from. It definitely wasn't me," said Amos. "He did some research on the weather station data last night which was very interesting."

"Hello, Jack, Jack, is that you?" Bernie said, closing the kitchen door.

"Yeah. Hi, sis, how are you, and did you get to visit Amos?"

"I'm fine, I'm with Amos right now and the kids and everything is OK. This is Elizabeth's phone, and there's not much battery left so it's gonna be a short call and the phone might go dead soon, so I'll hand you over to Amos... love you."

Bernie handed the phone over to Amos and took a sip of her coffee.

"Amos, how are you doing and how's that arm of yours?"

"I'm good, buddy; you didn't tell me Bernie was coming over."

"I did try Amos, but with the phone connection just dying when we spoke a few days ago," he replied apologetically.

"Anyhow, how's it going up on the rig; are you managing to hold the programme together with me away?"

"We're all good here, Amos, no more visits from the suits. But we've had an Arctic blast of cold temperatures and thundersnow up here these last couple of days, never experienced that before and it has slowed us up a bit. We heard that a ship has gone missing?"

"Yeah, we found that out yesterday as well."

"The snow just slows things down a bit, you know how it goes, but we've managed to crawl back to being basically only a day behind the programme, which is recoverable. Charles and his team have been an absolute wonder. I don't know what you've got where you are at the moment but—" The conversation stopped; the line had cut out... dead battery.

"Damn. Oh well, that's it then," said Amos, handing the cell phone back to Bernie. "I never knew they made phones this colour; it's seriously bright pink." He waved it about in his hands. "We will just have to make our way back to the hospital in the cars after breakfast when everyone is up."

He could see that Robert was stirring through the glass window in the kitchen door and gave him a wave. Robert got up and came into the kitchen.

"Hi, Mom, Dad, what have we got for breakfast?" asked Robert – the usual first words out of his mouth when they were away from home.

"Argh, that's a good point, Robert. We've not got much milk left," said Amos.

Ingrid made her way down the stairs and joined them in the kitchen.

"Morning, Ingrid," said Amos. "Robert is asking what do we have for breakfast?"

"Morning, Amos, Bernie. Well, we have about six *snegles* left. A little cereal and some salmon from yesterday, but that is all and some little milks. Two milks." She closed the fridge door. "So that is it, not enough. We go to the village shop and we can get our breakfast and then come back, yes?"

"That sounds sensible. Robert, do you wanna come with us?"

"I'll stay here and wait for Elizabeth and Henry to wake up, as they are still sound asleep; it was a long day yesterday," said Bernie.

"Er, yeah, Dad, I'm up for going out and getting breakfast," replied Robert.

"OK, let's wrap up warm as it looks pretty chilly out there," said Amos, taking a look out of the kitchen window. "Robert, can you bring in a basket of logs, please, for Mom so that she doesn't have to go out whilst we're down at the village shop. Thanks."

"Sure, Dad."

"How far is the shop, Ingrid?"

"You remember where we park? Well, it is about a minute or two by car, but ten, maybe fifteen minutes to walk. So we must wrap up warm and take walking boots because of the snow; we don't know how deep it is."

The three of them set off, well wrapped in coats and hats. Robert had found another interesting woolly hat, this one brown with a pair of eyes sewn on, with ears and reindeer antlers.

"Are you sure you wanna wear that? If anyone sees you they might take a pot shot."

"No one from school is here and it's cool."

He does look daft, thought Amos; they all smiled at each other.

"Come on, let's get going, I'm hungry," said Amos.

They set off from the cottage. Ingrid leading the way followed by Amos and Robert, taking crunchy steps into the freshly fallen snow, leaving Bernie standing at the front door. The slight wind was bitter on their faces and made their eyes water with the cold. They were wary of slipping and in particular the depth of the snow in places where the wind had blown the snow into drifts.

"We must keep close as the fog is still very thick and we don't want to lose anyone," said Ingrid, leading the way at speed. *She must also be ready and looking forward to breakfast*, thought Amos.

After following the footpath for a short while they approached the two cars parked next to each other.

"Looks like at least two or maybe three inches of snow," said Amos. "Hey, stop that," he shouted, holding a hand up and turning towards Robert. He had made a couple of snowballs and thrown them in his dad's direction.

"We cannot take the cars so we must walk. It is steeper from now on to the village shop," said Ingrid. "So be careful when you are walking, yes?"

They could still not see far in front of them; it was very restricting, but their vision was considerably better than last night. The *crunch crunch crunch* of their footsteps was the only noise. It was very quiet.

They reached a group of three cottages to the left of them, set slightly back off the road and there were no lights on; it was becoming eerie.

"Where is everyone? There's no sign of life or anything. How far is the village shop?" asked Amos.

"Only a minute now. It will be on the left as the sea is on our right."

They heard creaky scraping noises as they got close to the shop.

"What's that?" said Amos with concern in his voice. "Sounds like… I don't know." The intermittent scraping and creaking noises continued.

They reached the village shop.

Ingrid walked up to the door. "It is locked… huh… there is no one here," she said, peering through the shop window.

Amos then peered through the glass. "And not much food on the shelves either by the look of things. Where else is open?"

"That is strange. We could try the café down near the bridge," replied Ingrid with a concerned look on her face.

The creaking, scraping noises continued, followed by an occasional splash and rush of water up to the harbour wall.

"What's that noise again?" asked Robert as they got closer to the bridge. The fog swirling around was becoming disorientating. As he got closer to the bridge an image slowly appeared in front of Robert's eyes. "My God. Dad, look… Dad… Look!" Robert cried out. "And there… another and another – there are loads of them, all in the harbour."

The fog lifting for a short while, they were suddenly faced with an iceberg right up against the sea wall.

"Oh my God, this is terrible… this is why no one's here… they've all left the village," said Ingrid, bringing her hands to her mouth.

On reaching the bridge a gap appeared through the fog… The bridge. It was no longer there. The icebergs had broken through and were bobbing up and down on the other side, crashing into each other and a group of boats as they moved haphazardly away.

"There's hundreds of them… where did they come from?" asked Robert.

"Do you remember we looked at the shipping movements last night and we saw the shading which was the snow and fog and then all those areas of dots on the screen? I now know what those dots were. What on earth is… this is… just… incredible… unbelievable."

The three of them stood there aghast at the scene in front of them.

"This is one of the things I was telling you abouts… we are not treating the planet right. The planet is fighting back at us in the only way it can," said Ingrid with anger in her voice.

The three of them stood for a while motionless, close to where the bridge used to be, watching the bergs. They noticed that the bergs would build up at where the bridge used to be and then suddenly two or three of them would break away and make a rush for freedom through the gap and plunge through to the other side, bouncing in the water haphazardly, one then crushing a group of boats moored close to the harbour wall into matchsticks.

"Ingrid," said Amos after a few minutes of them all trying to take it all in, "are you going to tell me that this is the only way off the island?"

"Yes… we only has this bridge," she replied without looking back at where Amos was standing. She was still mesmerised at what she was seeing in front of her, as were Robert and Amos.

"What are we going to do, Dad?"

"A good question, Robert, a good question." He paused whilst thinking about a response, still looking from side to side, watching the bergs and shaking his head.

"Well, I think the first thing we should do is to go back to the others and get some breakfast and then we can discuss and decide what's the best thing to do."

They turned away from the devastation and walked away from the bridge towards the village café, which from a distance looked as empty as the village shop.

"Hello, anyone here?" shouted Amos. There was no reply.

"Everyone has left the island," said Ingrid.

They approached the front of the cafe and peered through the windows. The shelves were as sparse as in the village store. Amos was wondering what to do.

"Ingrid," said Amos, "I know you're not gonna like this, but it has to be done."

Amos wrapped his elbow with part of his coat and, using his elbow, broke the glass in the front door. Then he carefully pushed his arm past the glass and opened the lock to the door.

Ingrid looked at him in shock.

Amos looked back at Ingrid. "I'll pay for it, don't worry, we just need food for all of us."

On entering, they searched inside the café, but all they could find were jars of honey and an endless supply of tea bags, coffee powder and plastic window decorations. There were some cooking ingredients which, if needed, they could come back for. On opening the fridge they found one unopened bottle of milk, two blocks of butter and an untouched round-shaped cheese.

"Grab the food in the fridge, Robert, we'll need all of that, and see if you can find a bag to put it all in."

Having emptied the café of food, they exited and headed back to the village store with the unbelievable sight of the icebergs to the left of them. On reaching the door to the village shop, Amos did the same as he did at the café. Ingrid looked away again. Inside they had a little more success: tins of sardines, pickled herrings, which were not quite what Amos had in mind for breakfast but would probably be welcomed by Ingrid, a couple of apples and a bag of bread rolls.

"Right," said Amos. "That should do us for the time being; let's get back to the others before the fog closes in on us and before they start to get worried as to what's happened to us."

They made their way back up the hill towards the cottage, continually hearing the creaking and groaning sound of the bergs scraping against each other and the occasional cascading of ice falling off a berg and hitting the water. The snow had stopped as they walked past the two cars in the car park, but visibility had reduced again.

Bernie greeted them with a contented smile and welcome at the front door.

"Hey, I've been wondering where you guys had got to. I've got the table laid for breakfast," said Bernie, helping them in with the bags.

"Great. Thanks, honey," replied Amos.

"You won't believe what we've just seen," said Robert with excitement in his voice. "Icebergs down in the harbour, you know where we went over the bridge yesterday and—"

"Icebergs, are you serious?" replied Bernie, slightly taken aback by what Robert had said.

"Yeah, loads of them," replied Robert.

"Well, tell us about it when we sit down at breakfast, then we can all hear."

"I'm hungry, Mom," said Elizabeth.

"Me too, we've been waiting ages," said Henry.

"It's just arrived for both of you. Anyhow, you've had a *snegle* already, Henry; it's more than the rest of us."

"My favourite," said Amos, widening his eyes and looking down at Henry.

"There's still some left, Dad." Henry then ran into the lounge, jumping onto the sofa and hiding under the blankets with Elizabeth.

They removed their walking gear and took the remaining food bags into the kitchen.

"Hey, that's a lot of food for breakfast," said Bernie.

"Well, yeah," replied Amos, emptying the contents out of one of the bags, and Ingrid prepared the food for the breakfast table. "The good news, honey, as you can see is we've got food. Not much of a selection, but it will do us... The bad news, and you'd better all sit down for this, is that we are the only ones on the island, and the bridge has collapsed."

"What? How, Amos? This is crazy; you drag me all the way up here to somewhere in the middle of nowhere and – and – and now we're marooned? You've got to be kidding me," said Bernie, looking towards Ingrid and then Robert.

"Dad's right, Mom. We walked down to the shop, which was closed, and then down towards the harbour. The bridge, it's completely gone, demolished by the icebergs."

"Wow, can I go and see?" said Henry, popping his head out of the covers on the sofa.

"Yeah, we will, Henry, we will once you've had your breakfast," replied Amos. "Well, Bernie, to answer your question... last night me and Robert and Ingrid here, we were checking on the weather station computers and the data they collect and we could see where there were changes in water temperature, currents and shipping movements."

"And we saw where a ship, you know the one that the professor was enquiring about yesterday… well, it just disappeared off the screen," added Robert.

"And we also saw a lot of shaded areas of snow and fog on the screens and what appeared to be loads of dots on the screen all the way down to the harbour here and we've just seen what they are," said Amos.

"Icebergs," interrupted Robert. "Really cool, hundreds of them."

"Can I go and see them, please, please, Mom?" said Henry.

"Is that right?" replied Bernie, now looking towards Ingrid who nodded back at her.

"Mom," said Henry, tugging Bernie's jumper.

"Yes, it is right, and it is also not right; we sometimes maybe have some small remnants of ice out in the ocean but this is not heard of ever. This is what I have been saying is a problem man has created. I tell you yesterday." Ingrid looked at Amos. "Climate change, and it's a big change, it is happening right now, not tomorrow or the day after or next year but now. Perhaps people will start listening." Amos sensed that Ingrid was about to give them a lecture but she held back, probably reflecting on the potential impact and enormity of what she had seen.

"I agree with Ingrid. Can we go and see the bergs, please, Mom?" said Elizabeth.

"We will all go down later and have a look," said Bernie. "Now let's get breakfast going otherwise it will be lunchtime."

"After breakfast, Henry, we'll all go down, son, to take a look," said Amos.

"Yeah, great; Elizabeth, we're going to see real icebergs," said one very excited Henry.

"Ingrid?" asked Bernie.

"Yes," she replied after taking a sip of coffee.

"You say that you haven't had this sort of thing happen before?" Bernie asked her in the kitchen whilst Amos and Robert went to tend to the fire.

"No. Never. But this… this is extremely bad… Very bad. Not just for now, but for our futures and everybody's futures. All the five previous mass extinctions of life on earth were carbon-dioxide-related. We burns so much fossil fuel in the last hundred years, our atmosphere can't deal with it, it is too much, it is not natural and we create a planet out of balance. The weathers we have now and in the future will become more extreme. This amount of snow here is out of our regular season, and now this with the icebergs in the harbour. I now understand what we have been doing. Our summer sea ice in the arctic has been reducing every years and it is almost half of what it was a hundred years ago. But we make with the higher temperatures freshwater ice in the Greenland ice sheet melt so quickly we have then suddenly cold water which is then stopping the Gulf Stream. This is just one example. We create uncontrollable weather and turmoil, no seasons means less food. The bees will not know when to come out and pollinate. I am sorry, I am so cross and exhausted by all this." Ingrid was rubbing her hands together and pacing the kitchen whilst she was speaking. She now looked out of the kitchen window with a tear and sadness in her eyes.

"I do appreciate what you are saying, and I know you are right, Ingrid, but my immediate concern is how do we get off this island. What are we gonna do?" said a very concerned Bernie. "If the bridge is not there and the icebergs are blocking it, how do we get off the island?"

"Are we gonna die?" called out Henry from the lounge.

"No we're not, stupid," said Robert.

"Robert," said Bernie crossly. "Remember, he's only eight years old."

"Sorry, Mom."

Bernie walked back into the lounge and started to question Amos. "Well, Amos… what are we gonna do now that you've gotten us into this situation?"

"Well, I'm gonna first have my breakfast and then have another coffee whilst I have a think about all this," replied Amos.

"Ands we must keep the fire going in case we have to stay another night," said Ingrid out loud.

Henry started laughing again: her accent, and when Ingrid said "ands".

Bernie realised. "Henry, behave yourself," she said, giving him a gentle nudge. They all made their way to the breakfast table.

"This is really an adventure; wait till I tell Don," said Henry.

"Who's Don?" replied Amos, helping himself to a bread roll.

"He's Henry's best friend at school who always boasts about where he has been and what he's done," replied Elizabeth.

Henry's hand stretched across the table to reach the plate of *snegles*.

"Hey, Henry, you've already had one," said Robert.

"It's OK, I don't mind," said Amos. "He can have mine."

"*Snegles* are nice," said Henry, laughing with Elizabeth. "But we did save two others, one for Robert and one for Ingrid."

"OK, no worries; I need to lose a bit of weight," replied Amos. "Come on, everyone. Let's get breakfast out of the way and then we can discuss how we get off the island."

Whilst everyone was finishing off their breakfast, Amos got up and left the table and sat down by one of the computers with a blank screen, then looked out through a window to see the snow and fog outside.

"What are we gonna do?" he said out loud to himself, not expecting anyone to be listening. *No communications, no electricity, food running out, log pile almost non-existent now... And...*

"Hey, Dad."

Amos turned round sharply. "Woo... You made me jump, Robert."

"Sorry, Dad, I was just thinking: down by the harbour there are a lot of boats – maybe we could just use one to get over to the other side?"

"Good idea; that's if any are still seaworthy and with the bergs barging their way through the bridge, but we'd have to be careful. Some of those bergs we saw earlier are big, really big, and were moving all over the place. They could cause us a problem."

"Well, it's just an idea."

"Yeah, it's a good one, Robert. Thanks. Let's see what we can do when we get down there and have a better look." Amos stood up and patted Robert on his shoulder.

CHAPTER 13: HOSPITAL

Mary McKinnon sat behind the reception desk at the hospital in dismay, her hands over her face.

"Ooh dear, ooh deary, deary me, what have I done?" she said to herself.

One of the hospital's senior sisters was standing in the reception area, collecting a patient's notes.

"Morning, Mary. You don't sound very happy. What's the problem? Is there anything I can help with?"

"Ooh. Morning, Sister. I'm sorry," said Mary, putting a handkerchief to her nose and then wiping her eyes.

"What's wrong, Mary, this is not like you, what's happened? Why are you so tearful this morning?"

"Ooh I've done a terrible, terrible thing, Sister. Do you remember the family with three lovely children that arrived yesterday to see Mr Amos? I sent them over to Viðoy and… have you heard that the island has been cut off with terrible snowstorms and icebergs? Would you believe it, icebergs in the harbour, and on top of all of that the bridge over to the island has completely gone. Oh dear, deary me… and we've heard not a word since I sent them there yesterday afternoon, ooh I feel terrible." She wept into her handkerchief.

The sister comforted Mary. "I'm sure it will all be fine."

"But they are only a young family, a mother and her three young children. I feel terrible and no one has heard from them or from the doctor since lunchtime yesterday."

"Mary, I'm sure everything will be alright. The doctor's with Mr Amos and they will be OK, I'm sure," said the sister, giving Mary some further reassurance.

Mary wiped her nose with a tissue. "Yes, yes, Sister, of course. I'm sure you're right but look, look out there... You can't see beyond the end of your nose and we've snow, yes, snow now, so early in the year; we're not prepared for it... it can't be right."

The entrance door to the hospital reception opened and in walked Bill the helicopter pilot, stamping his feet on the entrance mat and shaking the snow off his coat.

"Morning, everyone, how are we all today?"

"Mary's upset because she sent Mr Amos's family over to Viðoy yesterday and you've heard that the island has been cut off?"

"No. How?"

"Well, apparently the bridge has gone and there's icebergs in the harbour. Would you believe it," replied the sister.

"Crikey, that's a first. Are you sure?"

"Yes, absolutely," replied a nurse at reception who joined them in the conversation. "My parents live on the island and they came over the bridge late yesterday evening and are staying with me. They were lucky they weren't stuck over there. A neighbour knocked on their door at about 6.30 in the evening saying that there were icebergs up against the bridge. My parents said they were one of the last, if not the last people to leave. It was so very foggy and shortly after they drove over the bridge, a berg pushed right through it. I can't believe it, I just can't; the bridge to Viðoy has gone."

"And I sent a young family over to the island yesterday afternoon and they've not been seen or heard of since," interjected Mary, who now started crying again, her handkerchief muffling her sobs.

"Isn't the doctor over there?" asked Bill.

"Yes, she went with Mr Amos; that's why I sent the family over to see him on Viðoy," Mary replied. "Oh dear, oh deary, deary me, what have I done?" Mary held her head in her hands again and continued weeping.

The nurse put her hand over Mary's shoulders and looked across at Bill.

"Mary, it'll be fine," replied Bill. "The doctor knows the island like the back of her hand and I'm sure they would have met up and be sorting things out right now; they've got shelter at the weather station and there's plenty of food over there."

"No there's not," said the nurse. "The delivery van was due over there this morning and it's parked up in the town just up the road right now."

"Have you tried to contact Ingrid?" asked Bill.

"Yes, yes, I've called dozens of times and there is no connection and I… I can't get through. There's nothing. The last we heard was a message from her saying that the weather is bad and the two of them might have to stay over and that everything is ok."

"Well then, Mary, there's nothing more you can do. You've tried as best you can; they will just have to stay warm until the fog lifts." *Maybe, just maybe, I can't promise anything, but I may be able to get the helicopter over*, thought Bill.

"But that could be days, Bill; we've already had two to three days of this blasted weather; we've not expected this and the wood stores throughout the islands are low at this time of year, they didn't have warm clothes with them, and we're all assuming that they have found the doctor at the weather station." Mary started to wail again.

Bill and the sister looked at each other. Bill was in a quandary as to what he could do to help the situation.

"Look, Mary. What I'll do is, I will go to the helicopter now and check the weather forecast and see if there is a window in the weather to let me fly over and rescue them, but, as you can see, I can't at the moment as we are fogged in."

Mary sniffled. "That will be good, thank you, Bill. I'm sorry, it's just… thank you." Mary put her hand on Bill's arm and then buried her face in her handkerchief again and gave a big blow to clear her nose.

Bill whispered to the nurse, "Can you keep an eye on Mary? She's obviously not in the best frame of mind."

Mary overheard. "I'm fine, Bill… and thank you for your concern; we just need to bring them back safely."

"Right, I'll see what I can do."

Bill nodded towards the nurse, directing her attention to keep an eye on Mary. The nurse nodded back and smiled at him.

"See you later, Bill, and thank you," said Mary.

"I'll be back in about twenty minutes or so, or I'll give you a call and tell you what's happening."

Bill left the hospital reception, back out into the cold and gloom. *I can't see me getting out of here today*, he said to himself, looking up and around the sky. *Just hope the family have found Amos; overnight in a car over there in this weather is not good for anyone*. The walk back to the helicopter pad took longer than Bill had expected, the crushed snow and icy conditions on the pavements making it difficult to get a footing.

At the helicopter, Bill turned on the ignition. The controls and screens lit up.

Right. Let's check the radar and see what it looks like up there... mmm... A blanket of low cloud and fog at the moment; that's not good... clearing at about eighty feet for a while... just need a bit of a breeze to take it away; what are we... a north-easterly at barely 1 for a while and then picking up... mmm... and we might... let's try the other screen with the main forecast...

One hour... mmm... well, it's lifting a bit, but... mmm... Two hours... argh...

Here we go... the weather's clearing up here... but they are still covered over on the island. But where are they?

Bill decided to give his co-pilot, Calum, a call to see what he thought about it.

Brr, brr... Brr...

"Hi. Calum speaking."

"Calum. Hi. Bill here. I'm over at the chopper checking if we can get over to Viðoy and back... You've heard that a group of people are stranded over there?"

"Yeah. Heard this morning," replied Calum.

"Well, I've checked the forecast and we may get a gap in this darn fog later this morning or possibly early afternoon... Just wanted to make sure you were around."

"Sure... like you, Bill, just waiting to get back to work; there's nothing much to do here when the weather closes in like this.

Where do you think we are gonna have to fly to?"

"They've got to be at the weather station... Argh, looking again at the radar... looks like around lunch time, maybe one-ish... Hey... Yeah... there's a window... Argh, damn it... but not here... mmm... this is going to take a lot of patience and probably a bit of risk... I don't like risk... Calum, could you check out your readings on the weather forecast for the next couple of hours and get back to me. Thanks."

"Yeah, will do," replied Calum. Bill turned his phone off and looked back at the helicopter's dashboard and the various dials.

Well, looking at this, said Bill to himself, *and with a bit of luck it looks like it might be at lunch time that we can get off the ground and search for them.*

Bill called the reception at the hospital.

Brr, brr... Brr, brr...

"Klaksvík Hospital, Mary speaking, can I help you?"

"Hi, Mary... Mary, it's Bill."

"Ooh, hello, hello, Bill, how are ye getting on? When can you go and get them off the island?"

"Well, Mary, it's not looking much good at the moment from what I've got on the screen here in front of me, but Calum is checking it out as well so there may be an opportunity at around lunch time... I'm gonna hang around here for a while to see if the fog lifts; remember it needs to lift both here and over on Viðoy for us to travel safely and then for us to return back again... safely, otherwise we'll be in trouble."

"Ooh, thank you, Bill, thank you. I'm very, very grateful to you."

"That's OK, Mary, I've got nothing else to do at the moment."

Mary put the phone down. "Ooh thank goodness for that, yer can always rely on Bill to come up with a solution."

"How are you feeling, Mary?" asked a nurse.

"A little better now, thank you, Nurse. Bill is at the helicopter now to see when he can go and rescue them; let's hope it's soon as I wouldn't like to have another day over on the island at the moment in these conditions."

"Yeah, my mother often says it can get quite wild over there when the weather turns and you just have to stay indoors. There's nothing you can do about it."

"God, I hope they've all met up and are together and safe," replied Mary.

"Right, I need to go to the ward now and check on Mrs Carmicalle; she's supposed to be leaving later today. I will see you later, Mary."

Brr, brr... Brr...

"OK, sorry, I've got to take this call. Klaksvík Hospital, Mary speaking, can I help you?"

***

Bill decided to leave the cold of the helicopter and grab a hot drink and warm up at a local café whilst he was waiting. As he walked along the street to the café, he noticed that the fog was definitely lifting a bit and there was a slight breeze picking up, which should help clear the fog. Bill reached the café and quickly opened and closed the door behind him.

"Brr, it's cold out there. Morning, Steffi, how are you?" he said, taking his gloves off and rubbing his hands together.

"Fine, Bill, thank you. No works for you today?"

"Not at the moment, but maybe a bit later... I just need the fog to lift. You heard about the bridge?"

"Yeah, very bad, very bad. Not good for any of us."

"Yeah, there's a family stranded over on Viðoy at the moment with Dr Svensen. Been there overnight, so Calum and I will hopefully go over once this lot lifts."

"And what would you like then, Bill?"

"A black coffee, please, Steffi."

"And anythings else?"

Bill paused. "Er, yeah... one of those *snegles* please." He pointed down at the display counter.

"You can have three for two if you like?"

"Hey, you fattening me up for Christmas now, Steffi?"

Steffi laughed. "We have not many people here today so...

Please… or they get thrown away."

"I know, I know… or you'll have to eat them!"

"Ha ha ha ha." Steffi laughed.

Bill didn't delay his response any longer. "Yeah, OK… how can I resist them?"

"I bring over for you, Bill, with your drink."

"Thanks." Bill removed his coat and made his way over to a table close to the open fire and a view through the window so he could keep an eye on the weather, acknowledging a number of other people in the café.

It's going to have to be a quick in and out, this one; I can sense it, thought Bill.

Steffi brought over the coffee and *snegles*.

"Here you are, Bill."

"Thanks, Steffi, that looks really good. Hey, how's your brother now that he's back from the Gulf?"

"Oh yes, he is good but goes straight away back again… it is busy there at the moment."

"What does he do again?"

"He makes a new rig for gas and they have problems with some delivery equipments so he comes back home and then suddenly the delivery arrives and so he then must go again."

"This is a lovely, lovely coffee, Steffi, thank you. Just what I needed," said Bill, wrapping his hands around the mug of coffee to warm them up and taking a sip.

"And the *snegles*?" asked Steffi.

"They are always good, Steffi, thank you. I will have one in a minute once I warm up; it's bitterly cold out there today."

"Yes, it has been for maybe a week now but you've not been here for a while now, have you?"

"Yeah, you're right. I brought a guy, Amos, over a couple of days ago, who injured himself diving on a rig; we were supposed to fly into Tórshavn but got diverted up here because of the weather there and have been grounded here now for three days."

"Auch, that must be frustrating for you."

"Yeah, and he's the guy stranded over on the island; hopefully he's met up with his family."

"How come?"

"Ingrid went over yesterday to check out the weather station and Amos joined her for the ride and apparently Mary at the hospital directed the family up to the weather station yesterday afternoon. They came over to visit him in hospital after his accident as the children were desperate to see their father."

Brr, brr. Bill's phone rang.

"Sorry, Steffi, I need to take this. Hello... Yeah... OK, I'll be over straight away." He put the phone down. "That was Calum, my co-pilot, saying that he's seen a window in the fog bank and that now might be a good time to see what's doing over on Viðoy."

"Ah, so that is good, yes," said Steffi.

"I'll take these with me if that's OK, Steffi." Bill stood up and picked up the remaining *snegles* from his plate and wrapped them up into a napkin. "And may I have another coffee to go?"

"Yes, that's fine; let me sort your drink out for you."

Bill put his coat on and Steffi returned with his drink to take with him. "You take care now, Bill."

"Yeah, sure; it's not really me you need to worry about... it's more what's happening over on the island, but the doctor's with them so I'm sure it'll be OK. She knows her way around."

Bill walked back to the helicopter. Calum was already there and they sat looking at the helicopter's screens again.

"I'll just give Mary at the hospital a ring as she's been very anxious about the situation."

Brr, brr... Brr, brr...

"It's gone to answer phone... Hello, it's Bill here with a message for Mary. I'm over with Calum at the helicopter and we're going to see if we can get up in the next hour or so; I'll keep you updated when I can... Right, Calum, what are your thoughts? Are we still looking good to go?"

Calum pointed at the screen. "Look, this bank of fog here; it is slowly moving south and clearing but there's another moving in from the north-west... Look at the prediction; it's swirling around all over the place."

Bill took a closer look and they reran the weather chart.

"Mmm... you're right, Calum, not looking very promising but, maybe, maybe half an hour... up and over to the island... If the wind picks up again then we've got a problem. We'll have to keep a close eye on that. OK, let's prepare ourselves and assume we can go so at least we are ready when the opportunity arises."

"OK, Bill, I'll get going with the pre-flight checks. That's gonna take a good twenty minutes anyhow."

Bill left Calum in the helicopter and strolled around outside with his coffee and the last of his *snegles*.

"Calum."

"Yeah."

"Do you wanna drink as I'm going to get another coffee from Steffi's?"

"No, I'm fine, thanks, Bill."

Bill walked back to the café, which was only a few minutes' walk away.

"Hi, Steffi, me again."

"That was quick; have you already been there? I didn't hears any noise."

"No, no. We've just been checking the weather charts and Calum is winding the helicopter up so we're ready to go when there's a break in the fog. Another coffee, please, Steffi." Bill placed his empty mug on the counter.

"As before?"

"Please, Steffi, thank you... and you'd better make that another couple of *snegles*."

Bill stood waiting and looking out of the café. *What a mess*, he said to himself.

CHAPTER 14: THE BRIDGE

At the cottage, they were sitting around the kitchen table enjoying a hearty breakfast, courtesy of what had been left in the village café and shop.

"Dad," shouted Henry across the table.

"Yeah."

"What's global warning?" asked Henry.

"Global warming, silly, not warning," said Elizabeth.

"Yes, that's what I said," replied Henry sheepishly, drooping his head back to his cereal bowl.

They all had a little chuckle of laughter at Henry's expense, which he wasn't pleased about until Ingrid stepped in to save Henry's tears.

"But I agree with Henry. I think 'global warning' is the right words," said Ingrid. "This is a warning… to all of us about the state of our planet and what we've all done to it. We are not looking after it. Well said, Henry."

"My teacher agrees with that as well," said Elizabeth. "She says that we need to be mindful of everything that we are doing. If we cut trees down then we must plant them. Did you know that in the UK they use thirty million trees a year just for new books and publications – that's just in the UK – and did you know that to produce a book it results on average about three kilos of carbon dioxide per book plus wastewater, plus transportation to deliver; so what we are doing at school is sharing books."

"That is good, Elizabeth," replied Ingrid encouragingly.

"And also we use ebooks. But rather surprisingly they are only slightly better with carbon dioxide emissions than sharing paper books. Anyhow, I think it's nice to know that it helps a bit."

"Yeah, well that's not gonna help much, is it," interrupted Robert.

"Hey, come on, Robert, that wasn't needed," said Bernie.

Elizabeth poked her tongue out at Robert and then looked away from him. Ingrid saved the situation developing into an argument between the two of them.

"I believe that every little helps and my motto is 'Let's not wait… just do it.'"

"That's very good," said Amos in a very supportive manner. Bernie gave him a brief questioning look but nothing more.

"Have you read Greta Thunberg's book, *No One Is Too Small to Make a Difference*?"

"Oh, I've heard of her," said Elizabeth excitedly. "She's the schoolgirl that is fighting for climate change. We're studying that book next term."

"Ethical living is what it is called, living sustainably. I try every day," replied Ingrid. "More tea or coffee, anyone?"

"Er, yeah… yes please, Ingrid, some more of that herbal tea," said Robert.

"How many cups is that?" asked Bernie.

"Just two; it's so nice and it's not coffee, Mom, if that's what you were thinking. Ingrid was telling me earlier that there are quite a few locally made natural teas made from moss and birch added to berries and some even using tree bark, but I like this one with apples and honey."

"Yeah, I also quite like it, it's very simple to make and warming inside as the coffee here is rather too strong for me," replied Bernie. "I also agree with you, Ingrid. We should all try to be more aware of our impact on the world; I'm trying with my cosmetic business, but it's hard work to keep the prices down and finding out where the products come from and their source, and how they have been produced and then delivery– it takes a lot of time and effort. But when I get back I'm going to take a genuine interest in all aspects of our daily life that affect the environment."

"But at least you are trying. It is so important how much nature and our planet is to our wellbeing. There are so many businesses and peoples that just ignore these issues and problems that we are creating for ourselves. We are so greedy and a throw-away society. If we don't like something we just throw it away and then buy something similar and new. I think that the earth is fighting back to survive; we make it hot, so it melts the ice to try to cool itself down. That's what I believe... and we make too much carbon dioxide and so the trees grow more and more... But at the moment they grow not quickly enough," said Ingrid.

"That's provided we don't cut all the trees down, then it will definitely be too late," added Elizabeth.

"Precisely," replied Ingrid enthusiastically.

"True, all very true. I'm starting to get my head around all this now," added Amos, much to the surprise of Ingrid and Bernie.

"My teacher thinks that the dinosaurs were made extinct because they ate all the world's vegetation," said Elizabeth.

Robert mimicked Elizabeth. "My teacher this... my teacher that."

"How do you mean?" asked Ingrid.

"Well, the dinosaurs wouldn't have known any different and just kept eating and eating and eating everything and reproducing more and more."

"This sounds like a very similar situation that we are in now. In the Serengeti in Africa when the food available goes down all the populations of animals and then peoples go down," replied Ingrid.

"I liked *Jurassic Park*; that was a really cool movie, especially when the eggs hatched and when the big Tyrannosaurus rex chased them," said Henry.

Robert and Amos chuckled together and continued with their breakfast.

"I liked that bit too and when—"

"Dad... Let me finish." Elizabeth was starting to get cross.

"Sorry," replied Amos.

"She said that the dinosaurs used up all the world's air and oxygen at the same time as they were spreading all over the land and kept eating all the trees and shrubs and bushes... everything. There was nothing but carbon dioxide."

"Everything?" said Henry.

"Yes, Henry, everything," replied Elizabeth in a very schoolteacher manner.

"Well, that's an interesting theory, Elizabeth... very interesting, and maybe more right than the asteroid theory," said Ingrid.

"Yeah, I liked that movie and particularly when—"

"Come on, Dad, let's get back to what's happening right here and now," said Elizabeth.

"Argh, come on, it was a good movie and..."

Bernie looked across at Amos, suggesting he didn't say any more.

"Yeah, well, let's... Let's just finish off our breakfast," said Amos.

"Dad. How are we going to get back to the mainland? Well? Hmm," said Elizabeth.

"I wanna see the icebergs," said Henry.

"Well," replied Amos after a quick bit of thinking around his response. "Er... When we went down to the harbour earlier there were boats there but the ones we looked at that were still intact didn't seem like they would make it if there was a collision. I also didn't feel it was safe to cross with the bergs moving around. Maybe they've stopped now, and we can use one to get across. We can have a better look when we walk down there later this morning. What do you think, Ingrid?"

"It is possible, yes, but maybe we will wait for people to come and collect us from Klaksvík or Tórshavn?"

"Collect us? What does she mean?" said Henry.

"She means that someone might rescue us, Henry," said Robert. Henry acknowledged by moving his eyebrows.

"Well, that's pretty unlikely at the moment," said Amos. "It's still so foggy out there we could be here for days." He looked out of the windows.

"OK, and what about food?" asked Bernie.

"When we went down to the village earlier we took the food from the café," said Ingrid.

"And..." added Robert, "we broke into the village stores." He mimicked Amos's elbow breaking glass.

"You did what?" said Bernie.

"That's cool," said Henry.

"Yeah, well, we had to… and I said to Ingrid at the time that I'd pay for any damage and any of the food we've taken as there was no one there to pay… I had to, Bernie, otherwise you wouldn't have had any food this morning," replied Amos, opening his hand and moving it across the table. "And there's not much food left in the village stores either."

"I wanna see the icebergs before they melt," said Henry.

"They are not gonna melt, Henry, honestly, they are so huge," replied Robert.

"OK now, everyone, finish up. We can clear the plates later. Let's get going and down to the village and take a look at how we can get off this island. Robert, could you put the remaining logs onto the fire and bring in some more. Thanks."

"There aren't any more, Dad; this was the last load."

Amos didn't reply but thought to himself that this was starting to get very serious.

Henry was first dressed and ready to go outside.

"Make sure you've got a hat and scarf and gloves, children, it's still looking very cold out there," said Bernie, buttoning up Henry's coat.

Robert had his reindeer woolly hat on again.

"Can I wear that, Robert?" asked Henry.

"Sure. But it might be a bit too big for you, Henry. I'll see if there are any others in the clothes bag."

"Amos, what are you thinking about?" asked Bernie.

"Nothing really… other than it's nice with all of us together… and a bit of an adventure."

"Yeah… Not quite what I was expecting." She looked across at Ingrid, who was bent down doing up the laces of her boots.

Robert returned to the entrance hall. "There you go, Henry," said Robert.

"What's that?" said Elizabeth.

"Well, it looks like another reindeer hat," said Robert.

"But I'm not sure it is," added Bernie with a questioning look on her face.

Henry took it from Robert and put it on. "I like it," said Henry.

"You do look so sweet, honey," said Bernie. "How are we all doing, are we ready to go?"

"We must take the log baskets with us as well, remember," said Ingrid.

"Ahh, yeah," said Robert.

"Robert, could you bring those with us, and we'll see what we can pick up on the way."

Bernie gave Amos a *What are you going to steal this time?* look.

"Honey, I know what you're thinking, but we need some logs to keep us warm, OK?"

They left the cottage; it had stopped snowing. But the fog and mist were still swirling around as they walked down towards the village and harbour, a sharp bite of cold in the air, particularly with the fog surrounding them.

"I think I know why it's so foggy," said Elizabeth. "It's because of the cold from the icebergs."

"You are right, Elizabeth," said Ingrid. The two of them were walking and chatting together, as were Amos and Bernie. The boys were making and throwing snowballs at each other.

"I think you learn a lot at your school. Did your teacher speak about the 2015 Paris Climate Change agreement and what America is doing?"

"Well, she did say that it was disgraceful that America had initially withdrawn from the agreement and that it was showing how irresponsible and ignorant some Western and supposedly 'advanced' countries are in addressing climate change. She said we should all be working together and that it might mean that we have a few years when companies have to contribute towards investing in clean energy provision, cleaner electric cars and planes, eating more vegetables and planting trees, but it will benefit us all in the future. I would be happy to put my money towards green projects and green initiatives. She worked out that if every person in the USA contributed just a hundred dollars a year, that would create a fund of about forty billion dollars every year. You could do so much too."

"You are right, Elizabeth, peoples need to open their eyes and take responsibility and be proud of it instead of shying away from the problems that we all know exist. Human beings have symb... symbio... Oh what is the word... symbiotic, that's right, yes, the word is symbiotic relationship with the planet, our planet where we both rely upon each other. Do you understand?"

"Wow. Yeah, Ingrid, I do; you know so much," replied Elizabeth.

"Symbiosis is the art of species living together for the mutual benefit of each other and providing helps for each other; but the relationship between man and the earth has changed from working together, to man being a parasite and causing harm to the planet, stealing resources and giving nothing back, and in doing so killing the planet's biodiversity. Do you know that the definition of a parasite is that it reduces the host's fitness and then causes the host's behaviour to change? That is what we are doing to the planet now. And parasites increase their own fitness by exploiting the host's resources for their own survival."

"That's very good, Ingrid, and I really do see where you are going with this," interrupted Amos as he and Bernie caught up with them.

"But it is so obvious," replied Ingrid with a sense of exhaustion again in her voice that Amos recognised from their evening at the restaurant.

"Hey. Robert," called out Henry after a snowball whizzed past his head.

"Yeah."

"Do you think there will be any polar bears?"

Now that got Robert thinking. He stood up whilst shaping another snowball. "Good point, Henry, I hadn't thought of that. No, I shouldn't think so; it's a long way for them to be stuck on a berg. Anyhow, if there were, then..." He wasn't sure how to answer that one. "Well, if there were any, they would have jumped off by now." *Mmm,* he was thinking to himself, *what if there were?*

"Robert."

"Yeah, Dad."

"There's some logs stacked outside that house up over there on the left; can you see them? And can you load up the two baskets with Henry and then leave them on the footpath. Thanks. We can pick them up on the way back."

"Sure, Dad." Robert opened the garden gate and the two of them walked up the footpath and started filling the two baskets.

"Amos," said Bernie.

"Yeah."

"Have you got a plan to get us off the island yet?"

"Not yet, honey; I'm working on it, but we're pretty close to civilisation so I would think we just have to hold out until someone comes to rescue us."

"What if they don't? We haven't much food, you know, and remember that there's six of us," said a concerned Bernie.

This is like a ghost town, thought Elizabeth to herself. *There's no one around and all you can hear is the creaky, creepy sound from the harbour area, it's scary.*

Amos looked towards Elizabeth and then back to Bernie. "As I said, we'll check in the village stores. We are almost there now and if there isn't much, then we'll have to think about getting off the island." Amos was now starting to feel the pressure of the predicament they were in.

Ingrid and Elizabeth moved ahead of Amos and Bernie when the boys came running up behind Amos and Bernie.

"Done that, Dad."

"Thanks, boys."

"Where are the icebergs?" said Henry.

"We're almost at the harbour, Henry. If the fog lifts a little more you'll be able to see them."

"Look, Henry, over there." Robert pointed into the grey.

"Cor... I can see one; it's so big. I never thought I would ever see one."

"Me neither," said Amos with a perturbed voice. "That's a big berg. They look a lot bigger than the ones we saw earlier; what do you think, Robert?"

"Yeah, you're right, Dad, and they seem to be moving quicker as well."

"Perhaps it's the passage they've created through where the bridge used to be."

They came up to the village store. Amos went in through the front of the store and rummaged around for a few minutes. The others waited outside looking at the icebergs building up on the other side of the harbour wall. The bergs were busily jostling for positions, trying to squeeze through the gap they had created.

"Look at that one, it's like a mountain." Henry pointed off to the left of where they were standing. The berg had just broken through and appeared to be bouncing in the water and steering itself towards an area where fishing boats were moored. The wash from the berg's movement splashed up and over the sea wall.

Bernie joined Elizabeth and Ingrid looking at the scene of devastation.

"Just unbelievable," said Bernie.

"Yes," replied Ingrid, the three of them almost gawping at the landscape in front of them. "It is not good, not good at all. Have you heard of the Thwaites Glacier? Not many people have… it's in Antarctica and it's a big glacier, as it is releasing fifty billion tonnes of ice every year into the oceans, and you know why?"

"Yes, because of the warming oceans," replied Elizabeth.

"You are right again, Elizabeth, and there is also another glacier called the Denman… If that breaks off, it could lead to a five-foot increase in sea level around all the world… Now that's serious and we just sit back and watch." Ingrid looked away from the harbour as a voice called out.

"Two tins of sardines and a dozen boxes of some sort of biscuits. We could have that with the cheese we got earlier," shouted Amos from the shop.

"The cheese has gone, Dad, we finished it off at breakfast," replied Robert. Amos paused, concern on his face, looking at Robert for a while and then went back inside.

Some firelighters… A handful of potatoes and… Amos was still rummaging around and talking to himself whilst the others were standing outside the shop close to the harbour wall, still watching with amazement the ice show.

"Bernie, you know the reason for the icebergs: it is global warming," said Ingrid.

"Yeah, just unbelievable," Bernie replied. "And it's probably only the start. How is this going to affect us?"

"We must rethink how we live our lives and ways of living sustainably and stop using the earth's resources like hungry wolves eating and eating until there is nothing left…" replied Ingrid.

"Yes, I agree. Henry, Henry, don't go so close; come away, you two," cried out Bernie all of a sudden. Robert and Henry had gone down the road to where the bridge used to be and were up on the harbour wall. They were within touching distance of a berg, Henry reaching out over the sea trying to touch one.

"OK, Mom," replied Robert, Henry quickly stepping back. The two boys slowly made their way back to the others.

"Where's Dad?" said Elizabeth.

"He's still inside the village store," replied Ingrid.

"Mom, I'm getting cold, can we go back now?" said Elizabeth. Hearing his name, Amos's head appeared out from the entrance to the store.

"Yeah, OK, honey. Amos, we're going back. Robert, can you see if your father needs any help and we'll see you back at the cottage."

"OK, Mom."

Ingrid and Robert walked back up the road and towards the door to the village shop and arrived just as Amos was coming out.

"Hey, you two, perfect timing; can you help me with these bags? Thanks."

"Looks like you got a lot of food in those bags, Dad."

"It looks more than it is, Robert, but it will have to do… I found some bread so we can make some sandwiches for lunch."

"OK, I will take these two bags and I see you back at the cottage." Ingrid took the bags from Amos and ran to catch up with the others.

Robert picked up another two bags that Amos had left by the door whilst Amos went back inside. He appeared shortly afterwards with a bag of cut firewood.

"That's a good find, Dad, and will help keep the fire going."

"Well, it will have to do for the time being; it's not gonna last that long."

The two of them stood on the road outside the shop, looking again at the scene in front of them. The bergs were on a mission.

"How are we gonna get back, Dad, as we have no means of telling anyone where we are with phones and power down?" asked Robert.

"I don't know at the moment although I have a few ideas. Whilst we are here let's take a look at some of those fishing boats down there." They left their bags in the road and walked the short distance to the harbour. It was a mess with a number of boats damaged. It was like the bergs had been playing pinball.

"Hey, there's a couple that look interesting further down; let's go and check them out," said Amos.

As they reached the boats, they noticed that there seemed to be only three that were undamaged.

"I'm sure we could get one of these started."

"Yeah, I'm sure you're right, Dad, but look at the speed of the bergs bouncing past; if we get caught in one of those we are gonna be in trouble and their movement is so sporadic."

Amos stood for a while and assessed the situation. "Robert, you may well be right; it'll be too risky and with the water cold as well... not good." Amos got off the boat he was standing on and stood next to Robert on the quayside.

"Dad, I've been watching the movement of the bergs after they reach the bridge... and if you look at them closely you'll see there is a pattern. They seem to build up at where the bridge used to be and then all of a sudden it's like they've been released and go bobbing off at a rate of about five or six of them at a time, more than when we looked at them earlier, and then after about ten minutes, it happens again. So we could try our luck between the surges?"

"Yeah, Robert, we could, but just look what happens when they break through; they disperse in such a haphazard way that we would struggle if we sailed in the wrong direction. Let's head back to the others," said Amos.

They collected their bags and walked back along the road parallel with the harbour wall. Amos then stopped in his stride. "Hold on a minute, Robert, let's just see what the bergs are like on this side of the bridge."

They both stood looking at them.

"Pick out a berg, Robert, any berg, and watch it down to the bridge and I'll do the same. See how long it takes to get to the front of the bridge once it joins up with the others waiting to break through."

"OK."

They stand there watching and timing the movements.

"Looks to me like once they've joined the group piling up at the bridge, they stack up and wait their turn to go through. There is at least forty-five minutes to an hour before they break free… and with six or so of them then breaking through each time. It happens about every ten minutes, then with the pressure building up from the others behind them… Yeah, so if we…"

No, thought Amos.

"Even on this side of the harbour it would be too tricky to use a boat," said Amos.

"That's assuming we can safely move one up to here, Dad," replied Robert.

All of a sudden Amos heard a noise. He was the first to pick it up; working on the rigs, it meant the expectation of letters from home or release from the prison of iron.

"Dad, a helicopter," said Robert.

The deafening *ratta-tat-ratta-tat-ratta* was soon overhead.

"Hey, someone's realised we're stranded on the island," shouted Robert.

"That could be Bill, my pilot friend who brought me over a few days ago."

"It's still very foggy, Dad; I can't see anything up there."

"Yeah, but maybe he's seen an area where he can land. We'd better get ourselves back to the others at the cottage."

Picking up their bags they walked as quickly as they could back to the others, listening out for the direction in which the helicopter was going. It was moving overhead rapidly, to and fro above them.

"It's heading towards the cottage, Dad, come on, hurry."

The noise slowly faded away as they headed back.

"Ah... come on," said Amos, dropping his bags on the footpath, exhausted.

"It's too foggy, Dad, isn't it."

"Yeah, for a moment I thought we were gonna be back on the mainland and a nice bed for the night."

They returned to the cottage.

"I'm ready for a hot drink, Robert, I don't know about you."

"Yeah, me too," he replied.

They were greeted at the open door by Henry and Elizabeth.

"Dad, Dad, did you hear the helicopter?" both cried out in unison.

"Yeah, we did."

"Are they coming to rescue us?" asked Henry.

"Well, I suspect they tried but with the fog being so thick, they had to go back. I'm sure they'll try again."

"But when, Amos, when? What are we going to do?" said Bernie with a very serious look on her face, then turning away from Robert and Amos and back into the cottage.

Amos stood for a while looking back into the fog and contemplative of their predicament... then entered the cottage and closed the door.

CHAPTER 15: BILL

Brr, brr… Bill's phone rang whilst he was sitting in the café with his coffee. He decided to save the *snegles* as he might need them later.

"Yeah, hello."

"Hi, it's Calum."

"How's it looking?" replied Bill.

"I think we're good to go, Bill, looking at the weather projections. I've checked them four times now just to make sure. We should be able to get away in about twenty minutes, maybe quicker if we are lucky and the wind picks up from the north-west. But we will need to set off shortly."

"OK, Calum, thanks, I'll be over in a couple of minutes." Bill drank the last of his coffee and put his coat on.

"Steffi. Thanks. I'll take these and be back later to finish off the rest of the *snegles*… if there's any left!"

"You be careful now, Bill; you know you can always go over tomorrow," she said with concern in her voice.

"Yeah, true enough… We'll be careful. Thanks, Steffi, don't you worry."

He closed the door to the café behind him and zipped up his coat and walked towards the helicopter pad. It was still too foggy for his liking. *But*, he thought, *it does seem to be clearing.* He got to the helicopter, opened the door and sat inside next to Calum.

"OK, Calum, so what have you got for me to look at?"

Calum ran the weather prediction on the helicopter's computer screen, showing fog movement for the next hour.

"Mmm… you're right, Calum, looks like we've got probably a thirty-minute slot to get up and over and then back again… at best, by the look of things, and that assumes we will be taking off in the next few minutes. You do realise it's still pretty foggy over there? Calum, have you been through all the safety checks?"

"Yeah, I did that earlier and then finished off whilst you were coming back."

"OK, it's cleared sufficiently. Let's go for it," said Bill. "We will need to check what the weather is doing for the journey home as well. Fire her up and let's get over there before the weather closes in."

Calum flicked the ignition switch and the blades started to turn and within a few seconds they were making the full turn before take-off. With their ear defenders on, Bill continued checking the weather forecast conditions to see if there was a window of opportunity to rescue them, but the fog was so dense in places. He continued to check a number of other dials on the dashboard, well aware they were taking a big risk.

"Let's hope the wind picks up and clears the fog."

"OK, here we go."

"Take it slowly now, Calum."

The engines roared and the helicopter slowly lifted off the ground.

Ten feet… twenty… thirty…

"Calum, hold it there a minute."

"OK."

"I think we should go back down… It's not clearing quickly enough… If the visibility doesn't improve up here we might be struck and then we really will have a problem."

Calum returned the helicopter to terra firma and the blades slowly came to a halt, but they kept the engine turning slowly on tick-over, ready for another attempt.

***

At the hospital, Mary could hear the helicopter and the sound of it lifting off the ground; she was used to the sounds, with patients being brought in regularly from some of the outer parts of the islands as well as the rigs.

"Oh, that's good," she said out loud, but then realised that something wasn't right as the helicopter noise remained at a constant *ratta-tat-ratta-ratta-tat-ratta*, the same noise for a short period of time. She took her phone earpiece off and stood up from her desk and walked towards the windows and entrance doors of the reception. "It's definitely clearing." The helicopter noise then slowly quietened down to nothing. "Oh dear, something's not right." She started fretting again and turned to walk back to her desk.

"What's the problem, Mary?" asked one of the nurses.

"Well, the helicopter's taken off and then returned to the ground. Something's not right."

"Well, I'm sure they have done the right thing, Mary. You shouldn't worry yourself; they know what they are doing."

Mary looked outside again, still with a concerned look on her face, pondering what, if anything, she could do to help.

"I know, I know, I know. But I just can't stop worrying."

***

Bill and Calum were sitting patiently in the helicopter, looking at the radar screen and keeping a close eye on the wind direction. It predicted a clearing of the fog here and a movement of the fog bank over Viðoy.

Bill then gave Calum a thumbs up.

"Let's go."

The helicopter's engines roared again and this time when they lifted off the ground they could see much more clearly. The town buildings started to appear and a few glimpses of hills in the distance… They could also see the fog bank over towards Viðoy; it looked very dense.

"Head straight for the bridge, Calum."

"OK."

Bill was constantly focused on the radar screen and the control panel dials, very mindful of the risk they were taking.

"We've got about ten minutes of this and then we should be

over the island."

As they approached, they caught very faint glimpses of the landscape through gaps in the fog and then roughly where the harbour was… Out to sea, they saw the white tips of icebergs.

"This is no good, Bill," said Calum, flying over where he thought the harbour and bridge would be. "We can't see anything and the fog bank… look, it's sweeping across towards us now. We're gonna have to abort and head back pretty much now, otherwise we'll get caught up here."

"Agreed. Let's turn her around straight away and head back. We'll give it another go later if it clears, or tomorrow."

As the helicopter turned, they could then see a second bank of fog in the distance… it was heading straight for them.

"Bill, do you see what I see?"

"Yeah… where did that come from… And so quickly. Out of nowhere." Bill looked down at the dashboard and it was showing that they would return to Klaksvík in seven to eight minutes. "We've got just enough time to get back. But we're gonna have to give it full speed all the way and no deviation from our course."

The *ratta-tat-ratta-tat-ratta* increased to a high-pitched roar as they raced against time to get back.

They caught glimpses of familiar buildings through the thickening fog. The helicopter returned back to the helipad next to the hospital just before the fog closed in.

CHAPTER 16: THE CLIMB

"Dad, Dad, why didn't they land? Are they going to come back to rescue us?" Henry asked, extremely disappointed as he was hoping to have a ride in a helicopter.

"Yeah, Henry. But I'm sure they would have landed if they could?" Amos looked across towards Bernie and then to Ingrid and breathed in and out deeply, very mindful that they were so close to getting off the island.

"Dad? When are we going to get back to the mainland?" asked Elizabeth. "I'm worried about what you and Mom were talking about earlier. We could be stuck here. Especially as the helicopter didn't land."

"We're all worried, honey," said Bernie, putting her hand over her daughter's shoulders and looking from Amos to Ingrid.

"Come on, Elizabeth," said Henry, grabbing her hand, "let's play hide." And they ran into the living room, diving under the blankets.

"It'll be soon, Elizabeth; once the fog lifts, they'll come for us, I'm sure of that," said Amos. "Anyhow, we've got plenty of food and firewood so no need to worry." Amos knew that it really wasn't enough for them but was trying to give everyone some reassurance about their predicament.

Bernie looked back towards Amos, Amos realising she knew that he had fibbed to Elizabeth.

"Is there another way to get back?" asked Bernie with a sense of desperation in her voice that Amos picked up on.

"There is only the one bridge. We could possibly use a boat to get across, Robert and I saw a few down by the harbour."

"Yeah, what's left of them," added Robert.

"When I am here by myself it is OK here, but now with so many of us it will be difficult with food but we can…"

"We don't appear to have much food left, even with the bags you brought up from the village stores. There isn't enough to last till tomorrow," said Bernie, emptying the contents onto the kitchen table. "Look, that's it."

They all stared at the different packaging on the table and then towards the fridge as Bernie opened the door.

"Well," said Amos, "there is possibly another way but it—"

"Anything to get off this bloody island," shouted Bernie.

"But it will be tricky," replied Amos.

"Go on, go on," said Bernie.

"When Robert and I followed up behind you earlier, we stood looking at the bergs for a while. We closely timed their movements from the sea to breaking through where the bridge used to be… there's a possibility we could climb around—"

"Climb around what?" Bernie snapped back. Amos paused and drew breadth,

"An iceberg," replied Amos.

"You've got to be kidding me. Of all the damn stupid ideas, Amos, you've had, that… that is the dumbest I've ever heard," said Bernie, waving her hands in the air and stamping her foot on the floor.

"I'm not doing that," came the muffled voice of Elizabeth from underneath the covers in the lounge, where they were still hiding under the blankets.

Henry's head popped out from under the blankets. "Cool, I want to do that, Dad," he said, smiling and then hiding again.

Amos looked back towards Ingrid, Robert and then Bernie. "It may be our only choice, honey. You've asked me to tell you about ways we could get off the island and that's one of them," he replied.

Bernie stood with her arms folded, shaking her head from side to side, and then proceeded to march up and down in the room. "That doesn't sound good, Amos, you know that."

"But if it's the only way, honey… How else are we gonna…" Amos stopped, realising that she needed to absorb what he had said and reconsider the proposal.

Bernie didn't reply and there was silence in the room for a few minutes.

"Ingrid?" asked Amos.

"Yes."

"Could we check what you've got here in the stores by the way of climbing gear and boots?"

"Well… we have everything here for climbing as the school parties and visitors, they come and climb the cliffs and rocks and walking so… yes, we have."

"OK, then, let's take a look."

Bernie still had her arms folded, her lips tense, looking out of a window and then turning to face Amos.

"I'm not doing it, Amos; I'd rather wait to be rescued. Why do we always get into situations like this, Amos. The grizzly bear followed us last year when we were in Canada… the canoe tipping over on the Campbell River… and what were we doing of all things? Chasing bloody salmon… why? And here we go again."

"Hey, that's not fair. It's not my fault. I don't know how long we are gonna be fogged in. One day, three days? A week, two weeks, who knows? We've got a roof over our heads and…" Amos stopped his sentence as he was about to say "firewood" but realised that that was also low.

"And then the time we went on a four-day hike and you forgot to pack the tent poles."

"We came out of that OK, didn't we?" said Amos sternly. "And we're gonna do the same here." He put the drying-up towel down and went over to give Bernie a reassuring hug.

She wasn't impressed and just shrugged her shoulders and then turned away.

"Look, Bernie, I did not cause this problem," said Amos.

Bernie looked at Amos, then towards Ingrid and then back to Amos again. Ingrid smiled slightly and lifted her eyebrows just a touch and carried on with the washing up.

"I'm just taking a look, Bernie, alright… to weigh up our options… it might be very simple. Otherwise we might just as well just sit here in the cottage and hope someone comes for us, with food running out. We could be here for days and that wouldn't be good for any of us."

Bernie walked out of the kitchen.

"I'm worried, Mom," said Elizabeth, popping her head out from under the covers.

"I wanna go climbing," said Henry. "It'll be fun, Elizabeth, come on." Henry gave Elizabeth a gentle nudge and then they were messing around under the blankets again.

"I'm sure that climbing around an iceberg will not be a problem. I'm gonna have a look at what equipment is available." Amos stood up and followed Ingrid out of the living room.

Ingrid was already opening up cupboard doors in the storeroom and dragging boxes out into the middle of the room.

"Here, we have the jackets and hats and… boots, I think, in this one. Yes, here they are. We will have the sizes, I think, for everyone, even for little Henry."

"That's good; do you think we're gonna need any ropes? What do you think, Ingrid?" asked Amos.

"Yes, I think so, and pins for fixing to the ice."

"What, really?"

"Yes. I think it is best, I think we will need them."

Robert and Amos started sorting out the equipment into the various sizes for everyone: jackets, boots, bright red helmets, life jackets and climbing ropes. They came across a box full of rubber dinghies which Amos immediately pushed to one side, thinking, *We are climbing, not white-water rafting.*

"Ingrid, have you got any flares?"

"None."

"That's a shame; that would at least tell people where we are. Ingrid, what do you think about us climbing around an iceberg?"

"I think it's straightforward as long as we have boots and gloves and rope for each other when we climb and we can wear life jackets in case of a fall in the water and helmet. What do you think, Amos? You know your family better than me, and those dinghies… we should take two with us if we can fit them in the backpacks as we may need them."

"Well, Robert. He's OK with climbing."

"Yeah. We did a bit of hiking and climbing in last summer camp," said Robert. "Do you remember, Dad?"

"Oh, yeah... yeah," replied Amos, slightly tongue in cheek as he only had a vague recollection of a school trip. "Bernie, she is strong... I think it's really Elizabeth that might be a problem... Henry should be OK but he'll need to be roped up."

"We all will, Amos," replied Ingrid, "big or small, experienced or not; we can all slip and then where will we be."

Being put in his place by Ingrid set Amos back.

"Well, if the plan is to climb around a suitably sized iceberg to the other side then we must take a good look down there now and choose which one or ones look climbable and also how long we've got to do it before they move again... I think we should go and have a look first before we decide that this is definitely what we are going to do," said Amos.

"If you want to try today, then we must go and see now otherwise we may not have the time before it gets dark and then we have to stay another night," replied Ingrid.

"We should head off now, then, down to the harbour. Robert, you coming?"

"Yeah, sure, Dad, I'm just getting the last of the wood we brought up from those houses so that Mom can keep the fire going whilst we're gone."

Ingrid decided that it would be sensible for her to stay at the cottage and finish off sorting all the equipment and rucksacks; that way, if they did decide to go that afternoon, they would have everyone kitted out. Amos and Robert were soon ready and out of the front door, making their way down to the harbour.

"We'll be back in about an hour," he called out from the front door of the cottage.

Elizabeth ran to the front door and called out, "Hurry up, Dad, I wanna go home..."

There was no reply from Bernie before the front door of the cottage slammed shut behind them.

As they made their way down to the harbour, Amos was running things over his mind, over and over again. *Do we wait? … Do we climb? … Do we use a boat? … Or walk to another part of the island and try to get across?* He eventually spoke to Robert. "Do you think this is sensible, trying to get across to the other side by climbing?"

"Yeah. Sure, Dad, I'm with you. We just need to keep a close eye on Elizabeth and Henry and make sure we choose the right bergs."

***

Ingrid returned to the living room and reassured Bernie that they had all the climbing and safety gear needed if it was decided that they were to climb. Bernie was still very reluctant about it despite the assurances given to her. She was trying to think of a reason not to leave the cottage. But there was the constant nagging reminder in her stomach… *Limited food, limited heat and… how long are we going to be stuck on the island?*

"Would you like to try on the equipment for our climbing?" Ingrid asked Bernie and the children, who were still happy playing under the covers.

"Yeah, yeah," shouted Henry. Elizabeth gave a more subdued response but still ran behind Henry, who was running into the storeroom. Bernie was a very reluctant follower.

***

Amos and Robert reached the harbour wall. Beyond, all they could see through the rolling fog was bergs and water. The icebergs were still following the same pattern as earlier: slowly moving in from the sea, stopping as they hit the bergs waiting at the old bridge. This was then followed by the periodic breakthrough of half a dozen or so bergs and the haphazardness on the other side of the icebergs once they were through the hold-up.

"Let's walk further along the sea wall, Robert, and get a better idea of timing. I suggest we each choose a berg that we think is suitable and watch it come in."

"OK, Dad, I've got that flat one with a sort of peak at the end; do you see it?"

"Right, I've got it... I'm on the one just to the right."

They watched patiently. The quiet was broken by the occasional sea bird and the rubbing of the icebergs against each other and the sea wall. After a few minutes, the two bergs then joined the bottleneck and stopped. They both waited patiently to see what would happen. There was a sudden break in the hold-up and a group broke through the old bridge to the other side.

That was similar to earlier... that's reassuring, Amos thought to himself, pondering now over the practicality of them climbing and that it may actually be feasible for them.

The two bergs they were keeping an eye on then moved closer and were shortly joined by others behind them. Seven to eight minutes later there was another "great escape" of bergs; this time a further eight bergs broke free.

The two bergs that they had been monitoring moved closer to the pinch point at the bridge.

They waited a further twelve minutes this time before the group of bergs broke through, their two chosen bergs moving closer to the old bridge.

"That's over twenty-five minutes so far, and there are at least two, maybe three more breakthroughs before ours... I reckon that we will have about an hour. Max."

"Yeah, I agree, Dad."

"Now I suppose we need to think how we are going to get on one of those blocks of ice?"

They both noticed that when the bergs came to a halt, there were always a few very close to the harbour wall, so they could perhaps scramble up onto the harbour wall, wade through the water and then climb up. *That's gonna be cold... and not a good start to the climb.*

"A ladder! That's what we need, Dad. It's simple. Place the ladder over the harbour wall, we climb up and we're on our way," said Robert, grinning from ear to ear, having solved the problem.

Well, he thought he had.

"Good thinking… but where do we get one of those from?"

"Dad. I think we should check out a few back gardens; there's bound to be a ladder in one of them that we can borrow," replied Robert.

The two of them headed up towards a group of cottages next to the village shop.

"You take the one on the right and I'll check this one out," said Amos.

After a few moments Robert called out, "Dad, I've got one. It's aluminium and it's a double; looks like it could be usable."

Amos joined Robert at the back of the house.

"Yeah, that looks perfect for the job, and a double in case we need to extend it. Nice."

They carried the ladder down to the harbour wall to try out the arrangement of connecting across to a berg. They worked out that they were going to have to climb over the wall with the ladder and then lean the ladder up against the berg… perfect.

"Right, let's get back to the others… We have a plan," said Amos happily.

Amos and Robert were greeted at the entrance to the cottage by Henry and Elizabeth, fully dressed up in their climbing outfits.

"OK, everyone, we have a plan. It's pretty straightforward as long as we all listen and stay together. If at any time there's someone who thinks it should be done differently then just say, OK? No moaning to yourselves; let's talk about it. That way we all get safely to the other side – you all got that?"

"Dad… What happens if we fall off?" asked Henry.

"That's a good question, Henry, and…"

"You have the life jacket, Henry… It is easy to pull the cord – here, I show you – and it keeps you afloat," replied Ingrid. Henry made a grab to pull the cord.

"Not now, Henry, only when you're in the water," said Amos sharply.

"And how, Dad, do we keep together?" said Elizabeth.

"We'll have a rope connected between us at all times, until

we agree to take it off. Got that? That way we are always safely together... Everyone got that? And always make sure that one of your two clips is connected to the rope. Do you see that, everyone...? Have a go at clipping on and off some rope so that you get some practice in now, as you will be doing it a lot once we're up on a berg."

"Food and water we have with us; Bernie has done that. But how do we get onto one of the icebergs, have you thought of that?"

"We found a long ladder that should do it, Ingrid."

She raised her eyebrows. "That sounds like you have thought of everything... So we get on, then we walk, then what... We climb and then...?"

"We get to the other side," said Amos, "and we're gonna need to get going soon before it starts to get dark, so let's get sorted and go before we end up having a change of heart and staying another night, which I know is not what you want to do."

"We're waiting on you now, Dad. We're all ready," said Elizabeth. Robert had been getting changed whilst Amos had been talking.

He smiled back. "Always the last one, hey."

Amos found a jacket and a pair of boots and changed in the storeroom. He picked up a large rucksack and joined the others.

"I suggest that Robert, Ingrid and Bernie have rucksacks... Bernie, if you put the food in yours and Robert, Ingrid and I will carry all the gear we need. That leaves Henry and Elizabeth free to climb without having to carry anything."

"Dad, you take the extra rope and the grappling iron... if you have any room, as it might help with climbing. What do you think?"

"We'll see; as you said, it depends on the amount of space we've got left in the bags."

"Look, Dad, there," said Robert. "Ingrid pointed them out earlier, dinghies, what do you think? I'm gonna take one if I can fit it into my backpack... just in case. Maybe we can't climb or whatever; we can always leave them down at the harbour if we don't feel we need them."

"It's a lot of space and weight, but... Yeah, OK then."

"I've got a three-man dinghy here and there's a smaller two-man dinghy you can probably get into your bag… I won't be able to fit any more in, Dad."

"You never said anything about boats, Amos," said Bernie, looking towards Amos.

Amos looked up from doing the shoelaces up on his boots.

"You know I'm not good at boats…"

"It's for safety; view it as a contingency plan, Bernie, just in case. Anyhow, that's why I didn't tell you earlier." Amos was having to think quickly on his feet; they couldn't afford any delay and discussion or argument… not now. But he admitted to himself that he hadn't thought that they would be needed. But there was always a possibility they might need them. *What if someone slips and falls in… What if we all do? Yeah, good call, Robert.*

"How are we getting on then?" said Ingrid. "Are we all ready?"

"Dinghies and climbing gear; what else do you suggest?"

"Well, you both need a life jacket – here you are, try these." Ingrid pulled two off the pegs, checking their sizes, and handed them over.

"Ah, yeah, thank you, Ingrid. You've done this sort of thing before?"

"Yes, I have been climbing in Norway many years ago and here there are bays with no footpaths… So I climb down so that I can clear the plastic from the beaches."

Ingrid was then stuffing netting into her bag, together with pins and a hammer. "It is good for climbing," she said. "I have the pegs and clips." Then she swung a coil of rope over her shoulders.

Amos picked up the coil of rope with the grappling hook on the end and waved it around.

"I've got space. You never know, we might need it."

"Yes, that is good." Ingrid nodded.

"I'm getting cold standing here waiting for all of you; can we please get going?" called out Elizabeth.

"Yeah, we're ready now." Amos and Robert emerged from the storeroom.

They took their last gulps of warm drinks and then left the cottage, Ingrid throwing the power switch and locking up on the way out.

"Robert, you look very silly," said Elizabeth. He was wearing his reindeer bobble hat over his climbing hat.

"Where's my bobble hat gone? I want to do the same," called out Henry.

"We haven't got time; come on."

"Leave it, Amos." Bernie asked Ingrid for the key and went to find Henry's bobble hat.

She returned and fixed it around Henry's climbing helmet, they could finally leave the cottage, Ingrid locking up behind her.

"This is fun," said Henry. "I've got gloves with pimples on them."

"That'll be good for gripping when you're climbing," Robert replied.

Now that they knew the route down to the harbour, it felt to all the family like it was only a short distance away. On reaching the harbour wall, Robert looked across the water. He still could not see any land on the other side of the harbour.

"From what I can see, Dad, it looks like we've got about thirty-five to forty bergs, queuing up and waiting to push through."

"Yeah. OK, that seems about right and about the same as we had earlier. Now all we've got to do is pick a berg. Preferably one that's close to us, and make sure that the ladder reaches across."

"You are checking the timing of the movements, yes?" asked Ingrid. "As they seem stopped for a while and then a lot of movement."

A series of splashes and rumbles out in the harbour reminded Amos that their journey was going to have some risks attached to it.

"Yeah, I know. Me and Robert have timed the movement of the icebergs and the time available to get across them before the iceberg breaks through where the bridge used to be. We've worked out that we will have about an hour to get across, perhaps an hour and a quarter, and that assumes a suitable iceberg comes along in the next twenty minutes, otherwise we are back to the cottage."

All of them were now looking at the bergs floating in, pointing and then discarding, following one and then as it came towards them realising it was not practical. It was becoming frustrating for them and getting darker. Time was running out. They needed to choose one that was coming up close to this side of the harbour, was not too high, and the flatter the better.

The two younger children were getting cold and impatience building up between them with the realisation that they would have to go back to the weather station and spend another night on the island.

"Look," shouted Robert, pointing out to sea. "Look. That one, that one there; it's coming across now." They all stood and observed it for a while.

"What do you think, Ingrid?" said Amos, pondering the shape, size and height and whether it had a place where they could get on.

"It is high in places, but there is a level edge around part of the sides. Let's see when it gets closer and how it joins the others."

There was a sudden bursting through of the bergs where the bridge used to be.

"That's another six," called out Robert.

"OK, let's just wait and see how this one joins the others; here it comes now."

The berg crashed into the other bergs, close to the harbour wall.

"It's twisted round; we've only got the steep face to try to get on. That's no good, we can't risk it even with the ladder."

"I'm cold, Dad," Henry shouted out.

"Me too; can we climb, please?" said Elizabeth. "Or I'm going back to the cottage."

"We've just got to wait a few more minutes," said Bernie. "Just think of it as having to wait for the school bus to take you to school. Sometimes when it arrives it's full up and you have to wait for the next one."

"Dad," Robert called out again, "I think there's a better one coming in. That's got to be the one; look at it – it's much bigger than the previous one, but it's got a ledge running around the side which will help getting across with the ladder."

They all watched it carefully as it glided past and came to a halt on the harbour wall with a thump and a flurry of ice falling off as it joined the queue of bergs.

"Ingrid. Can we get the ladder across? What do you think?"

"Yes, I think so. We should be able to but it's not in the best position on the harbour wall."

"We will just have to make do. Robert, let's get the ladder and lift it up over the wall and onto the berg," said Amos.

The ladder was positioned and angled across the gap. "It is good... let me see." Ingrid started shaking the ladder to check the supports were strong in their positions. "I go first and fix the rope and ladder, then everyone can follow... I think me, then Elizabeth followed by Bernie and then Robert, Henry and then Amos at the back."

The berg moved slightly... fortunately into a much more favourable position. The ladder held firm.

Amos felt he needed to repeat what Ingrid had said to make sure that his family understood the routine. "Everyone listen up: Ingrid will lead with the safety rope and fix it... and remember to keep your clips on the rope at all times, right... you all got that?"

"I'm scared, Dad. What happens if I slip?" said Elizabeth, a slight shudder in her voice combining a mixture of cold and apprehension.

"It'll be OK," said Amos confidently. But inside he was as apprehensive as the rest of them, except for Ingrid. She seemed to be taking it all in her stride. And then he thought about Robert; he was confident.

Ingrid explained, "The clip on the rope will stop you falling too far and your clip will run to the next pin or the next person behind you."

There was a rumble of ice and water splashing in the harbour.

"Now I go."

Ingrid climbed up and over the harbour wall, Robert and Amos holding the ladder steady. She carefully made her way across up the ladder, then started hammering in a pin safety rope connector into the ice wall. The ledge location on the berg they had chosen was about two metres higher than the harbour wall so climbing along the ladder was at an easy angle for them.

Ingrid secured herself and moved to get a better footing and fixed another pin, clipping herself on; she moved around the corner of the berg and out of sight disappearing from view for about a minute. There was no sound other than the hammering in of pins. They were wondering what to do when she reappeared and called over to them.

"It is good, very good; we can climb over now. There is a flat area behind me here that we can wait on when we are all across. OK, we are ready now – Elizabeth first."

"I don't wanna do it."

"Elizabeth, it is like you climb up a ladder; I have the rope and so does Bernie behind you – you are safes with us."

With that reassurance, within seconds Elizabeth was up and across the ladder and over to the berg, clipping herself onto the rope and working her way to the holding area, guided by Ingrid.

"Well done, Elizabeth, well done," called out Bernie, now realising it was her turn.

"Now that Elizabeth is over we should be OK, Dad," said Robert quietly.

"Yeah."

Bernie was next. She quickly reached the berg and carefully moved around the side to the safer area, followed by Robert as planned. The berg wobbled whilst he was on the ladder, shaking and juddering it down the face of the berg; it then stopped horizontally as he made his way across the final rungs on his hands and knees.

"Phew, made it," said Robert.

Henry followed after an adjustment to the position of the ladder, with Robert and Amos at either end holding it stable for him.

"Henry, over you go now, no hanging around," called out Amos.

Henry made it across easily, but whilst crossing there was a huge rumble and a splash as a chunk of berg broke away and fell into the sea. "Cor, did you see that?" said Henry.

Last to cross was Amos, with no support at the harbour wall end. It meant that Robert and Ingrid held the ladder as steady as they could as he made his way across. As he did so he was distracted by a movement in another berg and his foot slipped through a rung, twisting the ladder round on its edge. Robert and Ingrid desperately held on. Amos lifted his foot out and crawled across to them, stretching out his hand he was finally helped across by Robert, but his final movement and foothold onto the berg had loosened the support of the ladder. It fell away with a clatter against the sea wall. The berg moved slowly away from the harbour wall.

"That was good timing," said Robert, smiling at his father.

"There goes our escape route; no turning back now," said Amos to Ingrid and Robert.

The three of them joined the others, who were waiting impatiently to move on.

"Dad, my feet are cold," said Elizabeth, already shivering.

"We will get moving shortly. Remember, Ingrid here will lead on and we will follow behind, same order, and remember your clips… right… two on at all times when you're moving, and only take one off to connect around the next pin."

Moving forward, Ingrid stumbled and fell hard onto the ice.

She turned around, smiled and got up.

"Be carefuls, everyone, of the lumps – there are slippy ones here. Yes."

"Be carefuls… I like that," said Henry chuckling.

"Why is the berg moving so much, Dad?"

"It'll stop soon, Elizabeth," said Amos reassuringly, and hoping. Amos suddenly thought, *Oh my God… what if the berg flips over? … We've had it… we're all tied to this lump of ice.* The berg swayed and then jolted to a stop. *At least we have life jackets on.*

Amos looked up, and could just about make out the top of the berg through the flurries of snow… it was towering above them.

"Still looking rather hazy out there," said Amos aloud.

"I'm starting to see some of the other side of the harbour now," said Elizabeth, slightly further ahead and higher up than the others, "but it looks like there's still a long way to go."

Amos looked upwards past Elizabeth to what he could make out as being the shoreline. She was right, but it was a lot further than he had expected, and now realised the enormity of the situation he had got his family into.

Ingrid made slow progress along a ledge, they all hoped ran around the berg, otherwise they may well have to turn back and find another route. They followed Ingrid's voice and the hammering noise of the support pins being nailed into the ice. She called out to them to follow her quickly as she had found another safe holding position on the berg.

There were constant creaks and groans as the icebergs wobbled and scraped up against each other and onto the shoreline.

As Robert moved to catch up with his mother, he slipped and lost his footing on the ice and was held up by Bernie as she stretched out a hand on one side and his hand grabbed hold of the rope.

"Thanks, Mom, that was lucky."

"Just be careful and take it a bit slower, Robert." Bernie was becoming worried.

"Can I suggest we hold tight where we are at the moment?" called out Amos from the back. "As we haven't had a breakthrough of bergs at the bridge for a while and when they move we will all be moving and will need to hold on tight."

"Dad, I just wanna get to where Ingrid is standing and not hang around here. It's not very—" Elizabeth's voice stopped short.

The front line of bergs broke through. They all stopped moving and held onto the climbing ropes. The bergs in front of them started to move. They held their breath.

The berg next to them moved, and then theirs with a sudden jolt, followed by a wobble and swaying action in the water. The bergs were jostling for position and barging into each other. A huge thunderous crash of ice hitting the water and the sea wall, sent a torrent of water up and over where they were standing on the berg.

"God, that water is so cold," said Bernie, wiping the ice water off her face and jacket.

"That was scary," added Elizabeth.

"I liked it," said Henry nonchalantly.

"Where's Ingrid?" said a concerned Robert.

Her head appeared from around the corner in front of them. "I finish making the pitons for our next part of the journey."

"Pitons – what are they?" said Bernie.

"Pins, pitons, metal pegs or spikes for the rope to attach to," said Amos.

"Oh," replied Bernie with surprise in her voice at Amos's knowledge. "How do you know that?"

"Robert told me earlier," replied Amos.

Their berg came to a sudden halt, followed by a gentle movement from side to side.

"Wow, that was good," said Henry. "Glad I was holding on; that almost made me slip."

"Yeah... the only problem is we are facing in the wrong direction."

Ingrid had to swiftly make her way back to where Amos was standing at the back, clipping and unclipping as she clambered back.

"I don't wanna be at the back," came a cry from Elizabeth. With Ingrid heading towards Amos, Elizabeth was now by herself at the other end of the climbing rope.

"Honey, don't worry, we'll sort that out."

"I'll do it, Mom," said Robert.

"Be careful now, Robert, you've already slipped once."

He was quick and efficient with the clipping and unclipping along the rope. The only problem was where he had to pass the others. Ingrid was doing the same but going in the opposite direction.

"We need to move again, please, before the bergs change places again." Ingrid continued with her *tap tap... tap tap*, putting in the pins so that they could pull the climbing rope through. They followed behind, clipping and unclipping their safety harnesses.

Another shudder and movement of their berg and it had swivelled round... the direction that they needed to head in had now changed again.

"Shit, shit, shit," said Amos under his breath. *This wasn't meant to happen. What are we gonna do now?*

With the shift in position of the berg, Ingrid made her way to the front again, much to the relief of Elizabeth.

"We must all move quicker, please, otherwise we will run out of time." Ingrid was heard hammering in more pins at the front. Eventually, she called them through. Amos was now becoming extremely worried that they were not going to make it in time.

"OK now, everybodys," shouted Ingrid. "We now has to go to the next berg but we are waiting until they move again as there will be another rolling and swaying – hold tight."

The berg moved for a short while and then stopped.

"Robert, that will be the second of the four groups of bergs breaking through," said Amos.

"Yeah," he replied.

"OK, we go now, please," shouted Ingrid.

She hadn't said what they were going to encounter next, but it meant stepping over a chasm between two bergs.

"Oh my God!" shouted Elizabeth when she got there. The others soon joined her.

"Come on, I'll help you," called out Robert.

"I can't do it." Elizabeth started to cry.

"You have to," said Bernie, joining her and realising that there was no option. "Now, Elizabeth, otherwise we are gonna be separated."

Robert stretched across and held her hand and pulled her over as she jumped across.

"Mom, come on, quickly now you."

"Yeah, OK, I'm with you. Oh my God, my God."

"Bernie, now come on, we've got to follow you and I don't wanna be separated," said Amos. "Don't look down; just look across at Robert. You can do it."

She stumbled as she jumped but Robert's foothold and strength dragged her across. She held onto Robert tightly.

There was another huge crumbling and crashing sound of ice into water from a nearby berg.

"Come on, Henry, focus," said Amos, "it's your turn next."

"No problem, Dad," said Henry, looking across at Robert. "No fear."

"Be careful now, Henry," cried out Amos.

Henry jumped across and Robert caught hold of him, de-clipped and then re-clipped him to the rope. Henry made his way to join the others.

"Dad, quick now... ready – last one!"

"Yeah, I'm on my way but it's just very slippy over here..." The berg groaned and shook.

"Dad... come on, hurry up," screamed Elizabeth. "It's moving."

Amos took a big step to cross the divide. He stumbled and swayed backwards as his foot hit the ice... Robert steadied his father and then pulled him across by the rope to the second berg. Where Amos had been standing moments before suddenly moved away.

"Dad, untie the rope quickly," said Robert frantically.

Amos undid the knot and as soon as he did so the rope slipped through his fingers away with the berg that was now already a metre... now two metres, three metres away.

"Gee, that was close. That would have been interesting if I hadn't got across; thank you, Robert. I hadn't appreciated the amount of movement on the berg... It's steady for a while and then suddenly turns and jolts and judders." Amos felt a warm sensation down his arm, then blood dripping onto his hand; the stitches must have broken whilst stretching across from the berg on the rope.

They both looked around and realised that they were now surrounded by bergs.

Ingrid called out, "Is everyone all OK and ready to move on?"

"Thanks, Robert," said Amos, slapping his son on the shoulders. They moved to catch up with the others.

"Ingrid, are you sure which direction we have to take?" asked Amos.

"Dad. My feet are as cold as ice blocks," said Elizabeth.

"We can see where we have to go, everyone. Yes?" said Ingrid, pointing ahead and trying to encourage Elizabeth forward.

The berg jolted and started to sway again from side to side with a mesmerising motion.

"Hold tight, everyone, this might be a big one," shouted Amos. They waited… and waited… Nothing. They were all thankful that there was no further significant movement of the berg.

"Let's just get going," said Henry, interrupting the silence. Amos and Bernie looked at each other apprehensively and smiled, acknowledging Henry's enthusiasm.

"Make sure you helps each other and check with your clips, yes," said Ingrid, checking on Elizabeth's and then Henry's safety ropes.

"Dad. Daaaad. My hands are getting cold with all this standing around and waiting," cried out Elizabeth, visibly shivering.

"We must hurry now," said Ingrid, carefully moving past a projection of ice and disappearing out of sight. There followed more *tap tap tap*-ing… and hammering from Ingrid up ahead as she put in more pins. The family were huddled together to keep warm when Ingrid returned, having set the route for the next stage of their climb. They set off again. The route was taking them steadily further up the berg. Soon they were over thirty metres above the sea, and still climbing.

"I have to make for your feets around this next part of our climb for two places as there is no places for feets, so everyone, you must be very careful."

Bernie turned to Amos. "I hope you know what you are doing, Amos, getting us up here."

"Next one, please come, come quickly," called Ingrid.

Elizabeth, Bernie and then Robert followed with Henry and Amos bringing up the rear of the procession.

A sudden cracking and collapsing of ice in front of them was followed by a crashing into the water. This brought them all to their senses and the reality of where they were and what they were doing. Part of a berg to the left of them came crashing down, creating a huge wall of water which washed up and over them. They held on tightly.

"Glad that wasn't our berg," said Amos.

"Dad. I think part of it might have been. We've got to get going. Now."

"Yeah, you're right, Robert." *I hadn't put that into my plans either oh god*, said Amos to himself, his heart pounding with adrenaline.

The foothold distances didn't work well for Henry, he had to stretch his legs to reach the holes in the ice that Ingrid had cut. Whilst climbing around a projection of ice, he stretched and as he did so, his foot missed the foot hole cut by Ingrid. The clips around his waist holding him onto the rope. Despite screams from Bernie and Elizabeth, Henry didn't panic as he dangled over the cliff edge by his waist. With Amos and Robert either side of him, they held tightly onto the rope and the two of them gradually hauled him up to safety.

"That was tricky, but good fun," said Henry. "I liked that."

Amos and Robert looked at each other and smiled, shaking their heads from side to side. "Well done, Henry," said Amos. "Let's keep on going." Blood was now staining the arm on Amos's jacket.

Robert noticed that the berg they were on was getting much closer to where the bridge used to be.

"Dad. We're gonna have to get a move on, we're getting too close to where the bergs break through." Robert motioned with his head towards the bergs in front. They clambered around another projection of ice.

"Yeah," replied Amos.

"Come on, everyone, come on," called Robert, "keep going, we're almost there."

Ingrid was preparing the rope and pins for the route up to a ledge connecting them to the final berg. They followed her, and were relieved to be able to see clearer images of land on the other side through the fog. It wasn't far now.

A thundering noise and crashing of ice into the water rocked their confidence. A slice of the cliff immediately in front of Ingrid had sheared off and created another huge wave, the water shooting up high and over them as well as onto the land. This left a thirty to forty-metre cliff face of ice in front of them, dropping vertically down to the sea.

They took a while to recover from the scene. They had gathered themselves. "Where's Ingrid?" said Elizabeth anxiously looking around. "She's gone, Dad. She isn't in front of me any more."

"Ingrid?" shouted Amos and then Bernie.

"Ingrid? Oh God. No," said Bernie. She moved closer to where she had last seen Ingrid.

Bernie could see the rope disappearing over the ice cliff edge.

After what seemed an age to Bernie at the front, a hand slapped down on top of the ice and Ingrid called out.

"Ingrid's here," she called out with considerable relief. Robert swiftly moved to the front and helped Bernie pull Ingrid up. Her face appeared, scratched and bruised on one side but as always smiling. Scrambling up and onto her hands and knees, she smiled and looked up "Oh. That is good. The clips and safety ropes works. Thank you."

It was a huge relief for everyone. She had slipped when the ice cliff collapsed and the rope and safety pins held her from falling, after dangling for a short while she had frantically pulled herself up.

"We have a dead end. We cannot go any further," said Ingrid, now standing up.

Amos climbed up past the others and Ingrid and tentatively took a look for himself. He glanced over the edge and backed away quickly as he wasn't happy looking down.

Ingrid was recovering from her fall down the cliff face.

"Oh my goodness," said Amos, having peered over the edge down the face of a sheer cliff of ice.

"What is it, Dad?" asked Robert.

"Take a look Robert, but be careful." Robert gingerly crawled up and past Amos.

"That was a close thing," said Ingrid to Bernie and Elizabeth. "One minute the path was there and next... gone."

"Woo." Robert peered over the edge. "Glad we've got the dinghies; looks like we're gonna need them, Dad." He crawled back from the edge to his father and they made their way back to the others.

"Now what do we do Amos?" shouted Bernie. " We don't have time to go back. The berg has moved and we are faced with a sheer ice cliff down to the sea and ... and ... oblivion."

"Well, we brought the dinghies in case and they will now be needed," replied Ingrid.

"But how the hell do we get down to the sea?" asked Bernie.

There was another heavy jolt and movement of the berg... they all held tightly to each other and the safety rope.

Ingrid took off her backpack and pulled out the climbing netting.

"Here, now we must use this," she said, pulling the netting out onto the ice.

Robert then opened his backpack and pulled out one of the dinghies.

"It is good, yes?" replied Ingrid.

"Dad, this is brilliant up here, we are so high up," said Henry enjoying the view. Amos looked away he didn't want to look.

"I don't want to go down there," said Elizabeth. "I've had enough of all of this."

"You're gonna have to, honey," said Amos. "We'll have the dinghies ready for when we climb down."

"What do you mean, 'climb'?" Bernie screamed out. She moved tentatively closer to the edge of the ice to take a look. She looked down. "I'm not... no way, Amos," she called out, but she could also see the other side... land... that was the reward.

There was another shudder and shaking of the berg. They were now moving closer to the front line of bergs, waiting to break through where the bridge used to be.

"Dad," called out Robert.

"Yeah."

"Look... We're almost at the front row; it could be us next? We've got to go. We've got to go!"

Ingrid rolled the netting down the cliff after pinning it securely to the ice and looked over the edge.

"I think it will be goods," said Ingrid. This was followed by another chuckle from Henry, who still hadn't quite grasped the danger they were all in.

"Henry," said Bernie.

"It makes me laugh, Mom... 'goods'," replied Henry with a

giggle.

"That is fine; I don't mind. We are best of friends, yes?" Ingrid smiled back at Henry and then Bernie.

Robert checked the netting that had been dropped over the edge.

"The netting is fully down, Dad," called out Robert. The lower three rungs were splashing in the water.

"Phew, at least something is going our way," said Amos.

"We are going to end up in the water, aren't we, Amos?"

"Bernie. No honey, we're not so long as we are careful; it will be fine... Believe me," replied Amos.

Robert had unpacked the first of the dinghies.

Henry and Elizabeth were looking at what Ingrid was doing. Bernie holding the other end of the dinghy and pulling it out flat.

Ingrid yanked at the toggle on the dinghy, which automatically filled with air. "We climbs down the netting and then in the boat. Easy."

"That sure saves a lot of puff," said Bernie.

"Wow, that's a cool trick," said Henry.

"Yeah," added Elizabeth, now more interested, having seen the dinghy. "We should get one of these at home, Mom."

Meanwhile, Amos had been fixing more pins into the ice, to make absolutely sure the netting was secure.

"You make the climb sound so simple, Ingrid," said Bernie, now a bit more settled in herself with the plan.

"OK, I thinks I go first and then you pass the dinghy down to me, yes. Then Elizabeth, Bernie and Robert follow like that. As the second dinghy is only for two, that is for Amos and little Henry at the back."

Ingrid made her way to the top of the netting, removing her boots, giving the netting a strong tug to reassure herself and started to climb down. As she reached sea level, Robert lowered the dinghy down to her on a rope. After some flapping around in the air on the way down, she managed to grab hold of the dinghy.

There was a jolt of the berg as Elizabeth started to descend the netting and she held on tightly, paralysed. A chunk of ice landed with a splash in the water next to Ingrid.

"Come on now, Elizabeth, quickly." Ingrid clambered into the dinghy, holding herself and the dinghy close to the netting.

Elizabeth descended, following encouragement from Bernie. Bernie quickly followed her down… A swaying and movement of the berg got everybody worried… But the netting held steady.

"Robert, you go next and hurry, please; we've not got much time left," said Amos.

"OK, Dad, see you in a few minutes… remember you've got to pull the toggle to blow the dinghy up – it's there on the side." Robert pointed at the dinghy.

"Thanks."

Robert then disappeared over the cliff edge down to the others. There was a splashing sound as Robert got to the bottom of the netting. He had only partly managed to get into the boat, and clambered out of the water with the help of the others.

At the top of the cliff face, Amos pulled his and then Henry's life jacket toggles to inflate them and then the toggle to the dinghy.

"Henry, you ready? What we are going to do now is unclip ourselves from the rope and then slowly climb down the netting; you got that? And you do this properly and I'll give you a huge bag of your favourite sweets. Now that's your last safety link… You got that?"

"Yes, Dad. This is easy. I do this at school when we do physical exercise and circuit training and yes… I'm looking forward to the sweets."

"Well, Henry, you know more about this than I do," replied Amos, slightly taken aback again by Henry's continued confidence.

"It's OK, Dad, I'm fine. This is really cool."

Amos looked over the edge and saw the others safely in the dinghy and moving away from the berg. He removed both his and Henry's boots, knowing that if they hit the water with boots on it would make them heavy in the water.

"OK, let's climb down the netting, Henry."

The berg they were on suddenly came to life and was on the move again, now perilously close to breaking through where the bridge used to be. It was given a huge nudge by another berg and swayed vigorously from side to side, knocking Amos off his feet.

Where Henry and Amos were standing then started to collapse. The wave this created pushed the dinghy that the others were in away from the berg and towards the shoreline.

Amos grabbed Henry by one hand and yanked him into the dinghy. "Hold tight, Henry; we're gonna be getting wet."

The berg got jolted again and the ice disappeared from under their feet.

The dinghy followed the collapsing ice, sliding down the face of the ice cliff. They were catapulted into the air, flipping over and landing in the sea.

Henry landed close to the dinghy, holding onto the rope. Amos was nowhere to be seen.

"Where's Dad?" Elizabeth cried out, looking back at the berg with another wave coming towards them.

"Oh God… No…" said Bernie, her hands moving to her mouth. The first dinghy being driven to the shoreline by the waves.

After what seemed an age to those watching from the boat, Amos appeared up at the surface of the water and could breathe again. Amos got one of his shark flashbacks. Fired up with adrenalin, he swam frantically towards Henry, who was pulling on the rope connecting to the dinghy. With the strength he used for diving, Amos lifted his rucksack into the dinghy and pushed Henry up and out of the water and into the boat.

"Henry, now hold onto the rope on the sides of the dinghy, you got that?"

The berg they had been on was now heading in the direction of the gap through the bridge.

Amos looked across the water to the shoreline and saw the others being helped out by a number of local people who had come over to help, having seen and heard the commotion.

The bergs movement through the bridge, caused the current to pull the dinghy with the two of them towards the bridge.

"Dad, Dad, look," said Henry, pointing behind Amos towards a berg making its way towards them and now being dragged away from the shore by the current.

Amos pulled the dinghy towards him and then kicked and kicked with all his might… but he was making little headway. He remembered the rucksack in the boat – there was a lifeline.

"Henry, Henry," Amos called out in desperation. "Open up the bag… now… quickly."

Amos was still kicking in the water, trying to pull the boat away from the bergs, but it was useless; they were being dragged away from the shore.

Henry pulled out a rope with an anchor on the end.

"Henry, pass it over to me, quickly; come on, Henry, quick."

Amos pulled it out and tried to swing it towards the shoreline… but it landed short and in the water.

"Henry, can you pull that in, please, as fast as you can?"

Amos was kicking and kicking in the water, still trying to get closer to the shore but the current was getting stronger and pulling them away.

"I've done that, Dad," Henry called out and handed the rope back to his father.

Amos swung the anchor and rope again with all the effort he could muster and threw it as far as he could… they were now on the brink of being sucked through the break in the bridge… the anchor held on a rock. With one hand Amos was holding onto the boat and with the other the rope and anchor.

Other bergs were starting to close in on them.

"Dad, Dad, watch out."

A huge piece of ice collapsed off a berg, sending a wave of water towards them.

"Hold tight, Henry, we're gonna get wet again." As the water hit them, Amos pulled on the rope so that they kept themselves close to the shoreline when the water receded.

The water washed over them. Amos held the rope of the anchor and dinghy tight.

Robert, Ingrid and Bernie, having reached the shore, clambered out and ran to where Amos had managed to get the anchor secure, but Amos couldn't move without letting go of the rope or the dinghy.

"Dad," cried Elizabeth.

"Amos," called Bernie.

"I can't let go; you're gonna have to pull me in, there's... no other way," he shouted, taking another mouthful of water and spitting it out.

With Amos kicking in the water and wrapping the dinghy rope securely to his injured arm, he felt a rip in his arm, blood pouring out of his jacket. The stitches in his arm were torn apart. Despite the intense pain, there was no way he was letting go.

Robert, Ingrid and Bernie reached the anchor end of the rope and started to pull on it.

"It's no good," shouted Bernie. "We can't pull you in."

Two local men could see they were having difficulty and ran over to them, taking the rope from Ingrid and Bernie.

With three of them now holding the rope, they were able to hold Amos and Henry steady in the water and slowly pulled them to shore and safety.

With feet scrambling on the shoreline, Amos collapsed.

CHAPTER 17: THE WARMTH
OF THE OLD LADY

Bernie ran along the shoreline to Amos's motionless body and gently raised his head up onto her lap.

"Amos. Amos?" she shouted.

"Is there somewhere we can get warm?" Bernie called out towards some of the local people, with Amos shivering in Bernie's arms.

"I will find somewheres," replied Ingrid, running away from the shoreline towards a group of cottages.

Bernie held Amos close to her body. "Oh, Amos, Amos, you're alright? I thought…"

"Thanks, honey… yeah… I'm fine, just glad we're all OK and made it safely across." He held his injured shoulder.

Elizabeth joined them and gave her father a big hug. "Dad, have you seen your arm?"

Amos hadn't looked. He knew that the stitches had broken when he was in the water but didn't know the extent to which they had gone. Looking down at the amount of blood, he realised that it was bad.

Henry was helped out of the dinghy by Robert. Clambering out of the dinghy, he said, "Did you see me, did you see me, Robert? When – when… I went up off the berg and – and flew through the air with Dad and then went underwater. I really did have to hold my breath… we made such a big splash, didn't we?" Henry had his arms wrapped around his body and was shivering.

"I just wish I had my camera with me," replied a relieved Robert, now knowing that they were all OK and giving his little brother a hug.

The boys made their way over to their parents.

Amos's eyes closed, mightily relieved, and he heard voices in a language that he didn't understand. He realised when he opened his eyes that he wasn't in a dream, seeing Bernie and Elizabeth and the boys looking down at him, but it was local people speaking. He then heard the familiar voice of Ingrid.

"Yes," called out Ingrid, "I have found where we can go."

Bernie and Robert helped Amos stand up. They gingerly made their way off the shoreline, stumbling and crawling over slippery rocks and boulders. Ingrid was in front with Henry and Elizabeth leading the way, Henry non-stop talking about his experience.

"Your arm, Amos; it's really bleeding badly and we've got to get it seen to," said Bernie.

Up ahead of them, Ingrid could see a lady coming out of one of the cottages set back from the shore, she was walking down towards them holding a bundle of blankets. Ingrid ran up to her..

"Thank you." she said to the lady.

"I see you down in the water – please take these to keep warm and then you come back to me in my house."

"Thank you," said Ingrid, running back down to Henry and Elizabeth directing them up to the cottage and giving them each a blanket, then running down to the others. Ingrid immediately wrapped one around Amos and then Bernie.

"Dad, have you seen your arm?" said Robert.

Amos looked down at his arm, it was bleeding profusely. "Thanks, yeah… well, we made it, that's the important thing" he said to Robert. They embraced as best they could.

The old lady walked down and joined them and started speaking in a language that neither of them could understand.

Ingrid translated. "She says: 'In all the years I have lived here we have never seen anything like this. Over seventy years… Never, never, never have I seen." Tears in her eyes. She paused for a few moments looking out towards the harbour. "Are you all getting warm now? I'll make you some real Faroe soup and you can warms up by the fire in my house."

"Thank you, that would be lovely," replied Bernie with Ingrid continuing to translate.

A number of other local people helped them whilst walking along the footpath away from the waters edge.

The cottage was amongst a cluster of six houses, with sheet metal roofing, an ancient-looking wooden door and two small windows on the front stone elevation, with patches of light blue paint on cracked render where repairs had been carried out.

Standing at the front door, the old lady beckoned them into her house.

Both Amos and Robert had to duck whilst entering to avoid banging their heads and keep aware of the low beamed ceilings and doors inside the cottage. Amos stumbled on the step as he went in, Bernie just managing to hold him steady.

There was an open fire in the hearth facing them as they entered, which was just as well as there was an ice-cold wind blowing into the room until the front door was closed. The fireplace was surrounded with blackened cooking implements of various shapes and sizes hanging from wooden beams. Small black and white, browning pictures fixed in haphazard places on the walls. The old lady attended to the fire and added more logs from the pile in the adjacent alcove.

"This is so cosy," said Elizabeth, standing with a blanket around her, but shivering in unison with Henry.

"I'm sooo cold, Mommy," said Henry, his teeth chattering.

Ingrid then said something to the old lady in Faroese and the lady immediately disappeared up a set of stairs to the rear of the room.

Ingrid and Robert helped move Amos into the kitchen. Ingrid sat him down and strapped his arm to prevent it bleeding.

Bernie moved the two younger children closer to the warmth of the fire which was now roaring. "Stand by the fire, children, and keep rubbing your hands together and moving your feet; you'll soon warm up." Bernie intermittently rubbing Henry and then Elizabeth's back and shoulders.

When the old lady returned, she did so with a basket full of clothes. She then spoke a lot of words to them in Faroese.

Ingrid translated. "'Here you are, please, please help yourselves. They are from my sons and his children for when they come to stay here. Now I go make the soup that I promise you… If you wants to have a hot shower and then change, then i leaves the towels by the bathroom door – see?'" The old lady motioned with her head towards the far end of the room. She smiled at them, following Ingrid's translation.

"Go on, Mom, you first with Elizabeth… Henry and I will follow," said Robert.

"Go on, honey, we'll shower after you two," added Amos, now sitting by the fire. "My arm's in such a mess I had better go last."

They took turns to shower and change. Ingrid and Robert helped Henry to change out of his clothes close to the fire, leaving a pile of wet clothes, then wrapping him with a huge towel and vigorously rubbing his back and shoulders.

With Henry deciding he was now warm enough by the fire and didn't want to shower. Ingrid followed after Bernie and Elizabeth had finished.

Now warm and dry, Bernie, Elizabeth and Henry started rummaging in the basket of clothes that the old lady had brought them for suitable dry clothing.

Ingrid returned to the living room, rubbing her hair with a towel, one side of her face scratched and showing the bruising from her fall. She pointed towards Amos's arm.

"You have not seen?"

"No, what?" replied Amos.

"Your arm. It is bleeding badly again," she said with concern in her voice and walked over to Amos still rubbing her hair.

With everything else going on around him, Amos hadn't realised. Ingrid helped him take his jacket off and rolled his shirt sleeve up very gingerly to take a better look.

Everyone looked over towards Amos and could see immediately that the stitches had burst and the wound was now open and weeping heavily through the strapping that Ingrid had put on earlier. The mess on his jacket and shirt and now the floor made it look like he had been in a car accident.

"Laddie, let me see that," the old lady said in English.

Amos was shocked, as was everybody else in the room.

"Hey, you can speak English."

"Yes, but only when I know someone. I know you all nows."

Henry chuckled to himself.

The old lady must have been in her nineties, thought Amos looking closely at her, small, greyed, her skin wrinkled and leathered but still with a mischievous sparkle in her blue eyes. She took a hold of Amos's arm and carefully moved Amos closer to the window where it was brighter and could have a better look. She went to a drawer in the side cupboard and brought over a pair of scissors. She cut the arm off his shirt, leaving part of his wound exposed, together with the remains of the strapping Ingrid had put on and shirt holding his wound together.

"You're going to need more stitches in this arm; it is bad, you know. Ingrid, will you please see to the broth when you're ready and I'll get some plasters and bandages."

She pulled Amos's arm towards where she was now sitting. "Looking at this closely laddie, you're going to need a lot of new stitches, bigger ones if you're going to be climbing again."

"I won't be doing any of that for a while," replied Amos, looking at Bernie.

Bernie looked back at him with an expression on her face of *You had better not, Amos, or you'll be out in the doghouse.*

The fire continued to push out waves of heat into the living room with its low-beamed ceilings making it very cosy. Other than Amos, they were all now changed into warm clothing of various sizes, shapes and colours.

The old lady returned to where Amos was sitting and immediately wrapped plasters across the wound to try to hold it together with the remains of his shirt.

"Now go and shower and then I bandage it up properly."

Amos did what he was told. Ingrid nodded in agreement and reassuringly looked at Bernie to acknowledge that what the old lady was doing was for the best at the moment.

"I'll give it a proper clean when you're out of the shower and can have a better look at it. I was a nurse in the Second World War – yes, a long, long time ago – and that wound needs seeing to; it's a bad, nasty cut," she said looking at his arm and then into his eyes.

"Er, yes… thank you." Amos smiled back at her with a decidedly ashen look on his face and picked up a couple of towels as he went off to shower.

"Go on, Dad, hurry up. I can smell some lovely soup and I'm very hungry and showered. It's really nice and warm in here," said Elizabeth, pushing him towards the bathroom.

"Amos, do you need any help with your arm the way it is?" asked Bernie.

"No, I'll be fine, thanks, honey. I'll call out if I need any help."

Amos called out, from the shower "Wow, this is cold."

"It'll have to be cold for you, laddie." They all laughed together. The others had used up all the hot water.

Fortunately for Amos, he was used to cold showers on the rigs. The lukewarm water meant that Amos didn't stay showering for long and was soon dried and changed, the smell of the food luring him out.

The old lady ventured into the kitchen to see how Ingrid was getting on with the broth.

"That smells good, young lady." She dipped a spoon into the saucepan and sampled. "Where did yer learn how to cook Faroese broth?"

"I live here now for maybe four years by myself and works at the hospital so I learn a lot how to cook," she replied politely.

"Well you're very good and there – in the cupboard, that's it – we add some of my special ingredients ..." She opened the cupboard and took out a bottle that said, on the side, *Faroese rum*. "This will help." She poured some in and then a little extra. She smiled across at Ingrid.

"Do you need any help in there?" called Bernie from the living room.

"Yes, thank you. Please, the bowls are on the shelf over in the corner and you can bring those to use... I will see to your man's arm as he is finished in the bathroom now."

Amos walked into the lounge wearing a pair of rather oversized dark green trousers and a large yellow vest awkwardly holding one hand over his wound with the towel now bloodied, whilst trying to dry his hair with the other end of the towel. "Something smells good," he said, looking towards the kitchen.

The children and Bernie were already sitting up at the table. Ingrid joined them from the kitchen and placed the pot in the middle of the table, Bernie then scooping the Faroese broth into their bowls.

"You look really funny, Dad, in your clothes," said Henry from the table laughing with Elizabeth.

Steam poured off the soup. Ingrid brought in a platter of bread and *snegles*.

"Mmm, smells like there is something... er... interesting in there," said Bernie looking at the old lady and Ingrid.

"Yes, it is my special recipe... Good for peoples that are wet and cold... It will warm you ups."

"Not too much for Henry, now."

"I like it."

"Me too," said Elizabeth.

Amos stood up, admiring with contentment the scene in front him.

"Over here and now, please. You sits down, please," said the old lady, pointing towards Amos. "You can eat later after I see to this arm." She carefully pulled the blood stained towel away from Amos's wound and took a closer look through her spectacles.

"Yes. I would like some soup, that's assuming there will be any left," said Amos. "What do you want me to do with all the wet clothes?"

"I'll take them," said Bernie and added them to the pile of clothes by the fire.

"I will bag them for you in a minute, once i finish here" said the old lady, "and please call me Esta."

"That's OK," said Bernie, "I can do it."

"Please, you all sit and enjoy the soups and breads."

"This is all so wonderful; you are very kind, thank you," said Bernie.

"We're all very grateful. Thank you," added Amos. "Can we help pay for this as there's so much food and—"

"No, no, no… It is nothing, please… It is for you… Just make sure you come to visit me next time you come to Faroe for a proper holiday."

"Yes, we will. We definitely will," replied Amos.

"I've saved you some soup, Dad," said Robert, "and a *snegle*."

"Now you stays still," Esta said to Amos gently pushing him towards a seat. He duly sat down on an old wooden chair which wobbled on the stone flooring. Esta tried to take some more of the torn shirt away from the wound but decided not to. She cut some more of the shirt off after a bit of prodding and strapped some fresh sticky plasters around the remains of the shirt and wound. Finally wrapping a fresh bandage around his arm.

"There. This is the best I do for you; at the hospital you must see to your arm immediately when you are there, yes?"

Amos thanked Esta, got up and sat at the table. He sampled the soup they had saved for him and grimaced.

"Gee," he said wiping his hand across his mouth.

They all laughed.

"It is not nice?" said Esta.

"No it's not that, it's just so hot and I think I've burnt my tongue."

"Children," said Bernie, now smiling at Amos, "make sure you blow on the soup to cool it down before putting it in your mouth." Her humour had returned, much to Amos's relief. Henry took a third *snegle*.

"That's what we've been doing, Mom," said Elizabeth.

There was a knock on the door, and a voice that both Ingrid and Amos recognised.

"Can I come in?" A head appeared around the door.

"Hey, Bill, how are you? And good to see you, how did you know we were here?" said Amos.

"Word gets around very quickly in these parts. Good to see you too, buddy, and Ingrid. Hi, everyone, I'm Bill." He lifted his hand in recognition.

"This is my wife, Bernie; Robert, my eldest; Elizabeth and Henry, and this is… er…"

"Esta… I lives here; this is my family house."

"Er… yes, Esta, sorry, I didn't pick your name up earlier."

She shook her head, acknowledging with a beaming smile.

"Hey, you guys, I've heard a lot about you from Mary at the hospital. Glad to see you're all OK. Looks like you've been in the wars again, Amos, and by the sound of things had quite an adventure."

The children then went on to describe some of the challenges that they had faced over the last twenty-four hours.

"We've climbed an iceberg," said Henry, very proud of himself, "and Daddy's gonna get me some of my favourite sweets."

"And we climbed down an ice cliff; it was huge – just looking down made my stomach turn with the waves and pieces of ice falling off," said Elizabeth.

"Yeah, that was easy, wasn't it, Dad?" added Robert laughing.

"It started off well enough but the last couple of days have been, well…" said Amos, "quite…".

"Traumatic," interjected Bernie.

"And you were very brave, Elizabeth," said Amos.

"Yeah, and without Ingrid here we would still be over there on the island up in the fog somewhere or stuck on a berg somewhere floating the other side of the harbour and out to sea…" said Bernie.

"Looks like I arrived at the right time, then," said Bill, eyes wide looking at the dining table busy with plates of hot and cold food… a bowl of steaming soup in the middle and a pile of bread rolls and *snegles* slowly getting smaller… the children were tucking in, Henry's hand making its way for another.

"That smells like it's very tasty," said Bill.

"You may have somes if you like and then you must take this man to the hospital quickly to repair his arm," said Esta.

"Yeah, why not, but just a little as you guys need it more than me, and then I'll take you back to Klaksvík Hospital. Mmm, it smells good."

"Yeah."

"My special recipe," said Esta, pleased with herself. "With just a little bit of something in it to keep peoples warm."

"I like it as it is; you don't need to change the recipe," said Henry, grinning and taking another *snegle* from the table. "Are we going by helicopter?"

"No, I'm sorry, little man. I've driven here. It's too foggy for the chopper but maybe tomorrow if the weather improves."

"Did you try this morning?" asked Elizabeth.

"Yeah, I did. But we couldn't land and had to abort to get back before the weather closed in."

"We heard you," said Elizabeth. "Helicopters are very noisy, aren't they?"

"What happened to you?" asked Bill.

"Well… as you can imagine, it's a long story, Bill. How did you know we were here?"

"I got a call that someone needed rescuing but with no helicopter available… I decided to drive over anyway. As I got to the bridge I could see all the commotion and saw you being taken into Esta's."

"You know Esta?"

"Yeah, we go back a long way… Family connections, and everyone knows everyone here. There's no hiding away."

"As I say before, I've been here," interrupted Esta, "for over seventy years on Faroe, and I've never seen anything like this in the harbour since I have been living here."

"I am afraid it is the start of many things to come," replied Ingrid. "It is happening slowly… The change in weather… Changes in seasons… And we will soon find it more difficult for us to grow our foods."

"Yes, I agree with you, Ingrid," said Esta. "It's not the daily changes, but from one year to the next. You start to notice it when you get older and observe what is happening all around you."

"The planet is at the tipping point now. We still have the chance to change things but we must act now otherwise it is lost forever for the generations that follow us." Amos recognised the tone of Ingrid's voice was starting to get heated.

"And it's about time, Ingrid, you got yourself a man!" said Esta abruptly.

"Maybe… maybe soon… maybe not. I am happy as I am at the moment and maybe that time will come for me too," Ingrid responded in a confident manner.

They all thanked Esta for the soup, with an acknowledgement that it was delicious. Henry did not comment as by the look of things he was trying to eat the most *snegles* in a day.

"What shall we do with all the clothes we have borrowed from you?" Bernie asked Esta.

"That's OK," said Ingrid. "I will bring them back next time I'm over this way and come in and see Esta."

"Can we please pay at least something for our food and your hospitality?" said Amos, feeling slightly embarrassed by all the help they were being given.

"No, no, no, no. I say to you before. No." She put her hand over Amos's mouth.

"You're very kind and generous, thank you. It's really appreciated," said Bernie.

"Thank you," said Robert, followed by Elizabeth and Henry – Henry with part of a *snegle* in his mouth and the rest in his hand.

Ingrid touched Esta's arm.

"Right, you guys… if I'm gonna get Amos here back to the hospital today then we had better leave now otherwise you'll have another night to stay up here," said Bill, keen to get going.

"I don't mind staying here," said Henry, with a beaming smile on his face.

"But your father needs his arm seen to urgently," said Esta. "And as much as I enjoy having you all to stay here, I'm going to have to say goodbye to you."

They stood up from the table and gradually made their way to leave.

As Henry got to the front door, Esta came up to him and tapped him on the shoulder "Here, these are for you – some wee sweets for you to share with your brother and sister."

"OK, thank you. Thank you very much," replied Henry, and he

gave the lady a hug. "Look, Mom." He opened up the big bag of sweets to show his mother.

"Now, make sure you remember what Esta said to you about sharing," said Bernie.

"Yeah, I will, Mom."

Elizabeth and Robert came over to take a look at what was in the bag.

Bill was starting to get impatient. "Come on you lot, let's get going. By the look of things out there the fog is rolling in again and with it being almost dusk we need to hit the road, as we've got at least an hour on the road, maybe more if the conditions get any worse."

He had driven over in the hospital's Land Rover, so there was ample space for all of them. He suggested to Robert that he might want to sit in the front as he seemed the most awake of all of them.

"Yeah, definitely," replied Robert.

They were soon all sitting in the land rover and strapped in. Having said their final goodbyes, they waved to Esta from the vehicle. Looking back over their shoulders, they saw glimpses of the icebergs in the harbour through the fog.

"Want any sweets, anyone?" said Henry with a mouthful. "Bill, would you like one?"

"Yeah. I don't mind what you give me, Henry. Thank you." Bill changed gears and made his way carefully along the road well aware of the poor conditions. Henry gave him a sticky toffee sweet, which he duly started to chew on.

"I remember these. I can see I'm going to be in for a visit to the dentist. They're the ones that pull your fillings out"

Henry offered the bag of sweets to Robert in the front, and then to the others.

"Ingrid," said Amos. "Thank you for all your help back there; we wouldn't have made it without you."

"It's OK... I quite enjoyed the adventure. Ands... You have such a lovely family." She looked around at all of them in turn, wishing she had the closeness and family bond that there was between them all, despite Amos working away from the family for long periods on the rigs.

"Thank you, yes, I'm very lucky," replied Amos, looking across and smiling at Bernie.

The journey back was slow due partly to the weather conditions and combined with the winding roads. There were no fast stretches of road as visibility was restricted by the rolling mist and low cloud. Their journey continued and as they climbed a steep hill, and for a few fleeting moments, Amos could see landscape views out of the window, past the profile of Ingrid's face, looking out across the islands and then turning the other way towards Bernie. He held her hand. Bernie smiled back at him. Both Henry and Elizabeth had their heads down, working their way through the bag of sweets.

We are lucky, thought Amos, *very lucky. Not just today, but generally... we are lucky to be living in a time when there is plenty. But what about the future?*

His thoughts started to run away with themselves... *The icebergs, so far south; that's seriously worrying... the changing weather patterns... and all Ingrid has said about the environment and climate change... all that we were doing and the implications for the future of our planet.*

CHAPTER 18: REFLECTIVE TIME

Amos leant forward in his seat and tapped Bill on the shoulder. "Thanks, Bill. Thank you," he said, and then sat back in his seat.

Sitting between Ingrid and Bernie in the second row of seats, Amos fell asleep almost as soon as he leant back, slumping onto Bernie's shoulder. He was exhausted both mentally and physically. The movement of the vehicle made him stir every now and then, rolling his head from side to side, it was easy for him to fall asleep again. He could hear intermittent conversations in the background, usually after a sharp turn in the road or sudden braking of the car.

"Well, I'm glad I chose to drive and not use the helicopter," said Bill to Robert, who was sitting in the front passenger seat, "otherwise we would still be stuck back there... the fog had lifted at Klaksvík by early this afternoon, enough for me to get off the ground but looking at the forecast over here we decided that it would be too risky."

"I would have liked to ride in a helicopter."

"Hey... No worries Robert. As I said to your little brother earlier, if the weather's clear in the morning I'll take you both up and anyone else who wants to come."

"That would be brilliant," said Robert excitedly.

Bernie tapped Robert on the shoulder and put her finger to her mouth and whispered, "Your father's asleep."

"OK, Mom," he responded quietly.

Henry and Elizabeth were happy in the back seats, continuing to work their way through the sweets the old lady had given them. Bernie decided to leave them to it rather than create a scene trying to take the sweets from them.

"Anyhow, even if it's still a bit foggy," Bill continued, "we should still be able to get you a ride even if it's just straight up and down."

Ingrid sat on the other side of Amos; she had her arms folded and was leaning towards the window. She too was exhausted by the climb and the events of the last few days and was glad the responsibility for the family wasn't hers any more. She said very little on the way back and reflected on the events that had taken place. She was looking forward to getting back.

As they approached Klaksvík, the street lighting – what there was of it – became more of an eerie misty haze of orange. As they drove through the town towards the hospital, the fog rolled in in waves. Bill was relieved that they were getting closer to the hospital and glad that he had decided to drive; the helicopter would not have made it and there would have been a big problem finding a landing spot if he had used it.

The Land Rover came to a halt outside the hospital entrance. Bill leant back in his seat, thankful that the peering through the windscreen had finally stopped. Amos woke up with a start. Bernie smiled at him, holding his arm, and kissed him on the side of the cheek.

"Here already?" came the startled voice of Amos.

"Dad, you've been asleep ever since we left the cottage," said Elizabeth.

"We've saved you a few sweets, Dad," added Henry, chewing away happily.

"Yeah, but not many, Henry, I bet," said Robert from the front.

Ingrid was first out of the vehicle and she ran up the steps, bursting through the double doors and into the hospital reception. Mrs McKinnon looked up from her desk, then stood up and was the first to greet her.

"Ingrid, Ingrid… Oh, thank God; are you all back and safe?"

"Thank you, yes, all is good and safe. Could you call for a nurse, please, straight away."

"Why, what's happened?"

"Amos's stitches have broken and they needs renewing; his wound is opened and bleeding."

"Nurse to reception, please… nurse to reception, please…

now," bellowed Mary's voice over the tannoy.

"Mary, when the nurse arrives, sends her through to the patient cubicles and tell her I need sutures, polyglactin 910 Vicryl… and when the family comes in, can you get the duty doctor to see them, please, as soon as possible to check they are all OK… And ask the nurse to bring Amos through to me and I see to his wound."

"Surely the duty doctor can do that?" said Mary.

Ingrid stared back at Mary and then walked off to the staff washrooms to quickly shower and change.

"OK," Mary said to herself, realising she had said the wrong thing. A nurse responded promptly to the tannoy call, followed by the duty doctor and a number of other members of staff concerned about the urgency of the message from reception.

"Nurse… see that Mr Amos when he comes in is taken straight away through to the patient cubicle. Dr Svensen will see to him."

"Oh she's back; why doesn't the duty officer take care of it?"

"Yes. Thank goodness, they are all OK… and don't ask Dr Svensen about the duty officer doing the sutures; you'll get your head bitten off. She wants to do it," said Mary.

Amos sheepishly got out of the Land Rover, holding onto his arm. It was throbbing with pain, blood now dripping again from the bottom of his sleeve.

"Here they come up the steps; now go see to them, lass."

Bernie and Amos reached the entrance. She banged the doors open with her foot. Bernie supported Amos on one side. The adrenalin pumping around his body over the last four to five hours had disappeared and he was now feeling the pain in his arm and realising the damage he had done. The nurse ran up to Amos and took over from Bernie.

"Thank you," said Bernie. "Catch up with you in a minute, Amos; I'll see to the children."

Amos grimaced as someone else supported him, the sudden movement causing searing pain tearing through his arm.

"Argh, argh, that hurt," Amos cried out.

"Sorry," said the nurse, whilst walking him past the reception desk and towards the patient cubicle.

Mary stood up as the family came in and she walked around to the front. "Oh, I'm so sorry I sent you off, I really am so sorry..." she said.

"You've no need to apologise," replied Bernie.

"Oh. But I sent you and your children off into the wilds of Faroe and goodness knows what could have happened to you. Oh dear..." She started to cry again. Bernie comforted Mrs McKinnon with a hug.

"It's alright. Honestly. We're all back safe now."

The children, still working their way through the sweets that Esta had given them, had ambled behind Amos and Bernie and into the reception, Bill followed talking on his mobile phone.

"This way, please," said the duty doctor, "and we can check you over to make sure you're all OK, as I hear you've all had quite an adventure?"

"Yeah," replied Henry, speaking with a rather large boiled sweet to one side of his mouth. "We climbed around an iceberg and then went up into the sky" – he motioned with his hands – "and then splashing into the water."

Bernie looked across at the doctor and nodded when Henry responded and was explaining what they had done. She was sure that the duty doctor didn't believe him.

"OK, let's check out your mother first," said the doctor.

Bernie walked past the cubicle with Amos in. They said a brief hi to each other. The nurse had started to cut away the arm of the big dark green jumper Amos had borrowed and was using tweezers to pick at the shirt stuck to the wound...

"See you in a while, honey," said Amos.

Bill came running up behind Bernie whilst she spoke to Amos.

"I'll be with the children whilst you two are being seen to, OK?"

"Bill, that's kind of you," replied Bernie, "but you probably won't need to." She motioned her head towards reception and they both saw that Mrs McKinnon was showing them how the drinks and snack machines worked and pointing to where the canteen was for hot food.

They could just about hear what she was saying to them: "You choose what you like, now, children... whatever you like."

"Bill... Bill..." Amos called out from the cubicle. "Thanks again, buddy. I know I've said it a few times now, but it's really appreciated... particularly yesterday when you tried— Argh, argh, that hurt." The nurse was tearing a piece of shirt stuck in the wound, which now started to weep profusely. Amos looked away from it.

"I'm sorry, we have to remove it as best we can. I'll try not to hurt you but your arm, it's in such a mess..." said the nurse.

"OK... Yeah... we could hear you, Bill, but couldn't see anything."

"Yeah. That was a bit stupid on my part," replied Bill. "But hey... all OK now."

Amos couldn't quite see past the gap in the screen to see what his children were up to but could hear the buzz of excitement in their voices, telling Mrs McKinnon about their adventure.

"Ow..." Another strip of bloodied shirt was removed. "That really hurt."

"Sorry, but you have plasters across the wound now that are difficult... and I think it's best that I wait for the doctor before I do any more."

Amos smiled, looked down at the mess of his arm and looked away again; he hated the sight of blood.

"You OK, Amos? Sounded like someone was throttling you."

"Yeah, honey, thanks."

"Well, you're gonna need to close your eyes in a bit," said Bernie. Amos turned around and then realised what Bernie had meant. Ingrid walked through the curtains and instructed the nurse on the preparation of the injections.

The nurse prepared the needles and gave them to Ingrid one at a time, who proceeded to inject Amos in the arm.

"We need to do this, so we numb and then we can remove and clean and then re-stitch."

"Yeah, I understand, that's fine by me, Ingrid, thank you." He looked away and closed his eyes whilst Ingrid inserted the needles.

"We leave that for a few moments now... And then we can re-tie your wound together again. Good."

Bernie had finished being seen by the duty doctor and came into the cubicle. She put her arm on Amos's good shoulder and kissed him on the forehead. "There... no diving for you for a few weeks... which is good news. Perhaps we can now enjoy some real family time."

"I'll leave you to it, Ingrid, and thank you again; I need to go sit with the children while they are being checked over." Bernie exited the cubicle.

Amos could hear Bernie talking to Henry and then Elizabeth.

"Right, who's next to see the doctor?" Robert now returned to join the others. "Elizabeth, come on, you next, and boys, don't take advantage of Mrs McKinnon's good nature; this will come out of your pocket money."

There were chocolate and sweet wrappers on the chair and strewn on the floor. Mary was sitting down next to them telling stories of her childhood and which chocolates were her favourite.

"There's no charge, Bernie, please, this is on me."

"I appreciate that, Mary," said Bernie. "But you don't know my boys and you may not have any food left, and that's what worries me."

"Let's do what your mother says, now, boys, and I'll show you the hot food in the canteen."

Bernie joined Elizabeth, who was next to be checked out by the doctor.

"I thinks that is numb now," said Ingrid, prodding a finger around his wound whilst the nurse was stopping the blood from running down Amos's arm and onto the floor.

"Mmm," she said in a contemplative manner... and then seemed rather apprehensive. "Nurse, could you please ask the duty doctor to come in as this may be more difficult than I think."

"Yes, Doctor." The nurse quickly left the cubicle.

"Thank you again, Ingrid, for all you've done; we wouldn't have got back without you."

Ingrid looked at Amos and nodded with a slight tear in her eye.

The duty doctor appeared through the curtains with Elizabeth.

"You're fine, young lady," he said to Elizabeth.

"Hi, Dad. Ooh, that arm of yours looks horrible."

"Yeah. Thanks. Ingrid's going to sew it up again."

Elizabeth then walked off to see what her brothers were up to, and eating.

"Daughters," said Amos to Ingrid.

The duty doctor stood next to Ingrid and he started to prod and inspect the skin around the wound. The nurse continued to regularly dab around the wound and wipe the blood running off his arm.

"I think you're going to need two sets of stitches and some clamps where the old stitches were… That should hold it together and mean the scar is less protruding and should heal quicker."

"Did I hear you say two sets?"

"Yes," replied the duty doctor. "Two sets… the first wide of the wound to hold it generally together whilst the second finer set of stitches are put in; that way there's less chance of it bursting open."

"Well… You know best," said Amos, closing his eyes and looking away again. The duty doctor then left the cubicle.

"We will put ins the wider stitches first, please, Nurse."

Ingrid removed some further remnants of shirt and plasters as best she could with a smaller set of tweezers without opening the wound right up, working her way across the wound and clamping the skin together as she progressed, followed by the first set of stitching. Bernie returned back to the cubicle to see how Amos was. Seeing the nurse with a needle and Ingrid with the thread, she explained that Amos didn't like needles.

"Yes, we have found out." The nurse turned and smiled at Bernie.

Amos briefly smiled back at both of them, then looked away , closed his eyes and gritted his teeth even though his arm was numb to the stitching.

Having got the wider stitches in, Ingrid then proceeded with removing the plasters and remnants of the shirt from across the wound.

There was a yell from Amos, "Ow, that hurt!"

"Yes, removing the plasters has pulled some hair as well, sorry.

There is more to do."

His arm was really in a bad way, thought the nurse as they removed the last of the plasters. The nurse looked away towards Ingrid and then back.

"Thank you, Nurse; if you need to leave us for a while that's fine but I will need some help here."

"No, that's fine, I'm happy here."

Amos was still facing away from the two of them with his eyes closed.

"Another injection to kill any bugs… That's the last one."

"Thank goodness," said Amos.

"Yes, untils the next one… Joke!" said Ingrid. "Ha ha… it's OK, no more. We clean up, Nurse… and then I stitch good… yes."

The nurse finished cleaning the wound and Ingrid immediately commenced with the fine stitching. This was very delicate work and needed her full concentration.

"I'm glad I can't feel anything," said Amos.

"That is good. Because I am very busy here, but… you will feel something a bit later." She smiled at the nurse next to her. Ingrid continued, "Not many to go now." The nurse dabbed around the weeping wound. "Just a few more minutes and then we are finished."

The duty doctor joined them in the cubicle.

"How's it all going?"

"We are soon on the last row," replied Ingrid.

"That looks like a fine work of tapestry." He looked closely at Ingrid's workmanship.

"Thank you," replied Ingrid, briefly looking up.

"I know where to come now when I have a patient that needs stitches."

"That's reassuring, Doctor," said Amos, looking up and smiling at Ingrid.

"Finished… Nurse, please tidy up and dress the wound."

"Yes, Doctor."

Ingrid went to wash her hands at the sink. Bernie popped her head around the curtain to see how Amos was getting on.

"All finished, honey."

Bernie came in to have a closer look. "Gosh, that looks like Ingrid has been busy there... but ever so neat... thank you, Ingrid."

"Over eighty stitches," said the nurse. "I've been counting."

"Wow, and so much neater than the other ones on your side where the shark..."

"Yeah, yeah, thank you, honey, thank you for reminding me... you know it sends the shivers down me. And the doctor here is asking me to keep still."

They all smiled back at each other.

"Mrs McKinnon has given me a few shirts for you to try on as she wasn't sure of your size."

"That's kind of her; any will do," replied Amos.

"It's OK, you can look now that I have finished," said Ingrid. The nurse wiped the wound clean and started to apply a bandage.

Bernie helped Amos on with a vest and shirt then a thick cardigan. "Why a cardigan? Makes me look ancient."

"It's best for putting on and removing, because of your arm," said Ingrid.

"Ah right, yeah, yeah, thanks, good thinking."

Ingrid had put extra stitches in Amos's arm as she knew that he would probably end up diving with the children when they got back on holiday. Once he was dressed, Amos and Bernie joined their children in the canteen. Mary was continuing to entertain them.

"I see you've found where the food comes from, kids."

"Yeah, Dad, I didn't realise I was so hungry," said Henry. "There's some really nice pudding, Dad."

"Oh yeah, what is it?"

"Treacle sponge and custard... one of your favourites, Dad," said Elizabeth.

"Now you're talking."

Amos and Bernie sat down at the table.

"You both have lovely children," said Mary.

"Thank you," replied Bernie, taking a chip from Henry's plate.

"Hey, Mom, they're mine," said Henry, pulling his plate closer to him.

"I thought I would get some proper food down them," said Mary. "As they were eating quite a few sweets." There was a bag on the table. Bernie had a look inside… It was mostly sweet wrappers. There were so many, thought Bernie. Mrs McKinnon reassured Bernie that it was OK and there was no charge.

"Oh and if you're wondering where you are going to sleep tonight, I've booked you into the hotel next door here. I hope you don't mind but you're gonna need to stay somewhere."

"Mary, you're too good to us, thank you," said Amos.

"Yes, thank you," added Bernie.

"It's called Sjømannshjem… But it's easier just to call it Hotel Klaksvík… Not very original, I know, but it's just a two-minute walk. So I'll be able to see you in the morning before you go. Now I must get back to the desk in reception as someone has been covering for me."

She stood up to leave the family to catch up with each other and to finish off their meal.

"Children, remember you can choose whichever pudding you like… but make sure you leave some for your father." Mary's hand went up before anyone could speak and she looked towards Bernie and Amos. "I've told you it's all sorted… Now enjoy." She left the canteen.

"Dad," said Robert, "whilst you were having your stitches put in and we were waiting in reception, Mary let me have access to a computer, and I did some checking on the internet. You remember that professor guy that Ingrid mentioned up at the weather station…"

"Yeah… Hargreaves if I remember right."

"Well, he is actually a director of that oil company you mentioned, holds four hundred thousand shares and got paid a hundred and thirty thousand dollars last year by the company."

"Well, well, well, mmm," said Amos, shaking his head. "It looks like we may have found the culprit for not releasing information that should be available to everyone."

The family finished their meals. It was late, and they had had a very long, adventurous and tiring day.

As the children walked into the reception to pick up their coats, Amos pointed out to Bernie the children's pockets: bulging with sweets.

"Children, come on, that's way too many sweets; empty your pockets," said Bernie. "Give some back to Mary."

"No, no, no, no. It's OK, honestly." Mary gently pushed the handful of chocolate bars that Elizabeth was holding up to her mother back towards her.

"Thank you," said Elizabeth with a big smile on her face. Bernie shook her head from side to side and smiled.

They were putting their coats on and saying cheerio to Mary, when Ingrid came into reception. She hadn't wanted to interfere with the family and had left them to themselves, so had sat down quietly to calm herself.

"I see Mary has been looking after you?" She looked at the chocolates in Elizabeth's hands. "I will sees you all tomorrow before you go, yes… you are staying next door?"

"Yes, thank you, Ingrid. Mary has organised the hotel for us and thank you for all you've done; we would maybe not be here without you."

Ingrid nodded back to both Amos and Bernie, relief but also a hint of sadness in her eyes.

Bill was seated in reception and looked up from flicking through a magazine. "Good to see you are now back in one piece, buddy."

"Bill. Hi there," said Amos. "I didn't see you."

"Oh, and by the way, before I forget," interrupted Mary. "A man called Jack left a message. He said that everything was fine on the rig… and I told him that you and your family were reunited."

"Thanks, Mary," said Amos.

"That's very kind of you," said Bernie. "I don't know how to thank you all for looking after us."

Bernie was tightening the buttons on Henry's coat and putting his bobble hat on.

"And thanks for sorting out my arm, Ingrid… again." Amos lifted his arm slightly, winced and put it down awkwardly again.

"That is fine... please... it is my job. And you should be OK for maybe another hour or so but if the pain is too much then here are some painkiller tablets." She gave the tablets to Amos and then gave him a hug. Amos returned it with his better arm. She then gave Bernie a hug and each of the children. "Something I will never forgets," she said.

"Come along now, children," said Bernie, "let's get you all settled down in bed. We've all had a lot of excitement these last couple of days without much sleep; I know I need it."

"Aww, Mom, can we stay up a bit longer?" said a disappointed Henry.

"Come on, Henry, let's get going; we will see everyone in the morning," said Amos, moving his good arm over Henry's shoulder and gently pushing him towards the doors.

"Can Ingrid come and say good night?" said Elizabeth.

"I say good night here as I must go home too."

"It's a shame we have to go home tomorrow; I would have liked to have walked around Viðoy and explored some of the caves and climbed the cliffs," said Robert.

"Well maybes when you all come back next time for a proper family holiday to Faroe."

"That would be great," said Robert. "And climbing cliffs, not icebergs."

They all laughed.

"That's assuming that we are all able to... This iceberg phenomena, it is very worrying and the beginning of bigger problems to come. I only wish the politicians would stop, er... micro-thinking about themselves and their political parties and consider the bigger environmental impact and the need for them all to work together as countries and not just selfishly, and address the bigger climate changing issues. We will have, I fears, a lot of environmental pain, which will affect all of us before we actually wake up and then we tries to help make the planet recover. Our planet is a reflection of our health, so we must work together." Ingrid was now getting agitated and starting to pace up and down in reception.

"Do you really think it's that bad, Ingrid?" said Amos, pulling on his coat.

"My teacher at school says the same as Ingrid," replied Elizabeth. "She says that no one is listening or taking any positive action to stop damaging the environment. If a tree is cut down then others have to be planted to replace it so the carbon dioxide is absorbed that we are creating to try to balance what we are doing... in Brazil they are still cutting big areas of rainforest down every day and not replanting."

Ingrid smiled whilst Elizabeth spoke.

Robert then joined in with the discussion. "Even my geography teacher says that no one in authority is taking responsibility... they are just side-stepping the issues and pretending they are going to do something. Saying that they will 'deal with it tomorrow'. We are at or beyond the tipping point to allow the planet to recover. We ran a very simple straightforward program yesterday with all the statistics and data available and look at what we found: the change in direction of the currents bringing the cold and icebergs further south and the Gulf Stream potentially stopping in eight years' time, that's... actually stopping... that's unbelievable. Why hasn't this check been done before so we can all do something about it? Or maybe the professor has, but is not releasing his findings."

Bernie's eyes lit up, as did Ingrid's.

"Ingrid," said Amos, "you have two new recruits."

"She also says," added Robert, "that we will all be wearing breathing masks because of the poor air quality but that so many simple things could be done now to stop it happening."

"Planting trees. Easy," said Henry, joining in with the discussion.

"And what is stupid is that countries like Brazil have scaled back enforcement notices on deforestation. It is mindless," added Elizabeth.

"Yeah, that is right little Henry, plant trees," said Ingrid, "and I agree with Robert here that the constant procrastination and indecision... it's... it's..."

Everyone could see that Ingrid was getting cross and her blood pressure rising with her exaggerated arm movements.

"Now... We are like the dinosaurs... in fact we are the dinosaurs: eating all the food on the planet like parasites and giving nothing positive back and then there are no green plants to eat the carbon dioxide and methane and then we die. Anyway, it is my theory how they became extinct. Breeding and more breeding, not being able to think. We can think, yes, but we are like them; we are stupid and don't think about what we do. We have the knowledge... buts... we are not using our wisdom. We try to recycle but reuse is better. Yes?"

Ingrid tried to calm down and then apologised but also added that she was sure it was not just her but other people as well that were passionate about the need to repair "our" planet. "The Earth, our Earth, it already tells us many, many signals. We should live in harmony with our planet. You know that for every year since the year 2000, over 250 billion tonnes of water has been added to the sea, the result is a 10mm increase over 20 years in global sea-levels throughout the world from melting glaciers, not including Greenland or Antarctica. Islands will soon start to disappear. We all need to help nature now as it has helped us and we have left it behind; we must help nature to catch up again. I know all peoples and businesses and countries must be ready to change their thinking to a sustainable, carbon-neutral and ethical way of life. We need to reassess our values, money or environment and do it quickly one step at a time and not haphazardly. I believe we will all have to have a carbon credit card soon to buy things and that will show what each of us and our companies and then our actual countries' impact on the carbon dioxide in the environment. That would be good. Yes? Maybe to start with they can do this from satellites in space, we has the technology. You remember we had the Coronavirus lockdowns... well, it just shows we can do it... the air was cleaner... yes, that was like a humanitarian disaster... but maybe it was also a blessing in disguise? Well, the shutdown around the world proved it was possible. Much better than, say, food running out and the population dying... or the poles switching... or an asteroid hitting us... Whichever ways... oh, I'm sorry, I keep speaking so much." Ingrid finished and she sat down, exhausted.

Bernie went over and sat next to her.

Ingrid then carried on. "It's so very simple... plant trees... if I drive my car to work... then maybe I have to plant a hundred trees... or I can go see my parents in Denmark. Governments need to stop avoiding positive climate legislation. At the latest COP meeting of countries they agree to 'try' to limit global warming to 1.5C but that is not good enough to just try, we must do it, and reduce the temperatures. I say another thing," said Ingrid, "and then I stops, will keep quiet. The depth of the air around our planet that we breathe is about just 0.00028 per cent of the circumference of the earth. It is minute" – Ingrid showed with her fingers – "and we pollute it. We say that we must get to carbon neutral, but that is clearly not enough. As I say before, we are past the tip point and we need to be taking more carbon dioxide out of the atmosphere, *not* just keeping it the same. By taking more out we would actually be positive. We have had fifty years of too much carbon dioxide pushed into the atmosphere, now we must have fifty years less carbon dioxide in the atmosphere and help our planet recover."

Robert then gave an example. "You wouldn't put a fully grown salmon in an inch of water, would you? And that is what we are doing to ourselves."

"That is a very good example, Robert. I know it is not just me with these values and feelings and we must all change our behaviour. I love my planet, our planet. Let's put a value on how much carbon dioxide each of us and companies and countries minimise; if we have an emission we must match it as an absolute minimum..." said Ingrid.

"Perhaps," added Bernie, "we can from our experience tell people that we need to repair the environment now and not just sticky plaster over the problems every now and again."

Ingrid was now standing up again and began to pace up and down, screwing up the papers in her hand. She stopped at the entrance doors to the hospital, turned back round and threw them into a bin.

"I agree with you," said Bernie. "All industries, particularly yours, Amos, need to clean up their act now and not just think of dollars all the time."

Amos reassured Bernie that he was on her side and would look to see what he could do in his business.

"I can't say this enough, Ingrid, but I'm gonna... thank you for looking after us today and ensuring we got back safely, but the environmental issue is big... and... I'm not so sure..."

"That's the whole point, we are all in this together, animals, fish, trees, humans, water, air and dependent upon each other," said Ingrid. "I am not arguing with you but it's not being taken seriously enough."

There followed silence for a few moments. Everyone was expecting Amos to respond; he didn't. But he thought about how he was going to change his approach to work and do something positive and not just talk about it. Bill cleared his throat to speak and interrupted Amos's thoughts.

"I just thought that you would like to know that your flight out of Vágar Airport from Tórshavn to Edinburgh tomorrow is currently on time... weather permitting! And that we will have to be leaving here by midday latest."

"Right, kids, we really must go," said Bernie.

Amos thanked Ingrid again for sticking him together not just once but twice! And for an experience he would never forget. He moved towards her to shake her hand... she ignored it and just gave Amos a long hug.

When they released, Amos gave a brief shrug of his shoulders, looking towards Bernie.

"That's what we do here." Ingrid then hugged Bernie and Robert and thanked them both for their help and support. Then Elizabeth and "young Henry".

"I will sees you tomorrow before you go," said Ingrid.

They said their good nights and Mary added, "I hope you like the hotel; we've not got a great deal here."

"It'll be fine, thank you Mary, we just need a proper bed and some sleep."

Mary suggested to Bill that he should show them around to the hotel.

"Bye, everyone, and thank you, Ingrid, for all your help," said Bernie. They waved goodbye as they left the hospital.

Ingrid walked away from the reception towards the ward with a brief glance over her shoulder back towards the family. Amos caught her eye for a split second.

"Ingrid is very strongly opinionated about the environment," said Bernie on the walk to the hotel.

"Yeah," agreed Amos.

"And she's right," said Robert.

They looked up through breaks in the cloud to see stars for the first time... then more stars. So sharp and clear... they slowly disappeared, hidden again by fog.

"If it's clear in the morning, I'll see if we can give you your helicopter ride, Robert and Henry."

They reached the hotel.

"Thanks, Bill, for all your help and support. What time shall we meet you?"

"I will come and collect you after breakfast, at say, 9.30, then weather permitting we'll have time to take a flight in the helicopter before I take you to the airport."

"I liked what Ingrid said," chirped up Henry. "Look after planet earth first, each and every day... and our planet will look after us... we only have one."

***

To be continued in *Echo Bay*.

EPILOGUE

The health of our planet is being ignored. We each have a responsibility, personal, corporate, government and as countries. We are all responsible and we are all responsible.

Our planet may have already passed the stage of 'no return' or if we are lucky, still ticking; perhaps we are on borrowed time until we wake from our sleep to a big shift, such as poles switching, volcanic activity, rising sea levels, unpredictable seasons and temperatures followed by insufficient food. It will then be too late.

The book has lots of facts and information which on thinking about them may make you panic, it's not meant to, other than looking to make you aware of where we are going and the need to settle for no less than Carbon Neutral, preferably with Carbon Negative for us to survive. Balance your life with these thoughts in everything you do. Be mindful and consciously aware of the impact of what you do. Every effort, however small …. will help. Stay awake and engaged.

We have the knowledge and technology, so why not use our wisdom. Look after our planet and it will look after us.

That sounds like a good deal to me.

* * *

Echo Bay is the title of the book which follows *Time Bomb*.

Set 5 years later.

Will we still be around?

ACHNOWLEDGEMENTS

Considerable thanks to Curious Earth founders, Paul Davies, Conrad Langridge and Tom Brook and their passionate team of writers for their environmental and sustainability knowledge. Thanks also to Becca Allen editing and Carolina Frohlich, Charles Davies and Spiffing Covers for support, guidance, cover designs and publishing !

ABOUT THE WRITER

The first draft of the book, on various sheets and pads of paper I should add, was completed on 17 September 2004 on a train journey from London to Guildford.

Other demands on Philip's time as father, husband and a Chartered Quantity Surveyor meant he could only complete in 2021 and decided to self publish.

Considerable encouragement and support from his wife Ann, a gentle nudge (or two) from his eldest son, Paul, in January 2019 with comments and input to the book (plus IT guidance, and the loan of a laptop !); graphic design input from his son Charles and ideas from his daughter, Demelza, have enabled this book to be completed for your enjoyment and reflection.

Printed in Great Britain
by Amazon

79258329R00236